D0929923

The Science of

Bloodstock Breeding

B. Vijay

The Russell Meerdink Company, Ltd.
P. O. Box 485
Menasha, WI 54952
(800) 635-6499 in the USA and Canada
(414) 725-0955 Worldwide

Library of Congress Cataloging-in-Publication Data

Vijay, B., 1955 -
The Science of Bloodstock Breeding/ B. Vijay
Originally published: Madras : Curzon, 1986
Includes bibliographical references
ISBN 0-929346-14-9: $39.00

    1. Thoroughbred horse--Breeding 2. Racehorses--Breeding
I. Title.
SF293.T5V54 1991   91-38978
636.1's--dc20   CIP

Printed in the United States of America

Contents

Expansion of Abbreviations

R.W.I.T.C.	:	Royal Western India Turf Club
R.C.T.C.	:	Royal Calcutta Turf Club
M.R.C.	:	Madras Race Club
S.I.T.C.	:	South India Turf Club
Gen	:	General
Brig	:	Brigadier
Gr I/II/III	:	Group/Grade I/II/III
m	:	Metres
mi	:	Mile/s
f	:	Furlongs
B	:	Bay
Ch	:	Chestnut
Br	:	Brown
Gr	:	Grey
Ro	:	Roan
Dk	:	Dark

Bibliography

The Indian Turf Statistical Record, Volumes 1 to 6, published by The National Horse Breeding Society of India, 8 Nagar Road, Yeravada, Pune 411 006.

Fonn and Co's *All India Racing Record,* 1975-1976 to 1983-1984, edited, printed and published by S. R. Neogy for Molin Press (P) Ltd., 3, Prafulla Sarkar Street, Calcutta 700 072.

Original Vel Sporting News, November 1984 to April 1985, edited, printed and published by Smt. Radha Balasubramani, Original Vel Printing Works, 38, Davidson Street, Madras 600 001.

Catalogues of the Auction Sale of two-year-old bloodstock, 1975 to 1983, conducted by the Royal Western India Turf Club Ltd., Mahalakshmi Race Course, Bombay 400 034.

Register of Stallions in India, Volume 6 — 1979, published by the Royal Western India Turf Club Ltd., Mahalakshmi Race Course, Bombay 400 034.

Foreword

Horses have fascinated man from times immemorial. In addition to their traditional role, they have contributed greatly to sport and recreation. Equestrian sports, and racing in particular, have always been very popular. In the twentieth century organized racing developed rapidly throughout the world. The last two decades, in particular, have seen revolutionary changes in the structure of racing, methods of breeding and techniques of training. But still the twentieth century breeder, in spite of the explosion of knowledge, cannot claim to know far more than his predecessors! For we are playing a game of chess with nature, and nature does not yield her secrets easily. But nature is not ungenerous. All the great individuals who played this game scored significant victories. Their strategy, ideas and moves were at once sophisticated, powerful and subtle. For just as you can play a game of chess in a million ways, you can breed a horse in a million ways. But before you play any game you must know the rules. Similarly before you buy, or breed, horses you must know the rules. Since racing and breeding have been well documented for two centuries, Turf historians and breeders have been able to unravel a few of nature's secrets and lay down a few rules. But these are not rules in the dictionary meaning of the word. A better term would be "guide-lines". For bloodstock breeding is a probable science and not an exact science. But there is no need for us to feel ashamed as most sciences are probable sciences.

The twentieth century has given us a lot of leisure. This has enabled more and more people of every nationality to enter the sport; people who have absolutely no connection with the thoroughbred. This has made racing truly international, transcending all boundries. This book was written with such enthusiasts in mind.

In my college days we were often asked to prove theorems and solve problems from the "first principles" only. Likewise, I have developed every theory from the first principles. Therefore I am very confident that less experienced owners and breeders will be able to understand this book without the slightest difficulty. Throughout the emphasis is on first principles. But, hopefully, the more experienced will also have plenty of food for thought.

To enable readers get a firm grip on the subject, I have included several quizzes and exercises. These must be taken in a spirit of fun. But they are not meant for Turf historians or senior breeders. The answers to the quizzes are given.

I have divided the book into three parts. In the first part we will learn how to analyse a pedigree. Then we will study the basic characteristics of stallions, broodmares and maternal grandsires. The second part will take us into breeding proper. We will go deep into the behaviour of progenitors. We will understand the different forces at work. We will study different breeding techniques. The third part is a pot-pourri. I have given my views and opinions on different subjects.

Some of the horses mentioned in the book are in training. I have updated their race records as far as possible, but inevitably their latest victories have not been included.

I guess a few errors are unavoidable in a work of this magnitude. I would be most obliged if readers could drop me a line giving me the correct information.

MADRAS   B. VIJAY

PART I

CHAPTER 1

Introduction

There is no need for me to describe the structure of racing abroad. The principal racing countries have all adopted the "Pattern" race system. The Classics are obviously the most prestigious followed by other Group I races. Then come Group II and Group III events and other Stakes races. Then there are races of local importance and prestige, followed by races for average and inferior horses.

STRUCTURE OF RACING IN INDIA

A true Pattern race system has not yet been introduced in the country. Hence it is necessary for me to explain the structure of racing in some detail. The major racing season starts simultaneously in Bombay, Calcutta, Madras, Pantalone and Hyderabad (the principal racing centres) in November and ends in March. (In Bombay it starts a little later and ends a little later, and in Hyderabad it ends a little earlier.)

All the 5 centres conduct "classics", the details of which are given below:

BOMBAY

Race	Horses eligible	Distance
Indian 1000 Guineas	3-yr-old fillies	1600 m
Indian 2000 Guineas	3-yr-olds	1600 m
Indian Oaks	4-yr-old fillies	2400 m
Indian Derby	4-yr-olds	2400 m

The Indian St. Leger is run in Pune in the month of October for 4-yr-olds over 2800 m.

CALCUTTA

Calcutta 1000 Guineas	3-yr-old fillies	1600 m
Calcutta 2000	Guineas 3-yr-olds	1600 m
Calcutta Oaks	4-yr-old fillies	2400 m
Calcutta Derby	4-yr-olds	2400 m
Calcutta St. Leger	4-yr-olds	2800 m

1

MADRAS

South India 1000 Guineas	3-yr-old fillies	1600 m
South India 2000 Guineas	3-yr-olds	1600 m
South India Oaks	4-yr-old fillies	2400 m
South India Derby	4-yr-olds	2400 m
South India St. Leger	4-yr-olds	2800 m

BANGALORE

Bangalore 1000 Guineas	3-yr-old fillies	1600 m
Bangalore 2000 Guineas	3-yr-olds	1600 m
Bangalore Oaks	4-yr-old fillies	2400 m
Bangalore Arc de Triomphe	4-yr-olds	2400 m
Bangalore St. Leger	4-yr-olds	2800 m

HYDERABAD

Golconda 1000 Guineas	3-yr-old fillies	1600 m
Golconda 2000 Guineas	3-yr-olds	1600 m
Golconda Oaks	4-yr-old fillies	2400 m
Golconda Derby	4-yr-olds	2400 m

The Golconda St. Leger is also run in Hyderabad in the month of October for 4-yr-olds over 2800 m.

These races are all terms races with all horses carrying the same weight. In races for colts and fillies, the latter receive a sex allowance which is usually 1-1/2 kgs.

But the true "Derby" of the country is the "Indian Turf Invitation Cup" run over 2400 m. This race is run by rotation in the principal racing centres, and the best horses from each centre (i.e. the horses who have won or placed in the above classics) are "invited" to run. This race for 4-yr-olds is run in the first week of March. The colts carry 57 kgs and the fillies 55-1/2 kgs. The winner of this race is therefore the Champion of his generation. The day prior to the Invitation Cup is reserved for the "Sprinters' Cup" — a terms race for Indian horses 4-yr-old and upwards run over 1200 m, and the "Stayers' Cup" — a terms race for Indian horses 4-yr-old and upwards run over 3000 m. Again the best horses from each centre are invited to run. Therefore the winner of the former becomes the Champion sprinter, and the winner of the latter the Champion stayer of the country. Readers should note that the various Oaks, Derby and St. Leger races in India are for 4-yr-olds, unlike the principal racing countries. These races are held from January onwards and remember that all horses become a year older on January 1st.

The 2-yr-olds start racing only from November onwards at the principal racing centres, again unlike the principal racing countries. They run in terms races for Maiden 2-yr-olds / Maiden 3-yr-olds. They have about 5 months to break their maiden status. Horses who break their maiden status run in "Cup" races for 2-yr-olds / 3-yr-olds only. These races are from 1000 m to 1600 m. Therefore the horse who wins the most prestigious Cups can claim to be the Champion younger horse.

At the end of March racing ceases in the principal centres. Now the 3-yr-olds are "classified". In India all horses are divided into 6 "classes" — I, II, III, IV, VA and VB. Class I is the highest class, class II the next highest and so on, until class VB which is the lowest. These class races constitute over 90% of the races in the country, excluding the terms races for Maiden 2-yr-olds / 3-yr-olds. Do not equate these class races with Group races. They are all pure handicap events with the top-weighted horse carrying about 60 kgs and the bottom-weighted about 45 kgs. The 3-yr-olds are generally put in class VA, the better ones going to class IV or even class III. Now they can run against the older horses. They are expected to work their way up; if they win 2 races in a class they are promoted to the next higher class and so on, until they reach class I. But if a horse is not able to win 2 races in a class he does not go to the next higher class, and if he is not able to win a race in that class he is demoted to the next lower class. Therefore superior racers starting from class VA (or IV) reach class I by winning 2 races in each of the intervening classes. Average horses race in class III or IV. The substandard horses race in class VA and if they are not able to win even in this class, they are demoted to class VB.

The stake money increases as we go higher in class and is the highest for class I. All that readers need remember is this:

A horse who wins in in class I or II	is a	"superior" racer
A horse who wins in class III or IV	is an	"average" racer
A horse who wins only in class VA or VB	is a	"substandard" racer

A horse who has won a classic is automatically classified in class I or II. Therefore Indian horses from 3-yrs onwards will be running in any one of these 6 classes. These class races range from 1000 m to 2400 m with a few events over distances greater than 2400 m.

Apart from the classics and class races there are several valuable terms races, with or without penalties and allowances, for horses 4-yr-old and upwards. A few of them deserve special mention as they are the most prestigious and valuable and attract horses from all over the country. The details are as below:

Race	Centre	Distance
Calcutta Gold Cup*	Calcutta	1600 m
Guindy Gold Cup	Madras	1600 m
Idar Gold Cup	Hyderabad	1200 m
Queen Elizabeth II Cup	Calcutta	2800 m
R.W.I.T.C. Ltd. Invitational Cup	Bombay	2000 m
Maharaja's Gold Cup	Bangalore	2200 m
Governor's Cup	Bangalore	2400 m
Nizam's Gold Cup	Hyderabad	2000 m
President of India Gold Cup	Hyderabad	2400 m

* 3-yr-olds eligible

A number of prestigious terms races have been recently introduced for 2 and 3-yr-olds. I have made a special mention of these wherever necessary.

In April racing ceases in the principal racing centres, and the scene shifts to Ootacamund a hill-station in South India. Here racing takes place up to June with most of the races being class races. But 3 classics are held as below:

Nilgiris Fillies Trial Stakes	3-yr-old fillies	1400 m
Nilgiris Colts Trial Stakes	3-yr-old colts and geldings	1400 m
Nilgiris Derby	3-yr-olds	1600 m

Bangalore too, has a summer season (in addition to the principal winter season) from May to July with the following 3 classics as the main attraction:

Bangalore Fillies Trial Stakes	3-yr-old fillies	1600 m
Bangalore Colts Trial Stakes	3-yr-old colts and geldings	1600 m
Bangalore Derby	3-yr-olds	2000 m

Then Hyderabad, Mysore and Pune simultaneously begin another season which ends in October in the first two centres and in November in the third. The classic events there are:

HYDERABAD

Hyderabad Fillies Trial Stakes	3-yr-old fillies	1600 m
Hyderabad Colts Trial Stakes	3-yr-old colts and geldings	1600 m
Deccan Derby	3-yr-olds	2000 m

MYSORE

Mysore 1000 Guineas	3-yr-old fillies	1600 m
Mysore 2000 Guineas	3-yr-olds	1600 m
Mysore Derby	3-yr-olds	2000 m

There are no classics in Pune but there are valuable races for 3-yr-olds.

In November the horses return to their original centres and a new season begins, with a fresh crop of youngsters making their debut.

Readers would have noticed the large number of "classics" in the country — 25 winter classics + 12 summer classics. Strictly speaking we cannot consider all these races to be true classics. Most of them are events of regional and not national importance. The object of introducing so many classics was to stimulate the interest of owners in different parts of the country, and in that they have been eminently successful. We would not be wrong if we considered them to be the equivalent of true Pattern races abroad. But for the purpose of this book, I have considered a winner of any of the 37 classics to be a "classic" winner. In short:

A winner of the Indian Turf Invitation Cup, Sprinters' Cup or Stayers' Cup	is a	champion
A winner of any one of the 37 classics	is a	classic winner
A winner of a "class" race		as described earlier

NOMENCLATURE

A typical example of the nomenclature used is:

Belle Fill (filly, 1977, Three Wishes x Pretty Girl) : 12 wins, Mount Everest Cup, Allez France Cup, South India Gold Cup, Turf Club Cup (2400 m, classes II and III, Madras); 3rd Nilgiris Fillies Trial

Stakes, Tamil Nadu Commemoration Gold Cup (2000 m, classes I and II, Madras).

The year after the horse's name is the year in which she was foaled. Then come the names of her sire and dam followed by her race record. But the description does not mean Belle Fill ran 14 times won 12 races and placed 3rd twice. She ran a number of times, won 12 races and placed 2nd, 3rd and 4th on several occasions. To avoid cluttering up the book the details of place have been generally omitted unless it was a classic place. The 12 wins include the 4 "Cup" races mentioned. They have been specially mentioned as they are races of some significance. In this case they are class I or II events and they were the most prestigious won by the horse. This system has been adopted throughout the book. I do not expect, nor want, readers to ponder over the significance of the scores of cup races that are going to be mentioned. They have been included purely for the sake of continuity and record. Suffice to say they are all races of some significance and are invariably won by superior horses. In most cases I have made a specific mention of the long distance races won by a horse to indicate his staying ability. Different centres in the country organize races with the same name. To avoid confusion I have given the details of such races within brackets. Readers can now readily determine that Belle Fill was a superior racer of classic-placed standard with the ability to stay.

EARNINGS OF HORSES

I have scrupulously refrained from making any mention on the earnings of the horses concerned, as it is highly misleading. Every year there is a significant increase in prize money the world over. A winner this year would appear, in terms of earnings, to be vastly superior to a horse who had won the very same races five years earlier. Again a few horses manage to earn sizable amounts by placing frequently, or by winning a large number of small and insignificant races. Several outstanding horses have the mortification of placing 2nd or 3rd in several prestigious races. Their earnings are therefore relatively meagre. In all these cases a mention of earnings would be very misleading.

No attempt has been made to adopt "Black Type" nomenclature as a true Pattern race system is yet to be introduced in the country. Horses who ran in countries with a true Pattern race system have been classified as classic winners, champions, stakes winners or stakes-placed. Therefore readers will have no difficulty in judging the merit of the horses concerned.

CLASS AND APTITUDE

Before we plunge into the subject, we must understand the ideas of "class" and "aptitude". Class refers to the standard, the level, at which a horse raced. Did he distinguish himself in the classics and other prestigious races? Or did he run in races of average importance? Or was he content to run in races for substandard horses? Aptitude refers to the distance at which the horse excelled. We can conveniently divide all horses into 4 groups:

Horses who excel up to 1400 m	:	sprinters
Horses who excel from 1400 m to 1800 m	:	milers
Horses who excel from 1800 m to 2800 m	:	stayers
Horses who excel over 2800 m	:	extreme stayers

Now we can conveniently combine class and aptitude and describe a horse in a few words:

He was an outstanding sprinter.
She was an average sprinter-miler.
X was a classic winning stayer.
Y was a classic-placed miler.

And lastly we can describe horses who won from 1000 m to 2400 m or better still up to 2800 m — as those who won over the range of distances. If you categorize horses in this manner you need not bother to remember their exact race records.

Similarly we can say:

That stallion got average milers and stayers.
This broodmare produces superior extreme stayers.

Class is more important than aptitude! You have just purchased a costly youngster thinking that he would develop into a top class sprinter. But if he turned out to be a top class miler you would not be very unhappy. But if he developed into a very mediocre sprinter you would be extremely unhappy!

There is one more point of importance. I intensely dislike putting below average or substandard horses into the aptitudinal groups. You really can't call a substandard horse a "miler" or a "stayer". A substandard horse is a substandard horse. While we must classify superior and average horses, it is better to leave the substandard alone.

SPEED AND STAMINA

Throughout this book I have used the words "speed" and "stamina" in their strictly traditional sense, even though intrinsically they are both really the same. I have referred to horses who excelled up to 1400 m as speedy and those who excelled over distances greater than 2000 m as endowed with stamina. Horses who win over short distances but who cannot win over long distances lack stamina. Similarly horses who are not able to win over short distances lack speed. A horse with an ideal blend of speed and stamina excels from 1000 m to 2400 m or better still up to 2800 m.

QUALITIES OF A RACEHORSE

The thrilling victory of a horse in a prestigious race invariably brings out a variety of reactions. Pedigree enthusiasts will quickly point out his superior pedigree. Those who swear by conformation will urge one and all to try and fault his flawless physique. Admirers of the trainer and jockey will, no doubt, attribute his victory to systematic training and sympathetic riding. A few others may bluntly say that the opposition was substandard or that the going suited him. Another may emphasize the fighting qualities, tenacity and courage of the horse in question. We cannot disagree with any of these views.

To win races we need good horses. But a good horse cannot win races by himself. The care and attention he receives are equally important. Stable management must be of very high order. He must be well trained and ridden. We must pick the right races neither over-racing nor underracing him — something which is easier said than done. Then a lot depends on the manner in which the race was run, the going, the draw and the standard of the opposition. But all this is not going to help bad horses. We need good, superior horses to start with.

What exactly do we mean by a good horse? To many a good horse is a good pedigree. Is the horse really well-bred? Is his pedigree full of Derby winners and champions? Was his sire the champion sire? Is the tail female line really top class?

To others conformation precedes pedigree. They ask: "Would it not be infinitely wiser to look at the individual in question instead of poring over his pedigree?" Is he a horse of perfect conformation? Is he robust and healthy? Does he move well? Does he possess a certain vitality or "electricity"? — a quality which may be recognized but which is hard to describe. Therefore pedigree and conformation are the two major attributes that "shape" and "mould" a racehorse.

The third is temperament. Does the horse possess sound temperament? Is he intelligent and eager to learn? Is he bold and courageous and a fighter all the way? If the answers to all these questions are in the affirmative, the horse definitely has an edge. But we will know his temperament only when he starts racing.

We have noted all the beneficial qualities a horse can possess. They fall under "pedigree", "conformation" and "temperament". Therefore a good horse is one who possesses a good pedigree, conformation and temperament. To be sure very few horses score highly in all three categories and almost all the best horses had shortcomings in one category or the other. It is difficult to say one quality is more important or desirable than another. It is for you to decide on your priorities.

Conformation and temperament are out of the scope of this book. Therefore our first task is to study pedigree. This is done in the next chapter.

CHAPTER 2

Pedigree Analysis

MEANING OF THE PHRASE "WELL-BRED"

In the previous chapter I made mention of a "well-bred" horse. What exactly do we mean by the phrase "well-bred"? Every breeder claims his horses are well-bred. Owners as a rule get very upset and offended if anybody dare suggests that their horses are not well-bred! Surely you are not going to buy, or breed, indifferently-bred horses are you? Then if every alternate horse is well-bred, why bother about breeding and pedigree in the first place? And even if we have truly well-bred horses i.e. horses with top class pedigrees, we are not guaranteed success. For we will all readily agree that well-bred horses frequently fail and indifferently-bred horses come out on top. Then why all this fuss about breeding and pedigree in the first place? It is because:

The probability of a well-bred horse succeeding is far, far greater than that of an indifferently-bred horse.

In other words well-bred horses are inherently better racers. If a well-bred horse has a, say, 15% chance of success, an indifferently-bred horse will have at the most a 1% chance of success. Therefore we are all interested in well-bred horses.

Our next task is to identify and pin-point well-bred horses. To do so we must know the definition of the phrase well-bred. The phrase means so many things to so many people. But before we proceed further I would very much like readers to answer the questions below:

Which of the following horses are well-bred?

1) An Epsom Derby winner.

2) A half-sister to an Irish Oaks winner.

3) A horse who finished 3rd in the Indian Derby.

4) A son of an Epsom Derby winner.

5) A son of an Oaks winner.

6) A son of a Derby and an Oaks winner.

Truth to tell, none of the above horses are well-bred. Can we straightaway label an Epsom Derby winner as well-bred? If we do so it

10

follows that all Epsom Derby winners (and other classic winners) were well-bred. But readers will readily agree that this was not the case. Quite a few horses with average pedigrees (and a handful with substandard pedigrees) scored in the Epsom Derby and other classics. Therefore our first conclusion is:

The quality of a horse's pedigree i.e. his breeding is independent of his achievements on the track.

The act of winning a Derby, or an Oaks, or any other prestigious race does not make a horse well-bred. By the same logic the quality of a horse's pedigree does not diminish the moment he has lost a valuable race. A horse's pedigree and its quality is determined the moment he is foaled, or to be more precise, at the moment of conception. Then which horses are well-bred?

A well-bred horse is one whose sire was a superior sire, whose 1st, 2nd and 3rd maternal grandsires were superior maternal grandsires and whose 1st, 2nd, 3rd and 4th dams were successful broodmares who produced several superior racers.

Let us apply this definition to the above horses. Horses (1) and (3) need not be well-bred. A half-sister to an Irish Oaks winner need not also be well-bred. Suppose her sire was mediocre. Surely you are not going to call the offspring of such a stallion well-bred are you? This logic applies to horse (5) also. For we must ask, was the sire of that colt outstanding? Was the Oaks winner herself well-bred? Similarly horses (4) and (6) need not be well-bred. For no rule says that Derby winners must succeed in stud. Many were average and quite a few were failures.

Therefore when we are analyzing the pedigree of a horse, we are not bothered about the racing performances of the horses therein. They may have been classic winners, or average, or even substandard. As per the definition we are only concerned about their stud performances.

We can now lay down the procedure for identifying a well-bred horse. It is really simple. We must analyze his pedigree to come to a conclusion. Keeping his 4-generation pedigree in front of us, we must first study his sire. How successful was he? Did he get a large number of classic winners and superior racers? If he did he is superior. Then we must look at the dam — the bottom half of the pedigree. We can conveniently divide the bottom half into 2 parts — the maternal grandsires and the tail female line. We must determine whether the 1st, 2nd and 3rd maternal grandsires were superior i.e. whether their daughters produced a large number of superior racers including classic winners. We are not bothered about their performances as sires here. Then we must determine the quality of the tail female line. Were the 1st, 2nd, 3rd and 4th dams successful producers? Did they get a large number of superior racers? If the maternal grandsires and the dams in the tail female line were also superior, the horse is indeed well-bred.

Experienced readers would have noticed that the above definition is too severe. Literally only a handful of horses will qualify. It will be very difficult to use the definition practically. Hence it is necessary for us to modify it, simplify it. The first part of the definition can be easily satisfied — the horse must be by a superior sire. It is the second part that is difficult to satisfy. Firstly the dam of the horse must herself have a superior pedigree. Then she must have been a successful producer i.e. the horse in question is a half-brother or half-sister to a classic winner or superior racer. Let us assume that the dam has been very successful. She has produced a number of superior racers. Now isn't the quality of her pedigree a bit academic? Since she has proved to be a successful producer, we need not insist that her pedigree must be top class. (It may only be average.) We can automatically consider all her progeny out of superior stallions to be well-bred.

But not all mares would have produced a classic winner or superior racer e.g. mares whose progeny have just started to race. What about their progeny out of superior sires? Can we consider them to be well-bred? How can we judge them? In such cases we must study the maternal grandsires and tail female line. If both these sections are superior, the individual is well-bred. The logic is simple. Even though the dam of the horse in question is yet to produce a big winner, she definitely has the potential to do so as her pedigree is very strong. Therefore all her progeny out of superior stallions are well-bred.

There is a third alternative. We have a horse by a fair sire. His maternal grandsires too were only average and his tail female line is not outstanding. In short he is a horse with an average pedigree. But his full-brother was a champion who won several valuable races. Does his achievements alter the quality of the horse's pedigree? Yes, it does. For we can say: "Even though his pedigree is only average, another individual with the same pedigree excelled. Therefore this pedigree, this unique arrangement of names, is powerful. Hence we must consider the horse to be on par with well-bred horses. We must give him the status of a well-bred horse."

To summarize:

A well-bred horse is one who is a half-brother or half-sister to a classic winner, champion or superior racer by a superior sire.

or

A well-bred horse is one whose sire was superior, whose 1st, 2nd and 3rd maternal grandsires were also superior and whose 2nd, 3rd and 4th dams were successful, producing a number of superior racers.

or

A well-bred horse is a full-brother or full-sister to a classic winner, champion or superior racer.

We have just studied the phrase well-bred and defined it. We also saw the need to identify well-bred horses. To do so we have to analyze their pedigrees and see if they satisfy the definition. Therefore let us now rigorously analyze the pedigrees of two horses. There are other benefits too. We can determine not only the horse's class but also his aptitude. Will he be a sprinter or a stayer? Or will he possess an ideal blend of speed and stamina? Will he come to hand early or will he be late-maturing? Will he train on well? But remember pedigree is only one factor. Conformation and temperament are equally important.

The first horse is a bay colt by Prince Pradeep x Oh Calcutta.

Bay Colt (1976)	Prince Pradeep	Migoli	Bois Roussel — Vatout, Plucky Liege
			Mah Iran — Bahram, Mah Mahal
		Driving	Ratling Street — Fairway, Ranai
			Snow Line — Ujiji, Winter Sport
	Oh Calcutta	Paddykin	St. Paddy — Aureole, Edie Kelly
			Kilifi — Relic, Ethelreda
		Rockanella	Rock of Gibraltar — Rockefella, Toquade
			Superbe Rose — Tarquinius, Superbus, Rose Law

OH CALCUTTA: 1 win. This is her 1st foal.

ROCKANELLA: was not trained. Dam of:

Purple Heron: 3 wins.

Handicraft: 1 win.

Dominator: did not win.

Swiss Belle: unraced.

Storm Reine: did not win.

King's Law: did not win.

Oh Calcutta: as above.

SUPERBE ROSE: 1 win. Dam of:

Super Way: 3 wins.

Alkapuri: 8 wins, Governor's Cup (1 mile 1-1/2 furlongs, Hyderabad); 2nd South India 1000 Guineas.

Superbe Dust: 3 wins.

Allaudin: 1 win.

Pot-Pourri: 1 win.

Rose Rock: 6 wins, Sir Rahimtoola Chinoy Gold Cup.

Noble Venture: 14 wins (mostly in the lower classes).

Young Iraq: 1 win.

Supernatural: did not win.

Rockanella: as above.

ROSE LAW: ran only once in 2 yrs in Ireland. Imported into India as a broodmare. Dam of:

Tarquinne: 3 wins.

Arabian Night: did not win.

Superbe Rose: as above.

Let us first study his sire. Prince Pradeep was an outstanding racehorse and a phenomenal sire. His dam, a tail female line descendant of Toboggan, was imported into India "in foal" to Migoli and Prince Pradeep was foaled on April 9th, 1960.

Racing in Bombay he won the Indian Triple Crown and 6 other races. He was distinctly unlucky to finish 2nd in the Indian Turf Invitation Cup. He was undoubtedly the best of his generation.

Retired to stud his performance was awesome. He started getting classic winners right from his first crop. He was the champion sire in 1977-'78 and always finished "high-up" in the Sires lists — 2nd in 1978-'79 and

4th in 1976-'77. He was also the "unofficial" champion sire several times. (The National Horse Breeding Society of India started publishing the Indian Turf Statistical Record from 1975-'76 only. This is the authoritative publication and most of the data for this book has been extracted from its first six volumes. But racing under rules has been going on for decades. As authoritative records were not maintained, I refer to the champion sires and maternal grandsires during these early years as "unofficial" champions.)

Prince Pradeep's progeny possessed an over-abundance of class with an ideal blend of speed and stamina. Of sound conformation and temperament, they came to hand early and trained on well. For about a decade they held absolute sway over their rivals. His colts and fillies were equally good. His classic winners were:

Bright Hanovar (1967): 11 wins, champion, Indian Turf Invitation Cup, Indian Derby and St. Leger; 2nd Indian 2000 Guineas (on disqualification). Sire.

Royal Challenge (1967): 11 wins, won all the 5 classics in Calcutta; 3rd Indian Turf Invitation Cup.

Noor-E-Shiraz (1968): 7 wins, Indian 2000 Guineas and St. Leger (in record time). Sire.

Elegance (1967), **Heliantha** (1970), **Ghazab** (1972) and **Reprint** (1973) won the Indian 1000 Guineas and Oaks, while **Nectar Queen** (1970) and **Round Off** (1972) won the Bangalore St. Leger. **Reflect** (1974) won the Indian 1000 Guineas and Bangalore St. Leger. His other classic winners were:

Prince Blossom (1969): 8 wins, Calcutta Derby and 2000 Guineas

Beloved Prince (1974): 8 wins, Bangalore Arc de Triomphe, Mysore Derby. Sire.

Royal Double (1971): 5 wins, Calcutta 2000 Guineas, Bangalore Colts Trial Stakes. Sire.

Ipi Tombi (1974): 14 wins, Indian 2000 Guineas. Sire.

Princely (1969): 4 wins, South India 1000 Guineas.

Vox Populi (1975): 3 wins, Indian 1000 Guineas.

Skyline (1971): 2-1/2 wins, dead-heated for win in the Bangalore Derby. Sire.

In addition to the above horses Prince Pradeep got dozens of other superior racers. To own a Prince Pradeep was the ambition of most owners. His death at the age of 16 was a grievous blow to Indian breeding.

Oh Calcutta won only 1 race and placed. Since this is her 1st foal, we do not know her performance as a producer. We must therefore study her pedigree in great detail.

Her sire, the 1st maternal grandsire of the colt, Paddykin (1964) won 3 races in England. Imported into India and retired to stud, he was successful getting a number of superior racers. His best progeny included:

Fire Haven (1970): 8-1/2 wins, Bangalore and Deccan Derby, dead-heated for win in the Bangalore Fillies Trial Stakes, President of India Gold Cup. (She won the race as a 3-yr-old. Since then 3-yr-olds are not eligible.) Unfortunately she then had a setback in training and did not run in the winter classics. She was undoubtedly the best of her generation.

Shimmering Gold (1975): 9 wins, South India and Mysore 1000 Guineas, South India Oaks.

Green Goddess (1976): 5 wins, Bangalore Oaks.

Look of Eagles (1977): 5 wins, Deccan Derby.

His other superior racers included: **Noble Dancer, Red Regent, Resolution, Virginian, What More, Karmala, La Gitana, Amarantha** and **Young Moor.**

But we are not bothered about Paddykin's performance as a sire here. We are interested in his performance as a maternal grandsire i.e. in the performances of his daughters as broodmares. Were they successful producers? Yes, Paddykin is definitely making a mark, a big impact, as a maternal grandsire. His daughters are proving to be successful producers. He is already the maternal grandsire of:

Fire Flash (1979, Satinello x Fire Haven): 9 wins, Calcutta 2000 Guineas, Governor's Gold Trophy (1400 m, class 1, Mysore), Guindy Grand Prix (1600 m, 3-yr-olds, Madras); 2nd Bangalore Colts Trial Stakes; 3rd Bangalore, Deccan and Mysore Derby.

Vibrant (1980, Malvado x Fire Haven): 8 wins, Bangalore Triple Crown; 2nd Indian Derby.

Waynak (High Commission x Hi Sonnie): 8 wins, P.D. Bolton Cup, Monitor Cup.

Hilal (Republican x Hi Sonnie): 8 wins, Southern Command Cup, Richelieu Cup.

Vagabond (Lairg x La Gitana): 8 wins, Hovercraft Cup.

Wandering Minstrel (Young Lochinvar x La Gitana): 8 wins, Republic Cup (1600 m, classes I and II, Calcutta), Galstaun Cup.

Deejay (Disclose x Peridot): 6 wins, Nawabzada Rashiduzzafar Khan Trophy.

Kizzy (Hard Held x Paddy): 9 wins, Ardent Knight Trophy.

Abhinandan (Mighty Sparrow x Amarantha): 6 wins, Mayfowl Cup.

Obolensky (Simead x Amarantha): 4 wins, Calcutta Racehorse Owners Society Cup, George Williamson Indian Produce Stakes and Classic Cup — all in his first season at Calcutta, making him one of the best youngsters in the country.

It is clear that Paddykin is well on his way to becoming a very successful, if not outstanding, maternal grandsire. In fact the above results are all the more impressive, as only a handful of his daughters have got runners. Several of them have just entered stud and their progeny are sure to be equally talented.

The 2nd maternal grandsire Rock of Gibraltar (1951) too was very successful. He only placed in England. In India he won the Maharaja's Gold Cup, Eclipse Stakes, C.N. Wadia Gold Cup and 8 other races. He also placed in the Queen Elizabeth II Cup.

Retired to stud he was a staggering success. His progeny swept classic after classic almost unchallenged. We are going to study their performances in detail a little later. Here we are interested in his performance as a maternal grandsire. He was very successful always finishing high-up in the Maternal grandsires lists. Between 1975 and '81 he was within the top 10 except in 1979-'80. He was the maternal grandsire of:

Maltese Prince (1980, Zelenko x Queen of Gibraltar): 6 wins, Calcutta and Nilgiris Derby, Mysore 2000 Guineas.

Nectar Queen (1970, Prince Pradeep x Rocklie): 6 wins, Bangalore St. Leger, Eclipse Stakes of India; 2nd Indian 1000 Guineas and Oaks; 3rd Indian Turf Invitation Cup.

Wheels (1980, Satinello x Rock Haven): 3 wins, Calcutta 1000 Guineas; 2nd Calcutta Oaks.

He was also the maternal grandsire of the following superior racers:

King of Seers (Red Indian x Koh-E-Sina): 13 wins, Governor's Cup, Kashmir Gold Cup (2400 m, classes I and II, Madras), Nepal Gold Cup (2200 m, classes I and II, Calcutta); 2nd Bangalore and Hyderabad Colts Trial Stakes, Nizam's Gold Cup.

Tranquility (Red Rufus x Sparkling Rock): 13-1/2 wins, Mysore City Gold Cup (2000 m, 4-yr-olds and over, Mysore), Governor's Gold Cup (2000 m, classes I and II, Mysore) twice.

Running Blossom (Mossy Bear x Innocent): 11 wins, Karnataka Sub-Area Cup (2000 m, class I, Bangalore), Jayachamaraja Wadiyar Cup, Krishnaraja Cup.

Cannon Fire (Canton x Huntress): 11 wins, Air Force Cup, Mysore Race Club Cup (1400 m, class I, Hyderabad).

Replay (Prince Pradeep x Replica): 5 wins, Aga Khan's Spring Cup (1800 m, classes I and II, Bombay).

Sinn Fein (Baraloy x Alcmene): 5 wins, Gen. Obaidullah Khan Gold Cup (2000 m, classes II and III, Bombay); 2nd Byculla Club Cup (2800 m, classes I and II, Bombay).

Sweet Afton (The Wing x Roman Rock): 5 wins, Her Majesty Plate (2000 m, classes I and II, Bombay).

The 3rd maternal grandsire Tarquinius Superbus (1942) placed 3rd in his only start in England. Imported into India and retired to stud, he was successful getting among others:

Tosca (1951): 5 wins, Indian 1000 Guineas and Oaks, R.R. Ruia Gold Cup; 3rd Indian St. Leger.

Roman Dancer (1948): 5 wins, Indian 1000 Guineas.

Fiona: 7 wins; 3rd Indian 1000 Guineas.

Grecian Rose: 12 wins, Chikkavaram Gold Cup.

His daughters too made admirable broodmares. Tosca herself was the dam of classic winners **Fair Haven, Mica Empress, Mica Emperor** and **Rock's Son,** while Roman Dancer was the dam of classic winner **Roman Rose.**

Therefore the colt's 1st, 2nd and 3rd maternal grandsires were very successful.

Now we have to analyze his tail female line. We are eager to see if the female family is also top class, and whether it has produced a number of superior racers. But a careful study shows otherwise. The female line is definitely below average. Of the 20 horses produced by the 2nd, 3rd and 4th dams only 2 — *Alkapuri* and Rose Rock — were superior racers. Sadly the others were not even average; they were substandard.

We can now sum-up our findings. We have found that the colt's:

Sire : Outstanding
Maternal grandsires : Superior
Tail female line : Substandard

Therefore as per our definition the colt is not well-bred. His tail female line lets him down. It is the weak link in his pedigree. However since 2 of his 3 pedigree "components" are superior, his pedigree is marginally above average.

We must now try to determine his aptitude. It is clear that he will get a mile without difficulty as his sire and maternal grandsires were strong in stamina. But though his sire was a renowned sire of stayers we cannot say he will stay. For the weaknesses in his female line now become very real. It is not strong in stamina. Therefore our conclusion is:

The colt will be an average to marginally above average miler with a chance of getting longer distances. Like other progeny of Prince Pradeep he is bound to be sound and robust and train well. He is sure to win his share of races.

The colt named San Francisco did more than that. He was a genuine galloper and became Prince Pradeep's 18th classic winner. He broke his maiden status in his very first start as a 3-yr-old (on 1-1-1979). He then won the Champagne Stakes (1400 m, 3-yr-olds) and Grand Annual Handicap (1600 m, 3-yr-olds) at Calcutta. He then raced in Bangalore and won a 1400 m race in class III. Returning to Calcutta he developed further. He won the Calcutta 2000 Guineas and placed 2nd in the Calcutta Derby. He confirmed that he possessed high class stamina by winning the Bhutan Gold Cup (2400 m, classes I and II, Calcutta). In all he won 8 races and placed. He has been retired for stallion duties. Let us see how he will fare.

Oh Calcutta is proving to be a very successful producer. Her 3rd foal Baby Oh Baby won 5 races including the Maharaja of Morvi Cup (1400 m, 3-yr-olds, Bombay) and R.W.I.T.C. Committee Gold Cup (1200 m, class I, Bombay). He also placed 2nd in the Indian 2000 Guineas. Since Baby Oh Baby is by Valoroso, an outstanding sire, we can straightaway say he is well-bred. For he is a half-brother to a classic winner by an outstanding sire. Unfortunately Oh Calcutta's 2nd and 4th foals died. Her 5th foal a bay colt by Escapologist, Insignia, is in training and has won his first race.

The next pedigree we are going to analyze is that of a chestnut colt by Mr. Prospector x Hopespringseternal.

		Native Dancer	Polynesian / Geisha
	Raise a Native		
		Raise You	Case Ace / Lady Glory
Mr. Prospector			
		Nashua	Nasrullah / Segula
	Gold Digger		
		Sequence	Count Fleet / Miss Dogwood
Chestnut Colt (1978)			
		Tom Fool	Menow / Gaga
	Buckpasser		
		Busanda	War Admiral / Businesslike
Hopespringseternal			
		Princequillo	Prince Rose / Cosquilla
	Rose Bower		
		Lea Lane	Nasrullah / Lea Lark

HOPESPRINGSETERNAL: unraced. This is her 1st foal.

ROSE BOWER: 6 wins, Matron Stakes, Princess Pat Stakes. Dam of:

>**True Colors:** 6 wins, Round Table Handicap, Leonard Richards Stakes, Sword Dancer Handicap.
>
>**Spray:** 7 wins, Tri-State Handicap; 2nd Vivacious Handicap.
>
>**Over to You:** 2 wins in England, Intercraft Solario Stakes.
>
>**Cabin:** 6 wins; 2nd Berkely Handicap. Sire.
>
>**Forefather:** winner in Ireland and U.S.A.; 2nd Whitehall Stakes.
>
>**Rainbow Rose:** 2 wins.

LEA LANE: 4 wins, Durazna Stakes, Miss America Stakes (equalled track record), Pollyana Stakes; 2nd Arlington Lassie Stakes, Mademoiselle Stakes, Alcibiades Stakes, Kentucky Oaks. Dam of 8 winners including:

>**Foxy Quilla:** 2 wins; 3rd Princess Pat Stakes.
>
>**Ruffinal:** 2 wins; 3rd Garden State Stakes.
>
>**Manwari:** 4 wins in England; 3rd Gordon Stakes.

Involvement: 5 wins.

Contango: winner.

LEA LARK: 3 wins; 3rd Arlington Lassie Stakes, Ashland Stakes, Pimlico Oaks. Dam of 12 winners including:

Leallah: 10 wins, champion 2-yr-old filly, Arlington Lassie Stakes.

Shama: 5 wins; 2nd Cleopatra Stakes.

Lea Moon: 6 wins.

Let us go component by component.

The colt's sire Mr. Prospector won 7 races from 14 starts at 3 and 4. At 3 he won a maiden special weights race and 2 allowance races, establishing a new track record at Gulfstream. At 4 he won 4 races including the Whirlaway Handicap over 6 furlongs setting a new track record. He also placed 2nd in the Carter Handicap (Gr. II) and Firecracker Handicap (Gr. III) and 3rd in the Paumonok Handicap (Gr. III).

These victories do not reflect his true merit as he had bad setbacks in training. At 3 he was so brilliant and impressive that it was decided to train him for the Kentucky Derby. But he lost a preparatory race and was most unfortunately injured in the next. The injury ended the year for him and he was rested for more than 6 months. He started racing again and showed excellent form by winning the Gravesend Handicap beating a fine field. He was then beaten a nose in his next race, the Firecracker Handicap. Shortly after he fractured his sesamoid. This injury ended his racing career and he was retired to stud. The dominant impression was that he was a very speedy individual who excelled up to 7 furlongs.

He has proved to be a truly outstanding stallion. Among the leading sires, he is already the sire of 61 stakes winners. He started getting champions and Group I winners right from his 1st crop. His best progeny include:

Conquistador Cielo: 9 wins, Horse of the Year at 3, champion 3-yr-old colt, Belmont Stakes, Metropolitan Handicap (Gr. I).

It's in the Air: 16 wins, champion 2-yr-old filly, Vanity Handicap (Gr. I) twice.

Gold Beauty: 6 wins, champion sprinter, Fall Highweight Handicap (Gr. II).

Hello Gorgeous: 4 wins, William Hill Futurity (Gr. I), Royal Lodge Stakes (Gr. II).

Fappiano: 10 wins, Metropolitan Handicap (Gr. I).

The colt's dam Hopespringseternal did not race. This is her first foal.

Her sire — the maternal grandsire of the colt — Buckpasser (1963) was a stakes winner of 25 races including the American Derby, Jockey Club Gold Cup, Arlington Classic etc. Retired to stud he was very successful getting 35 stakes winners including several champions. But again we are not bothered about his performance as a sire here. Was he a successful maternal grandsire? Did his daughters produce a large number of superior racers? Yes they did. Among the leading maternal grandsires, he became champion maternal grandsire of North America in 1983. He is already the maternal grandsire of:

Coastal (Majestic Prince x Alluvial): 8 wins, Belmont Stakes, Monmouth Invitational Handicap (Gr. I), Dwyer Handicap (Gr. II).

Plugged Nickle (Key to the Mint x Toll Booth): 11 wins, champion sprinter, Florida Derby (Gr. I), Wood Memorial Stakes (Gr. I).

Try My Best (Northern Dancer x Sex Appeal): 4 wins, champion 2-yr-old in England, William Hill Dewhurst Stakes (Gr. I), Larkspur Stakes (Gr. III).

Believe It (In Reality x Breakfast Bell): 6 wins, Wood Memorial Stakes (Gr. I), Remsen Stakes (Gr. I); 2nd Florida Derby (Gr. I); 3rd Kentucky Derby, Preakness Stakes.

Private Account (Damascus x Numbered Account): 6 wins, Gulfstream Park Handicap (Gr. I), Widener Handicap (Gr. I).

The 2nd maternal grandsire Princequillo (1940) was truly outstanding. He was the leading maternal grandsire on no fewer than 8 occasions, a performance unsurpassed in the last 30 years. He was a stakes winner of 12 races including the Jockey Club Gold Cup, Saratoga Cup, Saratoga Handicap etc. He was also a very successful sire with 65 stakes winners. I do not think it is necessary for me to describe the achievements of his daughters in detail. Suffice to say over 200 of them were at stud. They produced about 1000 winners who won about 5000 races. They included over 150 stakes winners. About 65% of his daughters were stakes producing mares. I am sure readers would have easily grasped the magnitude of his achievements.

The 3rd maternal grandsire Nasrullah (1940) needs no introduction. At 2 he was champion 2-yr-old colt with victories in the Coventry Stakes and Great Bradley Stakes. At 3 he won the Champion Stakes and was 3rd in the Derby. His stud success is a legend. He was the sire of 99 stakes winners with over a dozen champions in England and U.S.A. His daughters too excelled. About 150 of them were responsible for about 600 winners who won about 3000 races. About 140 of them were stakes winners. Over a 100 of his daughters were stakes producing mares.

In short the 3 maternal grandsires of the colt are truly outstanding. There is plenty of talent in the tail female line too. His 2nd, 3rd and 4th dams were prolific producers. Rose Bower was a stakes winner and was the dam of stakes winners True Colors, Spray and Over to You. Lea Lane was also a stakes winner and was the dam of stakes-placed horses, while Lea Lark was the dam of champion Leallah and stakes winner Shama. Therefore out of the 34 foals produced by this tail female line, as many as 7 were stakes winners including 1 champion. In addition several were stakes-placed.

Summing up we have:

Sire	:	Outstanding
Maternal grandsires	:	Outstanding
Tail female line	:	Superior to outstanding

The colt's pedigree satisfies our definition. He is definitely well-bred. Now we must try to determine his aptitude. There are conflicting signs. His sire is proving to be versatile. In view of his own racing performance (and pedigree) it is not surprising that he has started getting excellent sprinter-milers. His progeny come to hand early and excel at 2. Then they train on well to win their share of valuable races at 3 and 4. But a few of his progeny like Conquistador Cielo are proving to be genuine stayers as well. But nevertheless a majority of Mr. Prospector's progeny are sprinter-milers. However there is no doubt at all about the stamina imparted by his maternal grandsires. They were the maternal grandsires of outstanding horses who excelled over the entire range of distances. But the tail female line is not strong in genuine, high class stamina. There is only a trace of stamina. I think we can safely say that speed, rather than stamina, is the principal characteristic of his pedigree. Therefore our conclusion is:

The colt is extremely well-bred. Like most of Mr. Prospector's progeny he is sure to come to hand early and excel at 2. He will train on well and win valuable races at 3 and 4. We can safely say that he will excel up to a mile. But we cannot rule out his chances of getting longer distances.

The colt named Miswaki ran very true to his pedigree. He was a Group I winner of 6 races. At 2 he raced in France and England winning the Prix de la Salamandre (1400 m, Gr. I) and Prix Yacowlef (1000 m). He was 2nd in the Prix Morny (1200 m, Gr. I) and 3rd in the William Hill Dewhurst Stakes (7 furlongs, Gr. I). At 3 racing in the U.S.A. he won 4 races including the Charles Hatton Stakes (6 furlongs) slicing 1/5th second of the course record. He also placed 2nd (by a neck) in the Fall Highweight Handicap (6 furlongs, Gr. II). He has been retired to stud.

Hopespringseternal subsequently produced a stakes-placed colt by Secretariat, a filly by Secretariat and a colt by Honest Pleasure who placed.

I am sure readers have understood the technique of pedigree analysis and can use it to identify well-bred horses without the slightest difficulty. The following procedure may be conveniently adopted:

First check whether the horse in question is a full-brother or full-sister to a superior racer. If so he/she automatically gets the status of a well-bred horse irrespective of the quality of his/her pedigree. Next study the sire and see whether he is superior. Remember only the progeny of superior sires (excluding horses in the above category) can qualify. Then study the dam and see whether she has produced at least one superior racer. If she has the horse is well-bred. If not study the maternal grandsires and tail female line, as we have done, and see whether they are superior. If they are the horse is well-bred. But even in the former cases you must analyze the pedigree fully in order to obtain more information about the horse.

I have deliberately selected horses from two different countries to show that the principles of pedigree analysis are the same throughout the world. You may analyze the pedigree of a Japanese thoroughbred, Kenyan thoroughbred or Canadian thoroughbred; the questions you are going to ask are the same: "How successful was the sire? How many big winners are there in the tail female line? How did the maternal grandsires fare?"

MISTAKES MADE IN PEDIGREE ANALYSIS

I have heard people say: "Look! This horse is well-bred! He has Nearco in the 3rd generation and Hyperion in the 4th!" They have conveniently forgotten that there are thousands of horses with crosses of Nearco and Hyperion. A few others will say : "She is a well-bred filly. She is a daughter of Mill Reef isn't she?" Or: "This colt is fabulously bred. He is a son of the great Nijinsky!" Needless to say all daughters of Mill Reef, or sons of Nijinsky, are not well-bred. You must not jump to conclusions. You must analyze his pedigree and see whether he qualifies. I am sure you did not commit these mistakes in the past and are not going to do so in future.

A very serious mistake is to confuse, mix up the different branches (stirpes) of the tail female line. Even experienced breeders and owners are guilty of this error. This will become very clear with an example. Let us go back to Oh Calcutta. We studied the Oh Calcutta — Rockanella Superbe Rose — Rose Law tail female line and found that it was substandard. But the same tail female line can be made to appear really top class as below:

OH CALCUTTA: 1 win. This is her first foal.

ROCKANELLA: was not trained. Dam of:

> **Purple Heron:** 3 wins.
> **Handicraft:** 1 win.
> **Dominator:** did not win.
> **Swiss Belle:** unraced. Dam of **Mitzi Lou,** 3 wins.
> **Storm Reine:** did not win.
> **King's Law:** did not win.
> **Oh Calcutta:** as above.

SUPERBE ROSE: 1 win. Dam of:

> **Super Way:** 3 wins.
> **Alkapuri:** 8 wins, Governor's Cup (1 mile 1-1/2 furlongs, Hyderabad); 2nd South India 1000 Guineas. Dam of **Red Satin** (13 wins, South India 2000 Guineas, Mysore Derby, Bangalore and Hyderabad Colts Trial Stakes), **Mighty Bear** (8 wins, Ramanatha Iyer Memorial Cup), **Om Shanthi** (6 wins, herself dam of the winners **Comedy Star, Impertinent** and **Vishwa Vijeta**) and other winners.
> **Superbe Dust:** 3 wins.
> **Allaudin:** 1 win.
> **Pot-Pourri:** 1 win. Dam of the winners Great Memories and Future Flash.
> **Rose Rock:** 6 wins, Sir Rahimtoola Chinoy Gold Cup. Dam of **Joint Venture,** 8 wins.
> **Noble Venture:** 14 wins (mostly in the lower classes).
> **Young Iraq:** 1 win.
> **Supernatural:** did not win. Dam of **Everything Nice,** 7 wins and **Climax,** 4 wins.
> **Rockanella:** as above.

ROSE LAW: ran only once at 2 yrs in Ireland. Imported into India as a broodmare. Dam of:

Tarquinne: 3 wins.

Arabian Night: did not win. Dam of the winners **Knight Companion, Jai Hanuman, Lovely Pet, Fighting Fury, Rebel Star, Sizzler** and **Golden Dream.** The last named was herself the dam of **Purse of Gold** (7 wins, Allez France Cup), **Ivanjica** (India) (8 wins, South India 1000 Guineas, Hyderabad Fillies Trial Stakes; 2nd South India Derby, Oaks and St. Leger) and **Sporting Tradition** (9 wins, Cecil Gray Cup, Glasgow Courser Cup).

Superbe Rose: as above.

How did this happen? The family now appears to be really top class with classic winners and superior racers! Did we err earlier? We did not. Here we have included all the other descendants of Rose Law even though they do not belong to the branch in question. How is this so? Consider Ivanjica (India). Her pedigree is given below:

		Star of Gwalior	Hyder Ali
	Buckpasser		Lady Emma
		Sans Peur	Prince Chevalier
Ivanjica (India)			Golden Flower
(Ch, 1974)		Babbanio	My Babu
	Golden Dream		Butterfly Blue
		Arabian Night	Tarquinius Superbus
			Rose Law

Study her tail female line carefully. Is it not that of Golden Dream — Arabian Night — Rose Law? Isn't this another branch of the Rose Law family? An offspring of Ivanjica will have Buckpasser (India), Babbanio and Tarquinius Superbus as his maternal grandsires and Ivanjica, Golden Dream, Arabian Night and Rose Law in his tail female line, while an offspring of Oh Calcutta will naturally have Paddykin, Rock of Gibraltar and Tarquinius Superbus as his maternal grandsires and Oh Calcutta, Rockanella, Superbe Rose and Rose Law in his tail female line. Therefore we cannot incorporate Ivanjica's achievements in Oh Calcutta's tail female line, thereby giving the entirely erroneous impression that it has produced a classic winner. It has not. Another branch of the Rose Law family produced Ivanjica. San Francisco is the first classic winner to be produced by the Rose Law — Superbe Rose — Rockanella — Oh Calcutta branch. By this reasoning Alkapuri's success as a broodmare too does not alter the quality of Oh Calcutta's female line. But again this information has been included in Oh Calcutta's pedigree.

The net result is Oh Calcutta's female line appears to be top class while it is not. We have seen that it is below average! Therefore you must separate the different branches of the tail female line and study the particular branch of the dam ignoring the others.

This is easily accomplished. Write down only the progeny of the 1st, 2nd, 3rd and 4th dams as I have done. Completely ignore the progeny of the other mares in the female line as they belong to different branches. Now judge the female line. This is the procedure I have adopted throughout the book.

Now imagine a daughter of Oh Calcutta in stud. What is the quality of her tail female line? We will have:

DAUGHTER OF OH CALCUTTA:

OH CALCUTTA: 1 win. Dam of:

San Francisco: as described

Baby Oh Baby: as described.

Insignia: as described.

ROCKANELLA: as described.

SUPERBE ROSE: as described.

It is at once superior to Oh Calcutta's. Oh Calcutta by her own merit as a broodmare has lifted her branch of the Rose Law family to almost above average standard. Therefore the quality of the tail female line of her descendants has gone up.

Mixing-up the different branches of a tail female line is a common error. It is done throughout the world unconsciously or consciously to make the female line appear better than it actually is. The moment you sort out the different branches, you will find that what remains is completely different from what originally appeared. Therefore you must not forget this very important step.

When must we study all the branches of a tail female line as a whole? It is when we want to study the performance of the mare as a foundation broodmare. Consider Rose Law. How did her descendants fare in a new country? To answer this question we must study all the horses in every branch of her tail female line. In doing so we find that she is the ancestress of 3 classic winners in Red Satin, Ivanjica and San Francisco. After some time as the different branches grow and expand Golden Dream, Alkapuri and Oh Calcutta will become foundation broodmares in their own right and Rose Law will fade into the background. This is how female lines grow and develop. It is a natural process.

PRACTICAL DIFFICULTIES IN PEDIGREE ANALYSIS

In the pedigree analysis of San Francisco and Miswaki I made a major assumption. I analyzed the pedigrees at the time of writing i.e. in 1984 in order to give readers the benefit of additional information. But when must we analyze a pedigree? Naturally when the horse is coming up for sale as a youngster. In the case of San Francisco it would have been necessary for us to analyze his pedigree during February 1978, as he was coming up for sale then in Bombay. Now let us analyze his pedigree as on February 1978. Would our analysis be different? Yes!

We would have no difficulty regarding Prince Pradeep as his 1st crop started racing in 1969. San Francisco was a member of his last crop. But we could not have judged Paddykin as a maternal grandsire then, as Oh Calcutta was a member of his 2nd crop and among the first of his daughters to go to stud. He was then making a name as a sire. We could not have even judged Rock of Gibraltar fully as a maternal grandsire as a large number of his daughters were active. Now suppose San Francisco was a member of Prince Pradeep's 1st crop. Pedigree analysis becomes impossible! For we have:

Sire	:	Too early to judge
Dam	:	Too early to judge
First maternal grandsire	:	Too early to judge

How can we analyze a pedigree when we cannot judge the horses in the three key positions? This problem must be faced when we consider the progeny of 1st crop or 2nd crop sires. Will he be a successful stallion in the first place? Then what will be his aptitude? If the stallion has made a bright start pedigree analysis will be a little easier, but otherwise? Then what about the maternal grandsire? Judging a maternal grandsire is really tricky as readers will learn in subsequent chapters. At this stage I will only say that all successful sires do not become equally successful maternal grandsires and average sires can become very successful maternal grandsires. Therefore we have to predict the performances of the sire, dam and maternal grandsire. In this even the experts are more often wrong than right. But nevertheless we cannot avoid the task. It is not always possible to buy horses with proven sires, dams and maternal grandsires. And every sire, dam and maternal grandsire was "unproven" at one time. But as we learn more about them we will find that the task is not hopeless. We can make an estimate of their behaviour.

The important thing for readers to note here is that there will be horses in a number of pedigrees whose stud performances cannot be judged at the time of analysis. You have to judge all the horses whose performances can be really and truly judged and estimate the performances of the others. As you go through this book you will surely be able to perform the task with success.

Another difficulty lies in studying the maternal grandsires. There is absolutely no difficulty as far as the sires are concerned. Their achievements are included in the auction catalogue itself in great detail. Similarly the tail female lines can be studied after separating the different branches. But what about the maternal grandsires? You would have noticed that auction catalogues do not give any information about them. They are apparently taken for granted. I request readers to wait till we come to the chapters on maternal grandsires where we will learn to appraise them.

CHAPTER 3

Stallions – 1

In this chapter we will make a detailed study of stallion behaviour. How do they behave? Is their behaviour more or less identical or does it vary a great deal? Can we measure their success precisely? What exactly do we want from them?

A stallion serves not one but forty mares every year. (A "book" of forty mares is the standard in the industry. Several may cover more; the less popular cover less.) The stallion's job is to get as many superior racers as possible out of his mares. To do so the stallion himself must be of the highest class.

Let us quickly write down the qualities a prospective stallion must possess. He must obviously be a top class racehorse who has won and placed in the classics and other prestigious races. He must be genuine, sound and tough. He must be a horse of excellent build and conformation. He must also possess good temperament. Above all he must have a top class pedigree. Apart from the above we would also like him to have the following qualities: An ideal blend of speed and stamina instead of a marked preference for one distance. Precocious speed i.e. "early" speed which enabled him to win valuable races as a 2-yr-old. Soundness throughout training and a true zest for racing. We would like him to have all these qualities so that he can, hopefully, pass them on to his progeny. Some succeed while others, alas, fail.

But how do we know that a particular stallion has succeeded and another has failed? It's simple! We only have to look in the "Sires lists". At the end of each year Turf historians write down all the winners (and placed) under their respective sires. Then the value of the races won by them (and the value of their places) is also written down and totalled. Therefore we know the money earned by the progeny of each stallion. This information is neatly listed to get the Sires list — total money earned.

In 1979-80 the progeny of Everyday earned Rs.24,77,563.* Since no other stallion had greater earnings Everyday became the champion stallion of 1979-80 — total money won. He was represented by 33 runners who started 251 times. All of them did not win or place. 27 of his runners won

* *Indian Turf Statistical Record - Volume 5.*

53 races among themselves. Therefore we have, in a nutshell, the achievements of the progeny of Everyday for the year 1979-80.

But this is not the only list. Another list is prepared which simply gives the total number of races won by the stallion's progeny. In this list Everyday is not 1st but 3rd. Satinello topped this list with 68 wins followed by Rapparee with 55. This list should be interpreted with care. A stallion whose progeny win a large number of races of average or even below average value will finish high-up here but not in the first list.

The third list gives the number of winners. Everyday, as mentioned, had 27 winners. This put him in 3rd place as Satinello and Rapparee had 33 winners each. This list is also very important. Frequently average or even indifferent stallions get 1 or 2 big winners who boost the stallion's rank in the first and second lists. But the third list will give a fairer picture of his ability, as his outstanding horse will count as 1 winner only.

The fourth list gives the average earnings "per start" A stallion finishes high-up in this list. What does it signify? It means the stallion's progeny were winning and placing in the most prestigious and valuable races. Therefore their earnings "per start" was very high. The opposite is also true. This means the stallion's progeny were competing in races of little or no significance. Therefore their earnings per start was low. In this list Everyday finished 2nd.

The four lists we have studied are:

1) Total earnings.
2) Number of races won.
3) Number of winners.
4) Average earnings per start.

These lists are extremely important. Readers should study each list carefully over a period of time — say 10 years — and see how each stallion has fared. See how young stallions climb up the lists while stallions past their peak drop down. See how last year's champion has fared this year. Identify the stallions who were consistently near the top. Was any stallion champion twice? Identify stallions on the fringe of top class.

The National Horse Breeding Society of India compiles and publishes these lists yearly in the Indian Turf Statistical Record. The Sires of Winners supplement to *The Thoroughbred Record* gives the lists (plus several others) for the stallions of North America (excluding Puerto Rico and Mexico City). All journals devoted to racing and breeding publish them. I urge readers to study them carefully and preserve them for future reference.

Our next task is to study the lists simultaneously and determine the performance and behaviour of different stallions. Let us determine the performance of Rapparee for the year 1979-80. His rank in the lists was as below:

Total earnings	:	4th with about Rs.11 lakhs
Number of races won	:	2nd with 55
Number of winners	:	1st with 33
Average earnings per start	:	31st with about Rs.3,000/-

His 45 runners started 366 times. 33 of them won 55 races.

What type of stallion was Rapparee? We can straightaway say he was very successful as he finished 1st, 2nd and 4th in different lists. He has certainly done what we first expect from any stallion — to sire a large number of winners. He got 33 winners from 45 runners which is very satisfactory. His progeny were talented, sound and tough. They were also admirably consistent, as out of 366 starts they won 55 times and placed 98 times, earning a sizable amount of about Rs.11 lakhs. But his low rank in the Average earnings per start list shows that his progeny were winning races of only average importance and value. But in these races they excelled, winning their share or even more than their share. In short Rapparee excelled in getting handicappers who were sound, consistent and with a zest for racing. They excelled in their class. We will study more about him later.

A study of the Sires lists, therefore, yields valuable information. It is the first step in identifying top class stallions and understanding their behaviour. In fact readers can determine the behaviour of any stallion listed. Once we have done so we can go deeper.

Having studied the Sires lists, we have identified all the superior stallions. What is our next step? How must we classify them for deeper study? What must be the basis, the yardstick, of our classification? Undoubtedly it is the ambition of every breeder, owner, trainer and jockey to be associated with classic winners. Therefore we will adopt the number of classic winners sired by a stallion as the basis of our classification.

A "Front-line classic" stallion is one who has sired 6 or more classic winners.

As we saw Prince Pradeep was a Front-line classic stallion. Young Lochinvar (1959) was also Front-line classic. His progeny who enabled him to qualify were:

Midnight Cowboy (1971): 13 wins, champion, Indian Turf Invitation Cup, Calcutta Derby and St. Leger, Mysore Derby, Queen

Elizabeth II Cup (twice); 2nd Calcutta 2000 Guineas, President of India Gold Cup, Queen Elizabeth II Cup, Calcutta Gold Cup.

Vamsi (1971): 4 wins, South India 1000 Guineas and Oaks; 2nd South India Derby, Hyderabad Fillies Trial Stakes; 3rd Nizam's Gold Cup.

Wide Awake (1973): 6 wins, Bangalore and Mysore 2000 Guineas; 2nd Bangalore Derby, 3rd South India Derby and 2000 Guineas.

Pure Honey (1969): 3 wins, South India Oaks.

Lovely Smitha (1971): 4 wins, Bangalore Oaks.

Young Lady (1972): 4 wins, Calcutta 1000 Guineas.

Pendragon (1967): 5 wins, Bangalore Derby; 2nd South India St. Leger.

Sombrero (1974): 5 wins, Bangalore Fillies Trial Stakes.

A few other stallions who qualified for Front-line classic status include: Everyday, Satinello and Knight of Medina. To be sure these stallions sired a whole lot of other superior racers as well.

But what about international breeding? The definition requires a slight change. In international breeding:

A "Front-line classic" stallion is one who has sired 6 classic winners, champions or Group I winners.

I do not think anybody will disagree with this definition. There are only 5 classics in countries like England, Ireland and France. A Group I winner is obviously a horse of the highest order. He is in the same class as a classic winner. Therefore his sire too must be given full credit. Let us give the broadest possible interpretation to the word "champion". Let us include champions according to aptitude (champion sprinter, champion miler etc.), champions according to age (champion 2-yr-old, champion older horse etc.), champions of either sex and even champion turf horse and champion handicap horse. Not all champions are Group I winners (especially among the younger horses) and obviously not all Group I winners are classic winners or champions. This definition is therefore broad enough to include all outstanding horses and not miss any.

Lyphard (1969) is a Front-line classic stallion. The horses bringing him in are:

Reine de Saba: 5 wins, champion 3-yr-old filly, French Oaks.

Dancing Maid: 5 wins, French 1003 Guineas, Prix Vermeille (Gr. I).

Three Troikas: 7 wins, Horse of the Year, champion older mare in France, Prix de l'Arc de Triomphe (Gr. I).

Monteverdi: 4 wins, champion 2-yr-old colt in England and Ireland, William Hill Dewhurst Stakes (Gr. I).

Durtal: 4 wins, champion 2-yr-old filly in England, Cheveley Park Stakes (Gr. I).

Pharly: 5 wins, Prix Lupin (Gr. I).

Sangue: 5 wins, Vanity Handicap (Gr. I).

Chain Bracelet: 9 wins, Top Flight Handicap (Gr. I).

Lyphard's Wish: 6 wins, United Nations Handicap (Gr. I).

Lydian: 4 wins, Gran Premio di Milano (Gr. I), Grosser Preis Von Berlin (Gr. I).

Al Nasr: 7 wins, Prix d'Ispahan (Gr. I).

Lyphard was the leading sire in France twice and is the sire of 38 stakes winners.

Similarly readers can easily determine that Northern Dancer, Nijinsky, Vaguely Noble, His Majesty, Mr. Prospector, Sir Ivor, Mill Reef, Habitat and others are Front-line classic stallions.

A "Border-line classic" stallion is one who has sired at least 3 classic winners.

Eagle Rock (1968) comes in this category. His classic winners were:

Zelda (1974): 6 wins, Calcutta 1000 Guineas and Oaks.

Turf Hawk (1976): 7 wins, Calcutta Oaks.

Young Rajput (1978): 5 wins, Bangalore and Nilgiris Derby, Madras Gold Vase (1400 m, 3-yr-olds, Madras), Owners and Trainers Association Cup (1400 m, 3-yr-olds, Madras).

Malvado (1972), a young stallion, has made an excellent start getting 4 classic winners already:

Vibrant (1980): 8 wins, Bangalore Triple Crown; 2nd Indian Derby.

Calibre (1980): 2 wins, South India 2000 Guineas.

Marchetta (1980): 3 wins, Indian Oaks.

Cartier (1979): 3 wins, Indian 1000 Guineas.

With several outstanding juveniles in training and many more years of stud duty ahead of him, he is sure to become a Front-line classic stallion.

Here I emphasize that classification is a dynamic process. Several stallions show their ability within their first few crops itself. If you feel the stallion is sure to reach the top, you can straightaway consider him to be Border-line classic. Then you must see whether he has a chance of becoming a Front-line classic stallion. The speed at which he qualified for Border-line classic status will be a definite and certain indicator. Stallions like Malvado who qualified within 3 crops are sure to become Front-line classic stallions. It is only a question of time. Therefore remember that these stallions are as talented as Front-line classic stallions. But on the other hand imagine a stallion who qualified in his 10th crop. Will he become a Front-line classic stallion? It is very unlikely.

For international breeding the definition requires the earlier modification.

A "Border-line classic" stallion is one who has sired at least 3 classic winners, champions or Group I winners.

Blushing Groom (1974) who has made such a phenomenal start straightaway falls in this category. His outstanding performers were:

Runaway Groom: 6 wins, champion 3-yr-old colt in Canada, Travers Stakes (Gr. I).

Blush with Pride: 6 wins, Kentucky Oaks (Gr. I), Santa Susana Stakes (Gr. I).

Too Chic: 4 wins, Maskette Stakes (Gr. I).

Rosananti: 2 wins, Italian 1000 Guineas (Gr. I).

His graduation to Front-line classic status is only a formality.

A "Good" stallion is one who has sired superior racers.

The progeny of these stallions are definitely not of classic or Group I standard. However many are superior racers. They are sound, tough and genuine gallopers who win their share of races. But when they run against classic winners and champions, they are fairly and squarely beaten. They are therefore a class inferior to the best horses. In a "non-classic" set they would hold their own. Note that we have dropped the condition of siring classic winners, champions or Group I winners for stallions in this category. We do not expect them to do so, even though a few may have got one or two such horses. Frequently progeny of these stallions place in the classics and Group I races. This confirms that their progeny are not of classic-winning standard, but a step below.

Lord Jim (1965), Noor-E-Shiraz (1968), Rapparee (1964) and others fall in this category. The first named was the sire of:

Aristocracy (1973): 8 wins, South India 1000 Guineas and Oaks, Bangalore 1000 Guineas; 2nd South India Derby. (His only classic winner.)

Silver Shoals: 4 wins; 2nd Calcutta 1000 Guineas.

Lord Ben: 4 wins, F.D. Wadia Gold Cup, Gen. Rajendrasinhji Cup (1800 m, 3-yr-olds, Pune); 3rd Indian 2000 Guineas.

Jamshid: 4 wins, Maharaja of Morvi Gold Cup.

My Smasher: 8 wins, C.D. Dady Cup.

Copper Dust: 7 wins, Akka Saheb Maharaj Cup.

Major General: 6 wins, Bengal Area Cup.

Heera: 6 wins.

Marlboro: 6 wins.

Rajput: 3 wins (died at 4).

Noor-E-Shiraz's performance was more or less similar:

Shibdiz (1979): 4 wins, Golconda Oaks. (His only classic winner.)

Noble Fella: 6 wins, Gen. Rajendrasinhji Cup, Jayachamaraja Wadiyar Gold Cup; 2nd Calcutta 2000 Guineas, Mysore Derby; 3rd Indian and Calcutta Derby, Bangalore Arc de Triomphe.

Ajaya: 8 wins; 2nd Indian and Bangalore 2000 Guineas.

Top Lady: 4 wins; 3rd Indian Oaks.

Ability: 6 wins, Eclipse Stakes of India (2000 m, 4-yr-olds and over, Bombay), R.W.I.T.C. Ltd. Invitational Cup.

Boogie Woogy: 7 wins.

Franak: 8 wins.

True Grit: 11 wins, Raj Bhavan Cup.

It is unlikely that Lord Jim or Noor-E-Shiraz will become classic stallions as both had sufficient opportunity. I think this is true for all the stallions in this category. If they do not become Border-line classic stallions within 6 crops, their chances of doing so are very remote.

This reasoning is equally valid for international stallions. Readers can easily identify stallions who have consistently sired superior but not classic racers.

The next category is made up of "Average" stallions.

An "Average" stallion is one who has sired average racers only.

The progeny of these stallions win races of little or no significance; they are completely outclassed when they run against superior horses. Readers may ask: "What is the difference between a 'Good' stallion and an 'Average' stallion?" The difference lies in the number of superior racers sired. A Good stallion is one who has sired a fair number of superior racers, while an Average stallion is one who has got no more than a handful. A few Average stallions may ultimately become Good Stallions.

We should not neglect these "non-classic" stallions. An average racer who has won his share of races has clearly fulfilled the purpose for which he was bred. He would have also rewarded his owners financially. And if the horse in question is a filly, she could be a valuable broodmare. Discerning buyers frequently buy such horses at average or even bargain basement prices. Can you buy an offspring of a Front-line classic stallion, who is out of an admittedly inferior mare and who has conformation defects, for a reasonable price? It is impossible. Even for such horses you must go to six or seven figures.

We now come to a crucial point. Frequently Good and Average sires become Front-line or Border-line classic maternal grandsires! The daughters of these stallions, though only of modest ability on the course, are able to become very successful broodmares. We are going to study this aspect of awesome importance a little later.

The last category is made up of "Substandard" stallions or "Failures".

A "Substandard" stallion is one whose progeny struggle to win and are able to win only in the lowest classes.

A few of them may get a couple of average or even superior racers, but this does not alter their classification. It is unnecessary for me to give examples for the last two categories.

Readers will now say: "All this is all right but when exactly must we classify a stallion?" My suggestion is to wait until his 3rd crop have run as 4-yr-olds. Now what do you think? In which category would you put him? Also see what his 4th and 5th crops are doing. You will invariably be correct in your classification.

But there are a few exceptions. We know that several stallions are a bit slow to "settle down" and acclimatize themselves in stud. Their first crops are very disappointing but later they are able to get a large number of superior horses. But if a stallion cannot get off the ground even in his 4th crop (3-yr-olds racing), his chances of success are definitely bleak. For breeders are sure to lose interest in him and the quality of his mares can only deteriorate.

A few other stallions begin their careers in small stud farms serving utterly substandard mares. But due to their inherent superiority they are still able to get a few superior racers, catching the attention of breeders and owners. Then they move to bigger farms and helped by superior mares develop into Good or even Classic stallions.

In the above section we classified stallions on the basis of the superior progeny sired by them. Our next task is to classify stallions taking into consideration all their progeny. We divided horses into three categories — superior, average and substandard. To these we can add one more category. We can put classic winners, champions and Group I winners in the "outstanding" category and leave all the other superior racers in the "superior" category.

We would like stallions to get only outstanding and superior racers. But this is obviously impossible. We must remember that competition is intense. There are scores of stallions and hundreds of broodmares who possess a lot of talent. Then we should not underestimate the risks, the hazards, in breeding. The foal of an outstanding stallion and mare may have a major conformation defect or a flaw in temperament. Illnesses and accidents take their toll. The environment — the weather, the air, the soil, the water and the grass may be very beneficial one year but detrimental the next. *Therefore even the best stallion with an outstanding book of mares will get average and substandard horses.* This is a natural law.

There is one more factor. A stallion serves a book of forty mares. All these mares are not going to be superior. There will be well-bred mares, indifferently-bred mares; stakes winners, non-winners; athletic mares, lazy mares; tall mares, short mares; strong mares, weak mares; intelligent mares, dull mares; sweet-tempered mares and foul-tempered mares. The stallion is therefore expected to get superior racers out of an almost infinite variety of broodmares. This is patently impossible. But several stallions have gone close. They have excelled year after year getting outstanding and superior racers.

If we therefore write down all the progeny of even the best stallion in the world, we will have outstanding, superior, average and substandard racers. This behaviour can be considered to be the "Normal" behaviour of stallions. Therefore our task now is to study Normal behaviour deeply. For only then will we understand the deviations from it.

Let us study two stallions who exhibited Normal behaviour. Strictly speaking we should study and classify all their progeny. But I have restricted myself to one crop only, for the crop I have selected is a true representative, a true sample, of all the crops of the stallion.

The first stallion I have selected is Young Lochinvar.

Young Lochinvar (Ch, 1959)	Elopement	Rockefella — Hyperion / Rockfel
		Daring Miss — Felicitation / Venturesome
	No Angel	Nasrullah — Nearco / Mumtaz Begum
		Fair Angela — Fair Trial / Pomme d'Amour

He won 4 races, the Upend Stakes (6 furlongs, Newmarket), Severals Stakes (1 mile, Newmarket), Old Newton Cup (1-1/2 miles) and Mentmore Stakes (1-1/2 miles). He also placed 2nd four times, 3rd six times and 4th twice from 27 starts. He defeated horses like Miralgo, Monterrico and Merchant Venturer. He had a Timeform rating of 121.

He was imported into India and retired to stud. We saw that he was very successful becoming a Front-line classic stallion. Let us study his crop of 1973* the details of which are given below:

TABLE - 1

	Horse	Sex	Race Record
1)	Dauntless	Colt	8 wins, winner in class II.
2)	Ever So Gay	Filly	2 wins, winner in class VA.
3)	Fondant	Colt	8 wins, winner in class I.
4)	Grand Aura	Filly	Placed.
5)	Salome	Filly	5 wins, winner in class I. (Set a course record over 1100 m in Calcutta.)
6)	Shenandoah	Colt	1 win (handicap for 3-yr-olds who had not won or placed 2nd).
7)	Sundance Kid	Colt	7 wins, winner in class II. He lost the Governor's Gold Cup (2000 m, classes I and II, Mysore) by a short-head after being left at the start.

* I have included only members of the crop who raced. Inevitably several foals did not race due to various disabilities. The percentage of runners from foals is a very important index of a stallion's ability and readers must make note of it.

TABLE - 1 (con't.)

Horse	Sex	Race Record
8) The Cavalier	Colt	4 wins, winner in class II.
9) Touch of Venus	Filly	4 wins, winner in class II.
10) Venumbaka	Colt	6 wins, winner in class II.
11) Wide Awake	Colt	6 wins, Bangalore and Mysore 2000 Guineas; 2nd Bangalore Derby; 3rd South India Derby and 2000 Guineas.

In this crop of 11 runners Young Lochinvar got 8 superior racers, a tremendous performance. They included a multiple classic winner, a course record holder and a winner in class I. The other 5 horses won comfortably in class II. Only 2 horses were substandard and Shenandoah may be considered to be average. He was a remarkably consistent stallion who sired numerous classic winners, classic-placed and superior handicappers. Inevitably some of his progeny were substandard. But in his case the superior horses outnumbered the average and substandard.

ORBIT

Orbit (B, 1962)	Crepello	Donatello II	Blenheim Delleana
		Crepuscule	Mieuxce Red Sunset
	Urshalim	Nasrullah	Nearco Mumtaz Begum
		Horama	Panorama Lady of Aran

He ran as Cielo in England. He won the St. Oswald Stakes (1 mile, Newcastle) and Blackhall Stakes (1-1/4 miles, Carlisle) at 3 years. In India he won the Cooch Behar Cup (2200 m) and Governor's Cup (2800 m, Calcutta). He was then retired to stud.

He was almost a Border-line classic stallion as he got 2 classic winners. He also sired a handful of other superior racers. Again let us study his crop of 1973*.

---

* *Indian Turf Statistical Record - Volume 2.*

TABLE - 2

Horse	Sex	Race Record
1) Black Swan	Filly	3 wins. Even though she won only thrice she was an excellent 2nd in the Indian Oaks. Therefore we must consider her to be superior.
2) Chota	Colt	7 wins, winner in class VA.
3) El Khobar	Colt	2 wins, winner in class VA
4) Nainital	Filly	1 win (3-yr-olds in classes IV and VA only).
5) Nalini	Filly	3 wins, winner in class IV.
6) Our Delight	Colt	3 wins, winner in class IV.
7) Solar Music	Colt	9 wins, winner in class II.
8) Sunbird	Colt	7 wins, Queen Elizabeth II Cup, Nepal Gold Cup, Army Cup (2000 m, 3-yr-olds, Calcutta); 2nd Calcutta Derby and St. Leger.
9) Veertha	Colt	6 wins, winner in class IV.

* Only horses who raced have been included.

In this crop he had 3 superior, 4 average and 2 substandard racers. Notice that the average racers outnumber the superior or substandard. This was his behaviour throughout. He produced a couple of superior horses every year with the rest being average or substandard.

Readers will quickly point out that there is a qualitative difference between Young Lochinvar and Orbit. While the former was among the best stallions in the country, the latter was only marginally above average. Then can we classify them together? The answer is we must for both sired outstanding, superior, average and substandard horses. The fact that the percentage of horses in each category is different does not alter this result. Therefore both of them exhibited Normal behaviour.

Then are there any stallions who exhibit "abnormal" behaviour? Yes there are. Stallions who fail to sire a particular category of horses can be said to "deviate" from Normal behaviour. Let us study these deviations in detail.

The first deviation from Normal behaviour is simple. Stallions who are unable to sire outstanding racers i.e. Good and Average stallions constitute this deviation. This deviation is very important to big owners who insist on buying horses who are potential classic winners or champions. They should not buy the progeny of these stallions, whatever may be their pedigrees and conformation, as they have clearly demonstrated their inability to get such outstanding horses. The best progeny of these stallions are only top-handicappers.

The second deviation is made up of Average stallions i.e. stallions who are unable to get outstanding or superior racers. No further explanation is necessary.

It is the third deviation from Normal behaviour that is truly fascinating. Imagine a stallion who gets a large number of outstanding and superior racers — classic winners, champions, classic-placed and top-handicappers and a large number of substandard racers, but very few horses in between. Now you have the type of stallions who constitute this deviation. But you will ask at once: "Isn't this illogical? Can there be a stallion who sires superior and inferior horses but not average horses? Surely a stallion who gets 3 champions and 4 Group I winners must get about two score average horses?" But no. This stallion is determined to swing between extremes. On one end he will have classic winners and champions and on the other end a large number of substandard progeny with very few horses in between. Again an example will enlighten.

VALOROSO

		Wild Risk	Rialto
			Wild Violet
	Vimy		
		Mimi	Black Devil
			Mignon
Valoroso			
(B, 1962)		Hyperion	Gainsborough
			Selene
	Bellaggio		
		Belleva	Stratford
			Passee

He won 6 races including the September Stakes (7 furlongs, Doncaster), Newbury Summer Cup (1-1/2 miles) and the Doncaster Spring Handicap (1 mile, 6 furlongs, 132 yards). He also placed 2nd in the Old Newton Cup (Haydock), Ebor Handicap (York) by a short-head and Queen Alexandra Stakes (Royal Ascot) twice. He also won 3 races under N.H. rules.

Retired to stud in India, he was very successful becoming a Borderline classic stallion. He was the champion stallion in 1976-'77 and was 2nd in 1975-'76. In order to understand his behaviour clearly, let us study two of his crops.

TABLE — 3

Horse	Sex	Year Foaled	Race Record
1) Coat of Arms	Colt	1973	8 wins, winner in class II.
2) Jaan-E-Man	Colt	1973	5 wins, winner in class VA.
3) Jwalamukhi	Filly	1973	3 wins, winner in class VA.
4) Knight at Arms	Colt	1973	2 wins from 2 starts. He was an extremely promising colt but unfortunately died soon after. Since he was impressive, we can safely consider him to be superior.
5) Midnight Blossom	Filly	1973	Ran unplaced in class VA.
6) Squanderer	Colt	1973	18 wins from 19 starts, champion, Indian Turf Invitation Cup, Indian Triple Crown, Bangalore Derby and St. Leger, President of India Gold Cup etc; 3rd Bangalore Colt's Trial Stakes.
7) Wild Blossom	Colt	1973	8 wins. He had the misfortune of being foaled in the same year as Squanderer. He followed him home in the Indian Triple Crown. He was a versatile horse well up to classic winning standard.
8) Diamond Queen	Filly	1974	3 wins, winner in class VB.
9) Kilimanjaro	Filly	1974	Placed in class VA.
10) Knight of Candy	Colt	1974	Placed in class VA.
11) Noblesse Oblige	Filly	1974	4 wins, winner in class II.
12) Queen Aidalena	Filly	1974	2 wins, winner in class IV.
13) Titanic	Colt	1974	6 wins, winner in class IV.
14) Tudor Vale	Filly	1974	1 win, winner in class VB.
15) Valmoss	Colt	1974	9 wins, winner in class I.

Therefore in these two crops Valoroso had:

Outstanding racers	:	2
Superior racers	:	4
Average racers	:	2
Substandard racers	:	7
		15

A truly remarkable distribution with an almost equal number of superior and substandard horses with only two average horses! This was his behaviour throughout his stud career. His other superior racers were:

Commanche (1972): 11 wins, champion, Indian Turf Invitation Cup, Indian Derby and St. Leger, President of India Gold Cup. He won from 1000 m to 2800 m. Sire.

Darado (1977): 6 wins, South India Oaks, Bangalore St. Leger; 3rd Indian Oaks. But her best performance was in the Indian Turf Invitation Cup in which she was an excellent 2nd. Therefore we can consider her to be the champion filly of her generation.

Shandaar (1972): 3 wins; 2nd Indian Turf Invitation Cup; 3rd Indian Derby and 2000 Guineas. He is a full-brother to Squanderer. Sire.

Happy Landing (1977): 6 wins, R.W.I.T.C. Ltd. Invitational Trophy; 3rd Indian Derby in a thrilling finish with only a head between 1st and 2nd, head between 2nd and 3rd and head between 3rd and 4th!

Commissar (1977): 6 wins; 2nd South India Derby.

Baby Oh Baby (1979): 5 wins; 2nd Indian 2000 Guineas.

Para Brigade (1977): 5 wins, Byculla Club Cup (2800 m, classes I and II, Bombay), Northumberland Cup (3200 m, classes I and II, Pune) — the longest race in the country.

Therefore when you buy the offspring of stallions who exhibit this deviation you must be extra careful. For you may get a champion and classic winner or an individual who struggles to win in the lowest classes. Therefore such stallions are not suitable for small owners. But owners who race large strings can go in for them. One classic racer will compensate for all the others.

STALLION EARNINGS AND AVERAGE EARNINGS INDEX

We saw that a handful of Valoroso's progeny excelled and made him a success. This fact is strikingly confirmed by the money earned by his progeny. Let us study their earnings for the year 1976-'77. He had 23 runners. 1 horse ran unplaced. The remaining 22 earned about Rs.1.6 million. But only 12 of them were winners. Among them Squanderer alone earned about Rs.9,00,000/- and Wild Blossom about Rs.2,70,000/- constituting more than 70% of Valoroso's earnings for that year. Therefore, as explained, studying only the total earnings of a stallion can be very misleading. We must note the contribution of each horse. Only this will give a clear picture of the stallion's behaviour.

From a stallion's total earnings and the number of runners who represented him, Turf-historians calculate his "Average Earnings Index". In India during 1976-'77, 1792 runners competed for a total prize money of Rs.3,84,37,460/-, giving each horse an "average earning" of Rs.21,449/-*. A horse who earned more can be considered above average in terms of earnings and a horse who earned less below average. Imagine a stallion with 8 runners. If these 8 runners had earned Rs.1,71,592/- (21,449x8) we can consider the stallion to be "average" in terms of earnings. If they had earned more the stallion can be considered above average and if they had earned less below average. The Average Earnings Index expresses this idea.

$$\text{Average Earnings Index} = \frac{\text{Sire's earnings}}{\text{Average earning per runner} \; \times \; \text{Number of runners for the sire}}$$

Thus a stallion with an index greater than 1 is above average, of 1 average and less than 1 below average.

$$\text{Therefore Valoroso's Average Earnings Index for 1976-'77*} = \frac{15,78,975}{21,449 \times 23}$$

$$= \underline{3.20}$$

But this impressive figure is almost entirely due to the earnings of Squanderer and Wild Blossom. Let us recalculate Valoroso's A.E.I. first ignoring Squanderer and then ignoring them both.

Earnings of Valoroso excluding Squanderer = Rs.6,76,059

$$\text{Therefore A.E.I.} = \frac{6,76,059}{21,449 \times 22}$$

$$= \underline{1.43}$$

---

* *Indian Turf Statistical Record - Volume 2.*

The A.E.I. falls by more than half. It falls even more if we ignore Wild Blossom.

$$\frac{\text{A.E.I. of Valoroso excluding}}{\text{Squanderer and Wild Blossom}} = \frac{4,05,046}{21,449 \times 21}$$

$$= \underline{0.9}$$

Therefore an above average Valoroso becomes a below average Valoroso!

I am not trying to minimize the importance of the Average Earnings Index. It is an excellent tool, an invaluable aid, to breeders. But it is most accurate for stallions who do not exhibit the third and fourth deviations from Normal behaviour. Valoroso's A.E.I. in 1977-'78 was 1.38 (again with Squanderer earning the most). In 1978-'79 and 1979-'80 when he had no outstanding runner his A.E.I. fell to 1.03.

The fourth deviation is made up of "unpredictable" or "erratic" stallions. These stallions are very inconsistent in their stud behaviour. They perform brilliantly one year but dismally during the next few years. Then they regain their brilliance only to lose it again. Their stud careers are marked by unbelievable and unpredictable highs and lows. It is not that they cannot get superior racers; they do get a sizeable number. But they appear at very irregular intervals. Again an example will illuminate.

ROMNEY

Romney (B, 1962)	Shantung	Sicambre	Prince Bib / Sif
		Barley Corn	Hyperion / Schiaparelli
	Romanella	El Greco	Pharos / Gay Camp
		Barbara Burini	Papyrus / Bucolic

Romney is no ordinary individual; he is a Shantung half-brother to the great Ribot.

He raced in Italy. At 2 years he placed 2nd once and 3rd once from only 3 starts. At 3 years he won 3 races: Premio Casperia (1 mile, 110 yards), Premio Villa Torlinia (1 mile, 3 furlongs) and Premio Mandela (1-1/2 miles). He also placed 3rd in the Premio Botticelli. He had a Timeform rating of 121. He unfortunately split a pastern and was retired to stud in England in 1966.

He got a few winners in England, but in 1969 was imported into India. He was successful getting 4 classic winners and other superior racers. He has had a long innings at stud and is still active at the time of writing. 14 of his crops have raced and the 1 5th is in training. But he has not had large crops. His crops ranged from half-a-dozen to a dozen. He did not get the best of mares but he had enough opportunity.

Let us study the performances of his progeny in detail. His best racer was Sun Prince (1971) whose 6 wins included the Indian 2000 Guineas. He also placed 3rd in the Indian Derby. This crop included another classic winner in Amberdue. A hardy individual, he won 24 races including the South India 2000 Guineas. His next best racer Rastafarian arrived in 1977. An excellent miler his 4 victories included the Nilgiris Derby. Artemis was foaled in 1975. She won the Calcutta Oaks in a time of 2 mins. 54 secs., which must be the slowest in the country for a classic over 2400 m. But in the Calcutta Derby she put up a vastly different performance, finishing a gallant second in a respectable time. She won 4 other races including 2 races over 2200 m. His other superior racers were:

> **Roman Eagle** (1971): 13 wins, Farrokh K. Irani Gold Cup (1200 m, class I, Madras).
>
> **Roman Flame** (1970): 10 wins, Race Club Cup (1400 m, class II, Hyderabad), Air Command Cup (1200 m, class II, Hyderabad).
>
> **Good Luck** (1970): 10 wins.
>
> **Lucky Barbara** (1970): 11 wins.
>
> **Lord Henry** (1972): 4 wins, Champagne Stakes, Black Buck Plate (2200 m, classes II and III, Calcutta).
>
> **Jungurra** (1975): 6 wins.

Then why is Romney an unpredictable sire? He has done well hasn't he? He is in this category because the quality of his crops varied widely. His crop of 1971 which had 2 classic winners was the best. Sadly he did not have another crop of similar quality. In a few crops he did not get any superior racer; these crops were dominated by very indifferent performers. Note that this is *not* Normal behaviour. Stallions who exhibit Normal behaviour get superior racers in *every* crop. Prince Pradeep, Young Lochinvar and Satinello produced superior racers in every crop. They were models of consistency throughout their stud careers. Romney cannot be classified with them.

Also notice that Romney's behaviour is different from Valoroso's. Valoroso was not an erratic stallion. Though he sired a large number of indifferent racers, he did get superior racers in almost every crop. Therefore, unlike Romney, he was consistent in getting superior racers.

Buying the progeny of stallions in this deviation is extremely difficult. We do not know, and cannot say, which crop will have superior racers. The stallion may have several crops without a superior racer. But at the same time it is difficult to ignore them as they have clearly demonstrated their talent. Those owners who are really interested in the stallion may take a chance.

APTITUDE OF STALLIONS

We were discussing the class and behaviour of stallions. Now let us study their aptitude. We can conveniently divide stallions into two groups — "versatile" and "specialist".

A "versatile" stallion is one who gets sprinters, milers, stayers and horses who excel over a range of distances.

A "specialist" stallion is one who gets horses who excel over a particular distance.

A few examples will be of interest.

Young Lochinvar was a versatile stallion. His best progeny had an ideal blend of speed and stamina. They included horses like Midnight Cowboy, Vamsi, Wide Awake and Tradition (11 wins from 1100 m to 2400 m, Bangalore Turf Club Gold Cup [2400 m, 4-yr-olds and over, Bangalore], Guindy Gold Cup, Mysore City Gold Cup [twice]; 4th Indian Turf Invitation Cup). But not all his progeny were versatile. He also sired a number of sprinters and sprinter-milers. Salome was one. The others included:

> **Young Cavalier:** 15 wins; 2nd South India 2000 Guineas, Bangalore Colts Trial Stakes.
>
> **Whiplash:** 14 wins, The Metropolitan (1200 m, 4-yr-olds and over, Calcutta), Maharaja Jagaddipendra Narayan Bhup Bahadur of Cooch Behar Memorial Cup (1400 m, classes I and II, Calcutta).
>
> **Philanderer:** 16 wins, Guindy Gold Cup, R.W.I.T.C. Cup (1400 m, class I, Bangalore), Karnataka Police Cup (1200 m, class I, Bangalore), Indian Express Gold Cup (1200-m, class I, Mysore).

Let us determine the aptitude of Valoroso. From the list of his superior racers readers would have guessed that he imparted a lot of stamina to his progeny. While his best get (Squanderer, Commanche and Wild Blossom) possessed an ideal blend of speed and stamina, the others did not. They were essentially specialist stayers who were at their best over distances greater than 2000 m. I do not think they could have beaten specialist sprinters or milers. (Baby Oh Baby was an exception.) Therefore we would not be wrong if we considered Valoroso to be a specialist sire of stayers and extreme stayers.

To further confirm our findings let us determine the aptitudes of all the horses of the two crops we studied earlier.

TABLE - 4

	Horse		Longest distance won
1)	Coat of Arms	:	1600 m
2)	Jaan-E-Man	:	2000 m
3)	Jwalamukhi	:	1400 m
4)	Knight at Arms	:	1400 m (did not run over longer distances)
5)	Midnight Blossom	:	—
6)	Squanderer	:	2800 m
7)	Wild Blossom	:	2nd over 2800 m
8)	Diamond Queen	:	1400 m
9)	Kilimanjaro	:	—
10)	Knight of Candy	:	—
11)	Noblesse Oblige	:	2200 m
12)	Queen Aidalena	:	1400 m
13)	Titanic	:	1800 m
14)	Tudor Vale	:	1000 m
15)	Valmoss	:	2000 m

The stamina Valoroso imparted to his progeny is clear. All the superior racers of these two crops (except Coat of Arms) stayed well. This was his behaviour throughout his stud career.

Let us study one more specialist sire. In doing so we can also determine his class and behaviour.

RAPPAREE

		Court Martial	Fair Trial Instantaneous
	High Treason		
		Eastern Grandeur	Gold Bridge China Maiden
Rapparee (Ch, 1964)			
		Ballyogan	Fair Trial Serial
	Libertine		
		Travelling Flash	Winalot Drifting Flame

In England he won the Englefield Green Nursery Handicap Plate (5 f), Forest Handicap Plate (6 f) and Newchapel Club Handicap (5 f) and placed. In India he won the M.D. Petit Plate (1400 m), Helping Hand Plate (1600 m), Olympic Plate (1200 m), P. Hadow Cup (1200 m), Southern Command Cup (1600 m) and Sir Charles Forbes Cup (1200 m) — all his starts.

We saw that he was a successful stallion who excelled in getting handicappers. To understand his behaviour let us study his crop of 1973, which was very typical of all his crops.

TABLE 5

Horse	Sex	Race Record
1) Burnt Amber	Filly	5 wins, winner in class III.
2) Candide	Filly	11 wins, winner in class II.
3) Carnival Queen	Filly	8 wins, winner in class II.
4) Fighting Force	Colt	8 wins, winner in class I, Indian Gold Vase (1200 m, classes I and II, Calcutta), R.C.T.C. Gold Cup (1400 m, class II, Calcutta); 3rd Mysore 2000 Guineas.
5) Fortune's Flame	Filly	2 wins, winner in class VA.
6) Honey Bunch	Filly	2 wins. She won her first 2 starts — races for Indian 2-yr-olds only, but then ran unplaced 3 times.

TABLE 5 (cont.)

	Horse	Sex	Race Record
7)	Jai Mala	Filly	3 wins, winner in class VA.
8)	Le Chaim	Colt	6 wins, winner in class IV.
9)	Mr. Mysterious	Colt	6 wins, winner in class III.
10)	Noble Shaara	Filly	5 wins, winner in class III.
11)	Olivia	Filly	She ran unplaced in her only start and was retired to stud.
12)	Padma Shri	Colt	6 wins, winner in class III.
13)	Philemon	Colt	3 wins, winner in class VA.
14)	Red Bud	Filly	Placed 4th twice in class VB, unplaced in her other starts.
15)	Repartee	Filly	7 wins, winner in class III.
16)	The Sting	Filly	4 wins, winner in class II, Golconda Cup (2000 m, class II, Calcutta).
17)	Turf Star	Filly	3 wins, winner in class IV.
18)	Winfree	Colt	6 wins, winner in class II, World Wildlife Cup, Turf Club Cup (1200 m, class II, Calcutta).

The crop included 5 superior, 8 average and 4 substandard racers and 1 horse who ran only once. This appears to be an excellent example of Normal behaviour. But note that not one of them was a classic contender in the truest sense of the term. Also among the 5 superior horses only one — Fighting Force — could win in class I. Carnival Queen and Winfree won in class II and were promoted to class I, but as they could not win in that class (they placed) they were demoted back to class II. This was the type of horses he sired throughout.

He did not get a single classic winner and only one of his progeny, Ocean Gold, was a real classic contender. His best racer, he was 2nd in the Bangalore 2000 Guineas and 3rd in the Bangalore Arc de Triomphe. Among the others Great Memories was 3rd in the Calcutta 1000 Guineas, Distinctions 3rd in the Nilgiris Derby and Fighting Force 3rd in the Mysore 2000 Guineas.

Therefore, in fairness, we can say that Rapparee's superior progeny were only slightly above average and certainly below top class. Hence he is an excellent example of a Good stallion and he is among those who constitute the first deviation from Normal behaviour.

Let us determine his aptitude. He was not a versatile sire. His progeny, irrespective of their class, excelled up to 1400 m only. Even 1600 m was out of their compass with only a handful winning over the distance. In the crop we studied Mr. Mysterious won over 1800 m and The Sting over 2000 m. (The latter was also 2nd in the Calcutta Oaks.) But they won in a slow time and beat only non-stayers. Hence they cannot be considered as true starters.

Between 1975 and 1980 his progeny won 230 races. As many as 215 of them were up to (including) 1400 m only. 2 were over 1500 m, 9 over 1600 m, 1 over 1800 m, 2 over 2000 m and 1 over 2400 m. This clearly shows the aptitude of his progeny. Since they really excelled over 1200 m we can say Rapparee was a specialist sire of sprinters.

I said earlier that we should wait until a stallion's 3rd crop have raced as 4-yr-olds before we come to any conclusions on his class. This is because several stallions — even the best stallions — require one or two years to "settle down" in stud. This settling down affects their aptitude also. The aptitude of a stallion in his settling down period is different from his true aptitude. Think of Nijinsky and his early progeny like Caucasus. Caucasus did not even race at 2. At 3 he won the Irish St. Leger defeating Quiet Fling. At 4 and 5 he won and placed in Group I races over 1-1/2 miles in the U.S.A. Quiet Fling was similar. He did not win at 2. At 4 he won the Coronation Cup (Group I) and at 5 placed 2nd in the same race. Can we therefore say that Nijinsky is a sire of late-maturing horses who develop into classic stayers? Obviously not. For after settling down he sired scores of truly outstanding horses who won as 2-yr-olds and who went on to win over the entire range of distances. This settling down process is very important today as horses are foaled in one country, race in another and go to stud in a third. I have seen the progeny of numerous stallions who were imported into the country specially for breeding. The performances of their first crops was extremely disappointing to say the least. Even their conformation was markedly below average. But once they settled down they were able to produce superior horses. The conformation of these horses was visibly superior. Breeders and owners must make note of this. We must therefore judge stallions (and broodmares) only after they have fully acclimatized themselves in stud.

Think of a stallion who has settled down well. Assume that he is a specialist sire of sprinters and milers. Now we can safety say that he will continue this behaviour throughout his study career. In other words stallions (excluding erratic stallions) do not change their behaviour in every crop. The above sire is not going to suddenly get stayers and extreme stayers. A sire noted for late-maturing extreme stayers is not going to suddenly sire a set of brilliant, precocious sprinters. A stallion who was average for a dozen years is not going to suddenly top the Sires lists. Therefore once a stallion has settled down we know his behaviour for life. We studied one exception i.e. a young stallion who moves to a bigger farm and gets vastly superior mares. His performance is bound to improve. The second exception is a stallion who changes countries. Then dramatic changes in behaviour can take place. Some stallions excel in their home countries but perform moderately abroad, while others are average in their home countries but excel abroad.

PROCEDURE FOR DETERMINING THE BEHAVIOUR OF STALLIONS

We now know how to determine the behaviour of stallions. We can conveniently rewrite what we have learnt in the form of steps as below. The advantage of such a procedure is that we will not miss any step.

STEP 1

Identify all the superior progeny of the stallion.
This will at once tell us his class.

STEP 2

Study the performances of all his progeny crop by crop.
This step is very important for it tells us whether the stallion's behaviour is Normal or not. If he has deviated, the nature of the deviation will become clear. The four deviations are:
1) Inability to sire outstanding racers.
2) Inability to sire outstanding or superior racers.
3) Sire of outstanding, superior and substandard racers but not average racers.
4) Erratic behaviour.

STEP 3

Determine whether his colts and fillies were equally talented. If not determine who performed better.

STEP 4

Determine the aptitudes of all his superior and average progeny. See whether he is versatile or a specialist.

STEP 5

Determine the quality of all his mares and identify the types of mares out of which he produced superior racers.

Readers can easily perform the first four steps. They can undertake the fifth a little later.

We can sum-up the performances of all the stallions we have studied in the following table which incorporates the first four steps.

TABLE 6

Stallion	Class	Behaviour	Ability of colts and fillies	Aptitude
1) Prince Pradeep	Front-line classic	Normal	Colts and fillies equally good	Versatile
2) Young Lochinvar	Front-line classic	Normal	Colts and fillies equally good	Versatile
3) Eagle Rock	Border-line classic	Normal	Colts and fillies equally good	Versatile
4) Lord Jim	Good	First deviation	Colts and fillies equally good	Specialist sire of sprinters and milers
5) Noor-E-Shiraz	Good	First deviation	Colts and fillies equally good	Versatile
6) Orbit	Almost Border-line classic	Normal	Colts and fillies equally good	Versatile
7) Valoroso	Border-line classic	Third deviation	Colts markedly superior than fillies	Specialist site of stayers and extreme stayers
8) Romney	Border-line classic	Fourth deviation	Colts markedly superior than fillies	Specialist sire of sprinters and milers. (He also sired a few stayers.)
9) Rapparee	Good	First deviation	Colts and fillies equally good, but the colts had a slight advantage	Specialist sire of sprinters and sprinter-milers

CHAPTER 4

Broodmares – 1

Broodmares are truly remarkable. A broodmare can have but one foal a year for, let us say, a dozen years. She competes against thousands; yet she is expected to make a mark, a big impact.

Let us study the odds against a broodmare. In 12 years she can have 12 foals. But the stallion she visited may have been infertile; she herself may have been unable to conceive; she may have slipped her foal or had twins. Therefore we must assume that in 12 years she will have only 8 foals. (This is the assumption made by all breeders — a broodmare will have 2 live and healthy foals every 3 years.) But all her 8 foals will not have near perfect conformation and temperament. Accidents and diseases take their toll. The mare will be lucky if 6 of her 8 foals start. It would be too much to expect all the 6 horses to excel. Remember competition is intense. Annual production of horses in the principal racing countries runs in thousands. Therefore we can safely say that 3 of her runners will be substandard, 2 will be average and 1 will be superior. One superior racer in 12 years! For a mare who is young and prolific; of reasonable pedigree and conformation. A mare who visits successful stallions and who is well looked after. If these are the odds against such a mare readers can well imagine the odds against admittedly inferior mares visiting average stallions.

Are you a bit disappointed? — one superior horse after 12 years of hard labour for the mare and breeder. Honestly even the above scenario is optimistic! For in these inflationary days it is unlikely that breeders will persist with a mare for 12 long years. They will expect her 1st, 2nd, 3rd or 4th foal to really succeed on the course. If so the mare has it made. She is sure to visit superior stallions. Her progeny will be in great demand in the auction sales and will invariably be sold to big owners. But if her early progeny fail to show promise her future is bleak — however *inherently superior she may be.* For breeders and owners are sure to lose interest. She will not visit the best stallions. Her progeny will not be in demand. They will have to fight their way to the top. Therefore to attract and sustain interest a mare must get a superior racer within her first 3 or 4 foals. If readers keep in mind the difficulties explained and the fact that there are thousands of mares, the tremendous odds against a brood-mare become obvious.

What about the broodmare we just studied — the mare who produced a superior racer in 12 years. Can we consider her to be a "success"? Keeping in mind the arguments till now readers will readily agree that she is a success. Now we can define a "successful" mare.

A "successful" mare is one who has produced a superior racer.

I want readers to take time and study the definition. This concept is extremely important and will be used frequently throughout the book. Notice that there is no mention of classic winners or champions. For it would be unfair to describe only the dams of classic winners, champions or Group I winners (who constitute only a microscopic minority of the broodmare population) as "successful" and all the others as "average" or "failures". A few others may feel that the definition is weak in another respect. They will say that a mare must get 3 or 4 superior racers to be considered a success. After all several have done so. My reply is: "We cannot consider a broodmare to be a stakes winner producing factory. Do not make the mistake of equating a broodmare who can have only 1 foal a year to a stallion who can have 40 or more. Mares who have produced classic winners, champions or Group I winners are the most superior and successful, but a mare who has produced 1 superior racer must also be considered a success."

Let us study the performances of 2 broodmares to understand clearly what we have learnt. The first mare I have selected is Alluvial (1969). She was the dam of:

Dancing Detente (filly, 1973, by Nijinsky): unraced, producer.

Ete Indien (colt, 1974, by Herbager): 2 wins in France.

Ammunition (colt, 1975, by Ack Ack): 2 wins in U.S.A. Sire.

Coastal (colt, 1976, by Majestic Prince): 8 wins, Belmont Stakes, Monmouth Invitational Handicap (Gr.l), Dwyer Stakes (Gr. II); 2nd Woodward Stakes (Gr. I); 3rd Jockey Club Gold Cup (Gr. I), Marlboro Cup Handicap (Gr. I). Sire.

Calender Stack (colt, 1977, by Ack Ack): placed.

Upper Cross Road (colt, 1978, by Reviewer): placed.

Gulf (filly, 1979, by Sir Ivor): 3 wins in U.S.A.

Slew o' Gold (colt, 1980, by Seattle Slew): 6 wins, Woodward Stakes (Gr. I), Wood Memorial Stakes (Gr. I) 2nd division, Peter

Pan Stakes (Gr. II); 2nd Belmont Stakes, Travers Stakes (Gr. I). In training.

Colt, 1982, by Mr. Prospector is in training.

(She was barren in 1983 and her colt [1981] by Seattle Slew died.) Her progeny included:

Classic winners, champions or Gr. I winners	2
Other stakes winners	–
Stakes-placed	–
Winners	3
Placed	2
Unraced	1
In training	1

We can easily understand the uncertainties and difficulties in breeding from Alluvial's stud performance. Even superior mares inevitably produce inferior progeny. These progeny may be even out of outstanding, very successful stallions. We just cannot expect every runner of a mare to develop into a superior racer.

The stud performance of Hiding Place (1963), who was another very successful producer, is as below:

Camouflage (colt, 1968, by March Past): 2 wins in England, Royal Hunt Cup. Sire.

Disguise (colt, 1969, by Klairon): 2 wins in England, Horris Hill Stakes (Gr. III); 2nd Prix Eclipse (Gr. III); 3rd Ascot 2000 Guineas Trial Stakes (Gr. III). Sire.

Ambuscade (filly, 1970, by Relko): 1 win in England. Producer.

Cache Cache (colt, 1971, by Alcide): 3 wins in England. Sire in Australia.

Smuggler (colt, 1973, by Exbury): 7 wins, Yorkshire Cup (Gr. II), Gordon Stakes (Gr. III), Princess of Wales' Stakes (Gr. III), Henry II Stakes (Gr. III); 2nd King Edward VII Stakes (Gr. II), Jockey Club Stakes (Gr. III); 3rd Coronation Cup (Gr. I) twice. Sire in New Zealand.

Hirzio (colt, 1974. by Alcide): 9 wins in Italy.

Cloak and Dagger (colt, 1975, by Amber Rama): placed in England.

Elusive Pimpernel (colt, 1976, by Blakeney): 3 wins in England, Hyperion Stakes.

Major Grundy (colt, 1977, by Grundy): 2 wins; 2nd Warren Stakes.

Little Wolf (colt, 1978, by Grundy): 6 wins, Jockey Club Cup (Gr. III), St. Simon Stakes (Gr. III); 2nd Great Voltigeur Stakes (Gr. II); 3rd Yorkshire Cup (Gr. II), Cumberland Lodge Stakes (Gr. III). At 5 he won the Ascot Gold Cup (Gr. I) and Goodwood Cup (Gr. II).

Sanctuary (filly, 1979, by Welsh Pageant): unraced.

Colt, 1982, by Final Straw is in training.

She was barren in 1972, 1980 and 1981 and slipped her foal in 1983.

Her progeny included:

Classic winners, champions or Gr. I winners	1
Other stakes winners	4
Stakes-placed	1
Winners	3
Placed	1
Unraced	1
In training	1

Our next task is to classify broodmares on the basis of their stud performances. We can conveniently divide broodmares into the following six categories:

Category I : A majority of the progeny of a mare in this category are outstanding or classic racers.

Category II : Majority of the progeny are superior racers.

Category III: Majority of the progeny are average racers; none of the others are outstanding or superior.

Category IV: Majority of the progeny are substandard racers; none of the others are outstanding or superior.

Category V : Progeny are outstanding, superior, average and substandard racers.

Category VI: Majority of the progeny are substandard racers, but a few of the others are outstanding or superior.

The idea behind this division will become very clear after a few examples.

CATEGORY I

Hoverplane (1952) was a huge success. Her progeny were:

Time Machine (colt, 1959, by Decorum): 10 wins, Calcutta Derby, Calcutta Trial Stakes; 3rd Indian Turf Invitation Cup, Queen Elizabeth II Cup. Sire.

Hovercraft (filly, 1960, by Golestan): 13 wins, champion, Indian Turf Invitation Cup, Queen Elizabeth II Cup; 3rd Bangalore Derby.

Helicraft (filly, 1962, by Golestan): 2 wins.

Gay Time (colt, 1963, by Hervine): 13 wins, H.M. Mehta Gold Cup, Eve Champion Cup, Idar Gold Cup (twice); 2nd R.R. Ruia Gold Cup (2000 m, 4-yr-olds only, Bombay); 3rd Indian Derby, Queen Elizabeth II Cup. He won from 1000 m to 2400 m. Sire.

Hydroplane (filly, 1965, by Golestan): 6 wins, Indian Produce Stakes, Grand Annual Handicap, Southern Command Cup (in record time); 2nd Calcutta 1000 Guineas, 2000 Guineas and Oaks; 3rd Calcutta Derby.

Veronique (filly, 1967, by Hervine): unraced.

Prime Time (colt, 1970, by Prince Pradeep): 12 wins, Poona City Cup, Idar Gold Cup; 2nd Indian 2000 Guineas and St. Leger, Maharaja's Gold Cup, R.R. Ruia Gold Cup; 3rd Indian Derby.

Her 7 foals included 1 champion, 1 Derby winner and 3 superior racers who placed in the classics. Truly a glittering record.

CATEGORY II

Khado Cham (1958) too had a very successful stud career but on a lesser plane. Though she did not get a classic winner or champion, she got 9 winners including several superior racers:

Kaka Son (colt, 1966, by King's Son): 11 wins, Vernon Fisher Memorial Cup, Padmaja Naidu Cup.

Joy Palace (colt, 1967, by Mangal): 12 wins, Sprinters' Cup (not to be confused with the Sprinters' Cup that decides the champion sprinter; this race was introduced much later), R.W.I.T.C. Gold Cup (twice), C.D. Dady Gold Cup.

Vilasu (colt, 1968, by Cornish Flame): 15 wins, Brig. R.C.R. Hill Memorial Cup.

Madonna (filly, 1969, by Premi): 5 wins, Kamala Veereshwar Rao Memorial Cup.

Whirlaway (filly, 1970, by Time Machine): 4 wins in a short racing career of one year and four months only.

Royal Charm (filly, 1971, by Royal Scot): 6 wins.

Flying Colours (filly, 1973, by King's Son): 6 wins, winner in class II; 3rd Hyderabad Fillies Trial Stakes; 4th South India 1000 Guineas.

Mr. Mighty (colt, 1974, by Canton): 3 wins.

Ardent Son (colt, 1976, by King's Son): 8 wins, Prince of Berar Memorial Cup; 3rd Golconda Derby.

There is a clear and distinct difference between Hoverplane and Khado Cham. While the former specialized in getting classic racers the latter specialized in getting top handicappers. But undoubtedly both had a lot of inherent merit. They got their superior racers out of different stallions.

CATEGORY III

We saw that mares in category I produce classic horses while mares in category II produce top handicappers. Mares in this category are a rung lower. They specialize in producing average racers nothing more. Payal Baje (1963) comes in this category. She was the dam of:

Pappa's Pet (filly, 1970, by Pindari or Pa Bear): 5 wins, Agumbe Cup; 2nd Nilgiris Gold Cup, Varanasi Cup.

Windsor Park (filly, 1972, by Zinosca): 4 wins, Davangere Cup, Ootacamund Cup.

Bold Hanovar (colt, 1974, by Bright Hanovar): 5 wins, winner in class III.

Never Fear (colt, 1977, by Mica Emperor): 3 wins, October Cup, Siddaganga Cup.

CATEGORY IV

Mares in this category are failures. Their progeny are all substandard. A few of them may be, at the most, average. These horses are permanent members of the lowest classes. I do not think an example is necessary.

CATEGORY V

Randia (1963) was the dam of:

Perlina (filly, 1968, by Jethro): 2 wins.

Budhni (filly, 1970, by Golden Horde): 3 wins.

Face the Facts (colt, 1971, by Jethro): 14 wins, President of India Trophy (1600 m, class I, Madras), Czechoslovakia Cup (1600 m, class I, Madras), South India Gold Cup.

Dur-E-Dashmesh (filly, 1972, by Landigou): 4 wins, Justice R.S. Bavdekar Cup (1800 m, class III, Pune), Independence Cup (2000 m, class IV, Pune).

Dur-E-Jehan (filly, 1975, by Everyday): 8 wins, Chief Minister's Cup, Nanda Devi Cup.

Law and Order (colt, 1976, by Jethro): 2 wins, winner in class IV.

Day of Deliverance (filly, 1977, by Jethro or Everyday): 3 wins, Maharaja of Parlakimedi Memorial Cup (1400 m, class III, Madras).

Fiery Force (colt, 1978, by Fair World): 3 wins, winner in class IV.

Dur-E-Deva (filly, 1980, by Shari): 3 wins, Golconda Oaks; 2nd Golconda Derby, Bangalore Oaks. She has just proved herself to be the champion filly of her generation by running a magnificent 3rd in the Charminar Challenge Indian Turf Invitation Cup.

Filly, 1981, by Shari is in training.

Randia's sincerity and dedication to duty was ultimately rewarded by Dur-E-Deva, her first classic winner. I would have been very disappointed if she had failed to do so, as I was following her career with great interest and was convinced that she had the required ability. Therefore Randia got:

Outstanding racer	1
Superior racers	2
Average racers	4
Substandard racers	2
In training	1

Notice that a majority of her progeny cannot be put in a single class. Their abilities spanned the entire spectrum — from classic to substandard. But there is absolutely no need for a mare to produce a classic winner or champion to belong to this category. It is enough if she has produced a superior racer.

Noor Mahal's (1962) stud performance is another excellent example. She was the dam of:

Perception (colt, 1969, by Pushp Milan): 5 wins.

Young Indian (colt, 1970, by Monkshood): placed, died at 3.

Prince Horizon (colt, 1972, by The Liquidator): 1 win.

Damavand (colt, 1973, by Whistling Glory): 5 wins.

Whistling Lass (filly, 1975, by Whistling Glory): ran unplaced.

Princess Polixena (filly, 1976, by Disclose): 4 wins, Griffin Cup (1200 m, 2-yr-old fillies, Madras), M.R.C. Cup (1400 m, 3-yr-olds, Ootacamund) in only one season of racing. Since she was an impressive performer we can consider her to be a superior racer.

Nation's Princess (filly, 1977, by Whistling Glory): 6 wins, winner in class II.

Thundering Gold (colt, 1978, by Thundering): 8 wins, Farrokh K. Irani Gold Cup (1200 m, class I, Madras), Hyderabad Silver Vase (1400 m, classes I and II, Madras).

Prince Karan (colt, 1979, by Thundering): 1 win, in training.

Open Sesame (colt, 1980, by Disclose): 2 wins, in training.

Colt, 1982, by Maratha Lancer is in training.

Her first 8 produce included 3 superior, 1 average and 3 substandard racers. 1 horse died at 3.

CATEGORY VI

The behaviour of mares in this category is similar to the stallions who constitute the fourth deviation from Normal behaviour. This behaviour is unusual and not at all "logical". Can a mare get a couple of outstanding or superior racers together with a large number of very indifferent performers? Yes, several mares have done so. Shararat (1952) is an excellent example. Her produce record is as follows:

Tienshan (colt, 1957, by Aawaz): 2 wins.

Shara Belle (filly, 1958, by Premi): 8 wins, Indian Oaks.

Mahbooba (filly, 1960, by Mahboob 11): 4 wins.

Mrag Gaminee (filly, 1961, by Ramillies): 2 wins in a brief racing career due to a fall.

Khesar (colt, 1962, by Two Pair): 3 wins.

Devotion (filly, 1963, by Gareeb Parvar): 2 wins.

Neutron (filly, 1964, by Mangal): 4 wins.

Jaimaal (filly, 1965, by Two Pair): 5 wins.

Sweet One (filly, 1966, by Dhola Maroo): 7 wins, Man on the Moon Gold Cup, Charity Gold Cup, Consolation Cup

Tres Nouvelle (filly, 1970, by Khan Saheb): 4 wins.

Notice that Shararat had the ability to get an Oaks winner. But most surprisingly all her other racers, with the exception of Sweet One, were very mediocre. If for a moment we exclude Shara Belle, Shararat becomes a failure — and a big one at that. But Shararat is not unique. Since several mares have exhibited this type of behaviour, they must be put in a separate category.

Bani Thani (1966) is another example. She got an Oaks winner but blotted her record by getting 4 very poor racers:

Bani Ho (filly, 1972, by Horatius): 2 wins.

Trudy (filly, 1974, by Landigou): 2 wins.

Tulipa (filly, 1975, by Royal Gleam): 5 wins, Indian Oaks, Eve Champion Cup, Idar Gold Cup (2400 m, 4-yr-olds and over, Pune); 2nd Bangalore 1000 Guineas and Oaks, Nilgiris Derby; 3rd Nilgiris Fillies Trial Stakes, Gen. Rajendrasinhji Cup.

Zonaki (filly, 1976, by Landigou): 2 wins.

Royal Power (colt, 1977, by Royal Gleam): 3 wins.

Sitabani (filly, 1982, by Royal Gleam): in training.

The fact that even dams of classic winners get very inferior racers confirms all our earlier findings. We emphasized the odds against a mare and stressed the intense competition among them. I emphasized that even outstanding mares inevitably get substandard racers. Now go back to Alluvial. Doesn't she belong to this category? Compare her other progeny with Coastal and Slew o' Gold. Aren't these two in a different world altogether?

Now what was the object of the above study? What have we gained from the above analysis? We have understood that broodmares perform differently and that even among the successful there are different degrees of success. But experienced readers will object strongly to the above analysis. They will point out that we have determined only the apparent behaviour of the mares in question and not their inherent behaviour. Consider Hoverplane and Khado Cham. The former had the good fortune to visit Decorum, Golestan, Hervine and Prince Pradeep all hugely successful classic stallions, while the latter visited King's Son, Mangal, Cornish Flame, Premi, Time Machine, Royal Scot and Canton. The last three named were indifferent and the second, third and fourth were only Good to Average. Only King's Son was a classic stallion and it is not a coincidence that her best progeny were by him. Therefore readers will argue: ''Had Khado Cham the good fortune to visit the stallions Hoverplane visited she might have done even better than her! With the limited opportunities Khado Cham had she has done really well. For all we know she may have been inherently more superior than Hoverplane! Therefore we really cannot compare the performances of broodmares in the above manner.'' This objection is very valid. I will not attempt to answer it fully here; I will answer in stages. But there can be no doubt regarding the following argument: Take any mare. Let her visit Nijinsky, Riverman and Mill Reef several times. Is she sure of producing a Derby winner or even a stakes winner? Obviously not. To get a superior racer your mare must also be talented and superior i.e. *an inherently superior and talented stallion and an inherently superior and talented mare have the greatest chance of producing a superior racer.* In other words both the sire and dam ''shape'' and ''mould'' the off-spring and not the sire alone. When we agree that mares are also inherently talented the classification is at once valid. Mares do not possess the same talent. There are different levels, different shades, of talent and this is what the classification shows.

But we must be careful. The progeny of a mare who has visited the very best stallions will exaggerate her own inherent merit. The converse is equally true. Think of a superior, talented mare who had the misfortune to visit very indifferent, substandard stallions. Inevitably her progeny would have been substandard. Can we therefore say that the mare is substandard and devoid of inherent merit? Obviously not. I will later give examples of top class broodmares who failed because they visited very mediocre, substandard stallions. All that readers need understand at this stage is this: Broodmares too play a role in shaping their progeny. But they are not equally talented; there exists different degrees of talent. This is manifested in their progeny as long as they have visited successful stallions.

It is easy to see the practical benefit of the above classification. When we are buying a horse we will naturally see how his dam has fared and determine the category to which she belongs. Was she the dam of any superior racer? If she was she belongs to Category I, II, V, or VI. Mares in category I are obviously the finest. We would all like to race their progeny only. But at any given moment there will not be more than a handful of such mares and naturally their progeny will be in greatest demand.

Our next preference would be for the progeny of category II mares. These mares too are numerically small in number. The major advantage is that such mares rarely produce inferior horses. We can be sure that their progeny will be superior, and if we are lucky they may be even better. We can safely say that mares in these two categories do well with all successful stallions.

Our next choice would be for mares in category V. But remember that they produce superior, average and inferior horses. Therefore we must be fully satisfied with the sire's credentials. Further the conformation of the individual must be near perfect.

Category VI is a special category. Here you must be doubly careful. You may get a classic horse or one who struggles to win in the lowest level. The entire investment on him may have to be written-off. You must be mentally prepared for this eventuality. A lot depends on your temperament. If you are "adventurous" you would like to buy the progeny of these mares, otherwise you would do well to leave them alone.

Therefore when you are analyzing the performance of a broodmare determine how many superior racers she has produced and classify accordingly. (Mares who are yet to produce a superior racer belong to category III or IV.) But we must classify a mare only after four of her progeny have run.

APTITUDE OF BROODMARES

We can study the aptitude of broodmares just as we studied the aptitude of stallions. Some mares are versatile while others are specialists. This idea will become very clear after the following examples.

VERSATILE BROODMARES

Randia was a versatile mare. Among her progeny Face the Facts was a true miler who excelled over 1600 m and 1400 m. But Dur-E-Dashmesh was a stayer. Her principal victories were over 1800 m and 2000 m. Dur-E-Jehan was a superior sprinter-miler who excelled from 1200 m to 1600 m. Dur-E-Deva, as explained, was a classic winning stayer and the champion filly of her generation. Therefore Randia has the distinction of getting sprinter-milers, milers and stayers.

Ballerina (1957) was another versatile mare. Her progeny were:

Bimbo (colt, 1964, by Matombo): 4 wins.

Houri (filly, 1965, by Monkshood): winner.

Turbo Jet (colt, 1967, by Rock of Gibraltar): 4 wins, Merchants Cup.

Black Ballerina (filly, 1968, by Flower Dust): 3 wins, Maharashtra and Gujarat Area Cup (2000 m, class IV, Bombay); 3rd Indian Oaks.

What Next (colt, 1969, by Pa Bear): 7 wins, South India Derby, Madras Gold Vase, Shanmuga Sethupathi Cup; 2nd South India St. Leger (by a neck). He won from 1200 m to 2400 m. Sire.

Mountain Lily (filly, 1970, by Cradle of the Deep): 6 wins, Calcutta 1000 Guineas, Indian Gold Vase.

So What (filly, 1971, by Sauce Piquant): unraced.

Her progeny included a classic winning stayer, a classic winning miler and another stayer.

We need not wait until a mare has finished her career in order to classify her. Consider Silent Screen (1967):

King Pin (colt, 1974, by Mica Emperor): 10 wins, winner in class III. He won up to 1600 m.

Big Time (colt, 1975, by Rapparee): 12 wins, Akravathi Cup, Hyderabad Cup, winner in class II. Even though he won the Bangalore Cup (2400 m, class IV, Ootacamund) and Hill Stamina Cup (2000 m, class III, Ootacamund) on objection, we cannot consider him to be a true stayer. For he won the above races in a very slow time and beat only non-stayers. On going through his race record it is clear that he excelled over 1400 m. But Silent Screen's next racer was a true stayer and a classic winner.

Big Deal (colt, 1978, by Never Never): 12 wins, Golconda Derby and 2000 Guineas, Guindy Gold Cup; 2nd Golconda and Bangalore St. Leger, Stayers' Cup, Queen Elizabeth II Cup; 3rd President of India Gold Cup; 4th Indian Turf Invitation Cup. (He won the President of India Gold Cup in 1984.)

Asset (colt, 1980, by Everyday): 5 wins, P.D. Bolton Cup (1200 m, class I, Bombay), R.J. Kolah Cup, in training. He is among the best sprinters in the country.

Colt, 1982, by Everyday is in training.

Therefore identifying versatile mares is not at all difficult.

SPECIALIST BROODMARES

Not all mares are versatile. Some specialize in producing racers of a particular aptitude. This behaviour can be very strong. A mare after visiting a number of stallions of different aptitudes may yet produce progeny of a particular aptitude. A few examples will be of interest.

Sea Wife (1962) specialized in getting sprinters and milers:

Arun (colt, 1966, by Loyal Manzar): 4 wins.

Wonder Worker (colt, 1967, by Flower Dust): 16 wins, M.R.C. Cup, winner in class I.

Sea Charm (filly, 1968, by Baraloy): 4 wins.

Sea Palace (filly, 1969, by Rock of Gibraltar): 3 wins.

Sea Shells (filly, 1970, by Baraloy): 12 wins, P.D. Bolton Gold Cup, Mathradas Goculdas Gold Cup (1400 m, class I, Bombay), Brindavan Cup (1400 m, class I, Mysore) carrying 61-1/2 kgs.

La Gitana (filly, 1971, by Paddykin): 6 wins, The Metropolitan, Douetil Memorial Cup (1600 m, class II, Calcutta); 3rd Calcutta 1000 Guineas.

Beach Comber (colt, 1972, by Riberto): did not win.

Sea Belle (filly, 1976, by The Wing): unraced, retired to stud.

Port of Call (colt, 1978, by Sagittaire): 2 wins, M.D. Mehta Trophy (1200 m, 3-yr-olds, Bombay); 2nd Bangalore Colts Trial Stakes.

Hustler (colt, 1979, by Paddykin): 4 wins, Kalied Handicap (1200 m, class III, Calcutta), in training.

Filly, 1982, by Ballymacarney is in training.

Romantica (1961) was another mare out of the same mould:

Remarkable (colt, 1969, by Pa Bear): 5 wins.

Recompense (filly, 1973, by Satinello): 4 wins; 2nd Bangalore Fillies Trial Stakes; 3rd Bangalore 1000 Guineas.

Sholay (colt, 1974, by Red Rufus): 17 wins, Bangalore 2000 Guineas, Guindy Gold Cup, Calcutta Gold Cup. He was one of the best sprinter-milers of his generation. Sire.

Response (filly, 1975, by Red Rufus): 5 wins, Hyderabad Fillies Trial Stakes, Asaf Jah VII Memorial Cup (1600 m, class II, Hyderabad), Ootacamund Cup (1600 m, class II, Madras).

Satin Romance (filly, 1976, by Satinello): placed.

Malavika (filly, 1979, by Malvado): 6 wins, R.W.I.T.C. Cup (1200 m, classes I and II, Calcutta), Soli and Gool Poonawalla Memorial Cup (1200 m, class II, Hyderabad). Even though she was a fair 2nd in the Calcutta Oaks, she cannot claim to be a true stayer. She excelled up to 1600 m only.

I want to emphasize strongly that Sea Wife and Romantica had ample opportunity to get genuine high class stayers. For the stallions they visited — Flower Dust, Rock of Gibraltar, Paddykin, Pa Bear, Satinello, Red Rufus and Malvado sired top class stayers. Therefore their inability to get stayers was not due to lack of opportunity. It was their inherent behaviour, their inherent nature, to get sprinter-milers.

Now let us study Donna Princess (1960) who excelled in producing genuine, top class stayers. Her progeny were:

Allegro (colt, 1965, by Klondyke Bill): 5 wins.

San Marco (colt, 1967, by Pieta): 7 wins, Kolar Cup, Air Command Cup, C.S. Loganathan Memorial Cup; placed Nizam's Gold Cup, National Horse Breeding Society of India Gold Cup.

Bharat (colt, 1968, by Pieta): 11 wins, Aga Khan's Cup, Moss Cup; placed C.N. Wadia Gold Cup (2400 m, classes I and II, Bombay). Byculla Club Cup, Gen. Obaidullah Khan Gold Cup.

Nafasat (filly, 1969, by Never Never): placed.

Lady Madonna (filly, 1971, by Never Never): 4 wins, Indian Oaks, Eve Champion Cup (2000 m, 4-yr-olds and over, Bombay) setting a new course record, C.N. Wadia Gold Cup, Homi Mody Gold Cup (2000 m, classes I and II, Bombay); 2nd Indian St. Leger; 4th Indian Turf Invitation Cup.

Trident (colt, 1973, by Never Never): 5 wins, National Horse Breeding Society of India Cup (2000 m, classes III and IV, Madras). His best performance was in the South India St. Leger where he was only 2 lengths behind the winner Kitty Bank, the only other runner, in a smart time. He was also 4th in the South India Derby, 7-1/2 lengths behind the winner Kitty Bank who equalled the course record

Dear Donna (filly, 1975, by Everyday): 6 wins, Stewards Gold Cup (1800 m, class IV, Bombay), Independence Cup (2000 m, class IV, Pune).

Regard (filly, 1976, by Never Never): 1 win.

Durango (colt, 1977, by Never Never): 2 wins, winner over 2000 m.

Abide (filly, 1978, by Everyday): 7 wins, Indian and Bangalore Oaks, Bangalore St. Leger, Mysore Derby and 1000 Guineas; 2nd Indian Turf Invitation Cup, Indian Derby. She was the champion filly of her generation.

Sir Don (colt, 1979, by Never Never): 4 wins; 2nd Calcutta Derby; 3rd Calcutta St. Leger. In training.

Resplendent (colt, 1981, by Road to Glory): 8 wins, Nilgiris Derby and Colts Trial Stakes, Mysore 2000 Guineas, Hyderabad Colts Trial Stakes; 3rd Bangalore Colts Trial Stakes, in training.

It is clear that genuine, top class stamina was the hallmark of the progeny of Donna Princess. Five of her progeny, out of three different stallions, stayed 2800 m with ease, with the greatest comfort. (To digress a bit — I consider only such horses to be true stayers. Several horses win over 2000 m. Are they stayers? By our definition they are. But ask yourself these questions: "How would he have fared over 2400 m or better still over 2800 m? Would he have won with similar ease? Would he have got the distance comfortably?" If you think he would, he is a true stayer. Readers must note that I am not referring to extreme stamina. Till recently the objective of every breeder was to breed such horses. But for reasons that are not clear to me, the St. Leger has gone out of "fashion" and breeders are unwilling to breed horses who can get 2800 m. This is very detrimental to the breed. I will come back to this subject later.)

Our next task is to determine the class and aptitude of a mare. This is very simple. We have to only combine the two procedures we just followed. I leave this exercise to readers in the quiz below. I have given the produce records of six mares. Study them carefully and determine their class and aptitudes.

QUIZ I

1) **INNOCENT** (1961) was the dam of:

Sriluxmi (filly, 1968, by Glasgow Paddock): 12 wins, Sprinters' Cup (not to be confused with the Sprinters' Cup that decides the champion sprinter), Turf Club Cup.

Bear's Rock (colt, 1969, by Pa Bear): did not win.

Red River (colt, 1970, by Exaggerator): 6 wins, Dr. A. Karmally Gold Cup, Balam Plate (1800 m, class II, Bombay); 2nd Kailashpat Singhania Gold Cup; 3rd Aga Khan's Spring Cup.

Charming Princess (filly, 1973, by King's Son): 5 wins, Independence Cup (1400 m, class III, Mysore), Brahmaputra Plate (1600 m, class II, Bangalore).

Running Blossom (filly, 1974, by Mossy Bear): 11 wins, Karnataka Sub-Area Cup (2000 m, class I, Bangalore), Jayachamaraja Wadiyar Cup (1600 m, class I, Bangalore), Krishnaraja Cup (1600 m, class II, Bangalore).

2) **ALKAPURI** (1956) was the dam of:

Om Shanti (filly, 1963, by Daneshill): 6 wins, Andhra Pradesh Stud Farm Cup.

Khabardar (colt, 1966, by Tiptree): 3 wins, Cole Motee Golden Jubilee Commemoration Gold Cup.

Dictatorial (filly, 1967, by Exaggerator): unraced.

Turf Bullet (colt, 1968, by Glasgow Paddock): 6 wins.

Mighty Bear (colt, 1969, by Pa Bear): 8 wins, Ramanatha Iyer Memorial Cup.

Our Emperor (colt, 1971, by Satinello): 1 win.

Dinky Do (filly, 1972, by Romiti): ran only twice and was retired to stud.

Red Satin (colt, 1973, by Satinello): 13 wins, South India 2000 Guineas, Mysore Derby, Bangalore and Hyderabad Colts Trial Stakes. Sire.

3) **HUNTER'S GIRL** (1968) was the dam of:

Cupid (colt, 1972, by Darling Boy): 15 wins, South India Derby, Calcutta Derby and 2000 Guineas, Nizam's Gold Cup, Calcutta Gold Cup. He won from 1000 m to 2400 m. He established a track record over 1400 m in Madras. Sire.

Artemis (filly, 1975, by Romney): 5 wins, Calcutta Oaks, Nepal Gold Cup, Pat Williamson Memorial Cup (2200 m, classes II and III, Calcutta); 2nd Calcutta Derby and St. Leger.

Blue Fire Lady (filly, 1977, by Romney): 1 win.

Young Rajput (colt, 1 978, by Eagle Rock): 5 wins, Bangalore Derby (in record time), Nilgiris Derby, Madras Gold Vase (1400 m, 3-yr-olds, Madras), Owners and Trainers Association Cup (1400 m, 3-yr-olds, Madras). Sire.

4) **CHRISTMAS EVE** (1962) was the dam of:

Richelieu (colt, 1970, by Pa Bear): 8 wins, Indian St. Leger, Maharaja's Cup, A.C. Ardeshir Gold Cup, Eve Champion Cup; 2nd Indian Derby.

Anaheeta (filly, 1972, by Horatius): 2 wins.

Santorini (filly, 1973, by Horatius): 1 win.

La Madelaine (filly, 1974, by Landigou): 1 win, H.M. Mehta Cup (1600 m 3-yr-olds which had placed 1st, 2nd, 3rd or 4th, Bombay); 2nd F.D. Wadia Cup, Gen. Rajendrasinhji Gold Cup.

Diorama (filly, 1975, by Royal Gleam): 3 wins.

Romanoff (colt, 1976, by Royal Gleam): 4 wins.

Christoffe (colt, 1977, by Landigou): 6 wins, R.R. Ruia Gold Cup, Gen. Rajendrasinhji Gold Cup; 2nd Indian Derby (by a head to Track Lightning, Happy Landing was 3rd by a head).

Christofina (filly, 1978, by Landigou): 2 wins.

Regal Gleam (colt, 1979, by Royal Gleam): 1 win, Jasdan Cup (1800 m, class III, Bombay); 2nd Breeders Produce Stakes (1400 m, 3-yr-olds, Bombay), Classic Trophy (1400 m, maiden 3-yr-olds, Bombay).

Colt, 1981, by Royal Gleam is in training.

5) **ROSE BUD** (1957) was the dam of:

Dew Drop (filly, 1967, by High Commission): 2 wins.

Sword Dancer (colt, 1969, by Glasgow Paddock): 3 wins.

Witty Answer (colt, 1970, by Pindari): 3 wins.

Satin Rose (filly, 1971, by Satinello): did not win.

Black Rose (filly, 1973, by Buckpasser [India]): 4 wins.

Black Superman (colt, 1974, by Romiti): 1 win.

Regency Bud (filly, 1975, by Red Rufus): 5 wins, Panchavati Cup (2000 m, class IV, Bangalore).

Buttinsky (colt, 1977, by Nijinsky [India]): 6 wins, Tamil Nadu Commemoration Gold Cup, Governor's Cup (2600 m, classes III and IV, Madras); 2nd Stayers' Cup; 3rd South India St. Leger.

Rubaiyat (filly, 1978, by Nijinsky [India]): 6 wins, Turf Club Cup (2400 m, classes II and III, Madras), Governor's Cup (2600 m, classes III and IV, Madras).

6) **GLORIANA** (1957) was the dam of:

Roanna (filly, 1965, by Roman Honey): 5 wins.

Scottish Venture (filly, 1967, by Scotch Crown): 10 wins, Chief Minister's Cup, R.W.I.T.C. Cup, Bangalore Gold Cup, Poonawalla Estates Gold Cup ; 2nd Calcutta 1000 Guineas; 3rd Calcutta Oaks.

Royal Gloria (filly, 1968, by Cheko): 7 wins.

Roxana (filly, 1969, by Cheko): 4 wins.

Beatrix Potter (filly, 1970, by Punjab): 7 wins; 2nd Akka Saheb Maharaj Cup, P.D. Bolton Gold Cup; 3rd Mathradas Goculdas Gold Cup.

Grand Marque (colt, 1971, by Punjab): 8 wins, Ashwapriya Cup (1200 m, class I, Bangalore), Hyderabad Silver Vase, Mount Everest Cup.

Trevi (filly, 1973, by Three Wishes): 10 wins, Stewards Cup (1200 m, class III, Ootacamund), winner in class II.

(Answers in page 97)

We have just classified broodmares on their performances as producers No doubt the exercise is useful. It helps us to pinpoint superior mares and understand their behaviour. But we cannot always insist on buying the progeny of mares who have proved to be excellent producers i.e. progeny who are half or full-brothers or sisters to outstanding or superior racers. We may be interested in the 1st or 2nd foal of a mare. But can we predict to a reasonable degree of accuracy that the mare will be a successful producer? Can we say that the mare has all the credentials necessary to succeed as a producer? Yes we can. To do so we must first identify all the qualities broodmares must necessarily possess in order to succeed in stud.

QUALIFICATIONS OF BROODMARES

We can safely say that a mare must possess good racing ability, pedigree, conformation and temperament to succeed in stud. Conformation and temperament are out of the scope of this book, but a few words are in order. A mare must possess such conformation and temperament that it enables her to produce sound and healthy foals. If so, half the battle is won. But this is not always the case. The progeny of a number of mares are predisposed to conformation and/or temperament flaws. The mare herself may not have the flaw. It may be due to a genetic defect. When such a mare visits a stallion with the same defect there is a chance of the defect appearing in the offspring. Genetic defects may result in abnormal feet, pasterns, hocks, knees, shoulders, eyes etc. All these defects may not be very serious and even the best horses have them to a certain extent. However the first prerequisite for a mare's success is that she must be free from major genetic defects and be able to produce sound, healthy foals. (For an excellent introduction to this subject read — ''Genetics — They may affect the soundness of your foal'' by Ann Leighton Hardman, *Stable Management*, Volume 18, Number 1, April/May 1981.)

Now we come to racing merit and pedigree. Let us first study the former in detail. In essence the question we have to answer is this:

"Is it necessary for a mare to excel on the course in order to succeed as a producer?"

The question is easily answered. All we have got to do is identify all the mares who were outstanding or superior producers over a period of time and see whether they were superior racers. Were they all 1000 Guineas or Oaks winners? Were they all stakes winners or were they, in general, talented racers? Is it not reasonable to assume that there is a direct correlation between the mare's racing ability and her progeny's? Better the mare better will be her progeny. But a quick look through previous records disproves the above assumption. My favourite broodmare of all time is Morganette, dam of the great Ard Patrick. How did Morganette — how dare Morganette — who was incapable of winning a race of any kind get Ard Patrick winner of the Epsom Derby? (The also-rans included the great Sceptre. He defeated her again in the Eclipse Stakes the following year.) How did Bastia who could not win get the towering Right Royal V winner of the French Derby and King George VI and Queen Elizabeth Stakes? Are these two very isolated examples of non-winning mares who produced classic winners? No, they are not. There are several others. In order to determine the correlation between the racing ability of mares and their progeny, I studied the racing ability of the dams of "Major European Stakes Winners" of 1979, '80 and '81. *The Thoroughbred Times* gives the complete pedigrees of the Major European Stakes Winners every year*. Therefore my task was simple. From them I had to only note down the racing performances of all the dams. These findings are given in Tables 7 and 8. I beseech readers to study them very carefully; there are a few surprises.

---

* 13th February, 1980 (for the Major European Stakes Winners of 1979)
11th February, 1981 (for 1980).
10th February, 1982 (for 1981).

TABLE 7

DAMS OF MAJOR EUROPEAN STAKES WINNERS OF 1979, '80 AND '81

S.No.	Mares' Race Record	1979 No	1979 %	1980 No	1980 %	1981 No	1981 %
1)	Mares who were unraced	14	8.5	20	11.6	12	7.1
2)	Mares who were placed or unplaced	21	12.7	18	10.4	30	17.9
3)	Winners	74* (74+1)	44.9	75* (75+4)	43.3	64* (64+1)	38.1
4)	Stakes-placed	17* (17+1)	10.3	22	12.7	18	10.7
5)	Stakes winners	39	23.6	37* (37+1)	21.4	44	26.2
6)	Mare's complete record not available	—	—	1	0.6	—	—
	TOTAL	167	100	178	100	169	100
		Stakes winners out of 165 mares		Stakes winners out of 173 mares		Stakes winners out of 168 mares	

(The percentages are for the number of mares and not for the number of Stakes winners got by them.)

TABLE 7 (cont.)

1979

* Among the "Winners" (category 3) 1 mare comes twice i.e. she was the dam of 2 Major European Stakes Winners.
* Among the "Stakes-placed" (category 4) mare comes twice.

1980

* Among the "Winners" (category 3) 4 mares come twice.
* Among the "Stakes winners" (category 5) 1 mare comes twice.

1981

* Among the "Winners" (category 3) 1 mare comes twice.

I have further subdivided the "Winners" (category 3) as follows:

TABLE 8

DAMS OF MAJOR EUROPEAN STAKES WINNERS OF 1979, '80 AND '81

S.No.	Mares' Race Record	1979		1980		1981	
		No	%	No	%	No	%
1)	Mares who won only once	38	51.3	39* (39+3)	52	32* (32+1)	50

TABLE 8 (cont.)

DAMS OF MAJOR EUROPEAN STAKES WINNERS OF 1979, '80 AND '81

S.No.	Mares' Race Record	1979		1980		1981	
		No	%	No	%	No	%
2)	Mars who won twice	19* (19+1)	25.7	14	18.7	13	20.3
3)	Mares who won more than two races	17	23	22* (22+1)	29.3	19	29.7
		75	100	79	100	65	100
		Stakes winners out of 74 mares		Stakes winners out of 75 mares		Stakes winners out of 64 mares	

(The percentages are for the number of mares and not for the number of Stakes winners got by them.)

1979

* Among the mares who won twice 1 mare comes twice (i.e. she was the dam of 2 Major European Stakes Winners.

1980

* Among the mares who won only once 3 mares come twice.

* Among the mares who won more than 2 races 1 mare comes twice.

1981

* Among the mares who won only once 1 mare comes twice.

The Tables are of extreme interest. They call for a detailed explanation. During the three years in question there was very little change in the percentage of mares in each category. Therefore we can say the racing merit of the dams of the Major European Stakes Winners was as follows:

TABLE 9

1)	Mares who were unraced	9.1%
2)	Mares who were placed or unplaced	13.7 "
3)	Winners	42.1 "
4)	Stakes-placed	11.2 "
5)	Stakes winners	23.7 "
6)	Mare's complete record not available	0.2 "
		100%

Our first surprise: Did you know that mares who were unraced and mares who failed to win a single race accounted for as many as 23% of the Major European Stakes Winners? The total absence of racing ability did not prevent them from becoming successful producers. 9% of them did not even see a racecourse. In these inflationary days I do not think anyone will keep a sound, fit horse unraced. Therefore we can conclude that there was something seriously wrong, radically wrong, with those mares. Their owners felt that training them would be a sheer waste of time and money and preferred to send them directly to stud. Yet in spite of all their handicaps they became successful producers! (We have got to keep in mind one more aspect. I do not think these mares would have visited the very best stallions or have received the best care and attention in stud, unless they were full or half-sisters to big winners. I think we can safely say that they made their own way in the world.)

Mares who won produced 42% of the Stakes winners. But about half of them won only once and a further fifth won only twice. Only the remaining (about 27%) won more than two races. Though these mares were winners, they were no great shakes on the racecourse. Like the mares in the earlier category, their lack of racing ability did not prevent them from becoming successful producers.

Let us now discuss the performance of stakes winning mares. They accounted for about a quarter of the Stakes winners. This is not at all surprising as these mares were outstanding racers, superior winners — the "real" racehorses. They were the stars of their time. But we must note that they would have visited the very best stallions and got the best care and attention.

A big surprise for me was that the stakes-placed mares accounted for only 11% of the Stakes winners. I imagined the figure would be much higher. Can we not say that the stakes-placed mares too had everything going for them? Surely they were also talented racers — definitely superior than average racers but only marginally inferior than the stakes winners themselves. Surely their pedigrees cannot have been bad. Being superior mares they too must have received good care in stud, and we must not forget that there can be twice the number of stakes-placed mares than stakes winning mares. Yet they produced only 11% of the Stakes winners. Compare this with the 9% of winners produced by mares who were unraced and 14% of winners produced by mares who could not win. I thought this category would be near the top, but it is near the bottom!

We can rewrite Table 9 in the following manner:

TABLE 10

Mares who were unraced, unplaced, placed and who did not win more than two races, i.e. mares without racing ability produced	53.5% of Stakes Winners
Mares who won more than two races, states-placed and stakes winners i.e. mares with racing ability produced	46.3% of Stakes Winners

A very neat split right down the middle! About half the dams of the Major European Stakes Winners were themselves inferior racers, while the other half were superior. Therefore an extremely important result from the above investigation is:

It is not at all necessary for a broodmare to possess superior racing merit in order to succeed as a producer.

As we have just seen, unraced mares, non-winners and minor winners can get superior racers. Remember their progeny were no ordinary horses; they were classic winners, champions and stakes winners.

I also studied the race records of the dams of superior winners in India to see whether the result held. My findings are as below:

There are no stakes races in the country as a true Pattern race system is yet to be introduced. But every year the National Horse Breeding Society of India designates a number of prestigious and valuable races (including all the classics) as ''Selected'' races. I therefore studied the racing performances of the dams of these selected race winners. (Here I have adopted a slightly different methodology; but it will not alter the result significantly.)

In 1978-'79 45 horses won the 82 selected races among themselves.

In 1979-'80 51 horses won the 95 selected races among themselves.

In 1980-'81 52 horses won the 90 selected races among themselves.

Since several horses won selected races in more than one year, the actual number of selected race winners during the three years was only 124. These 124 horses were the progeny of only 108 mares as several were full or half-brothers and sisters. (93 mares were represented by one selected race winner, 14 by two winners and 1 mare had the distinction of getting three winners.) The racing performances of these 108 mares is given below:

TABLE 11

1)	Got-abroad mares	25
2)	Classic winners in India	5
3)	Classic-placed and top handicappers i.e. superior racers	14
4)	Average winners	24
5)	Minor winners	16
6)	Mares who were placed or unplaced	7
7)	Mares who were retired to stud unraced	16
8)	Mare who raced in Delhi which is not a principal racing centre	1
		108

The got-abroad mares (i.e. mares not foaled in India) were imported for breeding. Some of them raced in their countries of origin and in India, but we cannot compare them with mares foaled in the country. Therefore we must exclude them, and the solitary mare who raced in Delhi, from our calculations. This leaves us with 82 mares and we have:

TABLE 12

1)	Classic winners, classic-placed and top handicappers i.e. superior racers	19	23.2%
2)	Average racers	24	29.3"
3)	Inferior racers and mares who did not win	23	28.0"
4)	Mares who were retired to stud unraced	16	19.5"
		82	100%

Again we have the same "surprises", and a remarkably identical distribution. We must now try to explain why mares of each category behaved as they did.

How did mares who were unraced and those who could not win manage to get so many stakes winners? Sheer strength of numbers helped them! For remember that such mares constitute a sizeable portion of the broodmare population. Since there are hundreds (if not thousands) of mares in this category it was inevitable that some of them succeeded. The second reason for their success is more important. Their pedigrees would have undoubtedly been a factor. Though these mares were very poor racers, several of them would have been well-bred. Therefore their superior pedigrees could have helped them succeed. There is yet another factor. Remember only the very best colts become stallions in the first place. Therefore we can argue that since stallions are outstanding in almost every respect, they definitely have the inherent capacity to get superior racers out of such inferior mares. Several among the hundreds of mares in this category would have visited such stallions, and among those matings a few were bound to be successful. Therefore substandard mares can become successful producers.

The above arguments hold for the winning mares too. They were responsible for 42% of the Stakes winners.

Now we come to the stakes winning and stakes-placed mares. They produced 35% of the Stakes winners. But do not forget that such mares constitute a very small portion of the broodmare population! We can safely say that less than 10% of the broodmare population consists of such mares. Yet they were responsible for about a third of all the Stakes winners! Even if we assume that they visited the very best stallions, the inescapable conclusion is:

The superior racing merit these mares possessed enabled them to become successful producers.

Combining our two findings we can say:

While racing merit is not an essential prerequisite for success as a producer, it does help. It is a big advantage. In other words everything else being equal a mare who was a superior racer has a greater chance of stud success than a non-winner.

A long and sometimes acrimonious debate has always gone on among breeders: ''Is it advisable to breed only from superior mares i.e. 'the best with the best' or also from other mares?'' As we have seen, even mares who were incapable of winning a race became very successful producers. But without a shadow of doubt the advantage lies with mares who possessed real racing talent.

I will end this section by posing this question: ''Stakes winning mares produced 24% of the Stakes winners while the stakes-placed mares, who outnumber the stakes winners, produced only 11%. I strongly feel the latter group should have produced more. How do you feel? Do you think the stakes-placed mares should produce more, equal or less Stakes winners than the stakes winning mares? '' One thing is certain. During these three years the stakes-placed mares have not done justice to themselves. My guess is the unraced and non-winning mares gained at the expense of the stakes-placed. Do you know why? But a similar study done over ten years, or better still over twenty years, is sure to yield different results. But it will not alter our fundamental findings. (What do you think will be the distribution in a ''normal'' year? I will not hazard a guess.)

PEDIGREE REQUIREMENTS OF BROODMARES

When we analyzed pedigrees in chapter 2 we went into the pedigree of the dam. We divided her pedigree into two parts — the maternal grandsire component and the tail female line component. The former component will be dealt with in great detail in the next chapter. Here we will study the latter. We noted that the term ''tail female line'' of a mare refers to her dam, grandam and great-grandam taken as a whole, as a single unit. We are interested in knowing how they fared as producers. Were they hugely successful or just average? What was the class and aptitude of their progeny i.e. the class and aptitude of the tail female line? Determining it is not difficult. We only have to determine the class and aptitude of each of the three dams as we have done and sum up.

We noted that the tail female line component (and the maternal grand-sire component) becomes very important in the case of young mares whose

progeny have just started to race, and in the case of mares who are yet
to produce a big winner. Suppose we are interested in the 1st or 2nd offspring of a mare. We naturally do not know her class or aptitude or even
whether she will be a successful producer in the first place. But if her
tail female line and maternal grandsire components are superior, we can
boldly say that, in all probability,she will be a successful producer.

In addition to the class and aptitude of the female line, readers must,
at this stage, grasp one more concept — the concept of ''depth''. The depth
of a female line refers to the number and regularity at which the three
dams produced superior progeny. Frequently we come across tail female
lines which have produced a couple of outstanding or superior horses at
very irregular intervals. These superior horses were accompanied by a
large number of indifferent progeny. In fairness we cannot say that such
a female line lacks class; but it definitely lacks depth. Most of the mares
of such female lines are failures, while the others behave like a mare who
produces one big winner together with a large number of indifferent racers.
In other words such female families are very erratic and extremely inconsistent in their stud behaviour. We have to be alert and identify such
families. In contrast there are scores of female families who may not have
produced a classic winner or champion, but who have produced a number
of superior racers generation after generation. It is for you to decide on
which lines to patronize.

I have given in the following pages the tail female lines of six mares.
I am sure you can easily determine their class, aptitude and depth and
classify accordingly.

QUIZ 2

1) SITTING PRETTY (1973): 6 wins.

GUL-E-MANZAR: unraced. Dam of:

> **The Fuehrer:** winner.
>
> **Chanakya:** 6 wins, Sub-Area Cup, Chamundi Cup, Ram Mahad-
> evan Gold Cup (1200 m, 3-yr-old colts and geldings, Madras);
> 2nd South India 2000 Guineas, Maharaja's Gold Cup. (Winner
> in class I.)
>
> **Aureus:** 6 wins, R.C.T.C. Gold Cup (1200 m, classes I and II,
> Calcutta), Bengal Area Cup (2200 m, classes II and III, Calcutta).
>
> **Sitting Pretty:** as above.
>
> **Filly,** 1982, by Gregarious is in training.

MANZAR: 4 wins; 2nd Ceylon Turf Club Cup; 3rd Indian Oaks. Dam of:

Tony Rome: 2 wins.

Gul-E-Manzar: as above.

PURVEZ: unraced. Dam of:

Paigham: 13 wins, Rajpipla Gold Cup; 2nd Maharaja Sir Harisinghji's Stakes, Chikkavaram Gold Cup.

Win Master: 5 wins, South India Derby, M. Ct. M. Chidambaram Chettyar Memorial Gold Cup.

Dhavalgiri: 11 wins, Surgeon General's Cup.

Pavan Doot: 6 wins, Poona City Cup.

Grand Slam: 7 wins.

Babul: 2 wins.

Prize Fighter: 7 wins, Sir Rahimtoola Chinoy Gold Cup, Rajaram Chhatrapati Gold Cup, Wellington Cup.

Blassbull: 1 win.

Manzar as above.

Heyz: did not win.

2) MOHINI (1975): 6 wins, Bangalore 1000 Guineas, Bangalore and Nilgiris Fillies Trial Stakes; 2nd South India 1000 Guineas and Oaks, Hyderabad Fillies Trial Stakes; 3rd Deccan Derby.

MOONSHINE: 6 wins. Dam of:

Urvashi: 7 wins, Tamil Nadu Commemoration Gold Cup (1600 m, classes I and II, Madras).

Mohini: as above.

Mukh Mohini: 2 wins.

Deepali: 4 wins, Indian 1000 Guineas, Sir Jamsetjee Jeejeebhoy (VI Bart) Trophy (1000 m, 2-yr-old fillies, Bombay); 3rd Mysore 1000 Guineas.

Goodness Gracious: winner, in training.

Filly (1982) by Everyday is in training.

ROSE BEAM: 2 wins in the only season she raced. Dam of:

Rock Haven: 11 wins, South India Derby, 1000 Guineas, Oaks and St. Leger, Bangalore Fillies Trial Stakes.

Rashtra Doot: 6 wins, Quincy Cup.

Mica Rose: 5 wins.

Young Moor: 6 wins, M.Ct.M. Chidambaram Chettyar Memorial Gold Cup (1800 m, classes II and III, Madras).

Fire Brand: 3 wins.

Irma La Douce: 3 wins, Calcutta Oaks and St. Leger; 2nd Calcutta 2000 Guineas; 3rd Calcutta Derby.

Moonshine: as above.

NEOLIGHT: 7 wins, Indian 1000 Guineas and Oaks, Jammu Stud Gold Cup; 3rd Indian Derby and St. Leger. Dam of:

Ocean Light: 3 wins.

Rose Beam: as above.

3) **GREY SATIN** (1974): 4 wins; 2nd Indian Oaks; 3rd Indian 1000 Guineas.

MARY STUART: unraced. Dam of:

Grey Satin: as above.

Winfree: 6 wins, World Wildlife Cup, Turf Club Cup (1200 m, class II, Calcutta).

Mary Palmer: unraced, at stud.

Jat Hero: 2 wins.

BOUDICCA : 13 wins, South India Turf Club Cup, M.Ct.M. Chidambaram Chettyar Memorial Gold Cup; placed Madras Gold Vase, Stewards Cup. Dam of:

Loving Cup: 3 wins, Orange William Cup; 2nd Calcutta Oaks.

Mary Stuart: as above, her only 2 foals.

REGAL FROLIC: placed 3rd at 2 years in Ireland. Won 3 races in India. Dam of:

Royal Frolic: 3 wins.

Regal Commission: 8 wins, Sangam Cup, M.Ct.M. Chidambaram Chettyar Memorial Gold Cup (2400 m, classes II and III, Madras); 2nd Hyderabad Gold Cup (2400 m, 5-yr-olds and over, Madras).

Domani: 5 wins, Stewards Cup, Philanthropist, Cup; placed in Stewards Cup.

Stylish Lady: winner.

Jericho: 6 wins.

Boudicca: as above.

4) **BETTER LATE** (1974): 2 wins, winner in class IV, dead-heated for 2nd place in the Calcutta Oaks in an extremely slow time.

OPPORTUNITY: 4 wins. Dam of:

Cannon King: 9 wins.

Opportunist: 5 wins.

Better Late: as above.

PILLAR TO POST: 5 wins, Indian 1000 Guineas, Aga Khan's Spring Cup; 2nd Indian Oaks, Eve Champion Cup. Dam of:

Southern Queen: 4 wins.

La Paloma: 2 wins.

Tenacity: 1 win.

Opportunity: as above.

Point to Point: placed twice in her short racing career.

SUZETTE: unraced. Dam of:

Post to Post: 5 wins.

Flying Arrow: 3 wins.

Havana: 2 wins.

Golden Orb: 6 wins.

Dream Park: 4 wins.

Suzerain: winner.

Pillar to Post: as above.

5) **GRETEL** (1971): 9 wins, Huntsey Estate Cup, M.Ct.M. Chidam baram Chettyar Memorial Cup (1200 m, class 111, Mysore).

GENTLE ART: 2 wins. Dam of:

Hallo Hallo: 6 wins.

Arabesque: 3 wins.

Not So Gentle: 7 wins, T.N. Banerjea Gold Cup (1200 m, class III, Calcutta), winner in classes II and III.

Gretel: as above.

ARTISTIC: 9 wins, Dam of:

Cauvery: 9 wins, Clive Stud Cup, Belgaum Cup; 2nd South India 1000 Guineas (by a short-dead).

Rembrant: 11 wins, Kumararajah M.A.M. Muthiah Gold Cup.

Gypsy Rose: 9 wins, Stewards Cup, winner in class II.

Margot Fontyn: 4 wins.

Mossart: 4 wins, Brig. R.C.R. Hill Memorial Cup.

Gentle Art: as above.

GOLDEN EVE: winner in England and placed in India. Dam of:

Roman Art: 14 wins, Turf Club Cup, Stewards Cup.

Loch Lomond: 7 wins.

Nightingale: 10 wins, Madras Gold Vase, National Horse Breeding Society Cup; 2nd South India 1000 Guineas and Oaks.

Cinderella: 2 wins.

Scarlet Prince: 19 wins, Queen Elizabeth II Cup, M.R.C. Hospital Cup, Burdwan Cup; 3rd South India 2000 Guineas.

Roman Princess: 4 wins.

Autumn Gold: 12 wins.

Artistic: as above.

6) REPRINT (1973): 6 wins, Indian 1000 Guineas and Oaks; 3rd Indian Derby.

REQUEST: 7 wins, Indian 1000 Guineas, A.C. Ardeshir Memorial Gold Cup; 3rd Indian Oaks. Dam of:

Garuda: 8 wins, R.C.T.C. Gold Cup, Chief Minister's Gold Cup; 2nd Gavin Johnston Cup, Spring Cup; 3rd Bhutan Gold Cup, Gen. Obaidullah Khan Gold Cup.

Remarque: 5 wins; 3rd Indian 1000 Guineas and Oaks.

Reflect: 8 wins, Indian 1000 Guineas, Bangalore St. Leger, Eclipse Stakes of India, Eve Champion Cup, C.N. Wadia Gold Cup; 3rd Indian Derby and Oaks.

Star Above: 1 win.

Reprint: as above.

REPAY: 7 wins. Dam of:

Reward: 7 wins, Indian Air Force Cup; 2nd Rajaram Chhatrapati Gold Cup.

Request: as above, her only foals.

SILVER LOAN: did not win. Dam of:

Firelight: 2 wins.

Ambassador: 5 wins, Oakfield Cup.

Rivaz: placed.

Dollar Crisis: did not win.

Repay: as above.

(Answers in page 97)

As we have just seen, and as readers will be aware, tail female lines vary widely in quality. The outstanding lines consistently produce classic winners, champions and stakes winners, while other lines produce top handicappers with the occasional classic horse. Still other female families are average and there are lines which have failed to produce a superior racer for generations.

Therefore mares with superior tail female lines have greater chances of success as producers.

But where does it all begin? Who were the founders of these successful female families? One broodmare — the "foundation broodmare" — was the founder of each of these female families. These mares were extremely talented and were very successful producers. They passed on their inherent merit to their daughters who also excelled, and who in turn passed on all their beneficial qualities to their daughters and so on. It would not be an exaggeration to say that a relatively small number of female families have greatly dominated the production of outstanding horses. Turf historians have found that several female families have been consistently producing classic winners and superior racers for over a hundred years! *Bloodstock Breeding* by Sir Charles Leicester, revised by Howard Wright, gives the performances of a number of such families. I urge readers to study them very carefully.

Here let us study the performances of the tail female line descendants of the great Sceptre (1899). From Sunny Jane (1914) who won the English Oaks to Weimar (1968) who won the Italian St. Leger, this family produced six other classic winners, two Ascot Gold Cup winners, two Eclipse Stakes winners, one Grand Prix de Paris winner and several other superior racers. Several horses from this family became successful sires. (Further four horses from this family had the misfortune of finishing 2nd in the Epsom Derby!)

The female line descendants of Gondolette (1902) were equally talented. From Ferry (1915) who won the English 1000 Guineas to Snow Knight (1971) who won the Epsom Derby, this family was responsible for seven other classic winners (including Hyperion), two Ascot Gold Cup winners and several other talented racers. Several horses from this family were outstanding sires.

Readers will certainly know the brilliant performances of the families of Americus Girl, Frizette, La Troienne, Marchetta and others.

Identifying foundation broodmares is not difficult. Their descendants form the leading tail female lines of today. When we open our auction catalogues we have the female lines of all the dams. We can easily identify the most superior amongst them. Then if we research deeper we will come to the foundation broodmare.

Just as it is necessary for readers to identify and determine the behaviour of all the classic stallions, it is also necessary to identify all the leading female families and pinpoint mares from them who are active today.

Dhun Kothavala* has identified the ten leading female families in Indian breeding. But I consider five of the families, plus one family not in the original ten,to be superior to the other five. These are the families founded by Stella Marina (1935), Aurelie (1945), Neolight (1953), Hoverplane (1952), Repay (1947) and Daring Dance (1932) — who was not in the original ten. The progeny of these foundation broodmares were hugely successful. They included scores of classic winners, champions, classic-placed and top handicappers. Each of the above six families (except Hoverplane and Repay) produced at least six classic winners, the criterion for their selection. They proved their inherent merit by producing superior horses generation after generation. All the above families are very strong today. In order to fully grasp the achievements of a foundation broodmare, let us make a slightly detailed study of Aurelie's family.

		Bacteriophage	Tetratema Pharmacie
	Teleferique		
		Beaute de Neige	St. Just Bellezza
Aurelie (Dk B, 1945)			
		Teddy	Ajax Rondeau
	Anne de Bretagne	Our Liz	William the Third Countess Resy

* "'The matriarchal foundation' — which are the best Indian lines?" Dhun Kothavala, *The Indian Racing and Stud Annual (No.3)*.

Aurelie was bred in Germany but raced in France, where she placed 7 times. In France she had two foals. She was then imported into India in foal to Worden II, by the Maharaja of Kashmir. It was a very inspired buy. Even more so when her two foals in France were:

Wayne II: 3 wins, Prix Frisky Matron; 2nd Prix d'Arenberg (Gr. III, Longchamp), Middle Park Stakes (Gr. I, Newmarket).

San Diego: won Prix de la Vastine.

Most fortunately for Indian breeding, Aurelie it seems had firmly decided to become a foundation broodmare. She held to Worden II getting Auroden. She then visited the best stallions in the country and proceeded to get a series of fillies as shown below.

Auroden (1955)	by	Worden II
Golden Pollen (1956)	"	Flower Dust
Fairlie (1957)	"	Fair Aid
Statue of Liberty (1958)	"	Ocean Way
Rocklie (1959)	"	Rock of Gibraltar
Mica (1960)	"	Flower Dust
Triveni (1962)	"	King's Barn

Instead of giving the race records and stud performances of the above fillies and their descendants, I have prepared a chart which lists the principal winners of the entire family. This is given in the next page.

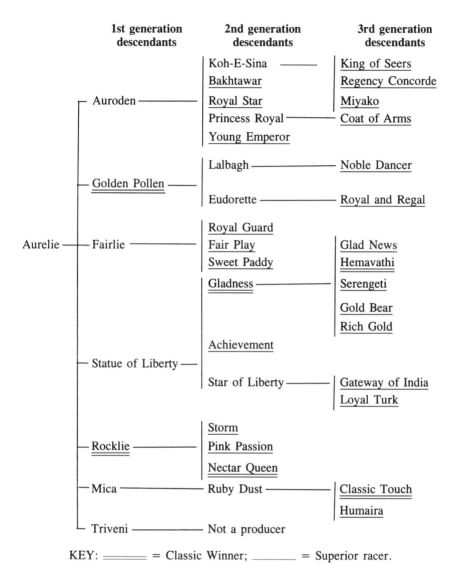

	1st generation descendants	2nd generation descendants	3rd generation descendants

Koh-E-Sina ——— King of Seers

Bakhtawar   Regency Concorde

Auroden ——— Royal Star   Miyako

Princess Royal ——— Coat of Arms

Young Emperor

Lalbagh ——————— Noble Dancer

Golden Pollen ———

Eudorette ——————— Royal and Regal

Royal Guard

Aurelie ——— Fairlie ——————— Fair Play   Glad News

Sweet Paddy   Hemavathi

Gladness ——————— Serengeti

Gold Bear

Rich Gold

Achievement

Statue of Liberty ———

Star of Liberty ——— Gateway of India

Loyal Turk

Storm

Rocklie ——————— Pink Passion

Nectar Queen

Mica ——————— Ruby Dust ——————— Classic Touch

Humaira

Triveni ——————— Not a producer

KEY: ═══════ = Classic Winner; _____ = Superior racer.

Within three generations Aurelie and her descendants produced 6 classic winners and 22 superior racers. The race records of the classic winners are given below:

Golden Pollen: 2 wins, South India Oaks, Hildebrand Memorial Cup; 2nd South India St. Leger.

Rocklie: 5 wins, Indian Derby, Poona City Stakes; 2nd Indian St. Leger and Oaks, R.R. Ruia Gold Cup; 3rd Indian 1000 Guineas.

Gladness (filly, 1963, by Matombo): 7 wins, Bangalore Fillies Trial Stakes, Douetil Memorial Cup.

Nectar Queen (filly, 1970, by Prince Pradeep): 6 wins, Bangalore St. Leger, Eclipse Stakes of India; 2nd Indian 1000 Guineas, and Oaks; 3rd Indian Turf Invitation Cup.

Hemavathi (filly, 1970, by The Wing): 6 wins, Replica Stakes for Bangalore 1000 Guineas; 3rd Bangalore Oaks.

Classic Touch (filly, 1979, by Everyday): 6 wins, South India St. Leger, Mysore Race Club Gold Trophy (2000 m, classes I and II, Mysore).

(Readers can quickly compare the achievements of Aurelie's family with Rose Law's.)

I am anxious to make a special mention of one superior racer — Bakhtawar (gelding, 1962, by Flower Dust).

Bakhtawar was a phenomenon the likes of whom we rarely see today. He was a complete contrast to the present-day thoroughbreds who masquerade as champions. He was an absolutely sound, robust, tough and genuine galloper who won 23 races. He was late in coming to hand; he recorded his first win only in his second season after being gelded. He then ran well in the classics, finishing 2nd in the Indian St. Leger and Indian Turf Invitation Cup, beaten by the great Red Rufus, the first winner of the Indian Triple Crown and Invitation Cup. He was also 3rd in the Indian Derby and 2000 Guineas. Racing till he was long in tooth, he won the Eclipse Stakes of India, A.C. Ardeshir Gold Cup and Maharaja Jiwajirao Scindia Gold Cup twice, C.N. Wadia Gold Cup thrice and the Byculla Club Cup once. Sadly we are not able to see such horses today.

I have described Aurelie's descendants in considerable detail. What are our conclusions? What must we learn from their achievements? The class, strength and depth of the female line is there for all to see. Can we not say that this female line has the inherent capacity to produce superior racers? A few readers may object to this straightforward conclusion. They will quickly point out: ''Aurelie and her descendants visited the very best stallions in the country and hence it is not at all surprising that they did well. Therefore the question of their ''inherent merit'' does not really arise. Aurelie's family merely utilized the ample opportunities they were fortunate enough to receive. Since other families did not get so many opportunities they could not do well.'' This objection can be easily answered. Stella Marina and her descendants too visited the best stallions (including many of the stallions visited by Aurelie and her descendants) but their performance was definitely better! We can easily write a book on their staggering achievements. Her tail female line is the best in the country. Then let us consider the five other families identified by Dhun Kothavala — the families of Caroline, Deepak Mahal, Fitna, Lady Emma and Queen Bess. Can anybody claim that mares from these families have been visiting inferior stallions? On the contrary they too visited superior stallions, but yet their performance was distinctly inferior to Aurelie's. Therefore our conclusion is:

Certain tail female lines are inherently talented. They have the ability to produce superior racers consistently. Mares from such families have greater chances of stud success.

THE DIFFERENT BRANCHES OF A TAIL FEMALE LINE AND THEIR DEVELOPMENT

I already made a mention of this subject but feel it is necessary to come back to it again. Let us quickly study the growth of two branches of the Stella Marina family — the Valkyrie and Flying Fairy branches. Incidentally both were daughters of Hawa Bibi. But straightaway I must say that their families have been developing on different lines.

VALKYRIE

Valkyrie (B, 1955)	Decorum	Orthodox	Hyperion Queen Christina
		Dignity	Sir Cosmo Happy Climax
	Hawa Bibi	Nasrullah	Nearco Mumtaz Begum
		Stella Marina	Noble Star Phalaris Girl

VALKYRIE: ran unplaced in her only start. Dam of:

Fairy Gold: 4 wins, Idar Gold Cup; 2nd Indian 1000 Guineas, Indian Oaks (by a short-head), Byculla Club Cup (by a short-head); 3rd Indian St. Leger.

Valamour: 13 wins, Champagne Stakes, Bhutan Gold Cup, Governor's Cup (2800 m, classes I and II, Calcutta), Sir Jehangir Ghandy Memorial Cup (2000 m, classes II and III, Calcutta).

Buland Bakht: 6 wins.

Volare: 4 wins.

Billion Crown: 4 wins.

Golden Harp: 9 consecutive wins, Eclipse Stakes of India, C.N. Wadia Gold Cup, Gen. Obaidullah Khan Gold Cup; 2nd Eve Champion Cup.

Valiente: did not win.

Golden Harp herself was the dam of:

Commissar: 6 wins, Ashoka Chakra Cup, Krishnaraja Cup; 2nd South India Derby.

Martial Air: 5 wins, A. Campbell Cup (2000 m, classes I and II, Pune); 4th Indian Oaks.

Colt, 1981, by Confusion is in training.

It is clear that the Valkyrie branch is developing into a family of high class stayers. In contrast let us study the performance of the Flying Fairy branch.

FLYING FAIRY

Flying Fairy (B, 1953)	Solonaway	Solferino	Fairway
			Sol Speranza
		Anyway	Grand Glacier
			The Widow Murphy
	Hawa Bibi	Nasrullah	Nearco
			Mumtaz Begum
		Stella Marina	Noble Star
			Phalaris Girl

FLYING FAIRY: 2 wins. Dam of:

Neon: 8 wins, South India Derby, Oaks, St. Leger, 1000 Guineas; 2nd Bangalore Fillies Trial Stakes; 3rd Kunigal Derby (this race was the forerunner of the Bangalore Derby).

Die Hard: 8 wins, Republic Cup, S.l.T.C. Cup; 3rd Guindy Gold Cup.

Gay Lover: 9 wins.

Noble One: 6 wins.

Nicene: 3 wins.

Naloma: 1 win.

Neon herself was the dam of:

Beandaz 15 wins, P.D. Bolton Gold Cup (twice), K.M. Munshi Gold Cup, Gen. Rajendrasinhji Gold Cup. He won from 1000 m to 1800 m. Sire.

Prince Jehan: 7 wins, Indian 2000 Guineas, Gen. Rajendrasinhji Gold Cup, A.C. Ardeshir Gold Cup; 2nd Indian Turf Invitation Cup, Bangalore Derby and Colts Trial Stakes; 4th Indian Derby.

Nouvola: 3 wins; 2nd Calcutta 1000 Guineas.

Next Move: 7 wins.

Interestingly the staying Neon did not produce any top class stayer (excluding Prince Jehan) even though she visited Frontline-classic stallions like Star of Gwalior (sire of Beandaz) and Zinosca (sire of Nouvola) who were sires of classic winning stayers.

Naloma's behaviour too has been similar. She failed to get any stayer even though she visited superior sires of stayers. She was the dam of among others:

Night Crown: 12 wins, Mysore 2000 Guineas, P.D. Bolton Cup; 2nd Mysore Derby.

Neola: 2 wins, Charminar Gold Cup; 3rd Mysore 1000 Guineas.

I personally feel the Flying Fairy branch is developing into a family of milers with the occasional stayer, while the Valkyrie branch is developing into a family of stayers and extreme stayers. This is not surprising. As the different branches of a female family evolve, generation after generation, they are bound to vary in class and aptitude. Branches which fail to produce superior progeny wither away while other branches flourish. A few other branches may be average. Therefore we must be careful. We have to determine the class and aptitude of the branch in question ignoring the others.

Coming back to Aurelie, a few readers may have noticed that she and her descendants constitute a branch of the Anne de Bretagne family. This family is really excelling, producing winners at the highest international level today.

ANNE DE BRETAGNE

	Teddy	Ajax
		Rondeau
Anne de Bretagne		
(B or Br, 1932)	Our Liz	William the Third
		Countess Resy

ANNE DE BRETAGNE: placed. She was the dam of:

Buena Vista: stakes winner of 3 races, Prix de la Foret (Gr. I); 2nd French Oaks. Producer.

Gades: 18 wins.

Norna: 1 win. Producer.

La Paix: stakes winner of 3 races, Prix Chloe (Gr. III), Prix Edgard de la Charme.

Louisville II: stakes winner.

La Paix (by Seven Seas) was the dam of 7 winners including several stakes winners. Her daughter Peace Rose (by Fastnet Rock) in turn got 7 winners including:

Roseliere: 5 wins in France, champion 3-yr-old, French Oaks, Prix Vermeille (Gr. I). She has made an incredible start in stud by getting 2 champions and I stakes winner as below:

Ile de Bourbon: 5 wins in England, champion 3-yr-old, champion older horse, King George VI and Queen Elizabeth Diamond Stakes (Gr. I), Coronation Cup (Gr. I). Sire.

Rose Bowl: 6 wins in England, champion 3-yr-old, champion handicap mare, Champion Stakes (Gr. I), Queen Elizabeth II Stakes (Gr. II) twice.

Rose Bed: winner including Prix Chloe (Gr. III)

ANSWERS
QUIZ 1

Mare	Class	Aptitude
1) Innocent	Category II	Dam of superior milers who also had the ability to get 2000 m.
2) Alkapuri	Category V	Versatile.
3) Hunter's Girl	Category I	Dam of outstanding horses who excelled over the entire range of distances.
4) Christmas Eve	Category V	Versatile.
5) Rose Bud	Category VI	Dam of stayers and extreme stayers. She made a disastrous start by getting six utterly mediocre racers (out of successful sires), but redeemed herself by getting a superior extreme stayer and stayer.
6) Gloriana	Category II	Dam of superior sprinter-milers.

QUIZ 2

Mohini and Reprint have really outstanding tail female lines. See the number of classic winners who have emerged. Horses from these two families excelled over the entire range of distances. Sitting Pretty and Gretel come next. Their families too have produced superior racers together with a few classic horses. A few of its members stayed well. Note the depth of these two families. Grey Satin's family too has done well. Notice the strong thread of stamina that is running through this tail female line. While its members have till now lacked the class to win a classic, they could very well do so in future. The female line of Better Late lacks class and depth. With the sole exception of Pillar to Post, its members were either average or substandard.

CHAPTER 5

Maternal Grandsires - 1

The maternal grandsire plays a unique and powerful role in the make-up of a thoroughbred. He is not directly involved — only the sire and dam are. He plays his powerful role behind the scenes, so to say.

Why must we make a separate study of the maternal grandsire in the first place? Isn't it enough if we study the sire and dam? I consider the maternal grandsire to be the connecting link between the "direct male line" and the "tail female line". As we shall see, this link is very important.

Who is the maternal grandsire? The maternal grandsire is the sire of the dam of the horse in question. But I have seen people use the incorrect expressions "broodmare sire" or "maternal sire" — which is even worse. For remember the "reference point" is the individual horse in question.

Horse in question	Sire	Paternal grandsire
		Paternal grandam
	Dam	Maternal grandsire
		Maternal grandam

He has a sire and dam and a maternal grandsire — one of his four grand-parents. The word "grand" in the expression "maternal grandsire" makes this abundantly clear. We can refer to his other grand parents in a similar manner as shown above. But the word "grand" is absent in the expressions "broodmare sire" and "maternal sire". Hence they are misleading. Therefore the correct expression is "maternal grandsire". Let us use it and insist on its use.

The maternal grandsire has remained a mysterious and elusive figure, lurking in the shadows. Extensive research has been done on sires, sire lines, broodmares and tail female lines, but comparatively little on maternal grandsires. In this chapter and later on in the book we will unravel the mystery and see what exactly the maternal grandsire is doing and is supposed to do.

Fillies who have been fairly successful on the course go to stud. Obviously they are by different stallions — outstanding, superior and average. But Turf historians noticed that daughters of a few stallions excelled, producing a number of classic winners, champions and stakes winners.

Therefore these mares — all daughters of a handful of stallions — seemed to possess some characteristics, some elements, which the others lacked; elements which enabled them to excel in stud. Therefore if you own a daughter of such a sire — a successful maternal grandsire — you are straightaway at a considerable advantage. The chances of your mare succeeding are far greater than most other mares.

Identifying successful maternal grandsires is not difficult. All we have got to do is study the "Maternal grandsires lists". In addition to the Sires lists Turf historians prepare Maternal grandsires lists every year. The "Gross earnings" list is very important. For example during 1979-'80 Asopo was the champion maternal grandsire in India in terms of gross earnings. His daughters' progeny won 70 races and placed 109 times earning about Rs.1.8 million. 41 horses by different stallions earned the above amount. They were the progeny of 30 Asopo mares — several of them had more than one runner. Since no other maternal grandsire had greater earnings Asopo became the champion maternal grandsire for 1979-'80.

This list clearly identifies stallions whose daughters excelled as producers. The other lists prepared are: "Number of winners", "Number of races won", "Average earnings per runner" and "Average earnings per start". Therefore the readers' first task is to diligently study all these lists for the last five years and identify the best maternal grandsires. By studying the lists simultaneously (as we did in the case of sires) readers can also determine the behaviour of different maternal grandsires.

THE TIME FACTOR

Before plunging into the subject we must understand the time factor. A young horse is retired to stud, say, in 1970. A year later his first foals would have arrived. Two years later they would have started racing. Three years later they would have been 5-yr-olds. At this stage taking into account his subsequent crops we would have had a fair idea of his ability as a sire. Imagine that a filly from his first crop went to stud in 1976. She would have foaled in 1977 and the foal would have started racing from 1979. He would have been 5 years in 1982, and by this time a few of his other fillies would have also gone to stud and become producers with their first foals racing. Therefore in 1982 we could have roughly determined the stallion's performance as a maternal grandsire. But to get a more accurate and fairer picture we would have to wait for three more years — till 1985. *In other words we will know the performance of a sire as a maternal grandsire only fifteen years after he has commenced his stud career.*

A stallion in his "younger years" is active as a sire only. In his "middle years" he is active as a sire and maternal grandsire. He himself is a producer and his daughters are also producers. Now suppose the stallion has finished his stud career. Notice that he will still be active as a maternal grandsire. For several of his daughters will still be active and fillies from his last crops will be entering stud to become producers. Therefore a stallion can make a big name for himself as a maternal grandsire long after he has finished his stud career.

Before proceeding further we must understand one fundamental truth. Since a horse's performance as a sire is known first, several jump to the conclusion that his performance as a maternal grandsire will be similar i.e. they assume that all successful sires will become successful maternal grandsires. *This tacit assumption is incorrect. We cannot predict a horse's performance as a maternal grandsire from his performance as a sire.* In other words a horse may be an average sire but an outstanding maternal grandsire while another may be a very successful sire but a disappointing maternal grandsire. But undoubtedly several are equally successful in both roles.

Here then is the reason why we should make a separate and detailed study of maternal grandsires. All our knowledge about a particular horse as a sire will not help us get an insight into his behaviour as a maternal grandsire, as his behaviour in this role can be entirely different.

Let us now identify the best maternal grandsires in the country between 1975-'81 from the Maternal grandsires lists in *The Indian Turf Statistical Record.* In 1975-'76, '76-'77 and '77-'78 Babbanio was champion. In 1978-'79, '79-'80 and '80-'81 Asopo was champion. He was also 2nd to Babbanio in 1976-'77 and '77-'78. Babbanio was 3rd in 1978-'79 and '79-'80. These two maternal grandsires towered over all the others. They were invariably followed by Exaggerator and Rock of Gibraltar. Glasgow Paddock, Flower Dust and Roman Honey too did well, finishing 2nd once during these six years. Then came Matombo and Star of Gwalior.

Therefore the list of best maternal grandsires during the period would read:

Asopo
Babbanio
Exaggerator
Rock of Gibraltar
Glasgow
Paddock
Flower Dust
Matombo
Roman Honey
Star of Gwalior

Now let us study some maternal grandsires in detail to understand their behaviour.

STAR OF GWALIOR

Star of Gwalior (B, 1952)	Hyder Ali	Hyperion	Gainsborough / Selene
		Eclair	Ethnarch / Black Ray
	Lady Emma	Nearco	Pharos / Nogara
		Divine Lady	Papyrus / Most Beautiful

He won 4 races including the Indian Derby and St. Leger. He developed into a Front-line classic stallion. His best progeny included:

Loyal Manzar (1958): 7 wins, Indian Triple Crown.

Glory of Andhra (1958) : 7 wins, South India Derby, Basalat Jah Cup, Owners' and Trainers' Cup.

Bade Miya (1969): 8 wins, Indian 2000 Guineas and St. Leger, Poona City Cup, Gen. Rajendrasinhji Gold Cup.

Gwalior Lass (1960): 7 wins, Indian Oaks, Maharaja Sir Harisinghji's Gold Cup; 3rd Indian Derby.

Buland (1964): 17-1/2wins, dead-heated for win in the Indian 2000 Guineas, Maharaja of Morvi Gold Cup, Maharaja Jiwajirao Scindia Gold Cup.

Buckpasser (India) (1965): 7 wins, Bangalore Derby, Maharaja's Gold Cup, Guindy Gold Cup.

Tenacity (1969): 10 wins, Deccan Derby, C.D. Dady Gold Cup, Sir Pratapsingh Gaekwar Gold Cup; 2nd Indian 1000 Guineas, Eclipse Stakes of India.

Beandaz: 15 wins, P.D. Bolton Gold Cup (twice), K.M. Munshi Gold Cup, Gen. Rajendrasinhji Gold Cup.

Jaandaar: 10 wins, R.W.I.T.C. Gold Cup (1400 m, class I, Bangalore).

He was also the sire of dozens of other superior racers. He was a versatile sire, getting sprinter-milers and stayers. His best progeny had an ideal blend of speed and stamina and an abundance of class. But his colts were to an extent better than his fillies.

His sons made admirable stallions. Glory of Andhra was almost Frontline classic with 5 classic winners, while Loyal Manzar and Beandaz were average. But misfortune struck two others. Buckpasser (India) made an excellent start getting classic winner Ivanjica (India) whose performance was described earlier (chapter 2, page 27). But most unfortunately he could not continue his stud career. Jaandaar too made a sensational start by getting champion Aztec (Stayers' Cup) but died soon after. There is no doubt that these two stallions were of the highest order.

As a maternal grandsire too, he has been equally successful. A Borderline classic maternal grandsire, he is till now the maternal grandsire of 4 classic winners:

Prince Ardent (1970, Ardent Knight x Mallika): 7 wins, Bangalore Arc de Triomphe, South India 2000 Guineas; 2nd South India Derby.

Sunray (1978, Lord of Light x Pistol Packer) : 8 wins, Calcutta 2000 Guineas. (He bettered Salome's course record over 1100 m in Calcutta.)

Priceless Polly (1977, King's Son x Etoile du' Ind): 6 wins, Golconda 1000 Guineas; 2nd South India 1000 Guineas, Golconda Oaks.

Regency (1971, King's Son x True Effort): 2 wins, Hyderabad Fillies Trial Stakes; 2nd South India 1000 Guineas.

His daughters also produced a number of superior racers:

Farz (The Famous x Hi Star): 12 wins, M.R.C. Cup, Sun Sip Gold Cup; 2nd Deccan Derby.

Corniche (Satinello x Retained): 4 wins, Mathradas Goculdas Cup, Chief Minister's Cup (1600 m, class II, Pune); 2nd Hyderabad Fillies Trial Stakes; 3rd Bangalore 1000 Guineas and Fillies Trial Stakes.

Gateway of India (Hervine x Star of Liberty): good winner including Rajpipla Gold Cup (1600 m, class I, Bombay), Maharaja Sir Pratapsingh Gaekwar Gold Cup (1600 m, class I, Bombay). Rajpipla Gold Cup (1600 m, class I, Bombay), Maharaja Sir Pratapsingh Gaekwar Gold Cup (1600 m, class I, Bombay).

Thundering Gold (Thundering x Noor Mahal): 8 wins, Farrokh K. Irani Gold Cup (1200 m, class I, Madras), Hyderabad Silver Vase (1400 m, classes I and II, Madras).

Turf Lab (Simead x Gorgeous): 9 wins, good winner in class II.

Miss Take (Zinosca x Turkish Star): 7 wins, Gavin Johnston Cup (1100 m, class II, Calcutta).

Torrential (Maratha Lancer x Tenacity): 3 wins, Greater Bombay Police Cup, in training.

Notice his aptitude as a maternal grandsire. While he was an excellent sire of stayers and horses with an ideal blend of speed and stamina, the evidence suggests that he has developed primarily into a maternal grandsire of sprinter-milers. Even though his daughters visited staying stallions, they have shown a preference for getting horses who were at their best up to 1600 m. Prince Ardent was an exception. Therefore readers must note: The aptitude of a horse as a Maternal grandsire can be different from his aptitude as a sire.

ROCK OF GIBRALTAR

Rock of Gibraltar (Ch, 1951)	Rockefella	Hyperion	Gainsborough Selene
		Rockfel	Felstead Rockliffe
	Toquade	Premier Baiser	Monarch Passez Muscade
		Tonkette	Dark Legend Tonka

I referred to him earlier (chapter 2, page 19). I mentioned that he was hugely successful and that his progeny swept classic after classic. He was the unofficial champion sire several times. To enable readers to fully grasp the magnitude of his achievements, I have given below the details of his classic winners and champions:

> **Prince Khartoum** (1968): champion, Indian Turf Invitation Cup, India; and Bangalore Derby; 2nd Indian 2000 Guineas; 3rd Bangalore Colts Trial Stakes. Sire.
>
> **Prince Royal** (1969): champion, Indian Turf Invitation Cup, Queen Elizabeth II Cup.
>
> **Fair Haven** (1965): she had the distinction of winning 8 classics in three centres. She won the Bangalore Fillies Trial Stakes, the 1000 Guineas, 2000 Guineas, Oaks and Derby at Calcutta and the Indian Oaks, Derby and St. Leger.

Star Haven (1968): she won all the 5 classics in Madras.

Rock Haven (1967): the 1000 Guineas, Oaks, Derby and St. Leger in Madras, Bangalore Fillies Trial Stakes.

Fair Court (1966): South India Derby and 2000 Guineas.

Rocklie (1959): Indian Derby; 2nd Indian Oaks and St. Leger.

The Phoenician (1966): Calcutta Derby.

Mica Empress (1963): South India 1000 Guineas and St. Leger, Queen Elizabeth II Cup; placed in Indian Turf Invitation Cup, South India Derby and Oaks.

Multirosa (1963): Indian 2000 Guineas and Oaks; placed in Indian Derby, St. Leger and 1000 Guineas.

Irma La Douce (1972): Calcutta Oaks and St. Leger.

Prince Jehan (1970): Indian 2000 Guineas; 2nd Indian Turf Invitation Cup, Bangalore Derby and Colts Trial Stakes.

Rock's Son (1970): dead-heated for win in the South India St. Leger; placed in Bangalore Arc de Triomphe, 2000 Guineas and St. Leger. Sire.

Rock Witness (1969): Indian Oaks, Bangalore Fillies Trial Stakes.

Foxbat (1974): South India Oaks; placed in South India Derby, St. Leger and 1000 Guineas.

Florina (1964): Indian Oaks; placed in Indian 1000 Guineas.

River Haven (1963): Indian 1000 Guineas; placed in Indian 2000 Guineas and Oaks.

Tudor Jet (1964): Bangalore Derby; placed in Bangalore Colts Trial Stakes. Sire.

Republican (1972): Mysore Derby; placed in Deccan Derby. Sire.

His colts and fillies were equally good. As seen they possessed an overabundance of class. They were all true stayers; all of them, without a single exception, could stay 2400 m and most of them could stay 2800 m. In addition to the above horses, he sired numerous other superior racers including several classic-placed. But I do not think he sired any specialist sprinter. Imparting high class stamina was his forte.

His sons too had the ability to excel in stud. Mention must be made of Prince Khartoum and Republican who have done well with very limited opportunities. We will study the former in detail later.

But how did his daughters fare? It is in their performances that we are interested. We saw that they were successful, but undoubtedly they did not rise to great heights. This is really surprising for two reasons. Firstly Rock of Gibraltar was the most successful stallion during his time, towering over all the others. Secondly breeders obviously valued his daughters highly; they were sure to have received the best care and attention. Yet he was not the finest maternal grandsire. No doubt he has always finished near the top in the Maternal grandsires lists: 4th in 1975-'76, 3rd in '76-'77, 4th in '77-'78 and 9th in '80-'81.

We already studied the superior progeny of his daughters in chapter 2. Special mention must be made of Rocklie and Rock Haven who really excelled. The former was also the dam of:

Storm (by Hervine): 6 wins, Governor's Cup (2000 m, classes I and II, Pune); 2nd Indian Turf Invitation Cup, Indian Derby and St. Leger, R.R. Ruia Gold Cup; 3rd Indian 2000 Guineas. Sire.

General Patton (by Prince Pradeep): 3 wins, H.M. Mehta Gold Cup. He was a very promising colt but unfortunately had a setback in training. Sire.

Pink Passion (by Prince Pradeep): 7 wins, Brindavan Cup (2000 m, class II, Bangalore).

Rock Haven was also the dam of:

Irish Love (by High Commission): 8 wins, R.C.T.C. Cup (1800 m, classes I and II, Hyderabad), Mysore Race Club Cup (1800 m, 4-yr-olds and over, Hyderabad).

Beau Geste (by Knight of Medina) : 12 wins, Farrokh K. Irani Gold Cup (1200 m, class I, Madras).

His aptitude as a maternal grandsire is very clear. It is identical to his aptitude as a sire. Since his daughters excelled in getting genuine high class stayers, he is a maternal grandsire of stayers.

I now want readers to take time and compare his performance as a sire with his performance as a maternal grandsire. By his high standards wasn't his performance in the latter role disappointing? I was convinced that his daughters' progeny would sweep everything before them. But it was not to be. Other maternal grandsires were more successful. *Therefore we must not assume that a horse's performance as a maternal grandsire will be identical to his performance as a sire.*

Let us go deeper and see why he could not do better as a maternal grandsire. One reason was that several of his classic winning daughters like Fair Haven, Star Haven, Multirosa and Florina were shy breeders.

But this cannot be taken as an excuse. I will be giving examples of stallions who did not sire any classic winner (or who sired only one classic winner) but became very successful maternal grandsires. And remember every sire has his share of daughters who are shy breeders. *Therefore we are forced to conclude that Rock of Gibraltar mares lacked certain qualities which prevented them from being even more successful.*

HORATIUS

Horatius (B, 1954)	Hyperion	Gainsborough	Bayardo / Rosedrop
		Selene	Chaucer / Serenissima
	La Goulue	Tourbillon	Ksar / Durban
		Galveston	Dastur / Galleon II

He won 2 races in England, the 2-yr-old Stakes and Cromwell Stakes. He was 2nd in the Mayflower Stakes and Curfew Handicap and 3rd in the Ayton Stakes. He had a short racing career. In India he won 2 races including the Rajpipla Gold Cup.

He was retired to stud in 1962. His superior racers included:

Sparkling Water (1964): 4-1/2 wins, Indian 1000 Guineas; 2nd Indian Derby and Oaks; 3rd Indian 2000 Guineas and St. Leger.

Sunbeam: 8-1/2 wins, Farrokh K. Irani Gold Cup.

Enterprise: 12 wins, Farrokh K. Irani Gold Cup, Owners and Trainers Association Cup; 2nd Indian Gold Vase.

Amontillado: 8 wins, Southern Command Cup (1800 m, class I, Pune), Abdullah Khairaz Cup (2000 m, classes II and III, Bombay).

No Worry: 10 wins, Golconda Cup.

Czardas: 8 wins, Chief of Kagal Cup, Rajaram Chhatrapati Gold Cup (1800 m, class II, Pune).

Lotus Princess: 8 wins, Maharani Tripurasundarammani Avaru Gold Cup, Tumkur Cup.

Riche Rich: 10 wins, Chief Minister's Gold Cup.

Flying Enterprise: 8 wins, Stewards Cup.

Rolls Royce: 7 wins. (She was full-sister to Enterprise and Flying Enterprise.)

Readers will have no difficulty in determining the class and aptitude of Horatius. He was only an Average-to-Good sire. He could get only one classic winner. In general his progeny won up to 1600 m, though Amontillado scored repeatedly over 1800m and 2000m and Czardas won over 1800 m. Compare Horatius' utterly mediocre performance with the glittering records of Rock of Gibraltar and Star of Gwalior.

Yet as a maternal grandsire he is definitely better than both of them! The progeny of his daughters have just started racing and the results are nothing short of astonishing. He is already the maternal grandsire of three classic winners:

Adelina (1979, Everyday x Three Little Words) : 9 wins, Calcutta Derby, 1000 Guineas, Oaks and St. Leger.

The King (1979, Cupid x Razia): 5 wins, Bangalore 2000 Guineas; 2nd Mysore Derby. (As a 3-yr-old he created a record of sorts when he won the Turf Club Cup over 2400 m for horses in classes III and IV in Bangalore. In general Indian horses do not run over 2400 m as 3-yr-olds. (Remember the classics over this distance are for 4-yr-olds only.)

Busy Lizzy (1979, Landigou x Bristol Cream): 5 wins, Indian Oaks, F.D. Wadia Cup (1400 m, 3-yr-olds, Pune).

He is also the maternal grandsire of:

Valour (Everyday x Hold the Bridge): 5 wins, C.D. Dady Trophy; 2nd Bangalore Arc de Triomphe.

Word-A-Day (Everyday x Mark My Words): 7 wins, Kanteerava Cup (2400 m, classes III and IV, Bangalore); 2nd Golconda Derby.

Riddle (Whistling Glory x Sparkling Water): 13 wins, Tamil Nadu Commemoration Gold Cup, Charminar Gold Cup.

Rollinsky (Nijinsky [India] x Rolls Royce): 5 wins, Madras Race Club Cup (1200 m, class II, Bombay).

We must all thank Horatius for teaching us a number of vitally important aspects. I beseech readers to follow the arguments below very closely as they are of awesome importance.

An average performance as a sire did not prevent Horatius from succeeding brilliantly as a maternal grandsire. Since he was only average, it follows that most of his daughters were only average or substandard on the course. Therefore they straightaway lack one very important prerequisite for success as a producer — a superior race record. Yet in spite of this major deficiency they made good in stud.

I stated that he was primarily a sire of sprinters, milers and sprinter-milers. I do not think he sired one top class stayer other than Sparkling Water. But look how he has fared as a maternal grandsire? Isn't he a maternal grandsire of classic stayers? Already a Border-line classic maternal grandsire, he is well on his way to Front-line classic status.

Therefore Horatius an Average-to-Good sire of milers has become an outstanding maternal grandsire of classic stayers!

In other words the class and aptitude of a horse as a maternal grandsire can be entirely different from his class and aptitude as a sire.

This is the principle I was emphasizing earlier and I have just given an example to illustrate it. I will give one more.

But a few readers will object strongly to this reasoning. They will say: ''Horatius had nothing to do with the high class stamina of Adelina, The King and Busy Lizzy — they inherited it from their sires.'' This objection is easily answered: First let us consider Adelina. Her sire the outstanding Everyday (whom we are going to study in very great detail) is, no doubt, a renowned sire of classic winning stayers. But he was not only a sire of stayers. He was also the sire of several superior sprinters and milers. And, as we are going to see, Everyday sired stayers mostly out of staying mares or mares bred to stay, and short-distance horses out of short distance mares. Landigou cannot claim to be a formidable sire of stayers. A Rock of Gibraltar, a Star of Gwalior or a Pa Bear yes; not Landigou. In fact he got only one other classic winning stayer in Makalu (Deccan Derby). Cupid's race record has been described (chapter 4, page 70). It is too early to comment on his performance as a sire. Therefore in all the three cases we cannot attribute the stamina of the horses concerned entirely to their sires. Their dams too undeniably played a role in shaping them. Therefore Horatius' daughters though non-stayers themselves are capable of getting classic stayers.

In essence what readers must understand is this:

Outstanding success as a sire is not an essential prerequisite for success as a maternal grandsire.

As we have seen, and are going to see, even average sires can become outstanding maternal grandsires. We also studied the second part of the above rule:

Outstanding success as a sire is not a guarantee for outstanding success as a maternal grandsire.

And we also saw that:

The class and aptitude of a horse as a maternal grandsire can be entirely different from his class and aptitude as a sire.

Coming back to Horatius, I would have boldly stuck out my neck and said he is sure to become champion maternal grandsire. But most unfortunately several of his best daughters — Bristol Cream, Lotus Princess and Queen Bee — are dead. (Incidentally do you know how many granddaughters of Hyperion are active today?) Let us see if he can still become champion.

Let us study one more horse who was only a Good sire but a classic maternal grandsire.

EXAGGERATOR

Exaggerator (B, 1953)	Hyperbole	Hyperion	Gainsborough Selene
		Avenue	Fairway Annabel
	Benjamine	Brumeux	Teddy La Brume
		My Dame	Littleton Estelle

He won 2 races in England and 8 races in India including the Eclipse Stakes. Retired to stud he was successful getting:

The Music Man: 6 wins, Bhutan Gold Cup; placed in Calcutta Derby.

Cambyses: 13 wins, Eclipse Stakes of India.

Romantica: 10 wins, C.D. Dady Cup, Sir Rahimtoola Chinoy Gold Cup.

Expresso: 13 wins, Nawabzada Rashiduzafar Khan Gold Cup.

Sai Rama: 11 wins, Stewards Cup (1200 m, class III, Madras), winner in class I.

Kecini: 8 wins, Rajpipla Gold Cup, Aga Khan's Cup, Gen. Obaidullah Khan Gold Cup.

Ferrari: good winner including Byculla Club Cup.

Flower Power: 3 wins, H.M. Mehta Gold Cup; 2nd Indian Oaks.

Red River: 6 wins, Dr. A. Karmally Gold Cup; 2nd Kailashpat Singhania Gold Cup; 3rd Aga Khan's Spring Cup.

Spellbinder: 8 wins, Douetil Memorial Cup, T.N. Banerjee Gold Cup.

There is no doubt that Exaggerator falls in the Good category. He was not a classic sire. He did not get a single classic winner. Very few of his progeny were classic contenders in the truest sense of the term. But there was one crucial difference between him and Horatius. Several of his progeny, unlike Horatius', were genuine stayers at the top handicap level.

As a maternal grandsire he has been very successful. A Border-line classic maternal grandsire, he was 3rd leading maternal grandsire in 1977-'78, 4th in '78-'79, 5th in '76-'77 and 7th in '75-'76. It is entirely possible that he topped the list earlier. As explained authoritative statistics for those years are not available. He was the maternal grandsire of:

Voluntary (1968, State Trumpeter x Water Music): 6 wins, Calcutta Derby and 2000 Guineas, Burdwan Cup. (The Calcutta St. Leger was not run that year.) Sire.

Sholay (1974, Red Rufus x Romantica): 17 wins, Bangalore 2000 Guineas, Guindy Gold Cup, Calcutta Gold Cup. Sire.

Miracle Chip (1976, Fey Legend x Silver Flight): 8 wins, Nilgiris Colts Trial Stakes.

Response (1975, Red Rufus x Romantica): 5 wins, Hyderabad Fillies Trial Stakes, Asaf Jah VII Memorial Cup, Ootacamund Cup.

Rage Royal (Lance Corporal x Punchi Nona): 8 wins, Shanmuga Sethupati Cup; 2nd South India 1000 Guineas; 3rd South India Oaks.

Statesman (Anybody Here x Preston's Girl): 8 wins, Guindy Gold Cup.

Yours Mine and Ours (Ardent Knight x Goldfinch): 6 wins, Jayachamaraja Wadiyar Gold Cup.

Mahalrathi (Nimble Lad x One We Love): 9 wins, good winner in class II.

Deep Secret (Rockwell x Dictatorial): 5 wins, J.B. Mallaradhya Memorial Cup.

Majestic Rock (Fey Legend x Silver Flight): 9 wins, Mysore Race Club Cup (1200 m, class I, Hyderabad).

Interestingly while Exaggerator was a sire of stayers, he seems to have made a name primarily as a maternal grandsire of sprinter-milers. I am not saying his daughters were incapable of producing classic stayers — Voluntary is an example. However I am convinced that they have shown a distinct preference for getting sprinter-milers. His behaviour is the reverse of Horatius, who was a sire of sprinter-milers but definitely a maternal grandsire of stayers.

We have just studied the performances of four horses — Star of Gwalior, Rock of Gibraltar, Horatius and Exaggerator as sires and maternal grandsires. The first-named was equally successful in both roles while the second was surely disappointing in the latter role. The third and fourth were only moderate sires but have excelled as maternal grandsires. Therefore we can divide all sires into three categories:

Category I : *Horses who perform equally well as sires and maternal grandsires.*

Category II : *Horses who are excellent sires but moderate maternal grandsires.*

Category III: *Horses who are moderate sires but excellent maternal grandsires.*

Now the question we have to answer is this: "Do an overwhelming majority of stallions fall in Category I? Are Category II and III sires very rare?" I am convinced the answer lies in between the two extremes. While a majority of sires may belong to Category I, Categories II and III sires are not uncommon. A significant number of sires definitely belong to these two categories. And remember even if an individual performs equally well in both roles, his aptitude in the latter can be different. As I emphasized earlier, when we analyze a pedigree we unconsciously judge the maternal grandsire as a sire and not as a maternal grandsire. One of the objects of this chapter is to point out this very major error. We have to judge him and determine his class and aptitude as a maternal grandsire. As we have seen this is not at all difficult. First see whether he has finished high-up in the Maternal grandsires lists. Then identify the progeny of all his daughters and determine their class and aptitude to get his class and aptitude as a maternal grandsire.

EXERCISE

Study the Sires lists about ten years back. Pick out three or four successful sires. Determine their class and aptitude. Now see how they have fared as maternal grandsires. To which categories do they belong? What are their aptitudes as maternal grandsires? Similarly study the last three years' Maternal grandsires lists. Pick out two or three maternal grandsires and determine their class and aptitude. Now study their performances as sires and see whether they exhibited the same class and aptitude.

Let us now study a maternal grandsire who is vastly superior to those we have just studied. He is in fact the best maternal grandsire in the country. His daughters are proving to be incredible broodmares producing classic winner after classic winner. Since many of them are just entering stud, and since the first progeny of several others have just started to race, the best is yet to come!

ASOPO

		Nearco	Pharos / Nogara
	Nimbus		
		Kong	Baytown / Clang
Asopo (Dk. Br, 1957)			
		Norseman	Umidwar / Tara
	Assamenta		
		Assylia	Plassy / Apulia

Asopo was an Italian classic winner. At 2 years he started only twice and placed 2nd in the Premio Gornate (6 furlongs, Milan). As a 3-yr-old he started by placing 3rd in the Premio Botticelli (1 mile, Rome). He was then a short-neck 2nd in the Premio Lazio (1 mi 2-1/2 f, Rome). He then won the Italian 2000 Guineas (1 mile, Gr.ll, Rome). In the Italian Derby (1-1/2 miles, Gr. I, Rome) he was beaten a neck by Fils D'Eve with Certaldo, Pueblo and Marguerite Vernaut behind him. He was then 3rd, beaten 1-1/2 lengths and a head, in the Group I Premio Presidente Della Republica. He was only twice unplaced in 8 starts. He was imported into India and retired to stud in 1962.

He was successful but not outstanding. His superior racers included among others:

Flying Saucer (1966): 4 wins, Calcutta 2000 Guineas ; 2nd Calcutta Derby and St. Leger (by a short-head).

Mabel (1964): 5 wins South India 1000 Guineas and Oaks.

Zeenie (1973): 6 wins, Calcutta Oaks.

Rare Gem (1963): 6 wins, Bangalore Derby; 2nd Bangalore Fillies Trial Stakes; 3rd South India 1000 Guineas.

Mumtaz: 3 wins; 2nd Indian Derby, Oaks and St. Leger, beaten by the great Fair Haven on all three occasions.

Princess Jani: 6 wins, The Metropolitan; 2nd Calcutta 1000 Guineas (by a short-head) and Oaks; 3rd Calcutta Gold Cup.

Mother's Son: 8 wins; 3rd Indian 2000 Guineas, Bangalore Derby.

Beauty Queen: 10 wins; 3rd Indian 1000 Guineas.

Foward Thrust: 10 wins, R.R. Ruia Gold Cup, Rajpipla Gold Cup.

Ek Nazar: 9 wins, K.M. Munshi Gold Cup, Kailashpat Singhania Gold Cup, Aga Khan's Spring Cup.

Roubaix: 2 wins; 2nd Indian 2000 Guineas.

His progeny had an ideal blend of speed and stamina with a zest for racing. I want readers to note that even during his peak there were several stallions superior to him.

But as a maternal grandsire he is in a class of his own. As explained he was champion for three years running — from 1978 to '81 and was 2nd in 1976-'77 and '77-'78. A Front-line classic maternal grandsire he is already the maternal grandsire of 8 classic winners as below:

Midnight Cowboy (1971, Young Lochinvar x Take Cover): 13 wins, champion, Indian Turf Invitation Cup, Calcutta Derby and St. Leger, Mysore Derby, Queen Elizabeth II Cup (twice); 2nd Calcutta 2000 Guineas, President of India Gold Cup, Calcutta Gold Cup, Queen Elizabeth II Cup. He won from 1200 m to 2800 m. Sire.

Aristocrat (1976, Everyday x Mumtaz): 15 wins, South India Derby and 2000 Guineas, Bangalore St. Leger, Deccan and Mysore Derby, Hyderabad Colts Trial Stakes; 2nd Indian Turf Invitation Cup, Bangalore Derby. He won from 1000 m to 2800 m. Sire.

Grand Parade (1974, Everyday x Mumtaz): 11 wins, South India Triple Crown, Deccan Derby, Hyderabad Colts Trial Stakes; 2nd Bangalore Derby and Arc de Triomphe. He won from 1000 m to 2800 m. Sire.

Enter the Red (1975, Red Rufus x Enter and Canter): 10 wins, South India 2000 Guineas, South India Gold Cup, National Horse Breeding Society of India Gold Cup (2000 m, classes III and IV, Madras).

Text continues on page 123.

TABLE 13

S.No.	Mare	Mare's race record	Quality of mare's tail female line	Mare's superior progeny and their race records	Class of the stallions she visited	Conclusion
1.	Jeevan Jyoti (1963)	6 wins	Above average	**Zelda:** as described	Eagle rock as described (chapter 3)	Success
2.	Mabel (1964)	As described	Above average	**Prince Mabel** by King's Son): Red Surprise Cup, Shivkumar Lal Memorial Cup (1400 m, class II, Hyderabad) twice. He won 12 races, he was her only runner.	King's Son was almost Front-line classic with 5 classic winners.	Success
3.	Moon Dust (1964)	3 wins	Above average	Nil	Superior and average	Failure
4.	Roopkosha (1964)	2 wins	Above average	Nil	Average	Failure
5.	Smitha (1964)	1 win	Above average	Nil	Superior	Cannot judge as she had only 2 foals, 1 runner
6.	Enter and Canter (1965)	3 wins	Above average	**Enter the Red:** as described	Red Rufus was Front-line classic.	Success
7.	My Baby (1965)	2 wins	Average	**Celesial Gift** (by Esquire): 2 wins, Monsoon Cup; 2nd Champagne Stakes. **Regular Guy** (by Esquire): 7 wins, Governor's Cup (2800 m, classes I and II, Calcutta), Bhutan Gold Cup. **Dear Baby** by Cradle of the Deep); 6 wins, Kailashpat Singhania Gold Cup (twice).	Esquire was a failure. Cradle of the Deep was Average to Good.	Success

8.	Mumtaz (1965)	As described	Above average	**Grand Parade** (by Everyday): as described. **Aristocrat** (by Everyday): as described.	Everyday is Front-line classic	Success
9.	Never So (1965)	unraced	Average to above average	**Ever True** (by Never Never): 6 wins, H.C. Clifton Cup (2000 m, class III, Bombay). **Filly** (1981) by Nijinsky (India) is in training.	Never Never was almost Front-line classic with 5 classic winners. Nijinsky (India) was almost Border-line classic with 2 classic winners.	Too early to judge as mare is active
10.	Starry Haven (1965)	3 wins	Slightly above average	Yet to produce a superior racer. Her **colt** (1982) by Arrogant Lad is in training.	Visited stallions who were at the most average. Arrogant Lad is Border-line classic.	Too early to judge as here progeny are racing.
11.	Take Cover (1965)	5 wins	Above average	**Midnight Cowboy** by Young Lochinvar): as described. **Tradition** (by Young Lochinvar): 11 wins, Bangalore Turf Club Gold Cup (2400 m, 4-yr-olds and over, Bangalore), Guindy Gold Cup, Mysore City Gold Cup (twice); 4th Indian Turf Invitation Cup. **Sundance Kid** (by Young Lochinvar); 7 wins; 3rd Calcutta St. leger. **Noble Memories** (by Young Lochinvar): 5 wins, Maharani Tripurasundarammani Avaru Gold Cup (1200 m, class II, Mysore).	Young Lochinvar and Orbit as described, Damastown was indifferent.	Success

TABLE 13 con't.

S.No.	Mare	Mare's race record	Quality of mare's tail female line	Mare's superior progeny and their race records	Class of the stallions she visited	Conclusion
11.	Take Cover (con't.) (1965)			**Irish Twilight** by Damastown): 4 wins, 2nd Calcutta Derby; 3rd Calcutta Oaks. **Easter Parade** (by Damastown): as described. **Moonglow** (by Orbit): 2 wins, in training.		
12.	Amigo (1966)	4 wins	Above average	Yet to produce a superior racer. Her **fillies** (1980, 1981) by Super Seer and Beloved Prince are in training.	Visited average stallions. The progeny of Super Seer and Beloved Prince have just started to race.	Too early to judge as mare is active
13.	Chic Baby (1966)	4-1/2 wins	Above average	Nil	Visited substandard stallions except King of Pippins who was almost Border-line classic with 2 classic winners.	Failure
14.	Antiquary (1967)	Unraced	Average to above average	**Track Master** by (Track Star): 4 wins, Committee Gold Cup (1400 m, class II, Mysore), Champagne Stakes, Grand Annual Handicap.	Track Star was at the most average	Success
15.	Fabiha (1967)	6 wins, Belfry Cup, Excelsior Stakes; placed in	Above average	**Nobility** (by Never Never): 5 wins; 2nd Indian 1000 Guineas and Oaks; 4th Indian St. Leger. Unfortunately she	Never never, Everyday and Malvado as described.	Success

#	Name (year)	Racing record	Rating	Progeny	Comments	Result
15.	Fabiha (con't.) (1967)	in Gen. Obaidullah Khan Gold Cup, Maharaja of Morvi Gold Cup, Gen. Rajendra-sinhji Gold Cup; 4th Indian Oaks		bolted before the Indian Oaks but for which she could have won.) **Flash Past** (by Everyday): as described. **Chamer** (by Malvado): 7 wins, South India Gold Cup (1400 m, class II, Madras), C.S. Loganathan Gold Cup, Nilgiris Gold Cup (1600 m, class IV, Ootacamund), a very prestigious race in that centre.		
16.	Mimion (1967)	3 wins	Above average	**Nation's Glory** by Paddykin: 7 wins, winner in class II.	Paddykin was Border-line classic.	Success
17.	Mystique (1967)	2 wins	Above average	Nil	Visited above average and average stallions.	Too early to judge as mare is active
18.	Golden Aura (1968)	Unraced	Above average	**Thunder Cloud** (by Young Lochinvar): 8 wins, winner in class I.	Young Lochinvar as described	Success
19.	Goodie (1968)	Unraced	Above average, full-sister to Mabel	**Young Lady** (by Young Lochinvar): as described. **Goodleigh** (by Lairg): 5 wins, winner in class III. **Young Character** (by Young Lochinvar): 5 wins, winner in class II. **Good Enough** by Young Lochinvar): in training. **Filly** (1981) by Mister Dan is in training.	Young Lochinvar as described. Lairg was at the most average. Mister Dan's progeny have just started racing.	Success

TABLE 13 (con't.)

S.No.	Mare	Mare's race record	Quality of mare's tail female line	Mare's superior progeny and their race records	Class of the stallions she visited	Conclusion
20.	My Mo (1968)	5 wins, Maharaja's Gold Cup	Average	Yet to produce a superior racer. Her **filly** (1981) by Al Marzouk is in training.	Visited stallions who were at the most average.	Too early to judge as mare is active
21.	Princess Saiqa (1968)	4 wins	Above average full-sister to Amigo	**Pride of Kiliyanur** (by Satinello): 7 wins, winner in class II.	Satinello is Front-line classic.	Success
22.	Sweet Sixteen (1968)	4 wins	Above average	Her 1st foal **Regency Bear** (by Mossy Bear) was retired to stud unraced. Her 2nd and 4th foals died. Her 3rd foal **Tradisteen** (by Tradition) is a winner. The mare is dead.	Tradition was disappointing.	Cannot judge as she had only 1 runner
23.	Versailles (1968)	3 wins	Above average	Nil	Visited superior stallions.	Too early to judge as mare is active
24.	Dear Barbara (1969)	5 wins	Above average	**Rajput** (by Lord Jim): 3 wins, October Handicap, winner in class III. He unfortunately died at 4 years. He was her 1st foal.	Lord Jim as described (chapter 3).	Has made a bright start
25.	Flying Splendour (1969)	4 wins	Above average	Nil	Visited superior stallions.	Too early to judge as mare is active
26.	Hatsoff (1969)	6 wins	At the most average	Her 1st foal died. Her 2nd foal a **colt** (1981) by Aliante is in training.	Aliante's progeny have just started to race.	Too early to judge as mare is active.

No.	Name (Year)	Race record	Assessment	Progeny	Remarks	Result
27.	Megh Jyoti (1969)	Unraced	Above average	**Minsky** (by Nijinsky [India]): 9 wins, winner in class I. He was a superior sprinter.	Nijinsky (India) as described.	Success
28.	Renaissance (1969)	1 win	Above average	**Ghazal** (by Mighty Sparrow): 6 wins, Gen. Obaidullah Khan Gold Cup. **Brown Bomber** (by Mighty Sparrow): 9 wins, winner in class II. **Chieftan** (by Dimead): 5 wins, winner in class III. **Sterling Moss** (by Mighty Sparrow): 10 wins, winner in class III. **Restoration** (by Zelenko): winner in training.	Mighty Sparrow was almost Front-line classic with 5 classic winners. Simead was Border-line classic. Zelenko's progeny have just started to race.	Success
29.	Eagle Eye (1970)	2 wins	Above average	Yet to produce a superior racer. Her 2nd foal a **filly** (1981) by Prince Khartoum is in training.	Prince Khartoum is above average.	Too early to judge as mare is active
30.	Handsel (1970)	7 wins Gay Talkie Cup	Above average, full-sister to Fabiha	Nil	Visited superior and average stallions.	Too early to judge as mare is active
31.	Periwinkle (1970)	Placed	At the most average	Nil	Visited superior and average stallions.	Too early to judge as mare is active
32.	Shubkamini (1970)	3 wins	Above average, full-sister to Jeevan Jyoti, Moon Dust and Enter and Canter	Nil	Visited superior and average stallions.	Too early to judge as mare is active

TABLE 13 (con't.)

S.No.	Mare	Mare's race record	Quality of mare's tail female line	Mare's superior progeny and their race records	Class of the stallions she visited	Conclusion
33.	Ask Me (1971)	6 wins	Above average, full-sister to Renaissance and Mystique	**Samantha** (by Simead): 4 wins, Kailashpat Singhania Cup (1800 m, class II, Bombay)	Simead as described	Success
34.	Hennessy (1971)	7 wins	Above average	Yet to produce a superior racer. Her 2nd foal died. Her 3rd foal a **colt** (1981) by Everyday is in training.	Her 1st foal was by an average stallion. Everyday as described.	Too early to judge as mare is active
35.	Judo (1971)	Unraced	Above average, full-Sister to Sweet Sixteen	Nil	Visited superior stallions.	Too early to judge as mare is active
36.	Mill Haven (1971)	3 wins	Above average	Yet to produce a superior racer. Her 3rd foal **Pillow Talk** (by Boris Godunov) is a winner, in training. Her **colt** (1982) by Lord of Light is in training.	Visited superior and average stallions. Boris Godunov's first progeny have just started to race. Lord of Light is almost Border-line classic with 2 classic winners.	Too early to judge as mare is active
37.	Willow Green (1971)	2 wins	Above average	**Wisdom** (by Thundering) her 1st foal has already won 3 races, P.R. Mehta Cup (1200 m, class III, Bombay), in training.	Thundering was almost Border-line classic with 2 classic winners.	Has made a bright start
38.	Georgian Gem (1972)	Unraced	Above average, full-sister to Mumtaz	**Exemplar** (by Young Lochinvar): 5 wins; 2nd South India Derby, Bangalore Arc de Triomphe; 3rd Deccan Deck	Young Lochinvar as described.	Success

38.	Georgian Gem (con't.) (1972)			**Carlos** (by Young Lochinvar): 7 wins, Maharaja's Gold Cup (1600 m, class I, Mysore).		
39.	Princess Jani (1972)	As described	Above average	**Zamindaar** (by Young Lochinvar) her 1st runner has already won 5 races, winner in class III. Her 2nd foal a **filly** (1981) by Mister Dan is in training.	Young Lochinvar and Mister Dan as described.	Has made a bright start
40.	Zeenat (1972)	Unraced	Above average, full-sister to Chic Baby and Eagle Eye	**None So Pretty** (by Young Lochinvar): She won 2 races and placed 3rd once from only 4 starts. She unfortunately died at 3. She would have definitely developed into a superior racer. **Princely Rock** (by Lairg): 6 wins, Mysore Race Club Cup (1600 m, class II, Hyderabad). Her **colt** (1980) by Lairg is in training.	Young Lochinvar and Lairg as described.	Success
41.	Maiden's Blush (1973)	6 wins	Average	**Apopca** (by Everyday) is a winner in training. Her **filly** (1982) by Road to Glory is in training.	Everyday as described. Road to Glory's progeny have just started to race.	Too early to judge as mare is active
42.	Padmani (1973)	Unraced	Above average	Her 1st foals (twins) died. Her 2nd foal a **colt** (1981) by Lairg is in training.	Lairg as described.	Too early to judge as mare is active

TABLE 13 (con't.)

S.No.	Mare	Mare's race record	Quality of mare's tail female line	Mare's superior progeny and their race records	Class of the stallions she visited	Conclusion
43.	Zeenee (1973)	As described	Above average	**Santini** (by Fair World) her 1st foal is a winner. Her 2nd and 3rd foals died. Her 4th foal a **filly** (1980) and her 3rd foal a **colt** (1981) by Young Lochinvar are in training.	Fair World is at the most average. Everyday as described.	Too early to judge as mare is active
44.	Nafeesa (1974)	Ran unplaced twice	Above average, full-sister to Padmani	Yet to produce a superior racer. Her 2nd foal a **filly** (1980) and her 3rd foal a **colt** (1981) by Young Lochinvar are in training.	Her 1st foal was also by Young Lochinvar, as described.	Too early to judge as mare is active
45.	Noble Love (1974)	Won once and placed thrice in a short racing career	Average to above average	Her 1st foal a **colt** (1979) by Mr. Mauritius is in training.	Mr. Mauritius is average.	Too early to judge as mare is active

Easter Parade 1978, Damastown x Take Cover): 5 wins, Calcutta St. Leger; 3rd Calcutta Derby. (He dead-heated for win in the Queen Elizabeth II Cup but was placed 2nd on objection.)

Zelda (1974, Eagle Rock x Jeevan Jyoti): 6 wins, Calcutta 1000 Guineas and Oaks.

Young Lady (1972, Young Lochinvar x Goodie): 4 wins, Calcutta 1000 Guineas.

Flash Past (1978, Everyday x Fabiha): 6 wins, Nilgiris Colts Trial Stakes, South India Gold Cup, Chief Justice's Cup (1200 m, 3-yr-olds, Madras); 2nd Deccan and Nilgiris Derby, Hyderabad Colts Trial Stakes.

In addition to the above classic winners, his daughters produced a large number of superior racers as described in the following pages.

We can now conclude by saying Asopo is an outstanding maternal grandsire But he is even more. To grasp fully the magnitude of his achievements and to further understand his behaviour, and the behaviour of maternal grandsires in general, we have to study the performance of each of his daughters. This is done in the following pages. I urge readers to study them very carefully. (A few of his daughters are just entering stud and a few others are yet to have runners. They have not been included in the Table.)

Analyzing Table 13 we find:

TABLE 14

	No.	Percentage
Successful mares	17	37.8
Substandard mares	3	6.7
Too early to judge	23	51.1
Mares who cannot be judged as they had only 1 runner each	2	4.4
	45	100

Let us study each category in detail. 17 of his daughters have already produced a superior racer. This in itself is very creditable. But it is not all. Several of his daughters like Take Cover, Mumtaz, Fabiha, Goodie, Georgian Gem, Renaissance and My Baby went higher. Each of them produced more than one superior racer. Their progeny included multiple classic winners, classic winners, classic-placed and a champion. This automatically puts them in Categories I or 11. This is one aspect that I want to strongly emphasize. Only the very best maternal grandsires. can get so many Categories I or II broodmares. And if a horse has so many of his daughters in these two Categories, he is obviously going to top the Maternal grand-sires lists not once but several times. In all these 17 broodmares produced no fewer than 30 superior racers. This shows their depth of talent. A word about Mumtaz, who was undoubtedly the best broodmare in the country. Grand Parade and Aristocrat were her only foals. She was earlier barren to Romiti and Red Rufus and died in foal to Ballo. If she had had a full stud career Lord only knows what she would have done!

Let us come to the "Too early to judge" category which has 23 mares (including the 3 mares who have made a bright start). While I am not go-ing to claim that all of them are going to succeed brilliantly, it is clear that Dear Barbara Willow Green, Princess Jani, Judo, Hennessy and Zeenee are going to do extremely well. Therefore about half his daughters can be considered to be successful broodmares, a tremendous achievement.

Readers would have noticed that Asopo mares produced a number of superior progeny out of Young Lochinvar and Everyday. This does not mean they did badly with other stallions. It was a question of opportu-nity. A greater number of Asopo mares visited Young Lochinvar and Every-day; hence these two stallions were more successful than the others. Closer examination of Table 13 clearly shows that Asopo mares were able to pro-duce superior racers out of several sires.

Readers would have easily determined his aptitude. He is a versatile maternal grandsire. His daughters have produced horses with an ideal blend of speed and stamina, stayers and sprinter-milers.

Did you notice one more very important facet of Asopo's behaviour? I will explain in detail later. Now let us try to determine why Asopo was a hugely successful maternal grandsire. Less experienced readers will be tempted to argue on the following lines:

"Daughters of Asopo visited superior stallions; hence they were suc-cessful."

This reasoning can be very easily demolished. Daughters of Star of Gwalior and Rock of Gibraltar too visited superior stallions. Then why weren't they successful? Roughly speaking they were only about half as successful as Asopo. This brings us to a very important point. Throughout this chapter on maternal grandsires, and elsewhere in the book, I have made the following assumption which I think is fair enough:

'' The daughters of all the horses in question received the same opportunities taken as a whole i.e. the daughters of Asopo taken as a whole, as a set, received the same opportunities as the daughters of Star of Gwalior, Rock of Gibraltar, Exaggerator and others.''

''Asopo mares were prolific breeders.''

There is nothing to suggest that Asopo mares were more prolific than other mares. He had his share of shy and problem breeders. He also had his share of talented fillies like Rare Gem and Beauty Queen who did not become producers.

''Daughters of Asopo had superior tail female lines. This was undoubtedly the major factor in their success.''

Undeniably a majority of Asopo mares possess superior tail female lines. This is because Asopo served superior mares. But Asopo mares are not the only mares with superior female lines. Daughters of Star of Gwalior and Rock of Gibraltar possessed equally illustrious tail female lines. But as we have seen they were only half as successful.

Hence we are forced to conclude that Asopo mares were successful because they were inherently talented producers. But why were they inherently talented? It is because:

Asopo was able to impart some characteristics, some properties to them which enabled them to be excellent producers. Other sires were not able to do so. Hence their daughters were less successful. Therefore a daughter of a successful maternal grandsire like Asopo, Horatius or Exaggerator has a greater chance of stud success than others. It is in our interest to buy the progeny of such mares, or better still breed from them.

I am sure the role of the maternal grandsire has now become very clear to readers. Having understood the behaviour of maternal grandsires we will now take up the study of two very powerful and extremely important concepts.

WELL-BRED MARES

We are now in a position to define a ''well-bred'' mare. What exactly do you mean by a well-bred mare? What are the pedigree requirements of broodmares? Are they different from the pedigree requirements of year-lings? Yes, they are. First and foremost a well-bred mare must be the daughter of a sire who was a successful maternal grandsire. There are no exceptions, I repeat, no exceptions to this rule. A filly may have won the Derby, Oaks and St. Leger,or she may be a full-sister to a champion; yet she need not be well-bred. Look at her sire and see whether he was a Front-line or Border-line classic maternal grandsire. If he was the filly now entering stud as a broodmare, has a chance of qualifying as a well-bred mare. But suppose it is too early to judge her sire as a maternal grandsire. Then what? Then we must use qualifying expressions like: "A mare who is in all probability well-bred" or"a mare who could be well-bred."

The second requirement a mare must necessarily possess in order to qualify for well-bred status is a superior tail female line. We studied this aspect in detail. We understood the importance of the female family and saw that a number of them have produced classic winners and champions generation after generation. A well-bred mare must therefore have such a superior tail female line.

Therefore the two requirements a mare must satisfy in order to qualify for well-bred status are:

1) *She must be the daughter of a sire who was a very successful maternal grandsire. Her 1st and 2nd maternal grandsires too must have been equally successful.*

2) *Her tail female line must be superior.*

Her racing merit does not come into the picture.

I once again repeat: "There are no exceptions to the above rules. A mare who satisfies only one requirement e.g. a mare who is the daughter of a sire who is an outstanding maternal grandsire, but with an average tail female line cannot be well-bred. Both the requirements must be satisfied in full."

Now let us go a step further and consider the racing merit of the mare. We saw that mares who were themselves superior racers, though numerically small in number, excelled in stud producing a large number of superior racers. Now think of two well-bred mares. The first was a superior racer, a stakes winner, while the second ran unplaced. Which mare has a greater chance of stud success? Naturally the former. For her pedigree is superior and she herself was a superior racer. We must consider such mares to be *Inherently superior.* Among all the broodmares they have the maximum chance of stud success. They have the greatest chance of producing classic winners, champions and stakes winners. Therefore an Inherently superior mare is one:

1) *Whose sire, 1st and 2nd maternal grandsires were very successful maternal grandsires.*
2) *Whose tail female line is superior.*
3) *Who was herself a superior racer.*

I want readers to study the definition very carefully. What is your opinion? How many mares do you think will qualify? Can a large number of mares qualify? Experienced readers would have immediately noted that the definition is very severe. Only a handful of mares will qualify. Can we honestly say that only these mares are inherently talented, that only these mares are going to produce superior racers, and that all the others are going to fail? No, we cannot. Hence it is necessary for us to modify the definition by relaxing the conditions we laid down. While the definition in the above form is theoretically impeccable, it is of little practical significance. It cannot be used by breeders and owners in their work. But how can we relax the definition? *I suggest that we consider mares who satisfy any two of the three conditions to be Inherently superior.*

Now there are three ways by which a mare can qualify:

A mare can satisfy conditions one and two i.e. she is a well-bred mare. *Therefore according to our modified definition all well-bred mares are Inherently superior.* We are not bothered about their racing merit here.

A mare can satisfy conditions one and three i.e. she was a superior racer and her sire, 1st and 2nd maternal grandsires were Classic maternal grandsires. Here her tail female line does not come into the picture. It can be average, marginally above average or even substandard. We will condone the weaknesses in the tail female line as she has satisfied the other two conditions.

A mare can also satisfy conditions two and three. Superior racers with solid tail female lines constitute this category. Here we will allow weak maternal grandsires. They can be average or even below average.

Finally do not forget that a handful of mares satisfy all the three conditions.

Our new definition makes it possible for a larger number of mares to qualify. But can this be justified? I am sure it can. Again think of the horses who go to stud as stallions. Weren't they outstanding gallopers, the champions of their generation? Don't they possess excellent pedigrees, excellent conformation? As explained, and as we are going to study in great detail, stallions have the inherent ability to overcome weaknesses in broodmares and still get superior progeny. Therefore we can relax one condition and accept one weak element, one weak component.

The three components of a broodmare as we saw above are:

1) Her race record.

2) Her sire, 1st and 2nd maternal grandsires.

3) Her tail female line.

(I have merely changed the order.)

What about mares with only one superior component or no superior component? Can we not consider them to be Inherently superior? No we cannot. For it will be difficult for a stallion however superior and "dominating" he may be, to overcome all the weaknesses and defects in utterly substandard mares and still get superior racers. I am not saying that mares with only one superior component or no superior component i.e. Inherently inferior mares cannot become successful producers. As readers will already be aware, they certainly can. (In the next part of the book I will explain clearly how Inherently inferior mares can and do succeed in stud.) What I am emphasizing is: The probability of an Inherently superior mare becoming a successful producer is several times greater than the probability of an Inherently inferior mare. Therefore we must breed from, and buy the progeny of, inherently superior mares.

SIGNIFICANCE OF INHERENTLY SUPERIOR MARES

Determining inherent merit is particularly important in the case of mares whose first offspring are coming up for sale. You are at an auction sale and an attractive colt catches your eye. You are impressed with his sire, but since he is the first foal of his dam you do not know her performance as a producer. Now study her three components and see whether she is Inherently superior, or better still whether all her three components are superior. If she qualifies you can buy the colt boldly, but if she does not you have to think twice. The dam is inferior. While such mares are not incapable of producing superior racers, they do so infrequently.

Once a mare has proved to be successful the question of her Inherent superiority becomes a bit academic. Since she has already produced a superior racer, there is absolutely no reason why she should not produce another. Such mares should be judged on their produce records. But mares yet to produce a sufficient number of racers must be judged on their Inherent superiority.

NEW DEFINITION OF A WELL-BRED HORSE

Our task now is to incorporate the concept of Inherent superiority in the definition of a well-bred horse. We defined well-bred horses as the progeny of outstanding, superior stallions out of successful or well-bred mares. In the latter case we ignored their race records. Now we can include them. We must substitute well-bred mares by Inherently superior mares in the definition. In other words we are broadening the definition. Since all well-bred mares are Inherently superior, their progeny out of superior stallions automatically qualify. In addition the progeny of superior stallions out of Inherently superior mares who are not well-bred (i.e. mares with superior race records and one superior pedigree component) also qualify. Therefore the improved definition of a well-bred horse is:

The offspring of a superior sire out of a successful or Inherently superior mare.
Or
A full-brother or sister to a superior racer.

APTITUDE OF BROODMARES

We learnt how to identify an Inherently superior mare. Now we must learn how to determine her aptitude i.e. the aptitude of her progeny. Is the mare predisposed to producing fine stayers? Or are you convinced that her progeny can win up to a mile only? To determine the aptitude of a mare we have to determine her own aptitude on the course, the aptitudes of her maternal grandsire and tail female line components and sum-up. Imagine a mare who was a stayer and who belongs to a family of stayers. Her sire too was a maternal grandsire of stayers. What will be the aptitude of her progeny? They are obviously going to develop into stayers. But determining aptitude will not always be this easy. Let us consider another mare. She was a miler, not a stayer. But her sire and maternal grandsires were maternal grandsires of stayers and there are traces of stamina in her female line. Is she going to produce stayers or milers? Honestly it is very difficult to predict. We have to wait till a sufficient number of her progeny have started racing.

Similarly determining the aptitude of a mare with a versatile pedigree is difficult. Her progeny may be versatile or specialists. But we can try one technique. Determine which of her three components is most superior, most dominant. There is a chance that the aptitude of her progeny will be similar to the aptitude of that component. But this technique is admittedly very imperfect. How can we say for sure that one component is the strongest, the most dominant? In general do not try to determine the aptitude of a mare unless two of her three components definitely have the same aptitude.

Determining aptitude by these methods is not necessary when a mare has had sufficient runners.

We have come to the end of the first part of the book. I am sure readers have understood all the concepts discussed without the slightest difficulty. After learning how to analyze a pedigree, we classified stallions, broodmares, tail female lines and maternal grandsires and studied their behiaviour. We then defined a well-bred mare and an Inherently superior mare. If any reader has not understood a topic, I urge him to study it once again, for all the concepts we have learnt till now will be used extensively in the second part, where we will go deeper into the subject.

PART II

CHAPTER 6
Stallions – 2

THE CONCEPT OF "COMPATIBILITY"

In the first part of the book we were able to identify superior stallions and mares. But superior stallions and mares do not always produce superior racers as breeders have learnt to their chagrin. And many a time average stallions and mares have come out with superior progeny. Therefore even if you breed from really top class progenitors you are not sure of getting superior racers. Apart from the "class" of the progenitors another factor, another dimension is involved. What is that factor? It is "compatibility" — compatibility between the sire and dam.

What exactly do we mean by compatibility? How powerful is its role in breeding? A stallion and broodmare are fully compatible if:

1) The speed and stamina of the stallion is compatible with the speed and stamina of the mare.

2) The pedigree of the stallion is compatible with the pedigree of the mare.

3) The conformation of the stallion is compatible with the conformation of the mare.

4) The temperament of the stallion is compatible with the temperament of the mare.

In other words the offspring of a compatible stallion and mare will have an ideal blend of speed and stamina, an ideal pedigree, conformation and temperament; in short he will be a superior racer. But can we predict that a particular stallion and mare are really and truly compatible? If we can we have an excellent chance of breeding superior racers. But how can we determine compatibility in advance? Imagine a young stallion who has made a bright start. He has already sired a number of superior racers. Now our task is to determine out of which type, out of which kind, of mares he got his superior progeny. Surely you are not going to claim that a stallion can get superior progeny out of every type of mare, are you? Can we not assert that most stallions, however superior they may be, invariably get superior progeny out of particular types of mares? In other words every stallion is most compatible with a particular type, or types, of mares. He has the greatest chance of producing superior racers out of such mares. Therefore our job is to determine the types of mares most compatible, most suitable, for him. The procedure we are going to adopt for doing so is simple. We will first identify all his superior progeny. Then we will look very, very closely at the dams of those superior progeny. What was their racing merit? What are the characteristics of their pedigrees, conformation and temperament? Do they have any characteristics in common? Frequently they will. Therefore can we not immediately say that a mare who has all these characteristics is most compatible with the stallion in question?

The class and compatibility of the sire and dam invariably decides the class of the offspring.

We learnt how to determine the class and aptitude of stallions and mares. Now let us learn how to determine which type or types of mares are most compatible with a particular stallion. The concept of compatibility will become very clear after the study of a few stallions. The first stallion I have selected is Everyday.

		Alizier	Teleferique
			Alizarine
	Jet Stream		
		Streamlace	Vatellor
			Straitlace
Everyday			
(Br, 1967)		Citation	Bull Lea
			Hydroplane
	Tomorrow		
		Until	Tudor Minstrel
			Visor

Everyday, a brown son of Jet Stream x Tomorrow, was bred in the U.S.A. He was sent to Ireland as a yearling and he started racing there.

As a 2-yr-old he covered himself with glory by running 2nd twice to the great Nijinsky. In the Erne Stakes he finished 2nd by only half-a-length at level weights. He then won his 2nd race, the Lucern Stakes by 8 lengths.

In his 3rd race, the Angelesey Stakes, he was again 2nd to Nijinsky. His 4th race was the Autumn Sprint Stakes which he won. He was rated only 13 lbs. below Nijinsky.

As a 3-yr-old he won once and was sent to France. He won the Prix du Clos Fleuri, placed 3rd in the Prix Maurice de Gheest (Group III) and 4th in the Prix de Meautry (Group III).

At 4 years he won the Prix d'Arromanches and placed. In all he won 3 races in Ireland and 2 races in France. He won from 1200 m to 1600 m. He was imported into India and retired to stud in 1973. He was an immediate success, getting a classic winner in his very first crop of only 3 runners! Since then he has gone from strength to strength and became a Front-line classic stallion with only 4 crops. He was the champion stallion in 1978-'79 and '79-'80 and 2nd in '80-'81. Within 5 crops he produced as many as 11 classic winners and 1 champion.

His progeny come to hand early and train on well. Sound and robust, they have a true zest for racing. In addition to an abundance of class, they also possess an ideal blend of speed and stamina. In the 1979 Bangalore Colts Trial Stakes the first five were his progeny — Aristocrat, Everynsky, Tehrani, Valour and Word-A-Day! They monopolized the finish of the Bangalore Derby too with Everynsky (1st), Aristocrat (2nd), Tehrani (3rd), Valour (5th) and Word-A-Day (7th).

By adopting the procedure formulated in the first part of the book let us determine his behaviour.

STEP 1

We have to identify all his superior racers.

First let us identify his classic winners and champions. The 11 classic winners and 1 champion in his first 5 crops (throughout this exercise we will restrict ourselves to his first 5 crops) were:

Everynsky (1976): 9 wins, champion, Indian Turf Invitation Cup, Bangalore Arc de Triomphe, Indian St. Leger, Bangalore Derby, President of India Gold Cup. He won from 1100 m to 2800 m. Sire.

Aristocrat (1976): 15 wins, South India Derby and 2000 Guineas, Bangalore St. Leger, Deccan and Mysore Derby, Hyderabad Colts Trial Stakes; 2nd Indian Turf Invitation Cup, Bangalore Derby. He won from 1000 m to 2800 m. Sire.

Abide (1978) : 7 wins, Indian and Bangalore Oaks, Bangalore St. Leger, Mysore Derby and 1000 Guineas; 2nd Indian Turf Invitation Cup, Indian Derby. She was the champion filly of her generation.

Grand Parade (1974): 11 wins, South India Triple Crown, Deccan Derby, Hyderabad Colts Trial Stakes; 2nd Bangalore Derby and Arc de Triomphe. He won from 1000 m to 2800 m. Sire.

Adelita (1977): 7 wins, Calcutta Derby, 2000 Guineas and 1000 Guineas; 2nd Calcutta Oaks and St. Leger.

Zeeba (1975): 4 wins, Calcutta 2000 Guineas, Champagne Stakes, Grand Annual Handicap; 2nd Calcutta and Mysore 1000 Guineas.

Star Asset (1978): 5 wins, Golconda 1000 Guineas and Oaks.

Mohini (1975) : 6 wins, Bangalore 1000 Guineas, Bangalore and Nilgiris Fillies Trial Stakes ; 2nd South India 1000 Guineas and Oaks, Hyderabad Fillies Trial Stakes; 3rd Deccan Derby.

Evita (1977): 6 wins, Bangalore and Mysore 1000 Guineas, Kunigal Stud Trophy; 2nd Bangalore Oaks.

Deepali (1978): 4 wins, Indian 1000 Guineas, Sir Jamsetjee Jee-jeebhoy (VI Bart) Trophy; 3rd Mysore 1000 Guineas.

Flash Past (1978): 6 wins, Nilgiris Colts Trial Stakes, South India Gold Cup, Chief Justice's Cup; 2nd Deccan and Nilgiris Derby, Hyderabad Colts Trial Stakes.

Everytime (1975): 11 wins, champion, Sprinters' Cup, Maharaja of Morvi Cup, Maharaja Sir Harisinghji Cup (1600 m, 4-yr-olds and over, Bombay) P.D. Bolton Cup. Sire.

Apart from these 12 horses he sired 18 other superior racers whose performances will be given a little later. He got these 30 superior racers from only 50 runners — truly an astonishing performance!

Percentage of classic winners and $= \dfrac{12}{50}$ x 100 = 24%
champions from runners

Percentage of superior racers $= \dfrac{30}{50}$ x 100 = 60%
from runners

Our finding at the end of this step is: Everyday is a Front-line classic stallion. He is a stallion of the very highest order. He is definitely among the top three stallions in the country.

STEP 2

We have to study the performances of all his progeny crop by crop and see whether his behaviour was Normal. If not we have to determine the nature of the deviation.

I have completed this step and to avoid a detailed exercise will just present the result: Everyday exhibits Normal behaviour. A remarkably consistent stallion, he has produced classic winners and superior racers in every crop. He has not changed his behaviour in any crop.

STEP 3

The class of his colts and fillies:

His colts and fillies were equally good.

STEP 4

We have to determine the aptitude of his superior and average progeny.

A quick look at his superior progeny itself reveals his versatility in no uncertain terms. He has sired outstanding sprinters, milers, stayers and horses who excelled over the entire range of distances. I have divided his superior progeny into two groups as below:

Sprinters, Milers and Sprinter-milers		Stayers
1) Urvashi	11) Cross the Floor	21) Grand Parade
2) Dur-E-Jehan	12) Evita	22) Dear Donna
3) Every Time	13) Let Me Fly	23) Aristocrat
4) Nobel Laureate	14) Two Little Winks	24) Beckoning Dream
5) Mohini	15) Black Tornado	25) Everynsky
6) Zeeba	16) Deepali	26) Word-A-Day
7) My Opinion	17) Ebonysky	27) Adelita
8) Tehrani	18) Flash Past	28) Moment to Moment
9) Valour	19) Prince O' War	29) Abide
10) Yucatan	20) Royal Game	30) Star Asset
	20	10

(I have classified Mohini, Valour, Evita, Flash Point and Prince O'War in the first category, even though they possessed elements of stamina. All of them placed in classics or prestigious races over 2000 m and above. But undoubtedly they excelled over 1600 m. Readers must note that several horses in the stayers category had an ideal blend of speed and stamina and excelled over the entire range of distances.)

STEP 5

We have to study all his mares in detail and determine out of which types of mares he produced superior racers. What was their racing performances, their pedigrees? I have given all his runners and their dams in Table 15. Then I have given their pedigrees and produce records. I urge readers to study them very carefully.

TABLE 15

PROGENY OF EVERYDAY WHO RAN (first 5 crops only)

Dam	Offspring

1974
(year offspring was foaled)

	Dam	Offspring
1)	Artic War	Pious Look
2)	Moon Shine	Urvashi
3)	Mumtaz	Grand Parade

1975

	Dam	Offspring
4)	Artic War	Wedding Present
5)	Donna Princess	Dear Donna
6)	Gangotri	Zeeba
7)	Golden Smile	Miles of Smiles
8)	Green Flame	Naughty but Nice
9)	Miss Rebecca	Nobel Laureate
10)	Moon Shine	Mohini
11)	Pashmina	Red God (India)
12)	Perfume	Every Time
13)	Randia	Dur-E-Jehan

1976

	Dam	Offspring
14)	Chamwort	Beckoning Dream
15)	Diamond Head	Glory of Kiliyanur
16)	Eye to Eye	Pick Me Up
17)	Gangotri	Tehrani
18)	Golden Smile	Yucatan
19)	Gold Paprika	Citistar
20)	Hold the Bridge	Valour
21)	Mark My Words	Word-A-Day
22)	Mumtaz	Aristocrat
23)	Not a Wink	Everynsky
24)	Perfume	Fantasy
25)	Queen O'Scots	My Opinion
26)	Shantiniketan	Amenity
27)	Star Above	Royal Jewel

TABLE 15 (cont.)

Dam	Offspring
1977	
28) Blue Butterfly	Let Me Fly
29) Diana	Moment to Moment
30) Eye to Eye	Tete-A-Tete
31) Gangotri	Bandolier
32) Green Flame	Adelita
33) Hold the Bridge	Come What May
34) Indian Rose	Cross the Floor
35) Little Wink	Two Little Winks
36) Mark My Words	Everyword
37) Martha Gunn	Evita
38) Nouvola	Any Time
39) Queen O'Scots	Tippu Sultan
40) Word Play	Richbru
1978	
41) Artic War	Prince O'War
42) Donna Princess	Abide
43) Enchantress	Ebonysky
44) Fabiha	Flash Past
45) Loyal Princess	Black Tornado
46) Mark Over	Royal Game
47) Moon Shine	Deepali
48) Never So	Ever So
49) Not a Wink	Star Asset
50) Zsa Zsa	Evangel

(Inevitably a few horses who belonged to the above crops did not race. They included: His Little Sister, Live to Fight, Immer Green, Reciprocity and Bo Derek.)

1) ARTIC WAR

		Prince Chevalier	Prince Rose Chevalierie
	Arctic Prince		
		Arctic Sun	Nearco Solar Flower
Arctic War			
(Ch, 1960)		Man o' War	Fair Play Mahubah
	War Memorial		
		Northern Belle	John P. Frier Marvella II

ARTIC WAR: was foaled in U.S.A. She was unraced. She was imported into India in foal to Le Levanstell and retired to stud. Dam of:

Another Jet: 5 wins, Indian Republic Cup, Parlakimedi Cup; 4th South India 1000 Guineas.

Neel Kamal: 2 wins.

Sandpiper: 2 wins in her short racing career.

Royal Ambassador: 9 wins, C.N. Wadia Gold Cup, Aga Khan's Cup, Chief of Kagal Gold Cup.

Ruby Royal: 5 wins, Bangalore Colts Trial Stakes; 2nd Guindy Gold Cup (by a neck), Kashmir Gold Cup; 4th Indian Turf Invitation Cup.

Observation: 4 wins, Indian Republic Cup (2000 m, class IV, Madras)

Pious Look (by Everyday): 2 wins, Ramanatha Iyer Memorial Cup.

Wedding Present (by Everyday): 3 wins, Alokananda Stakes (1200 m, 3-yr-old fillies, Calcutta).

Prince O'War (by Everyday): 5 wins, Sir Charles Forbes Cup; 2nd R.R. Ruia Gold Cup.

Artic Peace: 2 wins.

2) MOON SHINE

Moon Shine (Ch, 1964)	King's Barn	Persian Gulf	Bahram Double Life
		Wiston	Easton Chincona
	Rose Beam	Flower Dust	Pink Flower Brazen Molly
		Neolight	Bucephalus Belamina

MOON SHINE: 6 wins. Dam of:

Urvashi (by Everyday): 7 wins, Tamil Nadu Commemoration Gold Cup (1600 m, classes I and II, Madras. The distance was subsequently increased to 2000 m.).

Mohini (by Everyday): as described.

Mukh Mohini: 2 wins.

Deepali (by Everyday): as described.

Goodness Gracious (by Everyday): winner, in training.

Filly (1982) by Everyday is in training.

3) MUMTAZ

Mumtaz (B, 1965)	Asopo	Nimbus	Nearco Kong
		Assamenta	Norseman Assylia
	Georgiana	Fairy Fulmar	Fair Trial First Flight
		La Nouba	Goya II Gandara

MUMTAZ: 3 wins; 2nd Indian Derby, Oaks and St. Leger. Dam of:

Grand Parade (by Everyday): as described.

Aristocrat (by Everyday): as described.

4) DONNA PRINCESS

		Pink Flower	Oleander
	Wilwyn		Plymstock
Donna Princess		Saracen	Donatello II
(B, 1960)			Lovely Rosa
		River Prince	Rose Prince
	Gaztelupe		Vieste
		Nocturne	Noble Star
			Madrigal

DONNA PRINCESS: ran a few times in England and placed 2nd in the Summer Plate (Alexandra Park). Dam of:

Allegro: 5 wins.

San Marco: 7 wins, Kolar Cup, Air Command Cup, C.S. Loganathan Memorial Cup; placed Nizam's Gold Cup, National Horse Breeding Society of India Gold Cup.

Bharat: 11 wins, Aga Khan Cup, Moss Cup; placed C.N. Wadia Gold Cup, Byculla Club Cup, Gen. Obaidullah Khan Gold Cup.

Nafasat: placed.

Lady Madonna: 4 wins, Indian Oaks, Eve Champion Cup, C.N. Wadia Gold Cup, Homi Mody Cup; 2nd Indian St. Leger; 4th Indian Turf Invitation Cup.

Trident: 5 wins, National Horse Breeding Society of India Cup; 2nd South India St. Leger.

Dear Donna (by Everyday): 6 wins, Stewards Gold Cup, Independence Cup.

Regard: 1 win.

Durango: 2 wins.

Abide (by Everyday): as described.

Sir Don: 4 wins; 2nd Calcutta Derby; 3rd Calcutta St. Leger, in training.

Resplendent: 8 wins, Nilgiris Derby and Colts Trial Stakes, Mysore 2000 Guineas, Hyderabad Colts Trial Stakes; 3rd Bangalore Colts Trial Stakes, in training.

5) GANGOTRI

		Chamossaire	Precipitation
	Chmo		Snowberry
		Triskeles	Colorado Kid
Gangotri			Silver Star
(B, 1966)		Bear Dance	Big Game
	Ganga Mahal		Dancing Time
		Waikiki	Rajah II
			City Fare

GANGOTRI: placed in her short racing career. Dam of:

Mukurti: 7 wins, Stewards Gold Cup.

River Man: 7 wins.

Astro Turf: 2 wins.

Zeeba (by Everyday): as described.

Tehrani (by Everyday): 4 wins; 3rd Indian 2000 Guineas, Bangalore Derby and Colts Trial Stakes, R.R. Ruia Gold Cup.

Bandolier (by Everyday): 5 wins.

Pioneer (by Everyday): 7 wins, Asiad Cup (1800 m, classes I and II, Madras), M.Ct.M. Chidambaram Chettyar Gold Cup (2000 m, classes II and III, Madras); 2nd South India St. Leger; 3rd Calcutta Derby.

River of Hope: in training.

Filly (1982) by Gyrox is in training.

6) GOLDEN SMILE

Golden Smile (Ch, 1956)	Denturius	Gold Bridge	Golden Boss / Flying Diadem
		La Solfatara	Lemberg / Ayesha
	Sun View	Panorama	Sir Cosmo / Happy Climax
		Sunright	Solario / Democratie

GOLDEN SMILE: ran only twice in England. Dam of:

Gold Dust: winner in Germany.

Prasanti: 9 wins, Faridoon S. Chinoy Memorial Cup; 2nd South India 1000 Guineas.

Falcon: 8 wins, Cauvery Cup.

Interlaken: 8 wins.

Honorare: 4 wins.

Two Twenty: 5 wins.

Diamond Anita: 4 wins.

Tangerine: 3 wins in her only season to race.

No Bid: 4 wins.

Tres Jolie: 4 wins, Poona City Cup, April Handicap.

Gleam of Gold: 3 wins.

Touch of Love: 2 wins in her short racing career.

Miles of Smiles (by Everyday): 4 wins, Fillies Handicap Stakes.

Yucatan (by Everyday): 6 wins; 2nd Indian Gold Vase (1200 m, classes I and II, Calcutta), Golconda Cup (1400 m, class II, Calcutta).

Goodie Goodie: 5 wins.

Colt (1980) by Gyrox is in training.

7) GREEN FLAME

Green Flame (Ch, 1967)	Risby	Hard Sauce	Ardan Saucy Bella
		Persian Bubble	Persian Gulf Ballywellbroke
	Kordelya	Verso II	Pinceau Variete
		York Dale	Fairway Abbot's Glen

GREEN FLAME: 5 wins. Dam of:

Sunspray: 5 wins.

Naughty but Nice (by Everyday): 7 wins.

Adelita: (by Everyday): as described.

Malachite: 2 wins.

Fairworld's Flame: winner, in training.

8) MISS REBECCA

Miss Rebecca (B, 1963)	Dumbarnie	Dante	Nearco Rosy Legend
		Lost Soul	Solario Orlass
	Clara Rebecca	Neron	Nearco Love's Legend
		Aunt Clara	Arctic Prince Sister Clara

MISS REBECCA: placed once in England. Dam of:

Karthiayani: placed.

Tough Guy: 1 win.

Seer of Seers: 4 wins.

Reba: 3 wins, died at 3.

Czardas: 8 wins, Chief of Kagal Cup, Rajaram Chhatrapati Gold Cup.

Shoulder to Shoulder: 2 wins in a short racing career.

Terrific Victory: 3 wins.

Nobel Laureate (by Everyday): 7 wins, Governor's Cup (1600 m, 3-yr olds, Bangalore), Kunigal Stud Trophy (1200 m, 3-yr-olds, Bangalore), winner in class II.

His Little Sister (by Everyday): unraced.

Live to Fight (by Everyday): unraced due to injuries.

9) PASHMINA

Pashmina (B, 1959)	Fair Aid	Nasrullah	Nearco Mumtaz Begum
		Fair Portia	Fair Trial Trelissia
	Tosca	Tarquinius Superbus	Nearco Superbe
		Big Blaze	Barra Sahib Stella Marina

PASHMINA: placed 4 times from only 8 starts. Dam of:

Olympic Flame: 6 wins.

Sweet Memories: 11 wins, Indian St. Leger, Bangalore Fillies Trial Stakes, Mysore 1000 Guineas, President of India Gold Cup, Maharaja's Gold Cup, Governor's Cup. (She was undoubtedly the champion racer of her generation A setback in training prevented her from running in several classics.)

Fragrant Memories: 8 wins, Nehru Centre Cup (1600 m, class I, Bangalore).

Far Superior: 11 wins, Chief Minister's Relief Fund Cup (1600 m, class I, Bangalore).

Red God (India) (by Everyday): 1 win; placed 2nd thrice in his first season.

Shahtoosh: non-winner, retired to stud.

Purita: placed 2nd once from only 2 starts.

10) PERFUME

	Abernant	Owen Tudor
		Rustom Mahal
Gul Mohar		
	Fatimite	Mahmoud
		Sister Anne
Perfume		
(Gr, 1966)	Hyder Ali	Hyperion
		Eclair
Shantiniketan		
	Dilbahar	Steel Helmet
		Dancing Lilly

PERFUME: 5 wins, Kapila Cup, Basalat Jah Cup. Dam of:

Every Time (by Everyday): as described.

Fantasy (by Everyday): 1 win.

Silver Goddess: 3 wins.

Blossom a Day (by Everyday): 2 wins.

Colt (1982) by T.V. Sunday is in trainings.

11) RANDIA

	War Relic	Man o' War
		Frair's Carse
Relic		
	Bridal Colors	Black Toney
		Vaila
Randia		
(B, 1963)	Cobalt II	Teleferique
		Alizarine
Coruna II		
	Consolation	Foxhunter
		Bipearl

RANDIA: unraced. Dam of:

Perlina: 2 wins.

Budhni: 3 wins.

Face the Facts: 14 wins, President of India Trophy, Czechoslovakia Cup, South India Gold Cup.

Dur-E-Dashmesh: 4 wins, Justice R.S. Bavdekar Cup, Independence Cup.

Dur-E-Jehan: (by Everyday): 8 wins, Chief Minister's Cup, Nanda Devi Cup.

Law and Order: 2 wins.

Day of Deliverance: 3 wins, Maharaja of Parlakimedi Memorial Cup.

Fiery Force: 3 wins.

Dur-E-Deva: 3 wins, Golconda Oaks; 2nd Golconda Derby, Bangalore Oaks; 3rd Charminar Challenge Indian Turf Invitation Cup.

Filly (1981) by Shari is in training.

12) CHAMWORT

Chamwort (Ch, 1959)	Chamossaire	Precipitation	Hurry On / Double Life
		Snowberry	Cameronian / Myrobella
	Thoroughwort	Thoroughfare	Fairway / Brulette
		Larch Rose	Sir Cosmo / Prize Poem

CHAMWORT: unraced. Dam of:

Aceras: 3 wins in England, weighted in the Free Handicap.

Brahmachari: 5 wins.

Parashar Prince: winner.

Star Crest: 6 wins.

Orion: 4 wins.

Beckoning Dream (by Everyday): 4 wins, Totaram's Gold Cup (1800 m, class IV, Hyderabad), from only 5 starts. (He was a colt well up to classic winning standard but unfortunately suffered a setback in training.)

Jumbo Jet: did not win.

13) DIAMOND HEAD

	Balaji	Sayajirao	Nearco
			Rosy Legend
		Ashoka Kumari	Gold Bridge
Diamond Head			Organette
(Ch, 1965)		Cash	Winalot
	Solitaire		Florena
		On Appro	Apron
			Diomyth

DIAMOND HEAD: 1 win. Dam of:

Glory of Kiliyanur (by Everyday): 2 wins; 2nd Hyderabad Fillies Trial Stakes.

Diamond Gift: 1 win.

Colt (1979) by Whistling Glory is in training.

14) EYE TO EYE

	Jethro	Palestine	Fair Trial
			Une
		Jet High	Hyperion
Eye to Eye			Jet Plane
(B, 1970)		Firmament	Fair Copy
	Noor-E-Chashma		Stella Polaris
		First Royalty	Furrokh Siyar
			Madame Royale

EYE TO EYE: ran once unplaced. Dam of:

Mile A Minute: 9 wins, Magnanimous Cup.

Pick Me Up (by Everyday): 5 wins.

Tete-A-Tete (by Everyday): 1 win.

Blue Mist (by Everyday): 2 wins, Chief Justice's Cup.

Colt (1981) by Ballo is in training.

15) GOLD PAPRIKA

	Golden Cloud	Gold Bridge Rainstorm
Golden Horde		
	Cent Fois	Deux Pour Cent Fast Lady
Gold Paprika (B, 1970)		
	Caspian	Tehran Kindy
Pepita		
	Saraband	The Cobbler Lady of Legend

GOLD PAPRIKA: ran unplaced. Dam of:

Citistar (by Everyday): 3 wins.

Filly (1977) by Jethro is in training.

16) HOLD THE BRIDGE

	Hyperion	Gainsborough Selene
Horatius		
	La Goulue	Tourbillon Galveston
Hold the Bridge (Dk B, 1971)		
	Caspian	Tehran Kindy
Pepita		
	Saraband	The Cobbler Lady of Legend

HOLD THE BRIDGE: placed. Dam of:

Valour (by Everyday): 5 wins C.D. Dady Trophy (1400 m, class I, Bombay), Tippu Sultan Trophy (1400 m, 3-yr-olds, Bangalore), Ashoka (Chakra Cup (1400 m, 3-yr-old colts and geldings, Bangalore); 2nd Bangalore Arc de Triomphe (probably his best performance); 4th Bangalore Colts Trial Stakes.

Come What May (by Everyday): 3 wins.

Valiant: 4 wins, R.C.T.C. Cup (2000 m, class III, Bombay).

Protection Racket: in training.

Avant Garde: 2 wins, in training.

Hold Up: in training.

Colt (1982) by Fair World is in training.

17) MARK MY WORDS

		Hyperion	Gainsborough Selene
	Horatius		
		La Goulue	Tourbillon Galveston
Mark My Words (Ch, 1971)			
		Worden II	Wild Risk Sans Tares
	Word Play		
		Stage Fright	Big Game Bashful

MARK MY WORDS: unraced. Dam of:

Word-A-Day (by Everyday): 7 wins, Kanteerava Cup (2400 m, classes III and IV, Bangalore); 2nd Golconda Derby; 3rd Bangalore 2000 Guineas.

Everyword (by Everyday): 4 wins.

18) NOT A WINK

		Nearco	Pharos Nogara
	Narrator		
		Phase	Windsor Lad Lost Soul
Not a Wink (B, 1962)			
		Prince Chevalier	Prince Rose Chevalierie
	Princess Louise		
		Tropical Sun	Hyperion Brulette

NOT A WINK: won Knowkaney Plate (3200 m) at 4 years in England. She also won the Marly Knowe Fillies Plate but was disqualified and placed 2nd. Imported into India and retired to stud. Dam of:

Green Haven: 4 wins, Hyderabad Fillies Trial Stakes; 3rd Deccan Derby.

Little Wink: unraced.

Everynsky (by Everyday): as described.

Star Asset (by Everyday): as described.

19) QUEEN O'SCOTS

Queen O'Scots (Br, 1965)	Glasgow Paddock	Big Game — Bahram / Myrobella
		Annetta — Fairway / Caretta
	Big Bess	Hindostan — Bois Roussel / Sonibai
		Empress Catherine — Columcille / Bolarinia

QUEEN O'SCOTS: 6 wins, South India 1000 Guineas. Her first 2 foals died before racing. Her subsequent progeny are:

My Opinion (by Everyday): 9 wins, Galstaun Cup (1200 m, classes I and II, Calcutta), Governor's Trophy (1400 m, 3-yr-olds, Bangalore), Kunigal Stud Trophy.

Tippu Sultan (by Everyday): 3 wins, in training.

Lincoln (by Everyday): placed, in training.

20) SHANTINIKETAN

Shantiniketan (B, 1959)	Hyder Ali	Hyperion — Gainsborough / Selene
		Eclair — Ethnarch / Black Ray
	Dilbahar	Steel Helmet — Shell Transport / Hat Box
		Dancing Lily — Masked Jester / Silver Blessing

SHANTINIKETAN: 3 wins. Dam of:

Kadambari: 1 win in her short racing career.

Perfume: as described.

Royal Haven: 7 wins.

New Gold: did not win.

Amenity (by Everyday): 6 wins, Hyderabad Race Club Cup (1400 m, class III, Mysore).

21) STAR ABOVE

	Umidwar	Blandford Uganda
Hervine		
	New Moon	Solfo Selene
Star Above (Dk B, 1970)		
	Decorum	Orthodox Dignity
Request		
	Repay	Pay Up Silver Loan

STAR ABOVE: 1 win. Dam of:

Royal Jewel (by Everyday): 3 wins

Video Star: winner, in training.

22) BLUE BUTTERFLY

	Migoli	Bois Roussel Mah Iran
Prince Pradeep		
	Driving	Watling Street Snow Line
Blue Butterfly (B, 1972)		
	Hervine	Umidwar New Moon
Veronique		
	Hoverplane	Airborne Feriel

BLUE BUTTERFLY: unraced. Dam of:

Let Me Fly (by Everyday): 4 wins, Chief Minister's Gold Cup (1600 m, classes I and II, Mysore), Chief Minister's Cup (1200 m, class II, Bangalore; 3rd Indian 1000 Guineas

Cossack: 2 wins.

23) DIANA

		Hyperion	Gainsborough Selene
	Daybreak		
		L'Attaque	Big Game Spion Hill
Diana (B, 1968)			
		Khan Saheb	Atout Maitre Lady Emma
	Meherban		
		Meherunnissa	Donatello II Greek Muse

DIANA: 3 wins. Her first 2 foals died. Her subsequent progeny are:

Moment to Moment (by Everyday): 6 wins, K.M. Munshi Trophy (1600 m, class II, Bombay). His best performance was in the Indian Derby in which he finished an excellent 5th to Track Lightning. He won in class I.

Montevideo: 2 wins, in training.

24) INDIAN ROSE

		Migoli	Bois Roussel Mah Iran
	Red Indian		
		Red Briar	Owen Tudor Infra Red
Indian Rose (B, 1967)			
		Valerullah	Nasrullah Painted Vale
	Olipha		
		Dolcis	His Slipper Lady Olivia

INDIAN ROSE: 6 wins. Dam of:

Roses Roses: placed.

Cross the Floor (by Everyday): 6 wins, Chief Minister's Relief Fund Trophy (1200 m, class II, Bangalore).

Rising Rose: placed.

Colt (1982) by T.V. Sunday is in training.

25) LITTLE WINK

Little Wink (Ch, 1973)	Never Never	Never Say Die	Nasrullah Singing Grass
		Mixed Blessing	Brumeux Pot-pourri
	Not-a-Wink	Narrator	Nearco Phase
		Princess Louise	Prince Chevalier Tropical Sun

LITTLE WINK: unraced. Dam of:

Two Little Winks (by Everyday): 3 wins, Jayachamaraja Wadiyar Trophy; 2nd Nilgiris Gold Cup; 3rd Golconda Oaks.

Reciprocity (by Everyday): unraced.

26) MARTHA GUNN

Martha Gunn (B, 1969)	Scotch Crown	Jock II	Asterus Naic
		Sultan Mahal	Solario Firouze Mahal
	Village Girl	Selector	Fair Haven Painted Vale
		Fion Dearg	Hyacinthus Maighdean Mara

MARTHA GUNN: 2 wins. Dam of:

Crafty Admiral: 2 wins.

Evita (by Everyday): as described.

Erika: placed.

Battle Field: winner, in training.

Colt (1982) by T.V. Sunday is in training.

27) NOUVOLA

		Nosca	Abjer
			Capella
	Zinosca		
		Zina	Mirza II
			Drina
Nouvola			
(B, 1966)		Babbanio	My Babu
			Butterfly Blue
	Neon		
		Flying Fairy	Solonaway
			Hawa Bibi

NOUVOLA: 3 wins, Ramanatha Iyer Memorial Cup; 2nd Calcutta 1000 Guineas; 3rd Bangalore Fillies Trial Stakes. Dam of:

Flight to Glory: unraced.

Any Time (by Everyday): winner.

28) WORD PLAY

		Wild Risk	Rialto
			Wild Violet
	Worden II		
		Sans Tares	Sind
			Tara
Word Play			
(Ch, 1962)		Big Game	Bahram
			Myrobella
	Stage Fright		
		Bashful	Precipitation
			Saucy Sarah

WORD PLAY: ran at 3 years in England. She was then imported into India and retired to stud. Dam of:

Honee Boy: 4 wins.

Scrabble: 2 wins.

Gyrox: 1 win and once 2nd from only 2 starts. Sire.

Three Little Words: 2 wins.

Words of Wisdom: 7 wins, Kanteerava Gold Cup (2200 m, class III, Bangalore).

Give the Word: 8 wins, Aga Khan's Cup, Homi Mody Cup, Grand Western Trophy, Army Cup (1400 m, class II, Hyderabad); 2nd Indian Oaks; 3rd Indian and Bangalore 1000 Guineas.

Richbru (by Everyday): placed 3rd twice from only 3 starts.

29) ENCHANTRESS

Enchantress (Dk Br, 1969)	Glasgow Paddock	Big Game	Bahram Myrobella
		Annetta	Fairway Caretta
	Prestige	Sans Tache	Stardust Mouzelle
		Bleu de Ciel	Blue Booklet Sweet Lilac

ENCHANTRESS: 3 wins, Wiseman Cup, in her short racing career. Her 1st foal died. Her subsequent progeny are:

Ebonysky (by Everyday): 7 wins, winner in class II.

Filly (1979) by Al Marzouk is in training.

30) FABIHA

Fabiha (Dk B, 1967)	Asopo	Nimbus	Nearco Kong
		Assamenta	Norseman Assylia
	Eiram	Shahpoor	Solario Teresina
		Aunt Agnes	Lambert Simnel Cosmo Girl

FABIHA: 6 wins, Belfry Cup, Excelsior Stakes; 4th Indian Oaks. Dam of:

Mount Unique: 10 wins.

Divine Star: 2 wins.

Nobility: 5 wins; 2nd Indian 1000 Guineas and Oaks; 4th Indian St. Leger.

Flash Past (by Everyday): as described.

Charmer: 7 wins, South India Gold Cup, C.S. Loganathan Gold Cup), Nilgiris Gold Cup.

Casablanca: winner, in training.

31) LOYAL PRINCESS

Loyal Princess (B, 1972)	Cornish Flame	Hyperion	Gainsborough Selene
		Stratton Street	Fairway Devonshire House
	Frolic IV	Relic	War Relic Bridal Colors
		Freckle	Hyperion Fartuch

LOYAL PRINCESS: 3 wins. Dam of:

Black Tornado (by Everyday): 7 wins, Shantiniketan Cup (1600 m, class II, Bangalore).

Fashion Parade (by Everyday): won Hyderabad Free Handicap (1400 m, 3-yr-olds, Hyderabad), in training.

Filly (1982) by Everyday is in training.

32) MARK OVER

Mark Over (B, 1969)	The Wing	Major Portion	Court Martial Better Half
		Gondook	Chamier Rare Bird
	Big Bess	Hindostan	Bois Roussel Sonibai
		Empress Catherine	Columcille Bolarinia

MARK OVER: 7 wins, Stewards Gold Cup, Kumararaja M.A.M. Muthiah Cup; 3rd South India 1000 Guineas; Dam of:

Royal Game (by Everyday): 7 wins, Chief Minister's Cup (1200 m, class II, Bangalore), Maharani Tripurasundarammani Avaru Gold Cup, winner in class I.

Filly (1979, a twin) by Fair World, her last foal, is in training.

33) NEVER SO

		Nimbus	Nearco
Never So	Asopo		Kong
(Dk, Br, 1965)		Assamenta	Norseman
			Assylia
		Empyrean	Hyperion
	Never in Doubt		Ad Astra
		Manessa	Neapolitan
			Rhoda

NEVER SO: unraced. Dam of:

New Star: 1 win.

Starglow: placed 4th once from 7 starts.

Ever True: 6 wins, H.C. Clifton Cup.

Ever So (by Everyday): 2 wins, in training.

Filly (1981) by Nijinsky (India) is in training.

34) ZSA ZSA

		Crepello	Donatello II
Zsa Zsa	Orbit		Crepuscule
(Dk B, 1972)		Urshalim	Nasrullah
			Horama
		Tudor Melody	Tudor Minstrel
	Gavotte		Matelda
		Gayness	Merry Boy
			Denouement

ZSA ZSA: 5 wins, Indian Gold Vase, Turf Club Cup (1200 m, class II, Calcutta), Alokananda Stakes; 2nd Bengal Cup. Dam of:

Evangel (by Everyday): 4 wins.

(Readers may be wondering why a few horses by Everyday out of these mares have not been included in Table 15. It is because they are not members of his first 5 crops. They were foaled later. Several of these mares are still active and a few have again visited Everyday.)

Our first task is to determine how many of Everyday's mares are "Inherently superior". For this will clearly reveal his inherent merit. Studying his mares we find that most of them qualify. In determining Inherent superiority here, I made a slight modification. I included the entire tail female lines of all the mares (though I have not given them for reasons of space), but I did not include their 1st and 2nd maternal grandsires i.e. the 2nd and 3rd maternal grandsires of the progeny due to certain practical difficulties. I included only the sires of the mares i.e. the maternal grandsires of the progeny. By this criteria 21 mares qualify. (7 of them — Artic War, Donna Princess, Golden Smile, Miss Rebecca, Chamwort, Not-a-Wink and Word Play were got-abroad i.e. they were English, Irish or American mares. By Indian standards we can straightaway consider them to be Inherently superior.) But 13 mares — Gangotri, Green Flame, Perfume, Diamond Head, Eye to Eye, Gold Paprika, Hold the Bridge, Diana, Indian Rose, Martha Gunn, Enchantress, Loyal Princess and Never So-cannot claim to be Inherently superior. A few of them are definitely average, but by definition we have to consider all of them to be Inherently inferior.

Interestingly we find that Everyday produced classic winners and superior racers not only out of Inherently superior mares, but also out of Inherently inferior mares. This clearly reveals his "inherent" talent as a stallion in no uncertain terms. He not only gets classic winners and classic-placed out of Inherently superior mares (which is only to be expected — any successful stallion is sure to get superior progeny out of superior mares) but also out of average and substandard mares. He is so "dominating", so "powerful", that he is able to overcome, to cover-up, all the defects and weaknesses of substandard mares and still get superior progeny. This is the answer to the very important question we asked earlier:

"How do admittedly average and substandard mares i.e. Inherently inferior mares become successful producers?"

"Their success is entirely due to the outstanding stallions they were fortunate enough to visit."

It is unnecessary for me to repeat that only an outstanding horse — a horse with a superior race record, pedigree, conformation and temperament is going to become a stallion in the first place. Therefore it is not at all surprising that stallions have the power to get superior racers out of Inherently inferior mares. We can be sure that all successful stallions possess this power to some extent, but some are more powerful than the others. Let us precisely determine this power for Everyday and express it mathematically.

We already divided all the mares who visited him into two groups — Inherently superior and Inherently inferior. The 21 Inherently superior mares visited him 31 times producing 20 superior racers, while the 13 Inherently inferior mares visited him 19 times producing 10 superior racers. Therefore:

Percentage of success with   = $\dfrac{20}{31}$ x 100 = 65%
Inherently superior mares

Percentage of success with   = $\dfrac{10}{19}$ x 100 = 53%
Inherently inferior mares

The two quantities we have just calculated are of awesome importance. The first is easily understood. We have calculated his percentage of success with Inherently superior mares. Obviously higher the percentage the more successful the stallion is going to be.

But as we emphasized a stallion has got to serve average and substandard mares i.e. Inherently inferior mares as well. And since Inherently inferior mares outnumber the Inherently superior, a stallion's books are bound to be dominated by such mares. Only the very best stallions will serve a large number of Inherently superior mares. Therefore a stallion aspiring for success must possess the ability to get superior racers out of Inherently inferior mares. However we emphasized that as stallions themselves are outstanding or superior in most respects they do possess this ability. Biologists have named this ability. A stallion who possesses it is "prepotent." A prepotent organism can be defined as below:

A prepotent organism possesses a stronger fertilizing influence or power of transmitting hereditary qualities.

Therefore a stallion who has the ability to get superior racers out of Inherently inferior mares is prepotent. It is necessary for us to discuss this extremely important concept in depth.

The first point I want to emphasize is the aptitudes of the progenitors and the progeny do not come into the picture. Here we are referring to prepotence of class and not prepotence of aptitude. We will discuss prepotence of aptitude a little later. For example, a stallion who was a renowned stayer may well become a sire of sprinter-milers. If he is able to get superior sprinter-milers out of Inherently inferior mares, he is prepotent. The fact that some of those Inherently inferior mares possessed elements of stamina, or were stayers themselves, does not nullify or cancel his prepotence. He has got superior racers out of average and inferior mares; hence he is prepotent. *Therefore a stallion's percentage of success with Inherently inferior mares is a precise measure of his prepotence.* Note that his percentage of success with Inherently superior mares does not come into the picture.

Now think of another stallion. He has been able to get superior racers out of Inherently superior but *not* out of Inherently inferior mares. Is he prepotent? *No, he is not.* While he is a *successful* stallion, he is not a *prepotent stallion.* His success can be attributed to the high quality of his mares. Therefore these two percentages at once reveal a stallion's inherent capacity.

Let us go deeper and interpret these two vitally important percentages. Readers will readily agree that, in general, a stallion's percentage of success with Inherently superior mares is bound to be greater than his percentage of success with the Inherently inferior. Now think of two stallions. Both have the ability to get superior racers out of Inherently superior mares. But the former is prepotent while the latter is not. Which stallion will be more successful? Naturally the former. While he will get superior racers out of Inherently superior and Inherently inferior mares, the latter can get superior racers only out of Inherently superior mares. *Therefore prepotent stallions are invariably more successful than non-prepotent stallions.*

But there are a few exceptions to the above rule. Think of a stallion who is not prepotent but who has a very high percentage of success with Inherently superior mares. If he is fortunate enough to stand in a large stud farm and get superior mares year after year, he will become more successful than prepotent stallions. I will give an example of this type of stallion later.

The concept of prepotence does not apply to a few stallions. Think of a stallion like the great Nijinsky. From the very beginning his books have been truly outstanding. Therefore his magnitude of prepotence is bound to be very misleading as very few of his mares were Inherently inferior in the first place. But this does not mean Nijinsky is not prepotent. He did not get the opportunity to reveal his prepotence. Now it would be very foolish on my part to ask you to send some really substandard mares to him just to test whether he is prepotent or not. Therefore the concept of prepotence is hypothetical, inapplicable, in such cases.

Readers must note that these two percentages are independent of each other. One percentage is not a logical follow-up of the other. Frequently stallions excel with Inherently superior mares but do badly with Inherently inferior mares. Therefore a high percentage of success with the

Inherently superior does not guarantee a high, or even a reasonable, percentage of success with the Inherently inferior.

Now think of another stallion. He is prepotent — he has been able to get superior racers out of Inherently inferior mares. Now if we give him really outstanding mares will be automatically get a number of classic winners and champions? He need not. While he will get superior racers he may not get a classic or Group I winner. For there could be a ceiling, a limit, to which he can go. His maximum capacity is to get horses who are just above average, nothing more. He simply does not have the ability to get classic racers even out of outstanding mares. I will also give an example of this type of stallion.

A few readers may want to know whether any stallion excelled with Inherently inferior mares but not with Inherently superior mares. Such stallions are obviously very, very rare but a handful did exhibit this type of behaviour.

Finally we come to another extremely important point. *A stallion's percentage of success with Inherently superior and Inherently inferior mares is not independent of the total number of mares.* Suppose a stallion got 5 superior racers out of 25 Inherently superior mares i.e. his percentage of success is 20. Does this mean he will get 20 superior racers out of 100 Inherently superior mares? He need not. He may get only 17 superior racers or as few as 15 superior racers. It is unwise to assume that the percentage of success is the same for different numbers of mares. This is also true for Inherently inferior mares. This is because all stallions have a limit to which they can go. You cannot expect a stallion to sire a greater number of superior racers just because he has served a greater number of mares.

THE SIGNIFICANCE OF PREPOTENCE

I do not know whether readers have grasped the significance of prepotence But for prepotence racing and breeding as we know it would cease to exist. Why am I making such a sweeping statement? Imagine for a moment that the stallions of the world have lost their powers of prepotence. What does this mean? What will happen? This means *only* Inherently superior mares i.e. well-bred and/or well performed mares can get superior racers. Since such mares are not large in number the biggest owners are sure to buy up all their progeny. Therefore all the other owners are sure to lose interest as they cannot hope to own a superior racer. But happily this is not the case. Since stallions are prepotent, they have the ability to get superior racers out of average and substandard mares. Therefore a small owner who buys the progeny of these mares too has a chance of owning a superior racer. This sustains their interest and it keeps the sport going.

Coming back to Everyday we find that he is truly outstanding. He has excelled with Inherently superior and Inherently inferior mares. With such high percentages of success it is not surprising that he topped the Sires lists twice and finished second once. Note that his progeny out of Inherently inferior mares included 3 classic winners — Adelita, Zeeba and Evita and champion Every Time!

SPEED AND STAMINA COMPATIBILITY

Let us correlate the racing ability of the mares who visited Everyday with their progeny. Here we will completely ignore the pedigrees of the mares. The first step lies in identifying mares who were themselves superior on the course. Only 7 of the mares who visited him were superior. They were: Mumtaz, Not a Wink, Queen O'Scots, Nouvola, Fabiha, Mark Over and Zsa Zsa. Only 1 of them was a classic winner. These 7 mares visited Everyday only 10 times but with really spectacular results. The 10 visits yielded 7 superior racers including 5 classic winners!

Percentage of success with who were themselves superior racers $= \dfrac{7}{10} \times 100 = 70\%$

Percentage of success with mares who were themselves inferior racers $= \dfrac{23}{40} \times 100 = 57.5\%$

The percentage of success for mares who were inferior racers falls but not significantly. This clearly shows that Everyday has the ability to get superior racers out of well performed and badly performed mares. But I want to emphasize strongly that his best progeny were out of well performed mares. Mumtaz visited him twice producing multiple classic winners Grand Parade and Aristocrat; Not a Wink (a winner in England) visited him twice producing champion Everynsky and classic winner Star Asset.

We have again split his mares into two groups, as above, to see out of which type of mares he produced a greater number of superior racers. Readers must note that this division is different from the earlier one. Imagine a mare who was a superior racer. Assume that her sire was not a successful maternal grandsire and that her tail female line is not above average. In other words she is a mare who outran her pedigree. Therefore she is not Inherently superior and will not be included in that category. but she will be included in the category of mares who were themselves superior racers.

Let us go deeper. Two of his mares, Moon Shine and Green Flame, won 6 races and 5 races respectively. The latter won the Faridoon S. Chinoy Cup (1600 m, class III, Hyderabad). They are among the best racers in the category of mares who were themselves inferior racers. Moon Shine's first 3 visits to Everyday yielded 2 classic winners and Green Flame's 2 visits yielded a Derby winner! This further confirms our finding that Everyday excels with mares who demonstrated some ability on the course.

Let us correlate the racing aptitude of the mares who visited him with their progeny. A few readers may have guessed that Everyday gets genuine top class stayers only out of staying mares and short-distance racers out of short-distance mares. *In other words he is not prepotent for stamina i.e. he does not impart stamina to his progeny; he only consolidates the high class stamina of his mares in their progeny.* Mumtaz and Not a Wink are proof of the above. What would have happened if Everyday is prepotent for stamina? Then all his sprinter-milers would have developed into stayers. But as we have seen this was not the case.

PEDIGREE COMPATIBILITY

Once again we are going to split Everyday's mares into two groups — this time into well-bred and indifferently-bred mares. We already determined the criteria for a mare to qualify as well-bred. (Do not forget the modification I have made here. I have ignored the 2nd and 3rd maternal grandsires of the progeny.) Here we are ignoring their racing merit. Studying the pedigrees of all his mares we find that 21 are well-bred. These 21 mares are his 21 Inherently superior mares. But readers can easily understand that a stallion's Inherently superior and well-bred mares need not be the same, though in this case it is. We saw that these 21 well-bred mares visited him 31 times producing 20 superior racers. The 13 indifferentlybred mares visited him 19 times producing 10 superior racers. Therefore:

$$\text{Percentage of success with well-bred mares} = \frac{20}{31} \times 100 = 65\%$$

$$\text{Percentage of success with indifferently-bred mares} = \frac{10}{19} \times 100 = 53\%$$

Not surprisingly the well-bred mares have the advantage. But note that the indifferently-bred mares are not far behind. Therefore the pedigrees of the mares do not have a significant impact on the class of Everyday's progeny. He does almost equally well with well-bred and indifferently-bred mares.

But the pedigrees of the well-bred mares do influence the aptitude of his progeny. We saw that he sired classic stayers out of staying mares. But not all the dams of his stayers were themselves stayers. Then can we say that Everyday imparted stamina to his progeny? No, we cannot. For there are several sources of genuine high class stamina in the pedigrees of the mares who produced his stayers. In other words though these mares were non-stayers, they were bred to stay. Let us discuss each stayer individually.

> **Dear Donna and Abide:** We saw that their dam Donna Princess excelled in getting classic stayers.

> **Beckoning Dream:** He was definitely one of my favourites. A grand "old-fashioned" individual of the Captain Cuttle, Coronach type, the influence of the great Hurry On was very visible. The influence was obviously through his maternal grandsire Chamossaire, by Precipitation, by Hurry On. Sadly he . ran only 5 times winning 4 races. He did not get the chance to run in the classics. His legs could not support his massive frame — he was undoubtedly the heaviest horse in the country. He was retired to stud but unfortunately died after a couple of seasons. Sadly we do not see such horses today. We are definitely poorer by the loss.

> **Word-A-Day:** We say that his maternal grandsire Horatius is a maternal grandsire of stayers. There is stamina in his female line too. His 3rd dam produced Hardiesse who won the Cheshire Oaks; 3rd Yorkshire Oaks; 4th Epsom Oaks.

> **Adelita:** She seems to be the only exception to the rule. There are no sources of high class stamina close-up in her pedigree.

> **Moment to Moment:** Though his maternal grandsire Daybreak ran unplaced in England, he won 8 races in India including the Byculla Club Cup. His grandam Meherban too was a stayer. Her 8 victories included the Indian 1000 Guineas and Oaks.

While readers will not disagree with the above reasoning the more experienced will ask: "What about the mares who produced his sprinter-milers? Didn't any of them possess sources of genuine stamina?" The answer is they did. Mares like Moon Shine and Fabiha definitely possess sources of genuine stamina. Then why didn't they get stayers? The answer is their progeny too possessed some elements of stamina, for, as explained, they placed in the classics and other prestigious races over long distances.

Therefore Everyday sires horses who excel upto 2800 m out of mares strongly endowed with stamina, horses who excel upto 2000 m out of mares with less stamina and sprinter-milers out of mares with no stamina.

Let us now combine all our findings. What do we get? Everyday excels with well performed mares — an astonishing 70% success. If these mares are also well bred, well and good — 65% success with well-bred mares. But even if they are not well-bred it does not make a significant difference as he had 53% success with indifferently-bred mares.

In other words it is the racing merit of the mare and not her pedigree that plays a greater role in shaping her progeny.

Now we know the type of mares most compatible with Everyday.

Undoubtedly well performed and well-bred mares are the most compatible. Then come well performed mares. Next in line are well-bred but indifferently performed mares followed by indifferently-bred and indifferently performed mares.

We can base a stallion's "percentage of success" on an entirely different principle. Here we will ignore the mare's racing performance, pedigree and all other qualities. Instead we will focus our attention on her produce record. Was she a successful producer? How many superior racers did she get? Did she produce a superior racer by a stallion other than Everyday, or was her superior offspring by Everyday?

Among the 34 mares who visited Everyday at the time of writing, 7 are yet to have a runner by any other stallion. They are: Mumtaz, Mark My Words, Queen O'Scots, Little Wink, Nouvola, Loyal Princess and Zsa Zsa. Among the remaining 27 mares, 10 produced at least 1 superior racer by a stallion other than Everyday. Therefore:

Percentage of success for all the "Other stallions" taken as a whole $= \dfrac{10}{27} \times 100 = 37\%$

But 19 mares produced at least 1 superior racer by Everyday. Therefore:

Percentage of success for Everday $= \dfrac{19}{27} \times 100 = 70\%$

This single result alone confirms Everyday's prowess as a stallion. He has been able to get superior racers out of mares who failed to produce superior racers out of other stallions. In fact his percentage of success is almost double. Here we must note: A couple of mares produced superior racers out of stallions other than Everyday but not by Everyday. Several mares produced superior racers by Everyday and by other stallions, while other mares produced superior racers by Everyday only.

Therefore you must use all the methods available to determine a stallion's merit and behaviour. But do not mix up the different methods. When you are classifying mares on the basis of their race records, do not include a mare in the well preformed category just because she produced a superior racer. Similarly when you are classifying a mare on the basis of her stud performance, do not look at her pedigree or race record. Follow one methodology through and through.

CONCLUSION

I am sure readers have understood Everyday's behaviour without the slightest difficulty. His greatness lies in the fact that he has something to offer to every breeder. He is obviously the stallion for classic breeders. If you are fortunate enough to own really outstanding mares you would do well to breed them to him. The resulting progeny are sure to excel at the highest level. I wish to emphasize that he has very rarely "missed" getting stayers out of staying mares and mares bred to stay. And as we have seen he is also ideal for those interested in breeding sprinter-milers.

But it is not necessary for you to breed only outstanding mares to him. Since he is prepotent you can breed average and even substandard mares with very good results. Here conformation and temperament compatibility between him and the mare become very important.

Another hallmark of Everyday is his admirable consistency. He continues to excel. His 6th crop included 2 classic winners, Adelina and Classic Touch and 1 outstanding younger horse Kimberlite. His 7th crop produced Asset a superior sprinter. The members of his 8th crop are excelling. Lively Emprey won the Bangalore Derby and Arc de Triomphe while Eversun lifted the Indian 2000 Guineas. Idealist is developing into a good sprinter. *If there has been a slight fall in his performance, it is entirely due to the incompatible mares he served in the last few years.* Experienced readers would have noticed that his books included a distressingly large number of unraced and very badly raced mares. We have seen that such mares are not intensely compatible with him. To his eternal credit he has been able to get superior racers out of such mares also. But now that we have definitely determined the type of mares most compatible, breeders would do well to breed such mares to him. I am anxious that each of his future books should include at least a dozen mares of the calibre of Mumtaz, and there are such mares in the country.

He has made a splendid start as a maternal grandsire. He is already the maternal grandsire of Chaitanya Ratham (T.V. Sunday x Urvashi) Far And Above (Fair World x Dur-E-Jehan) and Robust (Road to Glory x Dear Donna) — 3 outstanding younger horses. He is also emerging as a sire of sires — Everynsky and Aristocrat have already started getting winners. There is no doubt that Everyday has raised the standard of the Indian thoroughbred considerably.

RAPPAREE

We studied Rapparee in some detail (chapter 3, pages 50-52). But I am coming back to him as I am anxious that readers know the quality of the mares he served. Further we have to determine the types of mares most compatible with him. His pedigree and race record have been given. We also determined his class and aptitude. Now let us study his entire stud career. As usual we will go step by step.

STEP 1

We have to identify all his superior racers.
They were:

Ocean Gold (1974): 9 wins, Jayachamaraja Wadiyar Cup, F.K. Irani Gold Cup (1400 m, class I, Mysore) ,Nanda Devi Cup, Governor's Gold Cup (1600 m, 3-yr-olds, Bangalore); 2nd Bangalore 2000 Guineas; 3rd Bangalore Arc de Triomphe.

Grizly (1976): 12 wins, Chief Minister's Cup (1200 m, class I, Bangalore), Mysore Race Club Cup (1200 m, class I, Hyderabad). (He was a top sprinter who won several races in class I.)

Vigoroso (1976): 8 wins, P.D. Bolton Trophy. (He was also a superior sprinter).

Fighting Force (1973): 8 wins, Indian Gold Vase, R.C.T.C. Gold Cup; 3rd Mysore 2000 Guineas.

Forever Glory (1974): he won 3 prestigious races in his first season including the Indian Produce Stakes (1200 m, 3-yr-olds, Calcutta) but unfortunately died.

Pancharathnam (1974): 11 wins, Maharani Tripurasundarammani Avaru Gold Cup, Shimoga Cup.

Big Time (1975): 12 wins, Hill Stamina Cup (2000 m, class III, Ootacamund), winner in class II.

Winfree (1973): 6 wins, World Wildlife Cup, Turf Club Cup.

Little Beaut (1975): 7 wins, Indian Produce Stakes, Karnataka Sub-Area Trophy (2000 m classes II and III, Mysore).

Carnival Queen (1973): 8 wins, winner in class II.

The Sting (1973): 4 wins, Golconda Cup.

Candide (1973): 11 wins, winner in class II.

Anmol Heera (1975): 12 wins.

Good Sort (1974): 9 wins.

Carson Troy (1977): 6 wins.

He had only 7 crops of 62 runners. Therefore:

$$\text{Percentage of superior racers from runners} = \frac{15}{62} \times 100 = 24\%$$

But let us go deeper. I classified the above 15 horses as superior, as they satisfied the definition. But among them only 4 — Ocean Gold, Grizly, Vigoroso and Fighting Force were genuine class I horses who won in that class. All the others were only class II winners. I then studied his average racers and found that 13 won in class III. Therefore in all fairness we can say that as many as 24 (13 + 11) of his progeny were marginally above average racers. Therefore:

$$\text{Percentage of marginally above average racers from runners} = \frac{24}{62} \times 100 = 39\%$$

I am sure readers have accurately gauged the calibre of his progeny. As explained he did not get a single classic winner. Only 4 of his progeny could win in the highest class. He specialized in getting good handicappers. Therefore he automatically belongs to the Good category.

STEP 2

We have to check whether his behaviour was Normal.

He was a consistent stallion who got superior and average racers in every crop except his last which had only 1 runner. He did not change his behaviour. But as he was unable to get classic winners or champions, he must be put among stallions who exhibit the first deviation from Normal behaviour.

STEP 3

The class of his colts and fillies:
His colts and fillies were equally good, but the colts had a slight advantage.

STEP 4

We have to determine the aptitude of his superior and average progeny.
We already determined that he was a specialist sire of sprinters and sprinter-milers. We saw that his progeny excelled up to 1400 m. Even though a few of his progeny won over long distances, they were not genuine stayers.

STEP 5

We have to study his mares in detail to determine out of which types of mares he produced superior racers, and identify the mares most compatible with him. Then we must correlate the racing performances and pedigrees of his mares with their offspring. This step is particularly important as it will tell us whether Rapparee's behaviour was "natural" and "inherent" or "artificial". What do I mean by this? We saw that he did not get a single classic winner or stayer. But this does not mean he was incapable of doing so. His mares may have been so bad that even the very best stallions may not have got classic winners out of them. His mares may not have included stayers or mares bred to stay, thereby preventing him from siring genuine high class stayers. In essence did Rapparee have enough opportunity to reveal his talent in full? The answer is an emphatic yes. He had excellent mares. He had ample opportunities. The weaknesses and deficiencies in his performance were entirely due to his own inherent lack of talent. Table 16 lists all his runners with their dams.

TABLE 16

PROGENY OF RAPPAREE WHO RAN (All his crops)

Dam	Offspring
1972	
1) Pot-pourri	Great Memories
2) Sea Dragon	Evergreen
1973	
3) Centre Court	The Sting
4) Cherie	Padma Shri
5) Cold Stream	Fortune's Flame
6) Gavotte	Carnival Queen
7) Iyella	Oliva
8) Kalied	Red Bud
9) Manna Hill	Turf Star
10) Mary Stuart	Winfree
11) Olipha	Philemon
12) Pandorea	Repartee
13) Princess Shaara	Noble Shaara
14) Roman Princess	Mr. Mysterious
15) Royal Way	Le Chaim
16) Shy Lass	Candide
17) Sona Lakshmi	Fighting Force
18) Sweetie Pie	Honey Bunch
19) Umberleigh	Burnt Amber
20) West Wave	Jai Mala
1974	
21) Bara Bibi	Luminous
22) Centre Court	Gonzales
23) Cherie	Subodhi
24) Gavotte	Nike
25) Home Work	Distinctions
26) I'll Make Up	Good Sort
27) Mary Poppins	Rhapsody
28) Om-Sakthi	Pancharathnam
29) Princess Huma	Forever Glory
30) Princess Shaara	Ocean Gold

TABLE 16 (cont.)

Dam	Offspring
1975	
31) Alexandria	Anmol Heera
32) Antiope	Romp Home
33) Centre Court	Pict
34) Good Year	Sher Beta
35) Gypsy Rose	Wanderer
36) Montana	Ocean of Love
37) Palace Girl	Harvester
38) Pandorea	Super Win
39) Princess Huma	Little Beaut
40) Silent Screen	Big Time
41) Subianca	Man About Town
42) Taking Ways	Conquest
1976	
43) Lovely Smitha	Cherry Hinton
44) Malina	Cantherisfly
45) Montana	Grizly
46) Noor Ul Ayn	Realert
47) Pure Heart	Victrix
48) Santham	Clique
49) Taking Ways	Vigoroso
1977	
50) Ardent Empress	Ardency
51) Fair Challenge	Strong Gale
52) Golden Dream	Grand Palace
53) Grecian Flower	Red Alert
54) Messenger Girl	Uncle's Love
55) Portrait Attachment	Outstanding
56) Princess Simoneal	Man of Vision
57) River Port	Shannon
58) Shiraz	Carson Troy
59) Super Money	Bhairavi Didi
60) Taletta	Expert Opinion
61) Tudor Rose	Bloodline
1978	
62) Streaking	Cinema King

As before our first task is to determine how many of his mares were Inherently superior. In order to save time and space I completed the exercise myself instead of asking readers to do it. 53 mares visited him 62 times producing 15 superior racers. The pedigree of I mare Princess Huma is unknown. (But she was a superior racer. Her 9 victories included the Maharaja's Gold Cup [Mysore] and Governor's Cup [Calcutta]. She also placed 2nd eight times.) Among the remaining 52 mares, 23 were Inherently superior. They included as many as 10 got-abroad mares: Gavotte, Iyella, Kalied, Olipha, Pandorea, Umberleigh, West Wave, Subianca, Taletta and Portrait Attachment. These 23 Inherently superior mares visited him 25 times but produced only 6 superior racers. The remaining 29 Inherently inferior mares visited him 35 times producing 7 superior racers. (Princess Huma and her progeny have been excluded from this calculation.) Therefore:

$$\frac{\text{Percentage of success with}}{\text{Inherently superior mares}} = \frac{6}{25} \times 100 = 24\%$$

$$\frac{\text{Percentage of success with}}{\text{Inherently inferior mares}} = \frac{7}{35} \times 100 = 20\%$$

Clearly Rapparee was prepotent to a certain extent. He was able to get superior racers out of average and substandard mares. *But surprisingly he was unable to take full advantage of all the Inherently superior mares (including several got-abroad mares) who visited him.* His percentage of success with Inherently superior mares is only marginally higher than his percentage of success with Inherently inferior mares. Doesn't this clearly show that there was a ceiling, a limit, to his capacity? Clearly his maximum ability was to get only marginally superior racers. Even out of got-abroad and outstanding mares he could not do better.

SPEED AND STAMINA COMPATIBILITY

Let us correlate the racing ability of the mares who visited him with their progeny. His mares included 14 superior racers:

Gavotte: 2 wins in England. 8 wins in India; 3rd Czechoslovakia Cup.

Iyella: winner at 2 yrs. in England. 3 wins in India. (She defeated top horses like Our Select and Bakhtawar.)

Kalied: winner and placed in England. 4 wins in India, Queen Elizabeth II Cup, Calcutta Gold Cup.

West Wave: placed twice in England. 6 wins in India, Czechoslovakia Cup.

I'll Make Up: 3 wins, Fillies Trial Stakes (Calcutta).

Om-Sakthi: 16 wins, South India Derby, Oaks and 1000 Guineas, Bangalore Fillies Trial Stakes.

Princess Huma: as described.

Gypsy Rose: 9 wins, Rajah Sir Annamalai Chettiar Cup, winner in class II.

Palace Girl: 5 wins, H.M. Mehta Gold Cup.

Subianca: placed at 2 yrs. in England. 8 wins in India, Indian Gold Vase (Calcutta), Indian Express Gold Cup, Chief Minister's Gold Cup. (She also placed in several prestigious races.)

Taking Ways: 5 wins; 2nd Calcutta 1000 Guineas and Oaks.

Lovely Smitha: 4 wins, Bangalore Oaks.

Grecian Flower: 8 wins, Gen. Obaidullah Khan Gold Cup, Asaf Jah VII Memorial Cup.

Portrait Attachment: 2 wins at 2 yrs. in England. In India she won the Southern Command Cup and placed 2nd in the Rajpipla Gold Cup.

These 14 mares visited Rapparee 16 times producing 6 superior racers. The remaining 39 mares visited him 46 times producing 9 superior racers. Therefore:

$$\text{Percentage of success with mares who were themselves superior racers} = \frac{6}{16} \times 100 = 38\%$$

$$\text{Percentage of success with mares were themselves inferior racers} = \frac{9}{46} \times 100 = 20\%$$

Clearly the well performed mares had the advantage.

Now let us determine the aptitudes of the mares who visited him. His mares included several genuine top class stayers like Kalied, Om-Sakthi, Princess Huma, Taking Ways, Lovely Smitha and Grecian Flower. *Therefore Rapparee had sufficient opportunity to sire stayers. The fact that he did not was entirely due to his own inherent inability.* In fact he could not even get genuine milers out of the above mares. His progeny out of them were no different from his other progeny. But these mares naturally produced classic stayers when they visited other stallions as below:

Om-Sakthi: dam of among others:

Arrangement (colt, 1976, by Red Indian) : 6 wins, Stewards Gold Cup (2400 m, classes II and III, Mysore), Governor's Cup (2600 m, classes III and IV, Madras); 2nd South India Derby and St. Leger.

Weight in Gold (filly, 1978, by Red Rufus): 6 wins, South India St. Leger, Maharaja's Gold Cup (1600 m, class I, Mysore), 2nd Bangalore 1000 Guineas and Oaks? Mysore City Gold Cup (2000 m, classes I and II, Mysore).

Taking Ways: dam of among others:

Black Swan (filly, 1973, by Orbit): 3 wins; 2nd Indian Oaks.

Lovely Smitha: dam of among others:

So Smitten (filly, 1979, by Gombos): 7 wins, Prince Khartoum Cup (1800 m, class II, Bombay), Turf Club Cup (2400 m, classes III and IV, Bangalore).

Grecian Flower: dam of among others:

Greek Tycoon (colt, 1980, by Gombos or Malvado): 3 wins; neck 2nd in the R.R. Ruia Gold Cup. (The horse who beat him, Charon, went on to win the Indian Turf Invitation Cup.)

It is clear that Rapparee completely cancelled all the elements of stamina in his mares.

PEDIGREE COMPATIBILITY

Rapparee's books included a number of well-bred mares. 21 well-bred mares visited him 23 times but produced only 5 superior racers. 31 indifferently-bred mares visited him 37 times producing 8 superior racers. Therefore:

Percentage of success with with well-bred mares $= \dfrac{5}{23} \times 100 = 22\%$

Percentage of success with indifferently-bred mares $= \dfrac{8}{37} \times 100 = 22\%$

(Princess Huma has naturally not been included in the above calculation.)

We find that Rapparee has done equally well with well-bred and indifferently-bred mares! Therefore the pedigree of the mare has no influence on the offspring. This result is not very surprising. Recall our first finding. We found that he did almost equally well with Inherently superior and Inherently inferior mares.

We saw that his mares included a number of stayers who also produced stayers. His mares also included a number of mares bred to stay but who did not stay. Needless to say he failed to sire stayers out of these mares also.

It is time for us to recapitulate all that we have learnt. First I will explain his limitations and then highlight his strength.

By any measure he had excellent mares. Very few stallions in India (till recently) had such high quality mares. 10 of his mares were got-abroad. They included mares like Gavotte (by Tudor Melody), Pandorea (by Princely Gift) and Iyella (by Eudaemon). 23 of his mares were Inherently superior. 14 were superior racers including winners in England and classic winners in India. 21 were well-bred.

Let us see how these mares fared with other stallions. Not surprisingly they excelled. 28 of them were able to produce at least 1 superior racer out of another stallion. And, as we saw, they included classic winners, classic-placed and several class I winners. But Rapparee was able to produce superior racers out of only 13 of them. (5 mares had runners by Rapparee only.) Therefore:

$$\text{Percentage of success for all the "other stallions" taken as a whole} = \frac{28}{48} \times 100 = 58\%$$

$$\text{Percentage of success for Rapparee} = \frac{13}{48} \times 100 = 27\%$$

A calamitous drop to less than half the earlier percentage!

Therefore, keeping all these factors in mind, Rapparee was very disappointing. He did not make use of the ample opportunities that were available to him. Other stallions were twice as good. It seems that he was not worthy of our patronage.

But let us not reject him in a hurry. We have yet to pinpoint the types of mares most compatible with him. Theoretically Inherently superior mares who were also well performed were most compatible. But practically no breeder would even dream of sending such mares to him if he is active. For would you not send such mares to the best stallions in the country and try to breed classic horses? Well performed mares come next, but again you will select vastly superior stallions for them. Now think of indifferently-bred mares who were average sprinter-milers. Remember such mares are large in number and can be cheaply purchased. You will not try to breed classic horses out of such mares. But you will definitely be anxious to breed average — above average — racers from them. *A stallion like Rapparee is most ideal for the purpose.* Remember 45% of his runners were marginally above average handicappers who won their share of races. They also earned significant sums of money in the process. Therefore progeny of Rapparee were in demand. They were sought after. This was his greatest strength.

There is a fascinating aspect of his behaviour. We saw that other stallions were twice as successful. But he was able to get superior racers out of 5 mares who failed to get superior racers out of other stallions. In other words Rapparee failed to get superior racers out of mares who produced superior racers by other stallions, but was, to an extent, able to get superior racers out of mares who failed to get superior racers by other stallions! Therefore Rapparee was to an extent suitable for mares who were disappointing producers.

The next question is: Among the hundreds of average and substandard mares, who would have been most compatible? In such cases conformation (and temperament) compatibility decides. We have to study the conformation of the stallion in detail and determine his strengths and weaknesses. The mare's conformation should be such that her defects can be overcome, as far as possible, by the stallion.

By the same reasoning when we are buying an offspring of a stallion like Rapparee, we must select an individual with perfect or near perfect conformation. For the pedigree of the mare is not the decisive factor. Therefore we will naturally "give" pedigree for conformation. We will prefer a horse with perfect conformation even if his dam is indifferently-bred, rather than a horse with defects in conformation even if his dam is very well-bred. But think of a stallion for whom the pedigree of the mare is the deciding factor. For the progeny of such stallions we will naturally "give" conformation for pedigree.

We have just discussed two stallions who were successful at different levels. But I want to emphasize once again that both had sufficient opportunities which they utilized in different ways. If a stallion has failed to sire a sufficient number of superior progeny, we will say he is moderate or even a failure. But before we pass this judgement we must check whether he had sufficient opportunity. Do we not come across talented stallions who had the misfortune of being very poorly patronized? They just did not get a chance. They were never popular, let alone "fashionable", at any stage of their stud careers. I said earlier that it is dangerous to give excuses for a stallion. He has got to fight his way to the top. While I have not changed my mind, I will now describe a stallion whom I consider to be very talented, although his performance has been modest.

PRINCE KHARTOUM

		Rockefella	Hyperion / Rockfel
	Rock of Gibraltar		
		Toquade	Premier Baiser / Tonkette
Prince Khartoum (Ch, 1968)			
		Elopement	Rockafella / Daring Miss
	Pink Bamboo		
		Paeonia	Palestine / Tenerezza

We saw that Prince Khartoum is a champion son of Rock of Gibraltar whose 7 victories, from only 11 starts, included the Invitation Cup in record time. He won from 1400 m to 2400 m. He was retired to stud in 1973.

STEP 1

His superior racers were:

Affreen (1975): 7 wins, Madras Cup (1400 m, class I, Bangalore); 3rd Bangalore Fillies Trial Stakes.

True Seven Hills (1976): 9 wins, Madras Cup (2000 m, classes I and II, Hyderabad), S.N. Reddy Memorial Cup, Red Indian Cup (2200 m, class III, Hyderabad); 3rd Golconda St. Leger; 4th Golconda Derby.

Be My Friend (1977): 12 wins, Asaf Jah VII Memorial Cup (beating Byerly Brigade who later won the Deccan Derby), Weight in Gold Cup (2000 m, class I, Ootacamund), Well Done Cup (2000 m, class I, Ootacamund). He was a colt well up to classic standard but unfortunately did not run in any classic.

First Flight (1974): 2 wins. In his first season he finished 2nd in 3 prestigious races in Bombay, his only starts: The India Cup (1200 m, 2-yr-olds), Ahmed I. Rahimtoola Gold Cup (1000 m, 3-yr-old colts and geldings) and the Excelsior Stakes (1200 m, 3-yr-olds). In doing so he defeated several superior racers including Muffin winner of the Indian Oaks. Sadly he did not run in the next two years indicating that he had a bad setback in training. If he had raced normally he would have definitely been superior. Therefore let us consider him to be a superior racer.

Fork Lightning (1975): 7 wins, winner in class II.

I have not calculated his percentage of superior racers from runners as his first 4 crops had only 18 runners.

STEP 2

We have to check whether his behaviour was Normal.

Since he has had very small crops we really cannot judge whether his behaviour is Normal or not. We have to wait till he has got a sufficient number of runners.

STEP 3

The class of his colts and fillies:
His colts and fillies were equally good.

STEP 4

The aptitude of his superior and average progeny:

Prince Khartoum is clearly a specialist sire of stayers. True Seven Hills and Be My Friend have been described. Others included Sudan Princess whose victories included the Freedom Fighters' Plate (1800 m, class III, Bombay) and J.K. Irani Plate (2400 m, classes III and IV, Bombay), Pardalis who won the M.D. Petit Plate (1800 m, class III, Bombay) and Fairway Prince who won the Baji Prasad Memorial Cup (1800 m, class III, Hyderabad).

Even though I wrote that it is unwise to classify inferior horses, I want to mention that quite a few of his inferior racers were also stayers. They included: Polygraph (winner over 2000 m), Real Smasher (winner over 1800 m) and Melinda (winner over 2400 m).

The exceptions were Affreen and Fork Lightning. The former excelled over 1400 m winning 6 of her 7 races over the distance. The 7th was over 1200 m. The latter won up to 1400 m.

STEP 5

We have to study his mares in detail to determine out of which types of mares he produced superior racers. Then we must identify the mares most compatible with him. But first we have to judge the quality of his mares as a whole and see whether he had sufficient opportunity. Table 17 lists all his runners with their dams.

TABLE 17

PROGENY OF PRINCE KHARTOUM WHO RAN (first 4 crops only)

Dam	Offspring
1974	
1) Fair Flight	First Flight
2) Golden Heaven	Sudan Princess
3) Pollyanna	Polygraph
4) Season's Greetings	Happy Day
5) Silver River	Princess Kirti
6) Spotted Beauty	Persian Beauty
1975	
7) Antiquary	Saboroso
8) Flash Lightning	Fork Lightning
9) Ma Bear	Pardalis
10) Vijayalaxmi	Affreen
1976	
11) Enchantment	Real Smasher
12) Fair Sailing	Fairway Prince
13) Matterhorn	True Seven Hills
1977	
14) Antiquary	Sorrento
15) Enchantment	Muezzin
16) Pretty One	Lucky Victory
17) Soorangana	Be My Friend
18) Sugar	Melinda

We have to determine the quality of these mares. Studying them I found that only 6 of the 16 mares were Inherently superior. Only 4 were superior racers and only 6 were well-bred. And as if to cinch the issue only 3 mares produced superior racers out of other stallions. Honestly what can you expect a stallion, however superior he may be, to do with such mares? This is not all. Ironically 4 of the 6 Inherently superior mares (Fair Flight, Pollyanna, Silver River and Spotted Beauty) visited him in his first year at stud when he had not settled down fully. Therefore he could not take advantage of them. Sadly his subsequent books included only 2 Inherently superior mares, Antiquary and Ma Bear. (These 2 mares are well-bred and they are also successful producers.) Yet out of such inferior mares Prince Khartoum produced 4 superior racers. In short Prince Khartoum produced superior racers out of indifferently-bred and badly performed mares who were also unsuccessful producers! Now can anyone deny that Prince Khartoum is very talented? Is he not prepotent? Is he not a stallion of tremendous inherent merit? Is he not sure to get classic winners and superior racers out of good mares? But these are not his only plus points. We will come across one more.

SPEED AND STAMINA COMPATIBILITY

We saw that the Prince has already sired a handful of stayers. But we also saw that his mares were utterly substandard. Obviously they do not possess sources of genuine, high class stamina in their pedigrees. *Therefore Prince Khartoum is prepotent for stamina i.e. he imparts stamina to his progeny.* Notice that this behaviour is different from Everyday's or Rapparee's. Everyday merely consolidated the high class stamina of the dam in the offspring while Rapparee cancelled all the stamina of the dam in the offspring. But Prince Khartoum gave stamina to his progeny. This is especially true in the case of True Seven Hills, Be My Friend and Sudan Princess.

We have just extended the concept of prepotence. You must not confuse prepotence of class with prepotence of aptitude i.e. in this case prepotence of stamina. A stallion who is prepotent for class has the ability to get superior racers out of Inherently inferior mares. The aptitudes of the stallion, mare and offspring do not come into the picture. But now think of a stallion who had the ability to get classic stayers out of Inherently superior mares who were not stayers and whose pedigrees were not strong in stamina. Is he prepotent? He is obviously not prepotent for class but he is prepotent for stamina. He has the ability to sire superior stayers out of non-staying mares.

Now think of a stallion who is prepotent for class and stamina. What will be his behaviour? He will be able to get superior stayers out of Inherently inferior mares who were non-stayers and who do not possess elements of stamina in their pedigrees! Can there be a stallion who is prepotent for speed? Yes, there can. A stallion who sires sprinter-milers out of mares who were specialist stayers or extreme stayers is obviously prepotent for speed. But a stallion who sires sprinter-milers out of mares who excelled over the entire range of distances is not prepotent for speed, as the mares possessed some speed.

Therefore when somebody tells you that a stallion is prepotent, you must at once ask him to elaborate whether the stallion is prepotent for class or aptitude or for both.

Readers must note that the concept of prepotence has been explained in other ways. These explanations include the aptitude of the stallion concerned. But I once again emphasize that the above explanation, which I feel is superior, does not include the aptitude of the stallion. For I have interpreted the word prepotent as follows: *The ability to give something to the offspring which the dam lacks.* A stallion who is prepotent for class gives class to his progeny i.e. he gets superior racers out of mares who lack class i.e. Inherently inferior mares. Similarly a stallion who is prepotent for stamina gives stamina to his progeny i.e. he gets stayers out of non-staying mares. The aptitude the stallion himself exhibited on the course does not come into the picture.

PEDIGREE COMPATIBILITY

We already noted that Prince Khartoum produced superior racers out of indifferently-bred mares.

I am sure readers now have a clear picture of Prince Khartoum's ability. Even though he is prepotent for class and stamina, staying mares and mares bred to stay are clearly most suitable for him. For his percentage of success with such mares is sure to be greater than his percentage of success with other mares. I am adamant that he has the ability to get classic winners. But sadly he has not been able to catch the eye of breeders. For reasons that are not clear to me, he seems to be active every alternate year only. In 1980 he did not have a single offspring entered for sale in the R.W.I.T.C. Auction at Bombay. In 1981 he had 5 progeny. But again in 1982 he did not have a single offspring. In the subsequent year 3 of his progeny were entered for sale. But even now I feel it is not too late. Breeders can still make use of his abundant talent.

Turf historians know a number of stallions like Prince Khartoum — enormously talented individuals yearning for half a chance. Definitely there must be a number of such stallions in your country. You would do well to identify them, especially if you are a small breeder or owner. Make a list of all the apparently average (and even substandard) stallions who have sired a handful of superior racers. Then, just as we did, investigate the quality of all their mares. You will surely find a few stallions who have done well with very poor mares. And if you can pinpoint their behaviour, all the better. With these stallions you can take on the big

breeders on almost equal terms. Nominations to these stallions are literally given away. Their progeny can be purchased at bargain-basement
prices. (These stallions are obviously not for market breeders.) But a word
of caution. You must be very thorough in your research. Otherwise all
your plans will end in a disaster. But what is more important is that you
must be emotionally prepared to patronize such stallions. (We feel so secure
when we buy the progeny, or breed to, "fashionable" stallions. After all
we are only following the footsteps of a large and distinguished group who
surely cannot be wrong. Then even if we fail we console ourselves by
saying that we gave ourselves every chance!) You must be prepared to
leave the main road and take a seldomly used by-lane with the fullest confidence. If you are prepared to do so the rewards can be great.

PUNJAB

Punjab (Dk B, 1963)	Pardal	Pharis II	Pharos Carissima
		Adargatis	Asterus Helene de Troie
	Indian Night	Umidwar	Blandford Uganda
		Fairly Hot	Solario Fair Cop

Punjab raced in England. At 2 years he ran only twice. At 3 years
he placed 2nd in the Gulford Stakes and Kennett Maiden Stakes, his only
starts. He was imported into India and retired to stud.

He developed into a Border-line classic stallion, getting 3 classic winners and several superior racers. He was the champion stallion in 1975-'76
In the same year he also topped in "Number of wins and places" with
74 and 144 respectively. He also topped the "Number of winners" list
with 27 winners. The next year he was 9th leading stallion. His peak was
in 1975-'76, but he did very well in the earlier years too.

STEP 1

His superior progeny were:

Pyare Miya (1971): won the Indian Derby. His career was truly
unique. He lifted the Indian Derby as a maiden and failed to
win a race afterwards.

Majolica (1972): 8 wins, South India and Bangalore 1000 Guineas, Bangalore Oaks, Tamil Nadu Commemoration Gold Cup (deadheat with Jugnu).

Grand Vision (1972): 7 wins, South India 2000 Guineas.

Glad News (1969): 8 wins; 2nd Calcutta Oaks.

Crepes Suzette (1970): 6 wins, Maharaja Jagaddipendra Narayan Bhup Bahadur of Cooch Behar Memorial Cup, Indian Gold Vase (twice); 2nd Calcutta 1000 Guineas.

Charlotte Bronte (1970): 12 wins, Rajyotsava Gold Cup, Sharavathi Cup; 3rd Bangalore 1000 Guineas.

Jugnu (1971): 13 wins, Tamil Nadu Commemoration Gold Cup; 4th Bangalore 2000 Guineas and St. Leger, Deccan Derby, Hyderabad Colts Trial Stakes.

Auro Flame (1973): 16 wins, Ardent Knight Cup (1400 m, class I, Bangalore).

Grand Marque (1971): 10 wins, Mount Everest Cup, Ashwapriya Cup.

Beatrix Potter (1970): 7 wins.

Punjabi Maid (1970): 10 wins, Chief Minister's Gold Cup.

Caterina (1972): 10 wins, Stewards Cup (2200 m, class II, Bangalore), Sharavathi Cup.

Sporting Life (1976): 10 wins, World Wildlife Cup (2000 m, class II, Calcutta), Bengal Area Cup (2200 m, classes II and III, Calcutta).

Character (1972): 12 wins, Chief Minister's Gold Cup (1600 m, classes II and III, Madras).

Great Seer (1972): 8 wins, Army Cup (1600 m, class II, Hyderabad).

Charlemagne (1972): 8 wins.

Great Parade (1978): 9 wins, Padmaja Naidu Memorial Cup.

Imperial King (1976): 8 wins, Indian Air Force Golden Jubilee Trophy.

Fire Dance (1971): 14 wins.

Grand Haven (1969): 7 wins, Turf Club Cup.

Citation [India] (1970): 7 wins, A.M.K.M.CT. Muthukaruppan Chettiar Memorial Cup.

Las Palmas (1971): 7 wins, Stewards Cup (1200 m, class III, Madras), winner in class II.

Not So Gentle (1974): 7 wins.

David Mike (1969): 6 wins.

He had large crops up to 1972. Then breeders seemed to have lost interest in him. (More and more imported stallions were taking up stud duties.) His latter crops were small. Inevitably his larger crops produced a greater number of superior racers. He is still active.

He produced the above 24 superior racers from 10 crops of 92 foals. Therefore:

$$\text{Percentage of superior racers from foals*} = \frac{24}{92} \times 100 = 26\%$$

* Here I have made a slight modification. I have calculated the percentage of superior racers from foals instead of runners.

STEP 2

Punjab's behaviour was Normal. He did not deviate in any way. In view of his excellent performance, it would be fair to say that he could have continued to do well in his later years too had he got the same opportunities.

STEP 3

His colts and fillies were equally good.

STEP 4

Punjab is a versatile sire. He has got sprinters, milers, stayers and horses who excelled over the range of distances. While Majolica was a filly with an ideal blend of speed and stamina, the same cannot be said of Pyare Miya. As mentioned the Indian Derby was his sole victory and he gained it entirely due to his superior stamina. (A few maintain that he was a "below average" Indian Derby winner. But I cannot altogether agree. His time was better than "above average" Indian Derby winners like Prince Khartoum or Commanche.)

His other stayers were Glad News and Grand Haven. Caterina's record is a bit surprising. She excelled over 1200 m winning 4 races, but was then switched to the Stewards Cup over 2200 m. She won the race by only a short-head but she beat a strong field which included several true stayers. The next year she went back to her favourite distance and won the Air Command Cup (1200 m, class II, Hyderabad). Charlemagne too was similar. He was essentially a sprinter-miler but managed to win the Vijayanagar Gold Cup (2200 m, class IV, Bangalore). Even though Sporting Life scored over long distances, we cannot consider him to be a true stayer. His principal victories were over 1600 m. Special mention must be made of one redoubtable stayer, Emperor of Kiliyanur. A specialist stayer, his 10 victories included 4 wins over 2000 m, 3 wins over 2400 m and 1 win over 2600 m — the Governor's Cup in Madras which was his most prestigious.

His specialist sprinters were Fire Dance, Auro Flame (he also scored over 1400 m), Not So Gentle and Great Parade (he won once over 1400 m). Most of his other progeny were sprinter-milers.

STEP 5

We have to study his mares and see out of which types of mares he produced superior progeny. Then we must determine the type of mares most compatible with him. I have completed this step and without going into details will just present the results:

On the whole he had excellent mares. Many were Inherently superior or well-bred. His mares also included winners in England and classic winners in India. Several were very successful producers. But inevitably some were inferior.

Studying the dams of his superior racers, we find that Punjab is prepotent. He got superior racers out of Inherently superior and Inherently inferior mares. He got 9 superior racers out of 8 Inherently inferior mares, a considerable achievement. But the Inherently superior mares had the advantage

SPEED AND STAMINA COMPATIBILITY

Let us study the racing performances of his mares. Only 6 of the mares who produced his superior racers were well performed:

Gladness: 7 wins, Bangalore Fillies Trial Stakes, Douetil Memorial Cup.

Great Campo: 2 wins in England.

Bia: 2 wins in England.

Crystal Crown: 10 wins, South India Oaks.

Om-Sakthi: as described (page 176).

Varctic: 1 win, McLean Cup; 3rd Goff's Sales Nursery Handicap.

Once again Punjab's inherent talent is obvious. 17 of his superior racers were out of mares who were average or substandard on the course.

At this stage readers will ask: "If Punjab is so inherently superior, he ought to have been more successful — like Everyday or Young Lochinvar. Why wasn't he? I will answer the question immediately. The well performed mares who visited him included classic winners like Om-Sakthi and Crystal Crown. (They were well-bred and were also successful producers.) But Punjab failed to get genuine high class stayers out of them. Om-Sakthi visited him twice getting Santham and Character. Neither were stayers. The latter, as explained, was a good miler. Crystal Crown produced Charlemagne who as explained was a sprinter-miler though. he won a 2200 m race in class IV. But like Rapparee we cannot say that Punjab cancels the stamina of his dams. For remember he sired genuine stayers like Pyare Miya, Majolica, Caterina, Grand Haven and Emperor of Kiliyanur.

But without a shadow of doubt he frequently "missed" getting genuine high class stayers out of staying mares. This is his major weakness. It is this weakness that prevented him from matching the performance of Everyday or Young Lochinvar.

Therefore Punjab sometimes cancels the stamina of the dam but sometimes preserves it enabling the offspring to stay.

PEDIGREE COMPATIBILITY

Among the 20 mares who produced his superior progeny, 12 were well-bred. They were: Beckford Belle, Gladness, Great Campo, Bia, Gloriana, Neemah, Crystal Crown, God Bless, Om-Sakthi, Varctic, Gentle Art and Mimion. They were responsible for 15 of his superior racers. Therefore we find that he has been able to get superior racers out of indifferently-bred mares as well. But well-bred mares had the advantage.

Many of his well-bred mares were bred to stay. But Punjab failed to take advantage of them and get superior stayers. Ironically his books included a number of such mares. Among them were: Green Sari, Home Work, Highland Fling, Not Guilty III, Heather Belle, Fair Verdict, Royal Highness and Mica. Many of these mares were dams of classic stayers out of other stallions.

CONCLUSION

Even though Punjab was the champion stallion once and sire of 3 classic winners, we cannot consider him to be outstanding. For clearly he has his limitations. We saw that he failed to sire superior stayers out of staying mares or well-bred mares bred to stay. A more serious limitation is his inability to take advantage of a number of really outstanding mares. *If he could not have got superior stayers out of them, he could have at least got superior sprinter-milers.* But he did not. In other words his percentage of success with Inherently superior mares was not high. Clearly there is a ceiling to his ability. *The fact that he sired some superior racers out of Inherently inferior mares does not alter this conclusion.*

Clearly his forte lies in siring sprinter-milers. Therefore well—bred and indifferently-bred mares predisposed to producing such horses are most compatible with him. They need not themselves be superior racers as he has done well with average and inferior racers. It would definitely be unwise to breed superior stayers to him as such mares can be reserved for classic stallions. He is without doubt an ideal stallion for average mares who, in all probability, are predisposed to getting handicappers only.

RED RUFUS

Red Rufus (Ch, 1962)	Dark William	William of Valence	Vatout Queen Iseult
		Nannie River	Irish Trout Templemoyle
	Red Belle	Redbay	Walvis Bay Rosebud
		Radnor Belle	Old Radnor Blue Print

Red Rufus was the first horse to win the Indian Triple Crown and Invitation Cup. A horse of perfect conformation, he was an outstanding galloper who won 9 races from 14 starts. He was unplaced only once. He won from 1000 m to 2800 m. He was retired to stud in 1967.

He has been very successful and has just qualified for Front-line classic status. His early crops were very small, but in spite of it he got big winners. His first crop included a classic winner. He then had slightly larger crops but was never really popular. He is an excellent example of a stallion who seizes all the opportunities he gets.

STEP 1

His superior progeny from 12 crops of 75 foals were:

Sholay (1974): 17 wins, Bangalore 2000 Guineas, Guindy Gold Cup, Calcutta Gold Cup. Sire.

Enter the Red (1975): 10 wins, South India 2000 Guineas, South India Gold Cup, National Horse Breeding Society of India Gold Cup.

Weight in Gold (1978): 6 wins, South India St. Leger, Maharaja's Gold Cup; 2nd Bangalore 1000 Guineas and Oaks, Mysore City Gold Cup.

Red Surprise (1968): 6 wins in a row including the Deccan Derby 2nd Indian 1000 Guineas. (She raced for only one season.)

Response (1975): 5 wins, Hyderabad Fillies Trial Stakes, Asaf Jah VII Memorial Cup, Ootacamund Cup.

Maandavi (1973): 4 wins; 2nd Bangalore Oaks; 3rd Bangalore 1000 Guineas.

Tranquility (1973): 13-1/2 wins, Mysore City Gold Cup, Governor's Gold Cup twice.

Blossom Shower (1969): 12 wins, Ghataprabha Cup, Karnataka Racehorse Owners Association Cup, Nalanda Cup.

Happy Time (1971): 8 wins, The Aga Khan's Cup (1800 m, class I, Bombay), Karnataka Racehorse Owners Association Cup (1600 m, class I, Bangalore),Peggy Banatwalla Gold Cup.

Beehive (1969): 9 wins, F.K. Irani Gold Cup, National Horse Breeding Society of India Gold Cup; placed Deccan Derby.

Red Success (1979): 7 wins, C.D. Dady Cup, Spellbound Cup, Chakori Cup.

Tuckahoe (1976): 6 wins, C.D. Dady Cup, Colts Handicap Stakes.

Al Mansour (1968): 8 wins, Bangalore Gold Cup, Swift Stakes.

Determination (1977): 7 wins, Krishnaraja Cup, Doncaster Plate (2000 m, classes I and II, Bangalore).

Honey Suckle (1976): 6 wins, Asaf Jah VII Memorial Cup; 2nd South India 1000 Guineas.

Burgundy (1977): 5 wins, Shantiniketan Cup, Tippu Sultan Gold Cup (2000 m, class III, Mysore).

Double Gold (1977): 5 wins, Gool Poonawalla Memorial Gold Cup.

The Conqueror (1979): 4 wins, Darley Arabian Stakes (1200 m, 3-yr-olds, Hyderabad), winner in class II.

The Parliament (1978): 3 wins. He had the mortification of finishing 2nd four times in class II. He was beaten by Amba Alagi (classic winner), Almagest (2nd in the Invitation Cup), Starry Night (classic winner) and Ability (an outstanding older horse). Earlier he was beaten by Simarow, another outstanding racer. He also finished 2nd in the Stewards Trophy (2400 m, classes II and III, Bangalore) by 3/4 length. Therefore we must consider him to be superior.

Vertex (1978): 2 wins. She was a very good filly who unfortunately got into the bad habit of getting left at the start thereby losing a number of valuable races. She was also 3rd in the Stewards Trophy (2400 m, classes II and III, Bangalore). We would not be wrong if we consider her superior.

His 13th crop included the classic winner Sheer Delight who won 5 races including the Golconda 1000 Guineas. His 14th and 15th crops are in training. Therefore:

$$\text{Percentage of superior racers from foals} = \frac{20}{75} \times 100 = 27\%$$

STEP 2

Red Rufus' behaviour was Normal. A consistent stallion he invariably produced superior racers in every crop.

STEP 3

His colts and fillies were equally good.

STEP 4

He was a versatile stallion. His progeny can be distinctly divided into sprinter-milers and stayers as below:

Sprinter-milers	Stayers
1) Al Mansour	12) Red Surprise
2) Blossom Shower	13) Beehive
3) Happy Time	14) Tranquility
4) Maandavi	15) Enter the Red
5) Sholay	16) Determination
6) Response	17) Weight in Gold
7) Honey Suckle	18) The Parliament
8) Tuckahoe	19) Vertex
9) Burgundy	___
10) Red Success	8
11) The Conqueror	___
___	
11	

Double Gold was his only specialist sprinter.

STEP 5

As usual we must determine the quality of his mares. Among the 17 who produced his 20 superior racers, as many as 13 were Inherently superior. These 13 mares were responsible for 16 of his superior racers. *Therefore Red Rufus cannot claim to be a prepotent stallion. He has not been able to get a significant number of superior racers out of Inherently inferior mares.*

SPEED AND STAMINA COMPATIBILITY

Among the mares who produced his superior progeny only 5 were well performed:

Sparkling Rock: 4 wins up to 2000 m, Poona City Cup, Surgeon General's Cup; 3rd Indian Oaks.

Romantica: 10 wins, C.D. Dady Cup, Sir Rahimtoola Chinoy Gold Cup; 4th Indian 1000 Guineas.

Mahasakthi: 4 wins, South India St. Leger; 2nd South India Derby and Oaks.

Victorious: 7 wins, Indian 1000 Guineas and Oaks.

Om-Sakthi: as described.

These mares (except Victorious) are also well-bred. Here we come to a very important aspect of his behaviour. We find that his very best progeny were out of these mares! Sparkling Rock was the dam of Tranquility Romantica was the dam of classic winners Sholay and Response. Mahasakthi was the dam of Determination and classic winner Sheer Delight. Victorious was the dam of Vertex and Om-Sakthi was the dam of classic winner Weight in Gold and The Conqueror. *Therefore Red Rufus excels with really outstanding mares i.e. well-bred and well performed mares.* But his other superior racers were out of moderately or badly performed mares.

When we correlate the speed and stamina of his mares with their progeny we find that Red Rufus' behaviour is similar to Everyday's. He sired stayers only out of staying mares or mares bred to stay, and sprinter-milers out of short distance mares. He was not prepotent for stamina. The dams of Determination, Weight in Gold and Vertex were classic winning stayers. The dam of Tranquility was also a genuine stayer. The tail female lines of Red Surprise, Beehive, Enter the Red and The Parliament contain at least one top class stayer. *Therefore Red Rufus only consolidated the high class stamina of his mares.* But here I must add a note of caution. He "missed" getting stayers out of a number of staying mares and mares bred to stay. Among them were Nanda Devi, Dear Heart, Taking Ways, Mallika and Multiplication. All these mares have very strong sources of stamina in their pedigrees. The 4th named was the dam of AL Mansour and the last named the dam of Red Success. Therefore Red Rufus cannot be considered a guaranteed source of stamina.

PEDIGREE COMPATIBILITY

We noted that his books contained a number of well-bred but moderately performed mares. Among the 13 Inherently superior mares who produced his superior racers, as many as 12 were well-bred. The quality of the mare's pedigree is therefore very important for Red Rufus. He produced superior progeny only out of well-bred mares. His performance with indifferently-bred mares was poor. *In short well-bred and well performed mares followed by well-bred mares are most compatible with him.*

But readers will query: "Such superior mares are bound to excel with other stallions also. Then what is special about Red Rufus?" My reply is: "His percentage of success, his 'striking rate', with Inherently superior mares is considerable. Therefore he is worthy of our patronage. He is an excellent stallion for classic breeders. A majority of his superior progeny were classic winners or winners in the highest class."

We saw that Red Rufus served a number of outstanding mares. They naturally produced superior racers out of other stallions also. The details are as below:

Mare	Superior offspring by other stallions
Mallika	**Prince Ardent** (by Ardent Knight): Bangalore Arc de Triomphe, South India 2000 Guineas; 2nd South India Derby.
Tartanella	**Coffee Blossom** (by Glory of Andhra): Bangalore 1000 Guineas; 2nd Bangalore Oaks; 3rd Indian Turf Invitation Cup.
Alwite	**Spellbinder** (by Exaggerator).
Sparkling Rock	**Thunder Shower** (by Pa Bear) and **Sparkling Princess** (by Prince Pradeep).
Romantica	**Recompense** (by Satinello) and **Malavika** (by Malvado).

Port Gang	**Port Royal** (by Orbit).
Montana	**Grizly** (by Rapparee).
Om-Sakthi	**Arrangement** (by Red Indian) and others.

Among the other mares River Port, Noble Queen, Bowl of Flowers, Victorious and Multiplication are active. The last named is the dam of classic contender Manino (by Manitou) winner of the McDowell's Premium Cup (1200 m, 3-yr-olds, Bombay). Even the 4 remaining mares who did not get a superior racer may well have, had they had full stud careers:

Some Surprise: had only 1 other offspring Banganga.

Tally Ho: had only 3 runners, the others being Sunila (by Tiptree): winner; placed 2nd seven times and Hemlata (by Glory of Andhra): 6 wins, winner in class III.

Enter and Canter: had only 4 runners, the others being Queen of Seer (by Red Rufus): 4 wins, winner in class III and Enter and Win (by Malvado): winner.

Mahasakthi: had only 1 other runner Retribution (by High Commission): 7 wins, winner in class III.

COMPARISON BETWEEN PUNJAB AND RED RUFUS

A comparison between Punjab and Red Rufus is very illuminating. On the surface it appears that they are identical. Both were equally successful and both were versatile. But here their similarities end. Punjab was prepotent. Red Rufus was not. Therefore Punjab must have been more successful than Red Rufus as inevitably both served Inherently inferior mares. But he was not. This is because he frequently missed getting superior racers out of Inherently superior mares. His ability to get superior racers out of average and substandard mares i.e. Inherently inferior mares did not help him score significantly with Inherently superior mares. On the other hand Red Rufus excelled with Inherently superior mares. His percentage of success was high. But this ability did not help him get superior racers out of Inherently inferior mares. This is what I meant when I wrote that a stallion's ability to get superior racers out of Inherently superior mares is independent of his ability to get superior racers out of Inherently inferior mares. One final point. We saw that Punjab frequently missed getting superior stayers out of staying mares and well-bred mares bred to stay. Red Rufus too missed getting superior stayers out of such mares but he frequently got superior sprinter-milers!

I am sure readers have easily understood the methodology used to determine the behaviour of a stallion and identify the mares most compatible with him. The method we have used can be applied to stallions in any part of the world. I have come across several owners and breeders who feel that only well- bred and well performed mares i.e. truly outstanding mares are most compatible with every stallion, and that only such mares can produce superior racers. As we have seen this simplistic view is incorrect. There are a few more variations in behaviour which we must learn to complete our knowledge.

You can easily divide the stallions in your country into Classic (Frontline and Border-line classic) and Good and Average. You would do well to research the latter also. Study all their mares and see whether they had sufficient opportunities. You are sure to come across stallions, like Prince Khartoum, who have the ability of classic stallions but who are languishing for want of opportunities. The object is to identify all superior stallions. If you feel the number is too large, you can restrict yourself to the stallions you are interested in.

The next step lies in identifying all the prepotent stallions; the stallions who were able to get an appreciable number of superior racers out of Inherently inferior mares. It is difficult for me to specify a number or percentage. It will vary from country to country. For the progeny of prepotent stallions, conformation is relatively more important than pedigree. You can boldly give pedigree for conformation as such stallions have demonstrated the ability to get superior racers out of Inherently inferior mares. But for the progeny of non-prepotent stallions, pedigree is relatively more important than conformation. It would be unwise of you to buy the progeny of such stallions out of Inherently inferior mares just because they have perfect conformation, as such stallions have clearly shown their inability to get superior racers out of Inherently inferior mares. Here you must give conformation for pedigree.

We studied five stallions who exhibited different behaviour. But, as I said, a few more variations are known to Turf historians. Let us note them.

SPECIALIST STALLIONS

As explained these stallions specialize in getting horses of a particular aptitude, irrespective of the aptitude and pedigree of the dam. Rapparee is an excellent example. But there is another very important type of behaviour within this category. This group is made up of specialist sires who produce superior racers only out of mares who themselves belong to that speciality, and very indifferent racers out of all the others. We saw that Rapparee sired specialist sprinters out of mares who were themselves sprinters, milers or stayers and mares who were bred to be sprinters, milers or stayers. But there have been a number of sires of specialist sprinters who produced their superior sprinters only out of mares who were themselves sprinters or bred to sprint. Similarly several specialist sires of stayers sired superior stayers only out of mares who were themselves stayers or bred to stay, and very mediocre progeny out of all other types of mares. I am sure readers can easily identify stallions who belong to these categories.

VERSATILE STALLIONS

Readers can easily and readily identify versatile stallions. Everyday was truly versatile getting sprinters, milers and stayers. But he got his sprinters and milers only out of short distance mares and stayers only out of staying mares or mares bred to stay.

He did not very often miss getting stayers out of staying mares or mares bred to stay. But this need not always be the case. We studied another versatile sire Punjab who was also a sire of sprinters, milers and stayers. But we saw that he frequently missed getting stayers out of staying mares and mares bred to stay. Therefore stallions in this category sire sprinters and milers out of short distance mares and sprinters, milers and stayers out of staying mares and mares bred to stay.

The next variation in behaviour is a bit more complicated. Think of a stallion like Punjab. Now what will happen if he is also prepotent for stamina? On one hand he will merrily miss getting stayers out of staying mares and mares bred to stay, but on the other hand will happily get genuine stayers out of non-staying mares to the utter consternation of breeders and owners! Therefore we really cannot predict the aptitudes of the progeny of such stallions. We can now summarize what we have learnt:

CLASS OF STALLIONS	**PREPOTENT:** Ability to sire superior racers out of Inherently superior and Inherently inferior mares.
	NON-PREPOTENT: Ability to sire superior racers only out of Inherently superior mares.

1) Sire of sprinters only out of sprinting and short distance mares.

2) Sire of milers only out of sprinting and short distance mares.

3) Sire of stayers only out of staying mares and mares bred to stay.

SPECIALIST

4) Sire of sprinters out of all types of mares.

5) Sire of milers out of all types of mares.

6) Sire of stayers out of all types of mares i.e. prepotent for stamina.

APTITUDE OF STALLIONS

7) Sire of short distance horses out of short distance mares and stayers out of staying mares and mares bred to stay.

VERSATILE

8) Sire of short distance horses out of short distance mares and short distance horses and stayers out of staying mares and mares bred to stay.

9) Sire of short distance horses and stayers out of short distance mares i.e. prepotent for stamina and short distance horses and stayers out of staying mares and mares bred to stay.

CHAPTER 7

Broodmares – 2

We divided broodmares into two groups — Inherently superior and Inherently inferior. The former group is made up of: Well-bred and well performed mares, well-bred but badly performed mares and well performed mares with a superior maternal grandsire or tail female line component.

Let us discuss some more aspects of the behaviour of Inherently superior mares. Theoretically all Inherently superior mares should be successful. But in reality many are not. Let us try to determine some of the reasons for their failure.

Several Inherently superior mares had the misfortune of visiting utterly indifferent, substandard stallions. You will readily agree that an Inherently superior mare, however talented she may be, can hardly be expected to get superior racers out of very bad sires. These mares simply did not get a chance to succeed. Their talents were definitely wasted. A few examples will be of interest.

LADY JOSEPHINE

Lady Josephine (B, 1956)	Ocean Way	Tiberius	Foxlaw / Glenabatrick
		Seaway	Fairway / Cachalot
	Queen Bess	Illuminate	Link Boy / Pamkins
		Minuet	Sheridan / The Minx

She won 13 races including the South India 1000 Guineas and Indian Republic Cup and was 2nd in the South India Oaks.

She was Inherently superior as she was a superior racer and as her sire Ocean Way was a very successful maternal grandsire. Ocean Way (1942) won the Governor General's Cup (1-3/4 miles, Calcutta) in 1948 and retired to stud. He was a successful sire and maternal grandsire. I am not going into details but readers can take my word that his daughters made superior broodmares.

Lady Josephine was the dam of:

Iron Duke (colt, 1966, by Horatius): 4 wins.

Lotus Princess (filly, 1969, by Horatius): 8 wins, Maharani Tripurasundarammani Avaru Gold Cup, Tumkur Cup.

Lady Sabina (filly, 1972, by Streak of Dawn): did not win, died in training.

Immortal (filly, 1973, by Red Royal): 4 wins; 2nd Calcutta 1000 Guineas. (Even though she placed 2nd in the above classic, she was not a superior racer. She won only in class III and not in the higher classes.)

Even though Lady Josephine produced a superior racer, her stud performance is not impressive. But it was not her fault. She had the misfortune of visiting indifferent stallions. Horatius as described was only Average to Good. Both Streak of Dawn and Red Royal were very bad sires. If Lady Josephine could get Lotus Princess out of Horatius and Immortal out of Red Royal think of what she would have got out of Front-line classic stallions. Would she not have got a classic winner or champion? But to an extent she was herself to blame, as she was a shy breeder. But undoubtedly she had the desire to excel. Ironically her lesser talented half-sisters Isis and Gloriana enjoyed considerable stud success! Their female lines are flourishing today.

My next example is the peerless Royal Challenge. Readers will recall that she was the very first foal of Prince Pradeep who went on to win all the 5 classics in Calcutta. Prince Pradeep's phenomenal achievements as a sire have been described. Even though the progeny of his daughters have just started to race, it is clear that they are very talented. Several have won in the highest class. Therefore we must consider Prince Pradeep to be a superior maternal grandsire. Hence Royal Challenge qualifies as an Inherently superior mare. (Again let us ignore her maternal grandsires.)

		Migoli	Bois Roussel
			Mah Iran
	Prince Pradeep		
		Driving	Watling Street
Royal Challenge			Snow Line
(B, 1967)		Royal Challenger	Royal Charger
			Skerweather
	Royal Puzzle		
		Bally Puzzle	Ballyogan
			Chinese Puzzle

Her progeny were:

Shakti Sri (filly, 1973, by Mica Emperor): 4 wins.

Mica Challenge (filly, 1974, by Mica Emperor): 1 win and placed, died.

Golden Falcon (colt, 1976, by Tristar): 2 wins.

Ratna Priya (filly, 1977, by Proboscis): placed once in her short racing career.

Own Option (filly, 1978, by Proboscis): 6 wins, B.D. Goenka Memorial Cup (1200 m, 3-yr-olds, Madras); 2nd Golconda 1000 Guineas (only 3 ran), South India Oaks (only 3 ran); 3rd South India 1000 Guineas (only 4 ran).

Royal Option (filly, 1980, by Arrogant Lad): in training.

Insat (colt, 1981, by Arrogant Lad): 3 wins, Charminar Challenge Gold Trophy (1400 m, 3-yr-olds, Bombay). He is in training and is one of the better youngsters in the country.

(All her foals, as she is dead.)

Again the disappointing performance of Royal Challenge was entirely due to her visits to mediocre stallions. Mica Emperor was a failure. Tristar was at the most average. Proboscis is Average-to-Good but unfortunately Royal Challenge visited him when he had just entered the country and had not yet settled down. Then at last she visited the Border-line classic Arrogant Lad and the result is there for all to see — Insat. Insat and, to an extent, Own Option are proof that Royal Challenge had the capacity to produce classic progeny. Therefore we must conclude that had she visited Front-line classic stallions she would have definitely produced classic winners and champions.

The next reason for the failure of Inherently superior mares is a bit subtle. It is not due to their visits to indifferent, mediocre stallions, but rather to their visits to incompatible stallions. These incompatible stallions may have been very successful in their own right. Om-Sakthi's stud performance illustrates this principle.

| | | Fighting Fox | Sir Gallahad III
Marguerite |
| | Fighting Don | | |
| | | Bird Nest | Mad Hatter
Tree Top |
| Om-Sakthi
(Br, 1961) | | Greek Star | Hyperion
Nebular |
| | Star of Vintage | | |
| | | Lyonnaise | Coup de Lyon
Rose Song |

We saw that she was a classic winner of 16 races including the South India Derby. We also studied a number of her progeny. Her complete produce record is as below:

Santham (filly, 1969, by Punjab): 8 wins.

Character (colt, 1972, by Punjab): 12 wins, Chief Minister's Gold Cup.

Mid-day Sun (colt, 1973, by Three Wishes): 8 wins, Kashmir Gold Cup, Tamil Nadu Commemoration Gold Cup. (Even though he won these long distance races, he cannot be considered a true stayer as he won in a very slow time.)

Pancharathnam (filly, 1974, by Rapparee): 11 wins, Maharani Tripurasundarammani Avaru Gold Cup, Shimoga Cup.

The Judgement (filly, 1975, by Voluntary): 8 wins, winner in class II.

Arrangement (colt, 1976, by Red Indian): 6 wins, Stewards Gold Cup, Governor's Cup; 2nd South India Derby and St. Leger.

Perseverence (filly, 1977, by Red Indian): 4 wins.

Weight in Gold (filly, 1978, by Red Rufus): 6 wins, South India St. Leger, Maharaja's Gold Cup; 2nd Bangalore 1000 Guineas and Oaks, Mysore City Gold Cup.

The Conqueror (colt, 1979, by Red Rufus): 4 wins, Darley Arabian Stakes, winner in class II.

Whims and Fancy (colt, 1980, by Young Pip): 3 wins, in training.

Killer Instinct (colt, 1981, by Young Pip): placed, in training.

Grand Entry (colt, 1982, by Red Rufus): in training.

Om-Sakthi's performance is awe-inspiring. Her 9 racers included 1 classic winner, 1 classic-placed and 5 superior racers. But without a shadow of doubt she could have done much better' For, study the stallions she visited. But before doing so ask yourself which class and type of stallions would have been most suitable and compatible for her. She was a well-bred classic winner. Therefore she was almost guaranteed to produce classic winners and champions. To do so she only had to visit Front-line or Borderline classic sires of stayers. Such stallions were obviously most compatible with her. By this criterion let us see how many of the stallions she visited were compatible.

Punjab was, no doubt, a Border-line classic stallion who sired stayers. But we saw that he frequently missed getting stayers out of staying mares. Therefore he was not fully compatible. Three Wishes and Voluntary were strictly Average, nothing more. Rapparee has been described. A friend of mine remarked after The Judgement had won a race (she won 1 race over 1000 m, 6 races over 1200 m and I race over 1400 m): "Though Om-Sakthi was herself a genuine stayer, she is incapable of getting a genuine stayer. Look at her first 5 progeny!" I quickly replied: "She is definitely capable of producing a classic winning stayer, but has not done so as she has been visiting incompatible stallions. Wait until she visits a compatible stallion, then you will see!" Happily for me, soon after I had spoken these words, Arrangement arrived on the scene and ran 2nd in the South India Derby and St. Leger. His sire Red Indian, whom we are going to discuss later, was most compatible. Then Weight in Gold went one better and lifted the South India St. Leger' Her sire Red Rufus was obviously another compatible stallion. *Though Om-Sakthi got 7 superior racers, her best progeny, Weight in Gold and Arrangement, were out of intensely compatible stallions.* (It is too early to comment on Young Pip as his first progeny have just started to race.) This conclusion is valid for all mares:

Though a mare can get average and superior racers out of several stallions, her best progeny will in all probability be out of intensely compatible stallions.

Suppose Om-Sakthi, instead of visiting Red Indian and Red Rufus, had continued to visit other successful but incompatible stallions like Punjab and Rapparee. What would have happened? No doubt she would have got marginally superior racers, but would she have got a classic winner? It is most unlikely. Then what would have been your judgement? You would have surely said: "Here is a Derby winning mare who visited successful stallions. Yet she could not produce a classic stayer. Therefore I am forced to say that her stud performance is disappointing.''

But on the other hand suppose she had, even at the outset, visited outstanding and, in all probability, truly compatible stallions like Prince Pradeep or Young Lochinvar. What would have happened? Would she not have got a Derby winner or even an Invitation Cup winner? Therefore can we not assert that though she was a very successful producer, she could have been even more successful?

Since Om-Sakthi was a Derby winner she had the ability to get marginally superior racers out of incompatible stallions. *But think of lesser mares. Will they possess a similar ability? Obviously not. Their progeny out of incompatible stallions are bound to be inferior.*

Therefore the success of an Inherently superior mare depends on two factors:

1) She must visit successful stallions.

2) Those stallions must also be compatible with her to some extent at least

If these two conditions are not satisfied Inherently superior mares may, in spite of their potential, turn out to be very disappointing producers. In other words they failed not due to lack of inherent ability, but due to lack of opportunity.

Having understood the concept of compatibility, we are now in a position to really analyze the produce record of a mare and determine whether her performance was ''actual'' and ''inherent'' or ''apparent''. To do so we have to determine whether she visited successful and compatible stallions. If she has, her performance is her actual or inherent performance. But if she has not, her performance is only her apparent and not actual performance. First let us discuss the former.

Consider any mare. By studying her race record and pedigree we can determine to a reasonable extent the types of stallions most compatible with her. Suppose that she has had half-a-dozen runners out of such stallions If they have done well, well and good. The mare is a success. But suppose they fared badly. Who is to blame? Naturally the mare has got to be blamed. She had everything going for her. She visited successful and compatible stallions; yet she could not produce superior or even average racers. Therefore she is undoubtedly a failure. We would not even think of buying her subsequent progeny. They are best left alone.

But on the other hand consider a mare who has been visiting incompatible stallions. (These incompatible stallions may be very successful in their own right.) Can she do well? Can she excel? It is most unlikely. Her progeny will be at the most average. Her produce record will be dismal. Would you buy the next offspring of such a mare? It is highly unlikely. You will at once point out her dismal produce record. But you will readily agree that her produce record represents only her apparent behaviour and not her actual behaviour, as she has been visiting incompatible stallions. Suppose she now visits an intensely compatible stallion. Isn't the resulting offspring on an entirely different foundation? Doesn't he have every chance to excel, even though his half-brothers and sisters were poor performers? Therefore can we not boldly buy him ignoring his half-brothers and sisters?

Let us analyze the produce record of a mare incorporating the above concepts. I have selected Koh-E-Sina, a granddaughter of Aurelie.

Koh-E-Sina (Ch, 1960)	Rock of Gibraltar	Rockefella	Hyperion / Rockfel
		Toquade	Premier Balser / Tonkette
	Auroden	Worden II	Wild Risk / Sans Tares
		Aurelle	Teleferique / Anne de Bretagne

She won only 2 races.

Let us analyze her pedigree. We saw that her sire Rock of Gibraltar was a successful maternal grandsire of stayers. We also saw that her tail female line is among the best in the country. Her grandam produced a Derby winner and an Oaks winner. Her dam too excelled in getting high class stayers. Clearly Koh-E-Sina was predisposed to producing classic stayers. Therefore stallions who excelled in getting classic stayers were most compatible and suitable for her. Keeping this in mind let us analyze her produce record.

In the beginning she was very unlucky. She did not visit compatible stallions. On the contrary the stallions she visited — Ivanhoe, Horatius and Courageous were most incompatible. For they were not superior in the first place and secondly they were not sires of stayers. Therefore she could not but help get 6 very indifferent progeny as below:

Sunny Smile (colt, 1966, by Ivanhoe): 2 wins.

Kohima (filly, 1967, by Horatius): 3 wins.

Midnight Angel (filly, 1969, by Horatius): 7 wins, (She raced until she was 8 years.)

Pamme Queen (filly, 1970, by Courageous): 10 wins. (She is 14 years old and is still racing and winning!)

Good Heart (colt, 1971, by Courageous): 4 wins.

Kohrisa (filly, 1972, by Courageous); 3 wins.

Then happily she visited the intensely compatible Red Indian, a specialist sire of superior stayers and extreme stayers. Naturally the resulting progeny King of Seers and Regency Concorde were superior racers. She then visited two other fairly successful stallions Landigou and Royal Gleam. These two stallions fall exactly mid-way between the earlier stallions she visited and Red Indian i.e. they were not intensely compatible but there were some elements of compatibility. Again she seized the chance and produced a superior racer out of Royal Gleam. These horses are described below:

King of Seers (colt, 1973, by Red Indian): 13 wins, Governor's Cup, Kashmir Gold Cup, Nepal Gold Cup; 2nd Bangalore and Hyderabad Colts Trial Stakes, Nizam's Gold Cup.

Regency Concorde (colt, 1974, by Red Indian): 8 wins, Shantiniketan Cup (1600 m, class II, Bangalore).

Paulina (filly, 1975, by Landigou): 5 wins.

Miyako (filly, 1978, by Royal Gleam): 5 wins, Royal Tern Cup (1600 m, class I, Bombay). (In 1981 82 she had the misfortune of placing 2nd five times.)

Having written so much about compatibility, I hope readers will not get offended if I say that mares do not always behave according to their aptitudes and pedigrees. This was brought home to me very forcefully by Floral Slipper.

	Pink Flower	Oleander
		Plymstock
Flower Dust		
	Brazen Molly	Horus
		Molly Adare
Floral Slipper (Br, 1963)		
	Solferino	Fairway
		Sol Speranza
Soldina Slipper		
	Bedroom Slipper	Morland
		Her Slipper

She did not race. Her sire Flower Dust was a very successful sire and maternal grandsire, and was also a maternal grandsire of stayers. Her dam was a superior winner of 5 races including the Gen. Obaidullah Khan Gold Cup. She also placed 3rd in the C.N. Wadia Gold Cup and Byculla Club Cup. Floral Slipper was her only foal. Therefore Floral Slipper like Koh-E-Sina was a well-bred mare bred to stay. Naturally we must presume that she was also predisposed to producing stayers and hence staying stallions were most compatible with her. But even though she visited a number of sires of superior stayers, she failed to get a genuine high class stayer! Her complete produce record is given below:

Classic Charcoal (filly, 1968, by Rock of Gibraltar): 6 wins.

Black Knight (colt, 1969, by Baraloy): 5 wins.

Gold Giver (colt, 1970, by Rock of Gibraltar): 8 wins, Turf Club Cup, Chief Minister's Gold Cup, Rajaram Chhatrapati Gold Cup, Peggy Banatwalla Gold Cup. (Even though he won over 2000 m, his principal victories were over 1400 m.)

What More (colt, 1971, by Paddykin): 7 wins, Stewards Cup (1400 m, class II, Hyderabad); 2nd Bangalore Colts Trial Stakes.

Diamond Slipper (filly, 1974, by Rock of Gibraltar): 8 wins, Kanteerava Cup (2400 m, class III, Bangalore).

Resolution (colt, 1975, by Paddykin): 7 wins, winner in class II. (He won upto 1400 m.)

Nation Wide (colt, 1977, by Sagittaire): 1 win.

Flor Fino (colt, 1978, by Sagittaire): 3 wins, winner in class II over 1200 m.

Classic Slipper (filly, 1979, by Malvado): 4 wins, winner in class II over 1200 m.

Colt, 1980, by Malvado is in training.

Clearly Floral Slipper had enough opportunity to get a stayer. She had 3 runners by Rock of Gibraltar, 2 by Paddykin and 1 by Malvado. Yet none of them was a *superior stayer*. They excelled up to 1600 m only. This clearly shows that she was predisposed to producing sprinter-milers. But it is virtually impossible for us to predict this. The breeder was on the right track. He reasoned that sires of stayers were most compatible with her and bred her to such sires. We could have known her predisposition only after 4 or 5 of her progeny had raced. In such situations breeders are faced with a tantalizing question. What would you have done? Would you have bred her to another sire of stayers convinced that she had the ability to get stayers, or would you have dramatically changed your breeding plan and bred her to a specialist sire of sprinter-milers? How would she have fared with such sires? Would she have produced champion sprinter-milers? Or the very same class of horses? Or would she have fared badly with such sires? There are no easy answers. But clearly Floral Slipper is not unique. Mares do not always behave according to their racing performances and pedigrees. Breeders must be very alert to pinpoint such mares. Then they can change their breeding programs if they so desire. Similarly buyers must also carefully identify such mares and determine their actual behaviour.

We must now analyze the reasons for the success and failure of Inherently inferior mares. We already determined one reason for their success. We saw that prepotent stallions, by definition, get superior racers out of Inherently inferior mares. Therefore an Inherently inferior mare who has the good fortune to visit a number of prepotent stallions may well become a very successful producer. But Inherently inferior mares who visit non-prepotent or average stallions are unlikely to succeed. They are bound to be failures. But a small number of Inherently inferior mares (and a larger number of Inherently superior mares) have managed to produce superior racers out of non-prepotent, average or even substandard stallions. How can we explain this? *In other words such mares are prepotent i.e. they have the ability to get superior racers out of out of average and substandard stallions.*

Prepotent mares can be divided into two groups: Inherently superior and Inherently inferior. The success of the former group can be explained without prejudice to our earlier arguments. Just as we argued that a stallion who is outstanding in every respect has the innate ability to overcome all the defects of substandard mares and still get superior progeny, several outstanding mares i.e. Inherently superior mares have the ability to overcome the weaknesses of average and indifferent stallions and still get superior progeny. But this argument cannot be used to explain the success of Inherently inferior mares. How do substandard mares manage to produce superior racers out of admittedly bad stallions? Uma is a mare who falls in this category. Let us study her performance and try to explain her success.

		Du-Bon-Air	Dubonnet
	Naya Daur		Symphony
		Navarra	Mas d' Antibes
Uma			Crimson Rambler
(B, 1968)		Chmo	Chamossaire
	Mica Star		Triskeles
		Indira	Bear Dance
			Chandra Kala

UMA: 1 win.

MICA STAR: 4 wins. Dam of:

Megha Pushpa: 1 win.

Texas Colt: 6 wins.

Uma: as above.

INDIRA: ran unplaced. Dam of:

Only One: 8 wins; 2nd South India Oaks.

Indraneel: 8 wins.

Poona Passenger: 8 wins.

Noviate: 1 win.

Fairy Boat: placed in her short racing career.

Mica Star: as above.

CHANDRA KALA: unraced. Dam of:

Khazana: 7ı1/2 wins.

Suhasini: did not win. Indira: as above.

NEW CROP: raced in England. Dam of:

Mansoor Beg: 5 wins, Indian Derby; 2nd Indian 2000 Guineas and St. Leger.

Shah Nawaz: 1 win.

Celebration: 1 win.

Senapati: placed.

Chandra Kala: as above.

UMA was the dam of:

Trinity (colt, 1974, by Mica Emperor): 2 wins.

Cherookee (filly, 1975, by Arizona Colt): 10 wins, Czechoslovakia Cup, Tamil Nadu Commemoration Gold Cup, Gool Poonawalla Memorial Gold Cup; 3rd Hyderabad Fillies Trial Stakes, the only classic she contested. She was a filly well up to classic winning standard but was unfortunately not entered in the other classics.

Milwaukee (filly, 1976, by Arizona Colt): 1 win.

Deep Water Blues (filly, 1977, by Red Indian): 7 wins, Calcutta Oaks, Northumberland Cup, Kashmir Gold Cup; 2nd Stayers' Cup, Bangalore and South India St. Leger, South India Oaks.

Byerly Brigade (colt, 1978, by Red Indian): 3 wins, Deccan Derby; 2nd Bangalore 2000 Guineas, President of India Gold Cup; 3rd South India 2000 Guineas.

Scintillation (filly, 1979, by Red Indian or Mr. Mauritius): 4 wins, Bangalore St. Leger; 2nd Bangalore Oaks.

Belmont (colt, 1980, by Orbit): 6 wins, Jayachamaraja Wadiyar Trophy; 2nd Bangalore Arc de Triomphe; 3rd Mysore 2000 Guineas.

High Rise (filly, 1981, by Loredaan): 2 wins, in training.

Filly, 1982, by Loredaan is in training.

Uma is not Inherently superior. On the contrary all her three components are markedly inferior. She could win only 1 race. Her sire Naya Daur failed as a sire and maternal grandsire. Her maternal grandsires too were not successful. Her 3 dams could produce only 1 superior racer. Only her 4th dam produced a racer of real quality. Hence her chances of success as a producer seemed almost non-existent. But has she succeeded! She has produced 3 classic winners, 1 classic-placed and 1 filly well upto classic winning standard. I want to emphasize that the stallions she visited were neither outstanding nor compatible. Arizona Colt was very indifferent. Red Indian and Orbit were no doubt successful, but I do not think anyone will claim that there was intense compatibility between them and Uma. They were not prepotent stallions. (It is too early to judge Loredaan.) *Therefore Uma's success was entirely due to her own efforts.* How can we explain her success? Here we have an utterly substandard mare — even her conformation is far from perfect — who produced classic racers out of indifferent and incompatible stallions. The theories we have developed till now cannot help us. Other factors were involved. What are they? As far as Uma is concerned we can assert: *Her success was almost entirely due to the care and attention she lavished on her foals.* In other words her performance as a broodmare was outstanding. She was able to provide an excellent environment to her foals, which enabled them to grow and develop into classic racers. This fact has been confirmed by a number of breeders.

We have just introduced a new variable, altogether a new dimension, in breeding: The quality of the environment a mare provides to her progeny. Undeniably a few mares excel in this respect while others do not. But how significant is this factor? Is it a major or minor factor? We cannot assert that a foal who grows up under the care of an ideal broodmare is going to develop into a superior racer. And paradoxically we all know that several foul tempered mares, who surely could not have provided an ideal environment to their progeny, have become very successful producers getting classic winners and champions. And is it possible for us to predict that a particular mare is going to provide an ideal environment while another is not? Considering all the evidence we must conclude that this factor cannot be decisive except in the rarest of cases like Uma. No doubt breeders will have a lot to say on the subject.

REASONS FOR THE FAILURE OF OUTSTANDING BROODMARES TO ESTABLISH STRONG TAIL FEMALE LINES

It is sad but true that several outstanding mares have failed to establish strong tail female lines. In other words they were not foundation broodmares. Two factors are primarily responsible for this.

The first factor is the infertility of the mares and their descendants. They were all shy breeders. They just could not establish a family. Prolific families have greater chances of producing superior racers, and once they do so breeders give them more opportunities, enabling them to get still more superior racers. Sheer strength of numbers works in their favour. The opposite is true in the case of shy breeders. Even when their families produce superior racers, breeders are not impressed. For such families are not "fashionable", they are not in the "news" so to say. Only the most determined breeder will persist with them. But we must not forget that such families too possess a lot of talent. Tudor Bouquet's family is an example.

		Owen Tudor	Hyperion
	Tudor Minstrel		Mary Tudor II
		Sansonnet	Sansovino
Tudor Bouquet			Lady Juror
(B, 1952)		Nearco	Pharos
	Grecian Flower		Nogara
		Bouquet	Buchan
			Hellesont

TUDOR BOUQUET: ran unplaced in England and placed in India.

GRECIAN FLOWER: 1 win; 3rd Marlborough House Stakes (Ascot) in her only season to race. Dam of:

Woodkote Lion: 1 win each in England and Malaysia.

Tudor Bouquet: as above.

BOUQUET: unraced. Dam of:

Airborne: 4-1/2 wins, Epsom Derby, English St. Leger, Prince of Wales Stakes; 3rd King George VI Stakes.

Fragrant View: 6 wins, and others.

Even though Tudor Bouquet did not win, her glittering pedigree automatically made her inherently superior. But very sadly for Indian breeding she was a shy breeder. She was the dam of:

Esparto: 2 wins, producer.

King Master: 14 wins, F.K. Irani Gold Cup, Madras Area Cup, Mysore Sub-Area Cup; 2nd M.R.C. Hospital Cup.

Rose of Tudor: 4 wins, South India Oaks; 2nd South India 1000 Guineas, Bangalore Fillies Trial Stakes (behind Fair Haven).

Rose of Tudor (1965) by Flower Dust had everything going for her. She was an Oaks winner. Her sire Flower Dust was a successful maternal grandsire. Her tail female line is of international standard. But sadly she too was a shy breeder. She had only 3 foals: Rose Riot (2 wins), Rose Parade (5 wins) and a colt (1982) by Subject to Raise who is in training. Esparto (by Rock of Gibraltar) had 5 winners: Rock Victory (7 wins), Thor (3 wins), Eos (1 win), Lara (3 wins) and Iron Goddess (1 win). Among these Rose Riot, Rose Parade, Lara and Iron Goddess are broodmares and they have the responsibility of keeping the line going. But had Tudor Bouquet and Rose of Tudor been more prolific, they would have surely established a strong and vigorous tail female line by now. They definitely possessed the inherent talent to do so. Both of them could have been foundation broodmares in their own right, but sadly were not.

The second reason is that several mares produce a number of outstanding colts but unfortunately fail to get outstanding fillies. When these average fillies go to stud they find it difficult to compete against other superior mares and are unable to establish strong lines. Frequently their lines die out or survive by a slender thread. The family of Aroma is an example.

		Solario	Gainsborough
			Sun Worship
	Solar Day		
		Trincomalee	Tetratema
			Dinner
Aroma			
(B, 1945)		Blenheim	Blandford
			Malva
	Bente Mira		
		Friar's Lady	Friar Marcus
			Lady Nairne

She won only once, but was a hugely successful producer getting 8 winners. Her progeny possessed an ideal blend of speed and stamina and an abundance of class. Unfortunately they were all colts:

Random Harvest (colt, 1956, by Bellrue): 12 wins, South India Triple Crown, Surgeon General's Cup, Abdullah Khairaz Cup.

Al Bashir (colt, 1959, by Hervine) : 11 wins, Ceylon Turf Club Cup, Byculla Club Cup (twice), Idar Gold Cup (twice).

Sun Deep (colt, 1961, by Golestan): 11 wins, Indian 2000 Guineas, Eclipse Stakes of India, A.C. Ardeshir Gold Cup, Maharaja of Morvi Gold Cup; 2nd in the Indian Derby by only a neck.

Her daughters who were producers included Orchis and Vinifera. The former (by Mubarak) won 8 races including the Griffin Cup and was the dam of 4 winners. Among them only Suntop (by Matombo) who won 4 races seems to be active. She has made a fair start by getting Al Amir who has won 7 races including the Stewards Trophy (2400 m, classes II and III, Bangalore.)

Vinifera (by Hervine) won thrice and got 4 minor winners. Among them only Vivre (by Horatius) who won 4 races seems to be a producer. Her progeny have just started racing.

Therefore the responsibility of continuing Aroma's tail female line falls squarely on Suntop and Vivre. While I am convinced that they are going to do well, I do not know whether they can match the magnificent achievements of their grandam and set the family on a really strong foundation.

Let us study the development of the female line of one more outstanding broodmare — Lady Emma, a daughter of Nearco. Her story is identical to Aroma's, but happily for her, one of her granddaughters performed brilliantly and saved the line from extinction.

		Pharos	Phalaris
			Scapa Flow
	Nearco		
		Papyrus	Havresac II
			Catnip
Lady Emma			
(Ch, 1940)		Papyrus	Tracery
			Miss Matty
	Divine Lady		
		Most Beautiful	Great Sport
			Rayon

Lady Emma only placed once each in England and Ireland. Retired to stud, she had the distinction of becoming the dam of three sires. Among them Star of Gwalior (1952) has been described. The others were Khan Saheb (1945) and Chhote Khan (1947).

Khan Saheb, by Atout Maitre, won only once in India but became a Border-line classic stallion. His progeny included: Win Master (5 wins, South India Derby), Akbar (6 wins, South India St. Leger; 2nd South India Derby), Meherban (8 wins, Indian 1000 Guineas and Oaks) and Nilanjana (9 wins; 2nd Indian 1000 Guineas and Oaks; 3rd Indian 2000 Guineas).

Chhote Khan, by Flag of Truce, too won only once in India but became a fair sire. His best racer was Nanda Deep who won the Indian 1000 and 2000 Guineas.

Since Lady Emma was so talented readers might assume that her female descendants too excelled and that her female family is among the best in the country. Astonishing as it may seem, her tail female line descendants fared very badly and the entire family was on the verge of extinction! Then an unlikely saviour arrived in the form of Ragamuffin.

		Arctic Star	Nearco
			Serena
	Lough Ine		
		Mindy	Mid-day Sun
			Rendezvous
Ragamuffin			
(B, 1966)		Hyder Ali	Hyperion
			Eclair
	Princess of Gwalior		
		Lady Emma	Nearco
			Divine Lady

She ran unplaced and was retired to stud. I do not know how many were confident of her success. But happily she has excelled:

Muffin (filly, 1974, by Nijinsky [India]): 7 wins, Indian Oaks, Sir Jamsetjee Jeejeebhoy (VI Bart) Gold Cup.

El Bravo (colt, 1975, by Satinello): 7 wins, F.D. Wadia Gold Cup, Rajaram Chhatrapati Cup, Southern Command Cup; 2nd Indian Derby.

Rasputin (colt, 1977, by Nijinsky [India]): 4 wins.

Bravissima (filly, 1979, by Gombos) : 2 wins, Thunder Storm Cup (1600 m, classes I and II, Bombay); 3rd Indian 1000 Guineas.

Gamin (filly, 1980, by Gombos): winner, in training.

Filly, 1981, by Sovereign Silver is in training.

Undoubtedly Ragamuffin, by her own efforts, has put Lady Emma's female family on firm ground. But think of her progeny. Who would have influenced them more — she or Lady Emma? Obviously she has played the dominant role in shaping and moulding them. Therefore can we not say that Ragamuffin's descendants belong to the Ragamuffin family and not to the Lady Emma family? In other words Ragamuffin is emerging as a foundation broodmare in her own right. For all practical purposes the tail female line of Lady Emma is dead (unless some of its other members perform spectacularly) and it has evolved into the tail female line of Ragamuffin. We emphasized that this is a natural process. A foundation broodmare establishes a number of branches. While some of them develop strongly, others wither away. Ultimately the different branches become distinct families in their own right.

DECLINE OF ONCE DOMINANT TAIL FEMALE LINES

Many have wondered why several outstanding tail female lines are now nowhere near the top. It is not difficult to answer this question.

Firstly we must not forget the "halving nature" of inheritance. Galton's "Law of Ancestral Contribution" states that both the parents between them contribute to half the make- up of the offspring, all the four grandparents a quarter and so on. Therefore the strong influence of the foundation brood-mare decreases by half every successive generation. How much influence will she have on her great grand-daughter? Very little. She must stand on her own feet. She must be a good winner, she must be Inherently superior. Do not forget that the tail female line is only one component, one factor. in the success of a broodmare.

Frequently the daughters of a foundation broodmare are slightly less talented than their dam, their daughters even less talented and so on. Therefore after a few generations the mares of the female line become average, no different from thousands of other mares. These average mares are unable to compete against other superior mares and the whole family slips into mediocrity.

Lastly we must not forget the odds against a broodmare and the intense competition among them. Keeping these factors in mind it is only natural that even the best and strongest tail female lines have their ups and downs. One family cannot dominate for a long time.

We now come to an important topic. Can we predict which mares are going to become foundation broodmares? I feel we can. A mare who satisfies the following criteria has a good chance of emerging as a foundation broodmare:

1) *She must have got three superior racers including one classic winner, champion or Group I winner, or four superior racers.*
2) *She must have also got a sufficient number of fillies to keep her family going.*

A potential foundation broodmare must possess such depth of talent if her family is to overcome the intense competition and flourish. The families of lesser mares will find it difficult to survive, let alone flourish. Readers should apply these two conditions and identify a number of potential foundation broodmares. All of them will not ultimately succeed but their principal branches are sure to do well.

I am anxious to make a mention of one more mare who can already claim to be a foundation broodmare. In any case her family has expanded rapidly and has consolidated itself strongly. It has already produced 3 classic winners and other superior racers and is sure to produce more. Yet I am not impressed. I personally feel the family does not possess inherent talent. If so how did it produce 3 classic winners? I am convinced it was due to the sheer strength of numbers working in the family's favour. Readers can judge for themselves. The mare in question is Stumped.

Stumped (Gr, 1958)	Djebe	Djebel	Tourbillon Loika
		Catherine	Tiberius Catherinette
	Wicket	Umidwar	Blandford Uganda
		Witchcraft	Wychwood Abbot Anadyomene

In England she won the Bryn Nursery Handicap and placed 3rd in the Earl of Sefton's Handicap. She was imported into India and retired to stud. She was a prolific producer who got 9 foals including 7 fillies. Her progeny included Lovely Smitha who won the Bangalore Oaks. Her daughters too were successful producers and they too excelled in getting fillies. Among them Jeevan Jyoti got Zelda who won the Calcutta 1000 Guineas and Oaks, and Enter and Canter got Enter the Red who won the South India 2000 Guineas. The Table below shows the development of the family.

TABLE 18

Progeny of Stumped	Fillies by Mare in Previous Column
Spotted Beauty (1962, by Torbido): placed. Dam of 4 foals, all winners.	Thundering Beauty (1971) Ideal Beauty (1972) Persian Beauty (1974)
Jeevan Jyoti (1963, by Asopo): 6 wins. Dam of 3 foals, 2 winners, 1 placed.	Su Lin (1970) Zelda (1974)
Moon Dust (1964, by Asopo): 3 wins. Dam of 4 foals, 3 winners.	Rose O'Lynn (1971) Cherry Pink (1973, dead) Saturday Night (1977)
Enter and Canter (1965, by Asopo): 3 wins. Dam of 4 foals, all winners.	Maandavi (1973) Queen of Seer (1974) Enter and Win (1979)
Young Princess (1969, by Young Lochinvar): winner.	Yet to have runners.
Shub Kamni (1970, by Asopo): 3 wins. Dam of 3 foals. 2 of them are in training and 1 has won. She is active.	Silver Tips (1977) Royal Trace (1978)

TABLE 18 (cont.)

Progeny of Stumped	Fillies by Mare in Previous Column
Lovely Smitha (1971, by Young Lochinvar): 4 wins. Dam of 3 foals, all winners. Her 2nd and 3rd foals are in training. She is active.	Cherry Hinton (1976) So Smitten (1979) My Colours (1981)
Bright Steel (colt, 1972 by Young Lochinvar or Ásopo): 8 wins.	——
Young Cricketer (colt, 1978, by Young Lochinvar): 8 wins, Hyderabad Silver Vase (1400 m, classes I and II, Madras), Stewards Cup (1400 m, class II, Hyderabad).	——

The Stumped family has within a relatively short span of about two decades established itself very strongly. In fact several of Stumped's grand-daughters are already producers. I have not described their progeny. Contrast this with the families of outstanding mares who are struggling to establish themselves even after three or four decades. But my object in describing her family was not just to bring out these facts. Readers in India may undertake the following exercise: Study carefully Stumped's 15 grand-daughters given in the 2nd column. Among them who do you think is going to become the most successful-producer? *Remember each of them can be considered to be a distinct "branch" of the Stumped family.* (No answer is given.)

We now come to an extremely important aspect. I divided a brood-mare into 3 "components" — 3 *equal* components and said that a mare who scores highly in any 2 components is Inherently superior. A mare who scores "moderately" in all the 3 components is *not* Inherently superior. She. is only average. But there is absolutely no need for you to follow this division. *You can formulate your own division.* One breeder may feel that all well performed mares can be automatically considered Inherently superior, irrespective of their pedigrees. In other words he is giving more weightage to racing performance and less weightage to pedigree. But another will insist that only a mare with an outstanding maternal grand-sire component together with another superior component can be considered Inherently superior. A third individual may give first priority to the tail female line, followed by racing performance and then by the maternal grandsires.

These different weightages are shown below:

I

	Points
Racing performance	70
Maternal grandsires	15
Tail female line	15
	100

II

Racing performance	25
Maternal grandsires	50
Tail female line	25
	100

III

Racing performance	35
Maternal grandsires	15
Tail female line	50
	100

It is necessary for every individual to sit down and formulate his weightages. Then he must consistently breed from such mares or buy the progeny of such mares. In the long run he is sure to be successful. But is it necessary to do so? Absolutely. Ideally we would all like to breed from, and buy the progeny of, only outstanding mares, mares who score very highly in all the 3 components. But this is impossible for even the biggest breeder. Therefore we are forced to compromise and breed from lesser mares. But instead of flitting from one type of mare to another, would it not be wiser to restrict yourself to one type of mares? Don't you think that those who do so are bound to be more successful in the long run?

IMPORTANCE OF BROODMARES

Experienced breeders and owners know the importance of broodmares. As I mentioned earlier, identifying superior stallions is easy. Even a schoolboy can rattle of the names of the leading stallions in the world. It will not be difficult for you to determine their behaviour. It is not necessary for you to own these stallions. You need not even be a share holder. You can simply buy a nomination. If you feel their services are too expensive, you can patronize young stallions who are rapidly making a name for themselves, or unfashionable stallions who in reality possess a lot of talent. The point is the services of the best stallions in the world are available to you. Therefore you must focus your attention on brood-mares. As I emphasized earlier, wouldn't it be wiser for you to breed from one type of mares instead of dissipating your energy on different types? I feel that a wise breeder should build up a broodmare band of one or two types and endeavour to breed them to outstanding and compatible stallions.

But several are sure to argue on opposite lines. Why should a stud farm have only one type of mares? Wouldn't it be better to have every type? Again it is for the individual to decide. But without doubt those who are consistent in their policies are sure to be more successful in the long run.

CHAPTER 8

Maternal Grandsires – 2

Let us discuss some more facets of the behaviour of maternal grandsires. Let us go back to Asopo. We saw that he is a Front-line classic maternal grandsire who topped the Maternal grandsires lists 3 times. Now let us determine how many of his daughters were Inherently superior. Studying Table 13 we find that most of them qualify on account of their superior tail female lines. (Only 4 mares — Periwinkle, Maiden's Blush, Hats Off and My Baby fail to qualify; My Mo qualifies as she was a superior racer.) Coming to their racing merit we find that Mabel and Zeenee were classic winners; Mumtaz and Princess Jani were classic-placed; My Mo, Fabiha and Ask Me were superior racers and Hennessy and Handsel won 7 races each. Therefore we have no difficulty in explaining the success of Asopo mares. Not only were they daughters of the best maternal grandsire in the country, they also had superior tail female lines. In addition several were superior racers. When such mares visit superior stallions they naturally produce outstanding progeny.

But Asopo mares went a step further. In addition to producing superior racers out of classic stallions, they were also able to produce superior racers out of average and indifferent stallions. *In other words several of his daughters were prepotent. Therefore we can consider Asopo to be a prepotent maternal grandsire.* In our study of stallions we found that several are prepotent. They have the ability to get superior racers out of inferior mares. Similarly we saw that broodmares too can be prepotent. Now we are introducing the concept of a prepotent maternal grandsire. *The sire of a number of prepotent mares is a prepotent maternal grandsire.* The following Asopo mares were prepotent:

Mare	Superior offspring	Inferior sire of the superior offspring
My Baby	Celestial Gift Regular Guy	Esquire
Take Cover	Easter Parade	Damastown
Antiquary	Track Master	Track Star
Zeenat	Princely Rock	Lairg

As emphasized earlier the daughters of a stallion are scattered far and wide. Asopo's daughters are distributed in stud farms throughout the country. Therefore they visit dozens of stallions every year. If the mare is lucky she will visit a superior and compatible stallion. But this will not happen every time. Inevitably several mares visit mediocre stallions. Now think of two sires, one a prepotent maternal grandsire and another who is not. Their daughters are bound to visit a variety of stallions. While the latter's daughters can get superior offspring only out of superior sires, the former's daughters can get superior offspring out of superior and inferior sires. This advantage, which they alone possess, frequently enables them to pull ahead and top the Maternal grandsires lists! This was one of the reasons why Asopo topped the Maternal grandsires lists 3 times. I am sure readers have clearly grasped the difference between a successful maternal grandsire and a prepotent maternal grandsire. The daughters of a sire who is a successful maternal grandsire get superior racers only out of superior sires, while the daughters of a sire who is a prepotent maternal grandsire get superior racers out of superior and inferior sires. In the chapter on stallions I explained that prepotent stallions need not always be more successful than superior stallions. *But prepotent Maternal grandsires are invariably more successful than superior Maternal grandsires due to the reasons explained above.* Therefore the leading maternal grandsires of every country are bound to be prepotent to some extent at least. It is precisely this prepotence that enabled them to top the lists.

We saw that Asopo was prepotent. Exaggerator too was prepotent. His daughter Preston's Girl produced Statesman out of Anybody Here and Ruffian out of Belmont's Prince, One We Love produced Maharathi out of Nimble Lad and Punchi Nona got Rage Royal out of Lance Corporal. Readers must identify leading maternal grandsires and determine their magnitudes of prepotence. But we must be careful. We cannot expect every daughter of a sire who is a prepotent maternal grandsire to be prepotent. Only a handful can be so.

Let us now study My Babu, a maternal grandsire who made a tremendous impact on international breeding.

		Toubillon	Ksar Durban
	Djebel		
		Loika	Gay Crusader Coeur a Coeur
My Babu (B, 1945)			
		Badruddin	Blandford Mumtaz Mahal
	Perfume II		
		Lavendula	Pharos Sweet lavender

My Babu was an outstanding 2-yr-old who won 5 races including the Champagne Stakes. At 3 he won the English 2000 Guineas and Sussex Stakes (Gr. I). Even though he was not a true stayer, his class enabled him to finish 4th in the Derby.

He was retired to stud in England. In 7 crops he got: **Our Babu** (4 wins, English 2000 Guineas), **Primera** (9 wins, Ormonde Stakes [Gr. II], Princess of Wales Stakes [Gr.II] twice; 2nd Irish St. Leger), **Milesian** (4 wins, Imperial Produce Stakes), **Babu** (National Produce Stakes [Curragh]), **Be Careful** (Gimcrack Stakes) and others. He was then exported to the U.S.A. where his best racer was **Crozier** (Santa Anita Handicap, Washington Park Futurity; 2nd Kentucky Derby). On the whole his performance was modest. In fact in the words of Peter Willett*: ''. . . in view of his excellence on the racecourse and his fine pedigree his stud record could only be called disappointing.''

But nobody can fault his performance as a maternal grandsire. His daughters have performed brilliantly. They produced horses who won repeatedly at the highest international level. It is unnecessary for us to study the produce records of each of them. We will restrict ourselves to their best progeny:

DAMASCUS (1964)

Sword Dancer	Sunglow
	Highland Fling
Kerala	My Babu
	Blade of Time

Damascus was a classic winner of 21 races including the Preakness Stakes and Belmont Stakes. At 3 he was Horse of the Year and champion handicap horse. He is among the leading sires with 39 stakes winners. He is now emerging as a sire of sires.

LITTLE CURRENT (1971)

Sea Bird	Dan Cupid
	Sicalade
Luiana	My Babu
	Banquet Bell

He won 4 races (2nd thrice and 3rd once) including the Preakness Stakes and Belmont Stakes from only 16 starts. He was champion 3-yr-old colt. He is already the sire of 16 stakes winners.

---

* ''Much-travelled Klairon reaps posthumous credit'', *Horse and Hound,* July 22, 1983.

GAMELY (1964)

Bold Ruler	Nasrullah
	Miss Disco
Gambetta	My Babu
	Rough Shod

She won 16 races including the Beldame Stakes twice. She was champion 3-yr-old filly and champion handicap mare twice. Gambetta was also the dam of Staretta.

STARETTA (1957)

Dark Star	Royal Gem
	Isolde
Gambetta	My Babu
	Rough Shod

She won 21 races including the Miss Woodford Stakes.

HIGHEST TRUMP (1972)

Bold Bidder	Bold Ruler
	High Bid
Dear April	My Babu
	Querida

She won 3 races in England and Ireland including the Queen Mary Stakes (Gr. II) and was 3rd in the Irish 1000 Guineas. She was champion 2-yr-old filly in Ireland.

ARTAIUS (1974)

Round Table	Princequillo
	Knight's Daughter
Stylish Pattern	My Babu
	Sunset Gun

He won 3 races including the Joe Coral Eclipse Stakes (Gr. I) and Sussex Stakes (Gr. I) from only 7 starts. He was also 2nd in the Prix du Jockey Club and Benson and Hedges Gold Cup (Gr. I). Sire.

NATIVE STREET (1963)

Native Dancer	Polynesian
	Giesha
Turkish Belle	My Babu
	Wood Fire

She won 10 races including the Kentucky Oaks, Sorority, Astoria and Jasmine Stakes.

BOLD LIZ (1970)

Jacinto	Bold Ruler
	Cascade
Turkish Belle	My Babu
	Taveta

She won 5 races at 2 years including the Hollywood Juvenile Championship and Hollywood Lassie Stakes. She was the second high-weighted filly in the Experimental Free Handicap.

CAPTAIN CEE JAY (1970)

Nashua	Nasrullah
	Segula
Colfax Maid	My Babu
	Tsumani

He won 7 races including the San Luis Obispo Handicap (Gr. II). He also placed 2nd in the Hollywood Invitational Handicap (1-1/2 miles, Gr. I, turf) by a head. Sire.

TYRANT (1966)

Bold Ruler	Nasrullah
	Miss Disco
Anadem	My Babu
	Anne of Essex

He won 13 races including the Delaware Valley Handicap and Carter Handicap. He is the sire of 15 stakes winners (excluding classic winner L'Attrayante).

It is clear that My Babu is a Front-line classic maternal grandsire. But this is not all. Can we not assert that he was also a prepotent maternal grandsire? When we do so, we can immediately answer a question raised by many: *"How did Sword Dancer a failure at stud get Damascus a classic winner who is now emerging as a sire of sires?"* The answer can be given in two words — "My Babu". Since he was a prepotent maternal grandsire his daughters had the ability to get superior racers out of inferior sires. Kerala was obviously one such daughter, producing Damascus. But My Babu's role is not yet over. Damascus was not only a classic winner and champion, but is also a Front-line classic sire with 39 stakes winners to his credit. Did My Babu play a role in his success as a sire? Yes he did! For My Babu is also a "maternal grandsire of sires". His daughters not only possessed the ability to get superior racers, but also the ability to get successful sires. For note that Little Current too has started very brightly getting Group I stakes winner Current Hope and other superior racers. Tyrant has been fairly successful and Artaius has also made a promising start. Without doubt My Babu is a maternal grandsire of sires.

Coming back to Damascus, there is a certain irony in his success. His success was vital and most necessary as his direct male line, the line of the great Teddy, was dangerously close to extinction. Teddy (1913) was an outstanding racer who won the substitute French Derby, San Sebastian St. Leger and Grand Prix de San Sebastian in Spain. Retired to stud in France he was a huge success getting among others: Sir Gallahad III (1920) and Bull Dog (1927) — full-brothers who were very successful sires in the U.S.A., Asterus (1923) another markedly superior sire, Ortello (1926) very successful sire in Italy, Brumeux (1925) sire and others. Hence there was no doubt that his direct male line would grow and prosper. But it was not to be. Leon Rasmussen explains in the *Daily Racing Form:* "It was certain that Teddy's male line would expand and flourish through Sir Gallahad 111 and Bull Dog. But their principal sons Roman and Bull Lea became outstanding maternal grandsires rather than sires of sires, Roman becoming champion maternal grandsire once and Bull Lea 4 times. (Actually this is not very surprising as Sir Gallahad III and Bull Dog were themselves outstanding maternal grandsires. Their sons apparently decided to take after them in this respect.) Therefore the line came dangerously close to extinction. But it survived through the relatively obscure stirp of Sun Teddy — Sun Again — Sunglow — Sword Dancer. Then happily Damascus arrived and he has set the line on a relatively strong foundation." But as we have seen, My Babu and not Sword Dancer was the principal architect of Damascus' success. It is appropriate that an outstanding maternal grandsire has saved a line that got into difficulty because its principal sires became outstanding maternal grandsires rather than sires of sires!

I am sure readers have understood the very powerful role played by maternal grandsires. When we are studying them we would do well to adopt the following procedure:

1) First determine his class and aptitude.
2) Then determine whether he is prepotent.
3) Finally determine whether he is a maternal grandsire of sires.

We need not wait until all his daughters have gone to stud. We must make a calculated guess.

EXERCISE

1) Identify all the successful maternal grandsires in your country and determine their behaviour. Then pinpoint prepotent maternal grandsires and maternal grandsires of sires. Also identify those who are closest to qualifying.

2) I want readers to make an in-depth study of another outstanding international maternal grandsire who was even more successful than My Babu. He was among the leading sires with 44 stakes winners. But as a maternal grandsire he is in a class of his own. The success of his daughters is mind-boggling. They were responsible for no fewer than 106 stakes winners (including a little individual who has won 31 races from 2 to 7 and who is still winning the biggest races in the world), enabling him to top the Maternal grandsires list 4 times and set a record in 1981. Readers must make every endeavour to answer the following questions:

a) How many of his daughters were producers?
b) How many of them were successful producers?
c) How many of them produced more than one superior racer and how many were category I or II broodmares?
d) How many produced a classic winner, champion or Group I winner?
e) What was the aptitude of their progeny? How many had an ideal blend of speed and stamina?
f) How many were prepotent?
g) Finally how many successful sires did they get?

We have so far been studying the behaviour of sires as maternal grandsires after their daughters had produced a large number of winners. But now we must learn how to predict which sires are going to become successful maternal grandsires in the first place. We saw the need for making such predictions.

First and foremost, the sire in question must be at least Average-to-Good. I am not going to claim that daughters of a substandard stallion are going to excel in stud. In all probability they will not even go to stud. Therefore throughout the following discussion the above condition holds. Now let us discuss, one by one, the factors which help a sire succeed as a maternal grandsire. Readers already know the first factor.

1) *A stallion whose sire was an outstanding maternal grandsire has more than the normal chance of success as a maternal grandsire.*

Primera, by My Babu, is an excellent example.

		Djebel	Tourbillon / Loika
	My Babu		
		Perfume II	Badruddin / Lavendula
Primera (B, 1954)			
		Deiri	Aethelstan / Desra
	Pirette		
		Pimpette	Town Guard / Arpette

His race record has been given. He was a successful sire getting among others: **Lupe** (Epsom Oaks, Coronation Cup [Gr. I], Yorkshire Oaks [Gr. I]) **Aunt Edith** (King George VI and Queen Elizabeth Stakes [Gr. I], Prix Vermeille [Gr. I]), **Attica Meli** (Yorkshire Oaks [(Gr. I]) and **Greengage** (Coronation Stakes [Gr. II]). He was then exported to Japan.

His daughters have proved to be admirable broodmares. I am not going into details, but among them were:

PRUDENT GIRL: 2 wins in England. Dam of among others:

> **Play It Safe** (filly by Red Alert): 4 wins in France, champion 2-yr-old filly, Prix Marcel Boussac (Gr. I).

> **Providential** (colt by Run the Gantlet): 6 wins, Washington D.C. International (Gr. I), Hollywood Turf Cup; 3rd Prix du Jockey Club, Premio Roma (Gr. I). Sire.

PRIME ABORD: stakes winner of 3 races in France. Dam of:

> **Super Concorde** (colt by Bold Reasoning): 4 wins, champion 2-yr-old colt in France, Grand Criterium (Gr. I), Prix Morny (Gr. I), now emerging as a top class international sire.

LUPE: dam of:

L'ile Du Reve (filly by Bold Lad): 2 wins, Cheshire Oaks (Gr. II).
Leonardo Da Vinci (colt by Brigadier Gerard): 4 wins in England and U.S.A., White Rose Stakes (Gr. III). Sire.

We saw that another son of My Babu, Babbanio, excelled as a maternal grandsire in India. But My Babu's influence in India was not entirely through him. He had four other sons — Bengali, Mary's Boy, Buskin and Babretto. They were only average sires but the first two named made a small impact as maternal grandsires!

Let us draw up a list of successful maternal grandsires who were by sires who were successful maternal grandsires.

Sire who was a successful maternal grandsire	Son who was also a successful materials grandsire
Sir Gallahad III	Roman
Bull Dog	Bull Lea
Big Game	Combat
Princequillo	Prince John
Double Jay	Bagdad
My Babu	Primera
Worden II	Bon Mot

Undeniably sons of sires who were successful maternal grandsires seem to have an edge.

2) *A stallion whose pedigree resembles that of a successful maternal grandsire has a good chance of success as a maternal grandsire.*

Peter Willett* gives the example of Klairon who was bred on identical lines as My Babu.

Klairon (B, 1952)	Clarion	Djebel	Toubillon / Loika
		Columba	Colorado / Gay Bird
	Klamia	Kantar	Alcantara II / Karabe
		Sweet Lavender	Swynford / Marchetta

---

* "Much-travelled Klairon reaps posthumous credit", *Horse and Hound,* July 22, 1982.

		Tourbillon	Ksar
	Djebel		Durban
		Loika	Gay Crusader
My Babu			Coeur a Coeur
(B, 1945)		Badruddin	Blandford
	Perfume II		Mumtaz Mahal
		Lavendula	Pharos
			Sweet Lavender

The similarities in their pedigrees are obvious. Klairon was a grandson of Djebel while My Babu was his son. Klairon was a grandson of Sweet Lavender while My Babu was her great-grandson.

Klairon was a classic winner of 6 races including the French 2000 Guineas and Prix Jacques le Marois (Gr. I). He was also 2nd in the Queen Elizabeth II Stakes (Gr. II) and 3rd in the English 2000 Guineas.

Retired to stud in 1957, he developed into a Front-line classic sire. His best progeny included:

Monade: Epsom Oaks, Prix Vermeille (Gr. I).

Altissima: French 1000 Guineas.

Luthier: Prix Lupin (Gr. I), Prix Jacques le Marois (Gr. I). Champion sire in France.

Lorenzaccio: Champion Stakes (Gr. I). Sire.

Shangamuzo: Ascot Gold Cup (Gr. I).

D'Uberville: King's Stand Stakes (Gr. I).

Caldarello: Prix d'Ispahan (Gr. I).

He was vastly superior to My Babu. (Peter Willett stresses his extraordinary versatility.)

As a maternal grandsire too, he has been equally successful. Already a Front-line classic maternal grandsire, his daughters have produced:

Irish River (colt, 1976, Riverman x Irish Star): 10 wins from only 12 starts, champion miler at 3 in France, French 2000 Guineas. He won three Gr. II races at 2 and four Gr. I races at 3.

Achieved (colt, 1979, Thatch x Last Call): another brilliant colt, he was champion 2-yr-old in Ireland. His 4 victories included the Gallaghouse Phoenix Stakes. (His full-brother Final Straw was a stakes winner of 5 races.)

     Quiet Fling (colt, 1972, Nijinsky x Peace II): 5 wins, Coronation Cup (Gr. I); 2nd Irish St. Leger, Coronation Cup (to Exceller by a neck). (Peace II also produced the stakes winners Armistice Day, Peaceful, Intermission and Peacetime.)

Now we come to **Habibti** and **L'Attrayante,** a pair of outstanding fillies. The former (1980, by Habitat x Klairessa) was champion 2-yr-old filly in Ireland. At 3 she won the William Hill July Cup (Gr. I). The latter (1980, Tyrant x Camerata) won the French and Goffs Irish 1000 Guineas.

Other superior runners by Klairon mares include the Grand Criterium winner **Satingo** and the William Hill Futurity winner **Sandy Creek**.

Earlier we saw that sons of sires who were outstanding maternal grandsires excelled as maternal grandsires. Must we not apply this rule to Luthier and Lorenzaccio? Luthier was the sire of 49 stakes winners and became the champion sire in France in 1976. His daughters are sure to do well. Lorenzaccio has announced his intentions in no uncertain terms. He is already the maternal grandsire of On the House, winner of the English 1000 Guineas.

    3) A stallion with a number of outstanding or successful maternal grandsires in his pedigree has an excellent chance of success as a maternal grandsire.

It is relatively easy for us to identify such stallions. Study closely the pedigrees of all the successful stallions. A few pedigrees are bound to be dominated by horses who were very successful maternal grandsires.

We are not bothered about their performances as sires here. In particular look at the two *"key" positions of a pedigree — the sire and maternal grandsire positions.* Are they occupied by horses who were outstanding maternal grandsires? If so the horse is sure to do well as a maternal grandsire. A few examples will elucidate.

		Mahmoud	Blenheim Mah Mahal
	The Axe		
		Blackball	Shut Out Big Event
Al Hattab (Ro, 1966)			
		Abernant	Gwen Tudor Rustom Mahal
	Abyssinia		
		Serengeti	Big Game Mercy

He was a stakes winner of 16 races. His victories included the Jersey Derby, Monmouth Invitational Handicap and Patriot Stakes (new track record).

He is a successful sire with 33 stakes winners. His Group I winners include **Silver Supreme** (6 wins, Brooklyn Handicap), **Roan Star** (8 wins, Prix de la Foret) and **Ali Oop** (7 wins, Sapling Stakes).

Now we have to study his pedigree and see how many horses in it were outstanding or successful maternal grandsires.

His sire The Axe is the first to qualify. He was definitely an un-fashionable stallion, yet he managed to get 36 stakes winners. But it is his performance as a maternal grandsire that is of interest to us here. Did you notice the way he is sky-rocketing up the Maternal grandsires lists? He was 58th in 1981, 33rd in 1982 and 9th in 1983. He is already the maternal grandsire of 31 stakes winners including:

> **Caveat** (colt, 1980, Cannonade x Cold Hearted): 6 wins, Belmont Stakes, Prince John Stakes; 2nd Breeders Futurity (Gr. II), Arkansas Derby (Gr. I), Tropical Park Derby (Gr. II).

> **Green Forest** (colt, 1979, Shecky Greene x Tell Meno Lies): 5 wins, champion miler in France at 3, champion 2-yr-old in Europe, champion 2-yr-old colt in France, Grand Criterium (Gr. I), Prix de la Salamandre (Gr. I), Prix Morny (Gr. I), Prix du Moulin de Longchamp (Gr. I).

> **Relaunch** (colt, 1976, In Reality x Foggy Note): 5 wins, Del Mar Derby (Gr. III), La Jolla Mile (Gr. III); 2nd San Luis Rey Stakes (Gr. I, by 1 1/2 1 to John Henry), San Antonio Stakes (Gr. I).

Without doubt his daughters are going to reach greater heights. Therefore we can consider The Axe to be a successful maternal grandsire.

Now consider the other horses close-up in his pedigree: His maternal grandsire Abernant, paternal grandsire Mahmoud and 2nd maternal grandsire Big Game. The presence of Big Game is of awesome importance as he is among the best maternal grandsires of the century. Mahmoud too was very successful and Abernant enjoyed more than his share of success. *Therefore Al Hattab's pedigree is dominated by horses who were outstanding or superior maternal grandsires.* In my opinion this guarantees Al Hattab's success as a maternal grandsire.

The logic we have just used applies to another son of The Axe — Hatchet Man.

Hatchet Man (Ro, 1971)	The Axe	Mahmoud	Blenheim Mah Mahal
		Blackball	Shut Out Big Event
	Bebopper	Tom Fool	Menow Gaga
		Bebop	Prince Bio Cappellina

He won 10 races including the Widener Handicap (Gr. I) and Amory L. Haskell Handicap (Gr. I).

At stud he has made a bright start getting in only 3 crops: **Half Iced** (6 wins, Japan Cup [Gr. I]), Woodchopper (3 wins, Louisiana Derby [Gr. II]; 2nd Kentucky Derby; 3rd Arkansas Derby [Gr. I]) and others.

Again it is his pedigree that interests us. The presence of Tom Fool is very significant. A very successful maternal grandsire, Tom Fool is sure to do for Hatchet Man what Big Game is doing for Al Hattab. Therefore I feel Hatchet Man too is sure to excel as a maternal grandsire.

My third example is a maternal grandsire in India who is headed straight to the top.

CRADLE OF THE DEEP

Cradle of the Deep (Ch, 1961)	Doutelle	Prince Chevalier	Prince Rose Chevalerie
		Above Board	Straight Deal Feola
	Papoose	My Babu	Djebel Perfume II
		Indian Call	Singapore Flittemere

He won the Bure Nursery Handicap at 2. His Timeform rating was 104. At 3 he won the Ditch Apprentice Stakes. In India he won the Calcutta Gold Cup, Burdwan Cup and Clifford Plate. He won from 1400 m to 2000 m. He was retired to stud in 1967.

He has had long innings — his 14th crop is in training. But I hesitate to call him a success. In all honesty we can say he was just a shade above average, even though he had good mares. His best progeny included:

Mountain Lily (1970): 6 wins, Calcutta 1000 Guineas, Indian Gold Vase.

Jee-O-Jee: 5 wins, Shanmuga Sethupathi Cup (2000 m, 5-yr-olds and over in classes I and II, Madras); 2nd South India Oaks (by a short-head), Bangalore St. Leger (by a head); 3rd Bangalore Oaks (by a head and neck).

Dark Orient: 7 wins, Governor's Cup (2800 m, classes I and II, Calcutta), Grand Annual Handicap; 3rd Calcutta 2000 Guineas.

Lorelei: 5 wins; 3rd South India 1000 Guineas.

Sports Page: 7 wins; 3rd Mysore 1000 Guineas.

The Wizard: 6 wins, Pat Williamson Memorial Cup, Rajcoomar Gujadhur Cup, P. Sreenivasan Memorial Cup.

His other superior racers were **Joint Venture, Victor, Guido, Dear Baby, Dynamic, Gulnaar, Ninza** and **Veni Vici.**

Most of his progeny were at their best between 1600 m and 2000 m. They did possess elements of stamina, but due to lack of class were only average or marginally above average stayers rather than classic stayers.

I do not know how many breeders had confidence in Cradle of the Deep mares after his lack-lustre performance as a sire. But I was supremely confident. Allow me to explain. The key positions of his pedigree are occupied by Doutelle and My Babu. My Babu has been described. Let us study Doutelle. He was a stakes winner of 7 races including the John Porter Stakes (Gr. II) and Cumberland Lodge Stakes (Gr. II). He was also 3rd in the King George VI and Queen Elizabeth Stakes (Gr. I) and Ascot Gold Cup (Gr. I). Sadly he was in stud for only four seasons. But within this brief period he demonstrated his ability as a sire, and later as a maternal grandsire, in no uncertain terms. He was the sire of **Pretendre** (Timeform Gold Cup; beaten by a neck in the Epsom Derby), **Canisbay** (Eclipse Stakes), **Fighting Ship** (Jockey Club Stakes, Greenham Stakes 3rd English St. Leger), **Amicable** (Nell Gwyn Stakes) and others. His daughters who excelled as producers include Ship Yard (Bustino, Oarsman), **Hiding Place** (Little Wolf, Smuggler and others) and **Amicable** (Example, Expansive and Amphora). Therefore Cradle of the Deep's sire and maternal grandsire were outstanding maternal grandsires. I was convinced that this factor would enable his daughters to excel.

This is exactly what is happening. His daughters have made an extraordinary start, already getting 3 classic winners:

Beat the Distance (colt, 1980, Knight of Medina x Dear Baby): 5 wins, Calcutta 2000 Guineas and St. Leger; 2nd Calcutta Derby, Queen Elizabeth II Cup.

Turf Hawk (filly, 1976, Eagle Rock x Phool Bagh): 7 wins, Calcutta Oaks, Army Cup (2000 m, 3-yr-olds, Calcutta), R.C.T.C. Gold Cup (2000 m, ciasses II and III, Calcutta).

Shibdiz (filly, 1979, Noor-E-Shiraz x Aimee): 4 wins, Golconda Oaks.

He is also the maternal grandsire of:

Peach of Gold (colt, 1976, Goldbricker x Pretty Peach): 3 wins, S.A.A. Annamalai Chettiar Cup. (A classic colt, he unfortunately had a setback in training.)

Royal Brute (colt, 1976, Satinello x Lorelei): 7 wins, K.M. Munshi Cup, Thunder Storm Cup.

Proud Image (colt, 1979, Gombos x Lorelei): 8 wins, Rastafarian Cup.

Renowned (colt, 1981, Malvado x Joint Venture): winner; 3rd Breeders' Cup (1400 m, 3-yr-olds, Madras). As I was rewriting this chapter, to my intense delight ,he won the Mysore Derby in a pulsating finish. But it was not all. He then toyed with his rivals in the South India Derby, 1985. He was then 2nd in the Bangalore Arc de Triomphe to Lively Emprey but was unplaced in the Indian Derby. His sudden death on the way to Calcutta for the Invitation Cup is a grievous blow to Indian racing and breeding.

But remember the best is yet to come! For the first offspring of a large number of Cradle of the Deep mares are just coming up for sale — eight mares had their first foals entered for sale in the Madras Auction Sale — 1984. Owners of Cradle of the Deep mares are in an envious position. They can breed classic winners and champions by sending them to superior stallions. (At the time of writing it appears that only Horatius is a better maternal grandsire.) Actually pedigree is not the only factor in his success. There is another factor which in all probability is more significant. We will discuss it a little later.

4) *A stallion on the fringe of top class has a good chance of becoming a successful maternal grandsire.*

What do I mean by a stallion "on the fringe of top class"? A name that immediately came to my mind was Nashua. A classic winner of 22 races (Preakness Stakes, Belmont Stakes), he was champion at 2 and Horse of the Year at 3. His stud career is now a legend. During a period of over 20 years he sired no fewer than 76 stakes winners. Then how dare I refer to him as on the fringe of top class? He was top class wasn't he? It is because I have a particular criterion in my mind for top class here. It is simply this: Stallions who sired a significant number of champions are top class. How many champions did Nashua get? Only two — Shuvee (16 wins, champion handicap mare at 4 and 5, C.C.A. Oaks, Mother Goose Stakes, Jockey Club Gold Cup twice) and Producer (10 wins in France and U.S.A., champion filly miler in France, Prix de la Foret, Prix de l'Opera). Compare this performance with say:

Nasrullah: 99 stakes winners, over a dozen champions.

Ribot: 66 stakes winners, 9 champions.

Bold Ruler: 82 stakes winners, over 10 champions.

Hail to Reason: 41 stakes winners, 7 champions (including 1 Horse of the Year).

Northern Dancer: 89 stakes winners, over 18 champions.

Nijinsky: 84 stakes winners, 9 champions.

Habitat: 71 stakes winners, 9 champions.

If we keep these stallions in mind we have to admit that Nashua was not really top class but only on the fringe of top class. He got plenty of superior racers but was unable to get many champions.

Such stallions frequently become superior maternal grandsires and Nashua himself is an example. He is consistently finishing high-up in the Maternal grandsires lists — 9th in 1980 and '82, 10th in 1981 and 11th in 1983. He is the maternal grandsire of among others:

Roberto (1969, Hail to Reason x Bramalea): 7 wins, Epsom Derby. Now a phenomenally successful sire.

Meneval (1973, Le Fabuleax x Nalee): 5 wins, Irish St. Leger, Hardwicke Stakes (Gr. II). Sire.

My Gallant (1970, Gallant Man x Predate) : 5 wins, Blue Grass Stakes (Gr. I); 2nd Flamingo Stakes (Gr. II); 3rd Belmont Stakes. Sire.

Tom Swift (1973, Tom Rolfe x Shuvee): 3 wins in only one season, Seneca Handicap (1-5/8 miles, Gr. II, turf) in a new course record. Sire.

Mr. Prospector (1970, Raise a Native x Gold Digger): stakes winner of 7 races. Among the best stallions in the world.

Raise a Cup (1971, Raise a Native x Spring Sunshine): stakes winner of 4 races from only 6 starts at 2. He has started brightly as a sire getting 15 stakes winners.

Marshua's Dancer (1968, Raise a Native x Marshua): stakes winner of 9 races. A good sire with 22 stakes winners.

Tanthem (1975, Tentam x Antigua Anthem): stakes winner of 15 races. Sire.

It is clear that Nashua has excelled as a maternal grandsire. What more, he is also a maternal grandsire of sires. I cannot assert that he is prepotent as I have not studied the performances of his mares in detail, but my guess is he is.

Let us recall all that we have learnt and consolidate our findings. Our object is to predict which sires are going to excel as maternal grandsires. We saw that sires who satisfied particular conditions excelled as maternal grandsires. Readers will at once ask: "If a stallion satisfies more than one condition, will he have a correspondingly greater chance of success?" The answer is an emphatic yes. Let us go back to Al Hattab. He satisfies three of the four conditions we laid down. His sire is a very successful maternal grandsire. His pedigree is dominated by successful maternal grandsires and he is on the fringe of top class. Therefore can we not assert that his daughters are going to excel in stud? But I will go further. I will be very surprised if he does not become a champion maternal grandsire and a world-leading maternal grandsire. (His early death is a very grievous blow to international breeding.)

Combat (Big Game x Commotion - a winner of the Epsom Oaks) was another individual who satisfied several conditions.

Combat (Br, 1944)	Big Game	Bahram	Blandford Friar's Daughter
		Myrobella	Tetratema Dolabella
	Commotion	Mieuxce	Massine L'Olivete
		Riot	Colorado Lady Juror

He was an unbeaten winner of 9 races. He was not a particularly successful sire, but interestingly made a mark as a maternal grandsire. This is not surprising as he was a son of Big Game. But do not overlook the fact that his maternal grandsire Mieuxce was also a very successful maternal grandsire!

I hope readers are convinced with the above methodology to some extent at least. I hasten to add that every prediction is not going to be correct, and several sires are sure to unexpectedly excel as maternal grandsires. But as I emphasized, it is virtually impossible for any of us to avoid making such predictions. When you buy the offspring of a mare whose sire is yet to make a name as a maternal grandsire, you are tacitly assuming — you are predicting — that he is going to be a successful maternal grandsire. Hence there is need for a framework, a methodology to make such predictions. This methodology will also help you in determining whether a mare is Inherently superior or not, especially in the case of mares who were inferior racers, or who did not race.

But this is not all. I said there was another factor, a very important factor, in the success of Cradle of the Deep. This factor also helped Big Game. What is this vital factor? Conformation! Several have tried to explain the staggering success of Big Game mares. But there is absolutely no doubt regarding one factor in their success — their conformation. Numerous experts have emphasized that they were all ''lengthy'' mares with plenty of ''scope'' and ''substance''. This particular type of conformation helped them become very successful producers.

Cradle of the Deep's daughters too possess similar conformation. I urge you to study closely the conformation of his progeny. The horse may be in class I or in class VB, it is immaterial. What do you find? Aren't most of his progeny very ''lengthy'' with plenty of ''scope'' and ''substance''? Since my knowledge of conformation is very limited I am unable to give a more accurate description. I have seen several of his progeny race in Madras during the last twelve years and with very few exceptions most of them possessed this type of conformation. Jee-O-Jee (class I) had it, Veni Vici (class II) had it, Deep Thoughts (class III) had it, Gala Girl (class IV) had it and even Line King (class VA) had it! A friend of mine hit the nail on the head when he looked at Line King parading in the paddock and exclaimed: ''But he is looking like a class I horse!'' This particular type of conformation did *not* help Cradle of the Deep's progeny to excel on the course, but it is definitely enabling his daughters to excel in stud

Conformation was also a factor in the success of Exaggerator mares. I must describe my personal experience as I remember everything vividly even today. It was my first visit to the Riding Club of Madras and naturally I was the first to arrive. About sixty horses were standing in two rows waiting patiently for members to arrive — truly an awe-inspiring sight for me. Interestingly one horse and only one horse, immediately "caught my eye". She possessed a certain beauty, a particular symmetry, which the others seemed to lack. She did not have the sleek lines of a racehorse; on the contrary she was rather rotund. But she was perfectly "put-together". The horse in question was I'am No Angel, a bay mare by Exaggerator x Thursday's Child. Sometime later I mentioned this rather casually to a veteran race-goer. He immediately told me that most of Exaggerator's progeny possessed such "perfect" conformation. It then struck me that conformation was one of the factors in the success of Exaggerator mares. But note that the conformation of his daughters was different from the conformation of Cradle of the Deep mares. (Sadly we do not know how I'am No Angel would have fared as a producer as she did not go to stud.)

Hence the conformation factor must also be incorporated in the methodology. In addition to satisfying the criteria we laid down, sires who are able to impart particular types of conformation to their progeny have greater chances of success as maternal grandsires. It is for veterinary doctors and other experts to research deeper and pinpoint the elements of conformation that help mares become successful producers.

Let us come back to criterion one. It says that a son of a sire who was a successful maternal grandsire stands a good chance of becoming a successful maternal grandsire. Now think of the converse of this condition. Can we not say that a sire who is an outstanding maternal grandsire will invariably have at least one son who will become a successful maternal grandsire? Let us apply this finding to the greatest maternal grandsire in the world today. Who is he? Even a school-boy will reply promptly: "The great Vaguely Noble." It is unnecessary for me to describe his victories on the course or achievements in stud. (We are going to study his pedigree in great detail later.) Here we have to note that his daughters are proving to be outstanding producers. He is already the maternal grandsire of three European classic winners — Golden Fleece, L'Emigrant and Touching Wood- besides other Group I and stakes winners. And as the progeny of a number of his daughters are just starting to race, the best is yet to come! Since he is really outstanding we can assert that at least one (or more) of his sons will become a successful maternal grandsire. Who will it be? *The Thoroughbred Record Sire Book* (1983) lists nine sons of Vaguely Noble: An Eldorado, Corvaro, Empery, Exceller, Inkerman, Noble Saint, Nomis, Royal and Regal and Vagaries. I want readers to apply the four criteria to the above stallions and determine who is most likely to succeed.

Val de Loir (1959) is another maternal grandsire who has made a tremendous impact on international breeding. He was a classic winner of 7 races including the Prix du Jockey Club. Retired to stud he was leading sire in France 3 times, getting 26 stakes winners. His progeny included Val de l'Orne (4 wins, champion 3-yr-old colt, Prix du Jockey Club), La Lagune (Epsom Oaks), Tennyson (Grand Prix de Paris [Gr. I] in record time) and others. But he is definitely a better maternal grandsire than sire. He is the maternal grandsire of the following Group I winners: Shergar (Great Nephew x Sharmeen), Green Dancer (Nijinsky x Green Valley), Hostage (Nijinsky x Entente), Vayrann (Brigadier Gerard x Val Divine) and Sun Princess (English Prince x Sunny Valley). Readers must therefore study all his sons at stud and identify those likely to succeed as maternal grandsires.

Stallions are always in the news. Their achievements are meticulously recorded and their behaviour analyzed to the minutest detail. X-Y-Z Stallion Guides and P-Q-R Stallion Registers sell like hot cakes! But I have yet to see, or hear, of a directory of maternal grandsires. Correct me if I am wrong. Does it mean that we know all that there is to know about maternal grandsires? I am sure publishers would have already taken my tip. A well-compiled directory of maternal grandsires is sure to be a best-seller!

BUYING A FILLY FOR "STUD VALUE"

We now come to a section which is sure to be of great interest to owner-breeders. Not long ago in the Madras Auction Sale a filly with noticeable defects was sold for a fancy price. When I was surprised a friend explained: "You see she was bought for her stud value. Her owner does not expect her to win many races, but since she is the daughter of a very successful sire, she is sure to excel as a broodmare." I went home and tried to figure out in what way the filly was superior; but I could not. True, she was the daughter of a successful sire, but unfortunately he was not a successful maternal grandsire. Further her tail female line was very mediocre. As expected the filly raaced sparingly in the lower classes, but was sent to stud with high hopes. Readers will not be surprised to hear that those hopes were never fulfilled.

This set me thinking. How can we buy a filly for stud value? What is the procedure to be followed? We would naturally like our filly to be Inherently superior. But when we are buying a yearling filly we obviously cannot assume that she is going to be a superior racer. But if her other two components are superior she naturally qualifies. Therefore when you are buying a filly for stud value, first and foremost make sure that her tail female line is superior if not outstanding. This is the first rule. Then we come to her sire. Which sires must we choose? Ideally we would like to buy a daughter of a sire who was champion maternal grandsire. But practically it will be very difficult to do so, as most of these sires would have finished their stud careers long ago. As an exercise I noted the top 25 maternal grandsires of 1980-81 from *The Indian Turf Statistical Record - Volume 6* and determined how many had progeny entered for sale in 1982. Among the 25 only 3 — Asopo (1st), Punjab (8th) and Paddykin (24th) had progeny entered for sale. But the first named had only a solitary colt entered for sale in Bombay. Similarly you must study the recent North American and European Maternal grandsires lists and identify individuals active today. Undoubtedly a few like Vaguely Noble are bound to be active. You can therefore go in for their daughters. But again there is a catch. Their fillies especially those with strong tail female lines are sure to sell for astronomical prices. Can you even dream of buying a daughter of Vaguely Noble cheaply today?

But there is an alternative. Making use of the techniques we have learnt you must identify sires most likely to excel as maternal grandsires and buy their daughters before they become ''hot''. But you will surely ask: ''Why all this fuss? Wouldn't it be infinitely easier and wiser to buy a daughter of a successful sire and hope that he is going to become an equally successful maternal grandsire?'' You may well do so, but again the price factor will frequently go against you. For these interested in building up a strong racing stable will be bidding for the filly you have in mind. But suppose after diligent study you prepare a list of sires most likely to excel as maternal grandsires. You will surely find that several of them are only marginally above average and that many are even unfashionable. (Horatius and Cradle of the Deep were never fashionable at any stage of their stud careers.) The daughters of these sires are frequently sold very cheaply. Identify their best daughters, daughters with strong tail female lines, and try to buy them. But do not expect such a filly to develop into a champion because she won't. She is by an average sire, but one who is going to become a superior maternal grandsire. When he ultimately makes his name as a maternal grandsire, your filly and her progeny will be worth a fortune.

Finally do not forget the conformation aspect. If you are convinced that the conformation of the daughters of particular stallions — or even the conformation of an individual — is ideal for stud success, you can boldly buy them.

CHAPTER 9

Nicks and Cancellations

We now come to the most fascinating aspect of thoroughbred breeding. In our endeavour to breed superior horses we understood the importance of class and compatibility of the sire and the dam. If the progenitors neither possess class nor are compatible their chances of producing average, let alone superior, racers are almost non-existent. But suppose we have with us a high class broodmare band and several outstanding stallions. The mares and stallions are definitely compatible: Therefore our chances of producing superior progeny are high. The odds are in our favour. But are there any methods, techniques, by which we can further tilt the odds in our favour? Happily for us, there are. We must breed for "nicks".

What exactly is a nick? How does it function? How vast is its scope? How can we make use of them? Experienced readers may have been wondering why I did not refer to nicks much earlier. It is because I had decided to reserve a full chapter for this extremely important phenomenon. Now let us make an exhaustive and in-depth study of nicks. At the outset itself I want to emphasize that *nicks are extremely powerful forces.* Anyone who is able to master their working can run rings round the others.

A nick has been defined as*:

The consistent ability of two bloodlines or crosses to produce superior individuals.

The definition is of awesome importance. Take your time and study it once again. What are the two "key" words in it? They are "consistent" and "superior". Here then is the means by which we can further tilt the odds in our favour. If we breed for a nick we are sure of not one superior racer but a number of superior racers! For note that as per the definition the two crosses *consistently* produce *superior* individuals. It seems all we have got to do is "latch on" to a nick and start producing stakes winner after stakes winner.

But first we have to identify a nick. How many nicks are there in thoroughbred breeding today? Before we can even attempt to answer the question we must know how many types of nicks there are. Historically

---

* Ann Leighton Hardman, "Genetics — They may affect the soundness of your foal", *Stable Management,* Volume 18 Number 1, April/May 1981.

two nicks have received a lot of attention and publicity and are known to one and all: The Phalaris x Chaucer and the Nasrullah x Princequillo. But are these two nicks of the same type? No, they are not. The former is an example of a sire (Phalaris) nicking with a maternal grandsire (Chaucer) while the latter is an example of a chef-de-race (Nasrullah) nicking with another chef-de-race (Princequillo). But are there only two types of nicks or are there more? Less experienced breeders and owners are under the impression that there is only one type of nick. They are not to be blamed. Turf historians have been using the word rather too freely. Therefore let us clear up the confusion here and now. Actually there are four types of nicks as below:

1) A sire x dam nick.

2) A sire x maternal grandsire nick.

3) A sire x chef-de-race nick.

4) A chef-de-race x chef-de-race nick.

Now let us study each of these nicks in detail and see how exactly it functions.

SIRE X DAM NICK

Turf historians know, and you too will surely know, a number of stallions and mares who seem to "hit it off" together, who seem to be made for each other. They produced not one but a number of superior racers, all obviously full-brothers and full-sisters. Therefore as per the definition we can say there is a "nick" between the concerned sire and dam. Let us study the nick between Red Indian and Nicola.

		Bois Roussel	Vatout Plucky Liege
	Migoli		
		Mah Iran	Bahram Mah Mahal
Red Indian (Gr, 1953)			
		Owen Tudor	Hyperion Mary Tudor II
	Red Briar		
		Infra Red	Ethnarch Black Ray
		Niccolo dell'Arca	Coronach Nogara
	Nicostratus		
		Exotic	Colombo Eastern Rose
Nicola (Ch, 1962)			
		Epigram	Son-in-Law Flying Sally
	Tasha		
		Dusky Maiden	Ximenes Double Rose II

NICOLA: 4 wins (including 2 wins in class VA) up to 1600 m.

TASHA: 2 wins. Nicola was her only foal.

DUSKY MAIDEN: unraced. Dam of:

Highway Patrol: 2 wins in England.

Shah Jehan: 1 win in England; 2nd Birdcatcher Stakes. 8 wins in North America.

Bayrum: 1 win in England.

Heir Presumptive: 6 wins in Germany.

Fair Councellor: 1 win in India.

Tasha: as above.

DOUBLE ROSE II: dam of 6 winners including:

Hafiz II: Queen Elizabeth Stakes (Ascot); 2nd Hardwicke Stakes, Cambridgeshire Stakes.

ROSY CHEEKS: winner. (Grandam of Dante [Epsom Derby] and Sayajirao [Irish Derby, English St. Leger]).

Nicola visited Red Indian on no fewer than eight occasions producing:

Warpath (Roan colt, 1968): 8 wins, Nizam's Gold Cup; 2nd South India St. Leger.

Red Divine (Grey colt, 1969): 5 wins, Bangalore Derby.

Great Gale (Grey colt, 1971): 5 wins, Owners and Trainers Association Cup, Kunigal Stud Gold Cup. (He was definitely developing into a classic contender but sadly had a setback in training.)

Canyon (Bay colt, 1972): 12 wins, M.R.C. Equine Hospital Cup (2000 m, class IV, Madras). (An average racer.)

War Cry (Roan colt, 1973): 8 wins, Rajpipla Gold Cup (twice), K.M. Munshi Gold Cup; 2nd Jiwajirao Scindia Gold Cup, Aga Khan's Spring Cup; 3rd Indian 2000 Guineas, R.R. Ruia Gold Cup. He holds the track record in Bombay for 1600 m. Sire.

Red Chieftan (Chestnut colt, 1975): 18 wins, South India, Deccan and Mysore Derby, Hyderabad Colts Trial Stakes etc. He also placed in several classics. Sire.

Nicolette (Grey filly, 1976): 11 wins, Golconda Derby and Oaks, Nilgiris Derby and Fillies Trial Stakes, South India, Bangalore and Mysore 1000 Guineas etc. She was never off the board in all her starts.

Nicolina (Dark bay filly, 1978): 3 wins, Narmada Cup (2000 on, classes III and IV, Bangalore). (An average racer.)

There was obviously a very strong and intense nick between Red Indian and Nicola. 3 of their progeny were classic winners and another 3 were well up to classic standard. Only 2 were average (and interestingly both were bays). All of them were genuine stayers, extreme stayers (with the exception of War Cry who was a miler, but with staying tendencies) who truly loved and excelled over a distance of ground.

We must now try to determine why Nicola nicked so strongly, so intensely, with Red Indian. First let us quickly study Red Indian. To save time I will straightaway describe his behaviour. He was definitely a specialist sire of high class stayers and extreme stayers, but only out of staying mares or well-bred mares bred to stay. He was therefore the ideal classic stallion. But tragically, most unfortunately, Indian breeders missed out on him, even though he was active for about fifteen years. (Remember he was also nicely bred: A son of Migoli out of an Owen Tudor mare who was a grand-daughter of Black Ray.) He had wretched books of mares, mares who were *incompatible* with him in every respect. Further his mares were always small in number. In my opinion very few stallions in India had such bad mares. Yet to his eternal credit, whenever a good mare came his way he seized the opportunity and produced a superior racer. His other superior racers were:

Young Turk (colt, 1967, by Reko): 7 wins, South India 2000 Guineas, Bangalore Colts Trial Stakes, Czechoslovakia Cup; 2nd South India Derby.

Deep Water Blues (filly, 1977, by Uma): 7 wins, as described.

Byerly Brigade (colt, 1978, by Uma): 3 wins, as described.

Arrangement (colt, 1976, by Om-Sakthi): 6 wins, as described.

King of Seers (colt, 1973, by Koh-E-Sina): 13 wins, as described.

Red Flame (colt, 1972, by Super Flame): 9 wins, Governor's Cup (2600 m, classes III and IV, Madras).

Notice that all the above horses were stayers or extreme stayers. Therefore staying mares or well-bred mares bred to stay were most ideal for him.

Let us apply this finding to Nicola and see whether she was compatible. She was not a stayer. But her pedigree, especially the maternal grandsire component, is of interest. She was the only produce of her dam. Her grandam was fair. It is difficult to judge her performance precisely as her progeny scored in four countries. But there is no doubt regarding the next two dams — Double Rose II and Rosy Cheeks. Their descendants are winning races at the highest level today. Let us turn to the maternal grandsires.

Nicostratus ran unplaced in England. In India he won 2 small races and retired to stud. His first crop was foaled in 1962. He had very few progeny. But look at the 2nd and 3rd maternal grandsires. Both were formidable extreme stayers. The former, Epigram, won the Ascot Stakes, Goodwood Stakes, Doncaster Cup and Alexandra Stakes (2-3/4 miles) while the latter, Ximenes, won the Rufford Abbey Handicap (1-3/4 miles) and was 2nd in the Goodwood Cup (about 2-3/4 miles).

Honestly there is nothing much to recommend in Nicola. She was not Inherently superior. She was at the most average. Modern-day breeders would recoil in horror on seeing the pedigrees of mares like Nicola and Tasha. But keeping in mind the extreme stamina in the maternal grandsire component, we can perhaps say that there was an element of compatibility between her and Red Indian. But you will ask at once: "When we are not even sure of the compatibility between Red Indian and Nicola, why did she visit him on no fewer than eight occasions? Surely the breeder must have guessed the nick in advance?'' It is unlikely, but obviously the breeder was sure that there were elements of compatibility between the two. He then followed a rule which we will discuss in detail below.

THE DERBY DICTUM

The ''Derby Dictum'' is the name given to a rule followed by the 17th Earl of Derby and several other eminent breeders. Stated simply it is this:

If a stallion and mare are compatible, they should be mated not once but several times, in order to obtain the full benefit of their compatibility.

It would be difficult to find a more useful rule in breeding. We are sure that a mare is compatible with a particular stallion. We are convinced that they can produce a superior racer. But suppose we breed only one offspring from them, and that individual is disappointing. Can we at once conclude that the stallion and mare are not compatible? Obviously not. For we simply cannot expect a stallion and mare to give their best in every mating. Do not forget the difficulties in breeding. But suppose the stallion and mare are bred four times, or at least a minimum of three times. Now can we not boldly say that at least one of the progeny will develop into a superior racer? Therefore instead of patronizing a different stallion year after year, would it not be wiser to select a couple of stallions who are, in all probability, the most compatible and breed the mare to them a minimum of three times? This rule has been followed with great success by a number of eminent breeders. I once again emphasize: We just cannot expect every offspring to develop into a superior racer. But at least one will do so.

The success with which you can use this rule depends entirely on your skill and experience. Remember the stallion and mare must be compatible in the first place. If they are not the results are bound to be disastrous, and no number of matings will help them produce a superior racer. But if they are compatible, the rewards will be very great.

Coming back to Red Indian and Nicola, the breeder convinced of the compatibility between them followed the Derby Dictum. But when even their first progeny showed talent in no uncertain terms, he wisely continued the breeding instead of experimenting with other stallions.

In other words a sire x dam nick is the ''total and intense compatibility'' between a sire and dam. Unless Red Indian and Nicola were totally compatible, compatible in every respect, they could not have produced so many superior progeny. While we cannot predict a nick, we can make use of all the principles we have learnt and confirm that there are elements of compatibility between a sire and dam. If we are lucky the elements of compatibility could be strong enough to constitute a nick.

Suppose that instead of a nick between Red Indian and Nicola, there were only elements of compatibility. Then what would have happened? Among their 8 progeny 1 would have been a classic winner, 1 classic-placed, 2 average and 4 substandard. The nick between them ensured that 6 of their 8 progeny were classic horses.

There is a nick between a stallion and mare if they produced a minimum of three superior racers.

A few readers will enquire: "No doubt the Red Indian x Nicola matings have been very successful. But suppose Nicola had visited Prince Pradeep or Pa Bear, she might have been even more successful' Does Nicola's nick with Red Indian preclude her from nicking with Prince Pradeep or Pa Bear?" No, it does not. But these nicks are mere conjecture. The Red Indian x Nicola nick is a fact.

From the above suggestion one more aspect of a nick is revealed: A mare can nick with more than one stallion, and a stallion can nick with several mares. Imagine a mare who produced 3 superior racers out of stallions A and B. Then as per the definition the mare nicked with stallions A and B.

KING OF PIPPINS X ONLY FOR YOU NICK

King of Pippins (Ch, 1953)	Persian Gulf	Bahram	Blandford / Friar's Daughter
		Double Life	Bachelor's Double / Saint Joan
	The Poult	Mr. Jinks	Tetratema / False Piety
		Golden Pheasant	Gold Bridge / Bonnie Birdie
Only For You (Ch, 1964)	Babbanio	My Babu	Djebel / Perfume II
		Butterfly Blue	Blue Peter / Glenfinnan
	Solar Princess	Solar Prince	Solario / Serena
		School Teacher	Rhodes Scholar / Baroness VI

ONLY FOR YOU: ran only once due to injury and was retired to stud.

SOLAR PRINCESS: 4 wins, C.N. Wadia Gold Cup; 2nd Aga Khan's Cup; 3rd Gen. Obaidullah Khan Gold Cup. Dam of:

Sun Child: 9 wins, T.V. Reddy Memorial Cup.
Sweet Bambina: 4 wins.
Vinto: 4 wins.
Harischandra: 2 wins.
Only For You: as above.

SCHOOL TEACHER: unraced. Dam of:

La Resistance: did not win.
Solar Princess: as above.

BARONESS VI: 14 wins in France. Dam of:

Blue Baron: 3 wins in England.
Lady Delhi: 1 win in England.
School Teacher: as above.

Only For You visited King of Pippins 8 times getting:

Benefactor (colt, 1968): 7 wins, Shantidas Askuran Gold Cup (1200 m, class II, Bombay), Sir Sultan Chinoy Gold Cup (1200 m, class III, Bombay).

Benevolence (colt, 1969): 5 wins; 2nd South India Gold Cup (by a short-head).

Emotional (filly, 1971): unraced, retired to stud.

Monopoly (filly 1972): 6 wins; 2nd Gool Poonawalla Gold Cup (1200 m, class II, Hyderabad).

Divine Jewel (colt, 1973): 8 wins, Army Cup (1200 m, class II, Hyderabad).

King's Bench (colt, 1974): 3 wins, Nevada State Racing Commission Trophy (1200 m, 2-yr-olds, Madras), Rajyotsava Cup (1200 m, class III, Bangalore); 3rd R.W.I.T.C. Cup (1600 m, class II, Madras) in only 2 years of racing.

Princess of Pippins (filly, 1975): 5 wins.

King Maker (colt, 1976): 10 wins, dead-heated for win in the State Bank Cup (1400 m, class II, Madras), Bombay Cup (1200 m, class II, Ootacamund), Random Harvest Cup (1200 m, class II, Madras).

She then visited two other stallions getting:

Only For Me (colt, 1980, by Romiti): 1 win, in training.

Sui-Generis (colt, 1981, by Malvado): 2 wins in his first season, Breeders Produce Stakes.(1400 m, 3-yr-olds, Bombay), Ahmed I. Rahimtoola Cup.

Let us study this nick. At once it seems to be qualitatively different from the Red Indian x Nicola. "Is there a nick at all", readers are sure to ask. The Red Indian x Nicola nick produced 3 classic winners. How many classic winners did this nick produce? Not even one. But recall the definition of a nick. Nowhere in the definition does it say a nick should produce classic winners or champions. It only refers to "superior individuals". Among the 8 King of Pippins x Only For You progeny, 3 were superior racers and another 3 can definitely be considered superior. Therefore there was a nick between King of Pippins and Only For You.

But a few will genuinely disagree. It is because of the way in which they visualize a nick. Whenever somebody mentions the word they immediately think of classic winners and champions. In other words they have unconsciously modified the definition into:

The consistent ability of two bloodlines or crosses to produce classic winners or champions.

Now think of this definition and compare it with the earlier one. Don't you think it is too severe? But if you still feel that this is the correct definition you can go ahead and use it in your work. But for the purpose of this book I will only consider the first definition.

Note that the intensity, the strength, of this nick was less than the Red Indian x Nicola. For the offspring of the nick were not the best offspring of either the sire or the dam.

King of Pippins won the Hull Handicap Plate in England. In India he won 7 races including the Czechoslovakia Cup, Berar Gold Cup, P. Natesan Memorial Cup and placed 2nd in the Rajpipla Gold Cup.

Retired to stud in 1963, he was almost a Border-line classic stallion with 2 classic winners and several superior racers. He had fair books of mares. He was a versatile stallion. His classic winners were:

Super Seer (colt, 1969, by Lady Orcades): 9 wins, South India 2000 Guineas and St. Leger, Owners and Trainers Association Cup; neck 2nd in the South India and Bangalore Derby. He won from 1000 m to 2800 m. Sire.

Galilee (colt, 1966, by Amukiriki): 9 wins, Bangalore Derby and Colts Trial Stakes (he was the first horse to bring off this double), Owners and Trainers Association Cup; 2nd South India Derby; 3rd South India 2000 Guineas. Sire.

His other superior racers included: **The Senator** and **Queen of Tamil-Nadu, Minnings, Mary Poppings** and **Moll Flanders, Floral Tribute, Lotus Prince, Best of Luck** and **Jigri Dost.**

It is difficult to say whether Only For You was Inherently superior. As mentioned her sire Babbanio was champion maternal grandsire. He was also a very successful sire. But the same cannot be said about her tail female line. Unfortunately she ran only once due to injury. Her racing performance may have enabled her to qualify. Note that her dam was a genuine high class stayer.

Even though Only For You nicked well with King of Pippins, her best offspring was by Malvado. For Sui-Generis by virtue of his victory in the prestigious Breeders Produce Stakes, has proved himself to be one of the best youngsters in the country. If he develops on normal lines he is sure to be superior than all the King of Pippins x Only For You progeny. Therefore Only For You was compatible with Malvado as well.

There is another interesting aspect of the nick. None of the progeny of the nick were stayers even though they were bred to stay. I emphasize that King of Pippins did get a handful of genuine stayers. Notice the superior stamina in Only For You. Her sire was a maternal grandsire of stayers and her dam was also a genuine stayer. Let us see if Sui-Generis develops into a classic stayer.

Finally we should ask: "What were the elements of compatibility between King of Pippins and Only For You? Why did they nick? Could we have predicted the nick?" In the case of Red Indian and Nicola we found that there was an element of compatibility. But here it is difficult to pinpoint the elements of compatibility. Only For You's major "asset" was her sire Babbanio. If we consider her tail female line to be superior, she qualifies as a well-bred mare. Therefore stallions who excelled with wellbred mares would have been most suitable for her. But there are dozens of such stallions including King of Pippins, and as we have seen another stallion Malvado was also compatible with her. Therefore we are forced to conclude that Only For You was compatible with a number of stallions and could have even nicked with them.

Our conclusions from this nick are:

The progeny of a nick need not be classic winners or champions. They need not even be the best progeny of the sire and dam involved. *In other words every nick will not be "strong" and "powerful ". The intensity of nicks varies. While some nicks are very strong others are only moderate.*

Let us study one more sire x dam nick, this time from international breeding: The Sharpen Up x Doubly Sure.

Sharpen Up (Ch, 1969)	Atan	Native Dancer	Polynesian / Geisha
		Mixed Marriage	Tudor Minstrel / Persian Maid
	Rocchetta	Rockefella	Hyperion / Rockfel
		Chambiges	Majano / Chanterelle
Doubly Sure (B, 1971)	Reliance II	Tantieme	Deux pour Cent / Terka
		Reliance III	Relic / Polaire II
	Soft Angels	Crepello	Donatello II / Crepuscule
		Sweet Angel	Honeyway / No Angel

DOUBLY SURE: placed.

SOFT ANGELS: 2 wins at 2 in England, champion 2-yr-old filly, Princess Margaret Stakes, Royal Lodge Stakes; 3rd Musidora Stakes. Dam of 5 foals, 2 winners:

Dulcet: winner; 2nd Prince of Wales Stakes.

Sancta: 3 wins in England.

SWEET ANGEL: stakes winner at 2 in England, Newmarket Stud Produce Stakes. Dam of 9 foals (all to race), 6 winners:

Sweet Moss: 6 wins in England, Dante Stakes, Gordon Stakes, Dee Stakes. Sire in Australia.

Sucaryl: 3 wins in England, News of the World Stakes; 2nd Irish Sweeps Derby; 3rd Prix Royal Oak. Sire in New Zealand.

NO ANGEL: dam of 8 winners including:

Young Lochinvar: 4 wins in England (as described), very successful sire in India.

Faust: 1 win in England; 2nd King Edward VII Stakes. Sire.

Crepes d'Enfer: 5 wins in England; 3rd Oxfordshire Stakes. Sire.

Doubly Sure's produce record is as follows:

Kris (colt, 1976, by Sharpen Up): 14 wins from 16 starts, champion miler twice, Sussex Stakes (Gr. I), Waterford Crystal Mile (Gr. II); 2nd English 2000 Guineas. Sire.

Pris (filly, 1978, by Priamos): unraced, at stud.

Risk (colt, 1979, by Reform): placed.

Diesis (colt, 1980, by Sharpen Up): 3 wins from 4 starts, champion 2-yr-old, William Hill Middle Park Stakes (Gr. I), William Hill Dewhurst Stakes (Gr. I).

Keen (colt, 1981, by Sharpen Up): in training.

Presidium (colt, 1982, by General Assembly): in training.

There is obviously a strong and very intense nick between Doubly Sure and Sharpen Up with 2 of their 3 progeny developing into champions. Even though a minimum of 3 superior progeny are necessary to constitute a nick, I think we can safely relax the rule here. Those mathematically inclined can determine the probability of a mare producing 1 champion and then 2 champions.

Sharpen Up was a stakes winner of 5 races in England. His performance as a sire has been entirely satisfactory: He has got 31 stakes winners including **Epsiba** (8 wins, Derby Belge, Horse of the Year in Belgium), **Sharpo** (7 wins in England and France, champion sprinter twice in England and France), **Sharpman** (3 wins in France; 2nd Poule d'Essai des Poulains), **Pebbles** (General Accident English 1000 Guineas) and others.

Doubly Sure's impressive pedigree automatically makes her a well-bred mare. No doubt she is compatible with a number of other stallions as well.

I am sure the functioning of this type of nick is very clear. I do not think any breeder would confidently predict a nick between a sire and dam. You must breed for as many elements of compatibility as possible. If your judgement is correct there could well be a nick. The performance of the first few progeny will clearly show whether you are on the right track. If they show promise you will be anxious to repeat the mating. There may be a very intense nick, a moderately intense nick or there may not be a nick at all. Only time will tell.

Readers must study the Nantallah x Rough Shod II nick. This nick produced 1 champion, 1 undefeated Horse of the Year at 2, 1 stakes winner and 1 stakes-placed filly. When the stakes-placed filly went to stud she promptly produced a champion and other stakes winners. Is there any significance in this?

SIRE X MATERNAL GRANDSIRE NICK

We all know this type of nick. Historically great emphasis has been placed on this nick and it has been studied in detail. Yet there are a number of aspects which require further study. Suppose stallion A nicks with maternal grandsire B.

A	VARIOUS
	VARIOUS
p, q, r,	B
s and t	VARIOUS

What does this mean? What are all the implications? How must we investigate the nick? What is the methodology to be adopted?

Applying the definition we understand that A will produce a large number of superior racers out of daughters of B. But there are several ways by which this can happen. Suppose that 3 daughters of B have each produced 3 superior racers out of A, while a fourth produced a superior racer. Is there a nick between sire A and maternal grandsire B? At first glance it appears that there is a nick, as A produced as many as 10 superior racers out of B mares. But on closer examination we find that only 3 mares were the dams of 9 superior racers. Therefore instead of a sire x maternal grandsire nick we really have three sire x dam nicks! The sire x maternal grandsire nick has collapsed! Frequently this is what happens. Many sire x maternal grandsire nicks are, in reality, three or four sire x dam nicks.

Then when is a sire x maternal grandsire nick really constituted?

Sire A nicks with maternal grandsire B when a sufficiently large number of daughters of B have produced at least one superior racer out of A.

Suppose that 7 daughters of B have each produced a superior racer out of and that another daughter has produced 3 superior racers. Since as many as 8 daughters of B have been successful, there is truly a nick between sire A and maternal grandsire B. But what about the mare who produced 3 superior racers? Her case is of special interest as her progeny had the benefit of two nicks! For she as an individual nicked with A i.e. Sire x dam nick, while her sire B also nicked with A i.e. a sire x maternal grandsire nick. We have just learnt a very important rule:

Two or more nicks can function simultaneously.

The greater the number of nicks functioning, greater the chances of success of the progeny. We will come back to this topic a little later.

Readers can easily pinpoint sire x maternal grandsire nicks by using the above principle. While every daughter of B is not going to produce a superior racer out of A, a significant number of them will do so. Again note that there is no mention of classic winners, champions or Group I winners. If the nick has produced such horses well and good, but even otherwise it is valid.

Let us go back to the stallions we studied and see whether any of them nicked with a maternal grandsire. Yes, a couple of them did. Prima facie, two nicks seem probable: The Young Lochinvar x Asopo and Everyday x Horatius. Both these probable nicks must be investigated. First let us study the former.

We saw that Asopo was a hugely successful maternal grandsire Studying Table 13 we find that several Asopo mares excelled with Young Lochinvar, getting, on the whole, 10 superior racers. In particular 5 Asopo mares produced at least 1 superior racer out of Young Lochinvar. (Take Cover produced 4 superior racers and Goodie and Georgian Gem 2 each.) Since stallions in India, till recently, had very small books we can definitely say Young Lochinvar nicked with Asopo. But now we must go a step further and test whether the nick is really valid. This is done as below. First we must determine the number of times non-Asopo mares visited Young Lochinvar and calculate their percentage of success in producing superior racers. Similarly we must determine the number of times Asopo mares visited Young Lochinvar and calculate their percentage of success. Then we must determine the number of times all the Asopo mares visited a stallion other than Young Lochinvar and calculate their percentage of success in producing superior racers.

In other words our objective is to determine the performance of Young Lochinvar and Asopo outside the nick.

This information is definitely relevant. Suppose Young Lochinvar had 20% success with Asopo mares and again 20% success with non-Asopo mares. Can we still say there is a nick between Young Lochinvar and Asopo? No, we cannot. For the definition of a nick also implies a higher "striking rate", a higher percentage of success. If Young Lochinvar had the same percentage of success with Asopo and non-Asopo mares, we cannot say there is a nick. *He has only performed in his usual manner.* But if his success with Asopo mares was significantly, or at least marginally, higher, we can boldly say he nicked with Asopo. Similarly the percentage of success of Young Lochinvar with Asopo mares i.e. the percentage of success of Asopo mares with Young Lochinvar, should be at least marginally greater than their percentage of success with stallions other than Young Lochinvar taken as a whole. While I have not carried out these two steps due to lack of authoritative data in a suitable form, I am convinced the Young Lochinvar x Asopo nick is valid.

Let us now see how Horatius mares fared with Everyday. Turning to chapter 5 we find that 3 daughters of Horatius — Hold the Bridge, Mark My Words and Three Little Words produced superior racers out of Everyday. Therefore as yet we cannot say there is a nick between Everyday and Horatius. But I have made a special mention as I feel there is every chance of a nick, or at least a "tendency" towards a nick. I am convinced the nick is in its incipient stage. If breeders follow up the nick is sure to develop strongly and blossom.

There is yet another nick which readers can investigate: The Raise a Native x Nashua. Raise a Native seems to have produced several superior racers out of Nashua mares.

EXTENSION OF A NICK

Whenever a nick is confirmed breeders not only rush to take advantage of it, but also try to "extend" its scope. Consider the A (sire) x B (maternal grandsire) nick. Surely the "reverse" nick i.e. daughters of A x B must be more than probable? Or how about a son of A x B nick? Sadly these extensions rarely work. The reasons are not hard to find. We know that a nick constitutes total and intense compatibility. Consider A's nick with B mares. A's unique race record, pedigree, conformation and temperament, and even his bone and sinew, are somehow intensely compatible with B mares. But a son of A will naturally have a different race record, pedigree, conformation and temperament. He is a distinct personality in his own right. He is not a carbon-copy of his sire. Where then is the question of a nick with B mares? This logic also applies to the reverse nick. A's intense compatibility with B mares does not guarantee B's compatibility with A mares.

SIRE X CHEF-DE-RACE NICK

This nick is identical to the sire x maternal grandsire nick. The only difference is that the sire, instead of nicking with the maternal grandsire in particular, nicks with a chef-de-race in the pedigree of the dam. Readers will at once ask: "Who is a chef-de-race? What does he do? We have not come across this phrase before." The concept of a chef-de-race is very fundamental and is extremely important. Now I must ask readers to turn to chapter 11 and study very carefully the concept of a chef-de-race. To put it simply a chef-de-race is one who was a "breed shaping" stallion in the truest sense of the term.

Turf historians have come across stallions who nick ·with mares who have a particular chef-de-race in their pedigrees. An example will help readers understand this nick very easily.

John P. Sparkman* has analyzed and explained the Mr. Prospector x Nasrullah nick. In essence, Mr. Prospector has produced a number of superior racers out of mares with a cross of Nasrullah. John P. Sparkman determined that 11 of Mr. Prospector's 27 stakes winners had a cross of Nasrullah. Further his very best progeny too had a cross of Nasrullah:

> **Conquistador Cielo** (1979, by K.D. Princess): 9 wins, Horse of the Year at 3, champion 3-yr-old colt, Belmont Stakes, Metropolitan Handicap (Gr. I).
>
> **It's in the Air** (1976, by A Wind is Rising): 16 wins, champion 2-yr-old filly, Vanity Handicap (Gr. I) twice.
>
> **Miswaki** (1978, by Hopespringseternal): 6 wins in France and U.S.A., Prix de la Salamandre (Gr. I).
>
> **Gold Stage** (1977, by Stage Princess): 5 wins, Breeders Futurity (Gr. II).

Since Mr. Prospector himself has a cross of Nasrullah in his 3rd generation, all the above horses are *inbred* to Nasrullah. But there is absolutely no need for a stallion to nick with only those chefs-de-race present in his pedigree. He can nick with any chef-de-race. One stallion may nick with Hyperion and another with Ribot. A third may nick with Native Dancer.

---

* "Speed, speed, more speed and now distance", *The Thoroughbred Record*, 9 June 1982.

To confirm the nick we have to adopt the procedure we used earlier. We must divide all the mares who visited Mr. Prospector and produced runners into two groups:

1) Mares whose 3-generation pedigrees are free from Nasrullah.
2) Mares whose 3-generation pedigrees have a cross of Nasrullah.

Then we must count the number of times mares in each category visited him and calculate their percentage of success. John P. Sparkman carried out this step (albeit in a different way) and found that Mr. Prospector's percentage of success with Nasrullah mares was slightly higher. By the same logic he determined one more very important aspect of Mr. Prospector's behaviour: His percentage of *winners* with Nasrullah mares was significantly higher than with other mares. The advantages of breeding a mare with a cross of Nasrullah to Mr. Prospector are now obvious. If the other elements of the mare are also compatible, and if everything goes well, we have an excellent chance of getting a stakes winner or even a champion. At worst, even if the mating does not really click, the offspring will in all probability be a winner. Therefore we have everything to gain but very little to lose.

We now come to an important point. John P. Sparkman specifies the position of Nasrullah in the pedigree of the dam: Her sire i.e. the maternal grandsire of the offspring should trace to Nasrullah in his direct male line. I feel this specification is quite unnecessary and needlessly restrictive. Let us therefore remove it. Let Nasrullah occupy any position within the 3-generation pedigree of the dam. Then the offspring will have the cross of Nasrullah within his 4 generations. Therefore for a sire x chef-de-race nick, the chef-de-race can occupy any position within the 3-generation pedigree of the dam.

CHEF-DE-RACE X CHEF-DE-RACE NICK

This type of nick includes one of the most potent influences ever in the thoroughbred: *The Nasrullah x Princequillo.* The functioning of this nick is radically different from the earlier nicks we studied. Its scope is vast and its sweep dazzling. Therefore our methodology here must necessarily be different. All the earlier nicks were limited to One stallion. The nick ended with that stallion. Not so a chef-de-race x chef-de-race nick Several stallions are involved and their sons and grandsons too may become powerful protagonists. For this is a nick that can be "extended" for two or three (or may be even more) generations. In essence, horses with a cross of each of the chefs-de-race within 4 generations have an excellent chance of developing into superior racers if not classic winners or champions. Let us study the Nasrullah x Princequillo nick in detail.

			Phalaris
		Pharos	Scapa Flow
	Nearco		
		Nogara	Havresac II
			Catnip
Nasrullah			
(B, 1940)		Blenheim	Blandford
			Malva
	Mumtax Begum		
		Mumtaz Mahal	The Tetrarch
			Lady Josephine

The great Nasrullah needs no introduction. Bred in Ireland by H.H. the Aga Khan, he won 5 races. At 2 he won the Coventry Stakes and was champion 2-yr-old colt. At 3 he won the Champion Stakes and was 3rd in the Derby which was run at Newmarket due to war-time restrictions. He was weighted 132 lbs. in the English Free Handicap, only 1 lb. below Derby winner Straight Deal. In all probability he was a better racer than what his record indicates. His training was entirely in Newmarket and it is said he disliked the place.

Retired to stud first in England, then in Ireland and finally in the U.S.A., he was a staggering success. He got 99 stakes winners including over a dozen champions. He was leading sire in North America 5 times. He was also leading sire in England. He was the first to become leading sire in both countries.

A sire of sires, his principal sons at stud were:

	Bold Ruler
	Never Bend
	Nashua
	Never Say Die
	Grey Sovereign
Nasrullah	Red God
	Jaipur
	On and On
	Fleet Nasrullah
	Nearula
	Princely Gift (and others)

Among these stallions I have selected Bold Ruler, Never Bend and Nashua for research.

BOLD RULER

		Nearco	Pharos
Nasrullah			Nogara
		Mumtaz Begum	Blenheim
Bold Ruler			Mumtaz Mahal
(Dk. B, 1954)		Discovery	Display
	Miss Disco		Adriadne
		Outdone	Pompey
			Sweep Out

An outstanding racer, Bold Ruler was a classic winner of 23 races from 33 starts. At 2, with wins in the Futurity and Juvenile Stakes, he was weighted 2nd-highest in the Experimental Free Handicap. At 3 he won 11 races (2nd twice and 3rd twice) including the Preakness Stakes, Flamingo Stakes and Wood Memorial Stakes. He was also 2nd in the Florida Derby and 3rd in the Belmont Stakes. He was champion 3-yr-old and Hhorse of the Year. At 4 he was champion sprinter with 5 wins.

Retired to stud he shattered all records by becoming the leading sire on no fewer than 8 occasions. He was also leading juvenile sire 5 times and leading sire of stakes winners 8 times. He got 82 stakes winners. He was also a sire of sires. What is of interest to us is that he excelled with mares who had a cross of.Princequillo getting among others:

Secretariat (dam Somethingroyal by Princequillo): 16 wins, American Triple Crown, Horse of the Year at 2 and 3, champion grass horse at 3. Sire of 18 stakes winners.

Syrian Sea (full-sister to Secretariat): 6 wins, Selima Stakes, Astarita Stakes, Colleen Stakes.

Misty Morn, an outstanding daughter of Princequillo (11 wins, champion 3-yr-old filly, champion handicap mare, Monmouth Oaks, Providence Stakes, Gallant Fox Handicap), excelled with Bold Ruler getting:

Bold Lad: 14 wins from only 19 starts, champion 2-yr-old, Champagne Stakes, Futurity Stakes, Metropolitan Handicap. Sire of 22 stakes winners including 4 champions.

Successor: 7 wins, champion 2-yr-old, Champagne Stakes, Garden State Stakes. Sire.

Bold Consort: stakes winner of 6 races.

Beautiful Day: stakes winner of 7 races.

Bold Bidder (dam High Bid, 2nd maternal grandsire Princequillo: 13 wins, champion handicap horse at 4, Charles H. Strub Stakes. Very successful sire with 40 stakes winners including several classic winners and champions.

Balance of Power (full-brother to Bold Bidder): unraced, sire of 15 stakes winners.

Title (dam Monarchy by Princequillo): stakes winner of 7 races.

Blade (full-brother to Title): stakes-placed winner. Sire of 30 stakes winners.

Chieftain (dam Pocahontas, 2nd maternal grandsire Princequillo): 13 wins, Governor's Gold Cup, Laurel Turf Cup. Sire of 27 stakes winners.

Key to the Kingdom (dam Key Bridge by Princequillo): 7 wins, Stymie Handicap. Sire of 8 stakes winners.

Big Advance (dam Stepping Stone by Princequillo): 5 wins from only 8 starts at 2 and 3, Sorority Stakes; 3rd Acorn Stakes, Adirondack Stakes.

Batteur (dam Bayou by Hill Prince by Princequillo): 12 wins, Santa Margarita Handicap, Santa Barbara Handicap.

NEVER BEND

		Nearco	Pharos
			Nogara
	Nasrullah		
		Mumtaz Begum	Blenheim
			Mumtaz Mahal
Never Bend			
(Dk. B, 1960)		Djeddah	Djebel
			Djezima
	Lalun		
		Be Faithful	Bimelech
			Bloodroot

Another outstanding son of Nasrullah, Never Bend was a stakes winner of 13 races. At 2 he won the Champagne Stakes, Futurity Stakes and Cowdin Stakes and became the champion 2-yr-old. At 3 he won the Flamingo Stakes, was 2nd in the Kentucky Derby and 3rd in the Preakness Stakes.

At stud he was very successful getting 58 stakes winners including 4 champions. Several of his sons too excelled at stud making him a sire of sires. Like Bold Ruler he too excelled with mares who had a cross of Princequillo:

Mill Reef (dam Milan Mill by Princequillo): 12 wins, European Horse of the Year at 3, champion 3-yr-old in England, champion older horse in France at 4, Epsom Derby, Prix de l'Arc de Triomphe, King George VI and Queen Elizabeth II Stakes, Eclipse Stakes; 2nd English 2000 Guineas. Outstanding sire of 21 stakes winners including several classic winners and champions. Now emerging as a sire of sires.

Riverman (dam River Lady by Prince John by Princequillo): 5 wins from only 8 starts, champion miler in France at 3, Poule d'Essai des Poulains, Prix d'Ispahan, Prix Jean Prat; 3rd King George VI and Queen Elizabeth II Stakes. Another outstanding sire with 35 stakes winners including several classic winners and Champions.

Fairway Fun (by Prince John) a stakes winner of 11 races nicked with Never Bend getting:

Torsion: 9 wins, Paumonok Handicap; 2nd Preston M. Burch Handicap. Sire

Fun Forever: 10 wins, Bowl of Flowers Stakes.

Fairway Fable: 3 wins at 2, Pocahontas Stakes; 2nd Alcibiades Stakes, Magnolia Stakes; 3rd Fantasy Stakes.

Full Out (dam Running Juliet by Round Table by Princequillo): 11 wins, Sapling Stakes. Sire.

Bends Me Mind (dam Top Round by Round Table): stakes winner of 5 races.

Gelinotte (maternal grandsire Princequillo): 17 wins, champion 2-yr-old and 3-yr-old filly in Venezuela.

Never Confuse (maternal grandsire Princequillo): 22 wins.

NASHUA

Nashua (B, 1952)	Nasrullah	Nearco	Pharos
			Nogara
		Mumtaz Begum	Blenheim
			Mumtaz Mahal
	Segula	Johnstown	Jamestown
			La France
		Sekhmet	Sardanaple
			Prosopopee

We referred to him earlier. He was champion 2-yr-old with wins in the Grand Union Hotel Stakes and Hopeful Stakes. At 3 he won the Preakness Stakes, Belmont Stakes and Flamingo Stakes and became Horse of the Year. He was also 2nd in the Kentucky Derby. At 4 he won the Jockey Club Gold Cup.

At stud he was very successful getting 76 stakes winners. He too did well with Princequillo mares getting:

Shuvee (dam Levee by Hill Prince): 16 wins, champion handicap mare at 4 and 5, American Filly Triple Crown, Beldame Stakes, Jockey Club Gold Cup (twice).

Nalee (full-sister to Shuvee): 8 wins, Black Eyed Susan Stakes, Santa Ynez Stakes; 2nd Acorn Stakes.

Diplomat Way (dam Jandy by Princequillo): 14 wins, Arlington Washington Futurity, Blue Grass Stakes; 2nd Louisiana Derby. Sire of 23 stakes winners.

Nashandy (full-brother to Diplomat Way): stakes winner of 14 races.

Guillaume Tell (dam La Dauphine by Princequillo): 3 wins from only 4 starts, Gordon Stakes. Sire.

Fairway Flyer (dam Fairway Fun by Prince John): 15 wins, Diana Stakes; 3rd Kentucky Oaks.

The object of the above exercise is to show that Nasrullah's sons produced outstanding progeny out of mares with a cross of Princequillo. I have not considered all the sons of Nasrullah and the lists of horses under the three sires considered are not exhaustive. But I am sure the evidence presented is sufficient to convince readers of the nick.

Now let us see how Princequillo's sons fared with mares who had a cross of Nasrullah i.e. the *Princequillo x Nasrullah* nick. Note that this nick is different from the Nasrullah x Princequillo which we have been studying till now. So far sons of Nasrullah were the sires and Princequillo and his sons were the maternal grandsires i.e. Nasrullah was in the top-half of the pedigree and Princequillo in the bottom-half. In this nick it is the other way around with sons of Princequillo as sires and Nasrullah and his sons as maternal grandsires. The Princequillo x Nasrullah nick is not an obligatory follow-up of the Nasrullah x Princequillo. The nick need not exist at all. But as we shall see, it does exist and is equally potent.

PRINCEQUILLO

Princequillo **(B, 1940)**	Prince Rose	Rose Prince	Prince Palatine Eglantine
		Indolence	Gay Crusader Barrier
	Cosquilla	Papyrus	Tracery Miss Matty
		Quick Thought	White Eagle Mindful

Princequillo won 12 races at 2, 3 and 4. His victories included the Saratoga Cup, Saratoga Handicap and Merchants' and Citizens' Handicap. At stud he was very successful getting 65 stakes winners. He was leading sire twice and emerged as a sire of sires. But as a maternal grandsire he was truly phenomenal. He topped the Maternal grandsires list on no fewer than 8 occasions. His principal sons at stud were:

Princequillo

        Round Table
        Prince John
        Dedicate
        Hill Prince
        Third Brother
        Prince Blessed (and others)

Among these stallions we will study Round Table in detail.

ROUND TABLE

Round Table **(B, 1954)**	Princequillo	Prince Rose	Rose Prince Indolence
		Cosquilla	Papyrus Quick Thought
	Knight's Daughter	Sir Cosmo	The Boss Ayn Hali
		Feola	Friar Marcus Aloe

A phenomenal galloper who raced from 2 to 5, Round Table won no fewer than 43 races (2nd eight times and 3rd five times) from 66 starts. His victories included the Breeders' Futurity, Hollywood Gold Cup,

American Derby and Santa Anita Handicap. He was champion grass horse at 3, 4 and 5, champion handicap horse at 4 and 5 and Horse of the Year at 4.

He was a hugely successful sire with 81 stakes winners. He was leading sire in 1972 and leading sire of stakes winners in 1973 and '74. He nicked very strongly with mares who had a cross of Nasrullah as below:

Drumtop (dam Zonah by Nasrullah) : 17 wins, Hialeah Turf Cup, Bowling Green Handicap, Camden Handicap, setting a new course record in each of these races.

Take Your Place (full-brother to Drumtop): 3 wins at 2 in England, Observer Gold Cup; 2nd high-weight in the English Free Handicap.

Zonely (full-sister to Drumtop and Take Your Place): stakes-placed winner of 4 races.

Apalachee (dam Moccasin by Nantallah by Nasrullah): 4 wins from only 5 starts, champion 2-yr-old in England and Ireland, Observer Gold Cup; 3rd English 2000 Guineas. Sire of 13 stakes winners. His full-brothers were also talented as below:

Indian: stakes winner of 4 races.

Brahms: stakes winner of 2 races, Railway Stakes.

Targowice (dam Matriarch by Bold Ruler): 5 wins, champion 2-yr-old colt in France, Eclipse Stakes (Gr. III, Saint Cloud), Prix Thomas Bryon. Successful sire of 21 stakes winners.

King Pellinore (dam Thong by Nantallah): 11 wins in Ireland and U.S.A., Gallinule Stakes, Champions Invitational Handicap, Oak Tree Invitational Stakes; 2nd Irish Sweeps Derby, English St. Leger. Sire.

Tell (dam Nas-Mahal by Nasrullah): 9 wins, Hollywood Derby. Sire of 24 stakes winners.

Upper Case (dam Bold Experience by Bold Ruler): 6 wins, Florida Derby, Wood Memorial Stakes; 2nd Flamingo Stakes; 3rd Gotham Stakes. Sire.

Circle (dam Vicerullah by Nasrullah): 12 wins, Monterey Stakes, Governor's Handicap, Speed Handicap. Sire.

King's Bishop (dam Spearfish by Fleet Nasrullah): 11 wins, Carter Stakes (new course record), Fall Highweight Stakes, Michigan Mile and One-Eighth Handicap. Sire of 19 stakes winners.

Borzoi (dam Respectful, 2nd maternal grandsire Nasrullah): 6 wins in England and U.S.A., John o' Gaunt Stakes, San Bernardino Handicap. Sire.

Poker (dam Glamour by Nasrullah): 7 wins, Bowling Green Handicap, Ventnor Handicap; 2nd San Luis Rey Handicap. Sire of 15 stakes winners.

Table Run (dam Theonia by Fleet Nasrullah): 6 wins, Longacres Derby Handicap, Hayward Stakes.

Shore (dam Delta by Nasrullah): 6 wins, Bewitch Stakes; 2nd Indian Maid Handicap. She set two course records. She was full-sister to:

Canal: 33 wins from 2 to 8, Chicago Handicap twice (once setting a new course record), Meadowland Handicap, Oceanport Handicap twice (once setting a new course record).

Cabildo: 22 wins from 2 to 7, New Orleans Handicap, Midwest Handicap. Sire.

Knightly Manner (dam Courtesy by Nasrullah): 16 wins, Laurel Turf Cup (setting a new course record), Brighton Beach Handicap (twice). Sire of 11 stakes winners.

Star Sprangled (dam Kingsland by Bold Ruler): 11 wins, San Bernardino Handicap (setting a new course record), Inglewood Handicap (twice); 2nd Hollywood Invitational Handicap, Century Handicap (twice). Sire.

Table Flirt (dam Gigi, 2nd maternal grandsire Nasrullah): 7 wins, Lilac Stakes; 2nd Long Island Handicap.

The above list is by no means complete. Readers can similarly research other sons of Princequillo and determine to what extent they nicked with Nasrullah.

Where do we stand now? We have clearly shown that Nasrullah's sons excelled with mares who had a cross of Princequillo and that at least one son of Princequillo excelled with mares who had a cross of Nasrullah. But does this confirm the nick between Nasrullah x Princequillo and Princequillo x Nasrullah? Remember we have not yet satisfied the second part of the definition. Did the stallions concerned get superior progeny ''consistently''? In my opinion this part of the definition does not apply to chef-de-race x chef-de-race nicks. For compare the scope and range of this nick with the earlier nicks. This nick is so powerful that it extends to subsequent generations. With such depth, I feel it is quite unnecessary to calculate percentages of success. The second reason for not doing so is the sheer class and dazzling ability of the horses involved. They were not just stakes winners. If they were, nobody would have even thought of a nick between these two chefs-de-race. Just look at the horses below: Secretariat, Bold Lad, Successor, Bold Bidder, Mill Reef, Riverman, Shuvee, Apalachee, Targowice, San San and Natashka. The records of the last two are as below:

> San San (by Bald Eagle [a son of Nasrullah] x Sail Navy by Prince-quillo): won Prix de l'Arc de Triomphe in 1972.
>
> Natashka (by Dedicate x Natasha by Nasrullah): 8 wins, Co-highweighted 3-yr-old filly, Alabama Stakes, Miss Woodford Stakes, Monmouth Oaks.

Aren't they among the finest thoroughbreds of the 20th century?

EXTENSION OF THE NICK

We have been studying the Nasrullah x Princequillo and Princequillo x Nasrullah nicks. Here readers must note: The Nasrullah x Princequillo nick does not imply that sons of Nasrullah were incapable of producing superior racers out of mares *free* from Princequillo. In fact all of them did so. We are only saying that they were more successful with mares who had a cross of Princequillo. This is also true for sons of Princequillo. All of them produced superior racers out of mares free from Nasrullah.

But how did grandsons and grand-daughters of Nasrullah and Prince-quillo fare? Did they also nick? I am convinced they did. Looking at the pedigrees of recent stakes winners, I find that a number of them have crosses of Nasrullah and Princequillo within 3 generations. Some of them are:

> Talking Picture: 6 wins, champion 2-yr-old filly, Spinaway Stakes, Matron Stakes, Adirondack Stakes, Schuylerville Stakes.
>
> Quack: 8 wins, Hollywood Gold Cup Invitational Handicap, California Derby.
>
> Screen King: 5 wins, Ak-Sar-Ben Omaha Gold Cup Stakes; 2nd Wood Memorial Stakes.
>
> Shamgo: 10 wins, El Cajon Stakes; 2nd Swaps Stakes; 3rd Hollywood Derby.
>
> Revidere: leading American 3-yr-old filly, Coaching Club American Oaks.
>
> Sweet Candy: 10 wins, champion 3-yr-old colt in Venezuela, Clasico Simon Bolivar.

Other stakes winners include **Bold Roll, Due Diligence, Gala Harry, Honest Moment, Island Sultan, Know Your Aces, Moleolus, Princely Pleasure, Verbatim** (successful sire) and **Prince Tenderfoot.**

But we must be careful. We are sure to find a number of superior racers with crosses of any two principal chefs-de-race within their 3-generation pedigrees. We cannot immediately conclude that there is a nick between the chefs-de-race concerned. But as the nick between Nasrullah and Prince-quillo is so strong and intense, we can safely say that its influence can be felt for one more generation.

Therefore the criteria for a chef-de-race x chef-de-race nick are:

1) A large number of truly outstanding horses must have the chefs-de-race within their 3 generations.

2) A large number of stallions and mares must have participated in the nick. The nick must not have been confined to a couple of stallions and half-a-dozen mares.

It is not necessary for the reverse nick to hold.

FACTORS RESPONSIBLE FOR THE NASRULLAH X PRINCEQUILLO AND PRINCEQUILLO X NASRULLAH NICKS

The intensity of these two nicks suggests that very powerful factors were at work. What were they? Can we identify them? In this case happily we can. A.B. 'Bull' Hancock has clearly explained the success of Round Table with Nasrullah mares: "Nasrullah was a horse of fiery temperament; Round Table was phlegmatic. Round Table was not a very big horse; Nasrullah mares were big and rangy." *In other words there was perfect conformation and temperament compatibility between Round Table and Nasrullah mares.*

This explanation is undoubtedly valid for the whole nick. In the words of Howard Wright*: "To the fire and vitality of Nasrullah were added the toughness, stamina and soberness of Princequillo and in several notable cases the two complemented each other to perfection; to such extent that their individual qualities persist through several generations, and have established the most important international nick in modern times."

Peter Willett has proposed another chef-de-race x chef-de-race nick — The Ribot x Hyperion. Ribot himself produced a number of superior racers out of mares who had a cross of Hyperion: Long Look, Ragstone,

---

* *Bloodstock Breeding,* by Sir Charles Leicester, revised by Howard Wright, J.A. Allen and Co.

Ribocco and Ribero, Graustark and His Majesty and others. Ribot's sons too seem to have carried on the nick producing horses like Morston and Alice Frey. His Majesty, in particular, has done well with mares with Hyperion getting Cormorant, Mehmet, Andover Way and others. In the words of Peter Willett*: "The fact that Hyperion outnumbers the almost ubiquitous Nearco in appearances in the pedigrees of leading winners by Ribot and his sons may be regarded as significant." Readers should investigate this nick further and also determine whether there is evidence in favour of a Hyperion x Ribot nick.

I am sure readers have understood the functioning of the four types of nicks without the slightest difficulty. Our next task is to learn how to identify nicks and to incorporate them in a breeding program. But before doing so I would like to emphasize, at the risk of repetition, that several nicks can function simultaneously. Consider the Bold Ruler x Misty Morn matings which produced two champions and two stakes winners. How many nicks were operating? The answer is three! Bold Ruler as a sire nicked with Misty Morn i.e. a sire x dam nick. We would not be very wrong in saying that Bold Ruler also nicked with Princequillo as a maternal grandsire i.e. a sire x maternal grandsire nick. In addition his sire Nasrullah nicked with Princequillo, a chef-de-race x chef-de-race nick. Therefore the progeny of Bold Ruler and Misty Morn had three nicks going for them, which is why they were so successful.

IDENTIFICATION OF NICKS

Having understood the mechanism of nicks, our next task is to identify as many nicks as possible. This is a part of a Turf historian's job and whenever they come across a nick in their research, they immediately study it and publish their findings. Therefore you must make it a point to read all the journals and magazines devoted to thoroughbreds and keep yourself abreast with current knowledge. But there is absolutely no reason why you too should not try to pinpoint nicks. The best time for doing so is when you are studying the behaviour of stallions. You can easily see whether a stallion has nicked with a mare. Then when you are studying his mares,keep an eye open and see whether he has nicked with any maternal grandsire or chef-de-race. Here I must emphasize: *Do not expect every nick to be strong and intense.* The nick may be of moderate intensity only. Or there may not be any nick as such, only a "tendency" towards a nick.

---

* "Ribot's temper was far from 'pleasant'", *Horse and Hound,* September 18, 1981.

In my opinion even these relatively "mild" nicks and "tendencies" are important and can be utilized very profitably. But admittedly it is a matter of conviction. I may feel that sire A nicks with chef-de-race C while you may disagree. Similarly I may not be convinced by a nick proposed by you. The point is you must always be alert for nicks and tendencies toward nicks. If you are fully convinced of a nick you can use it, otherwise you need not.

Chef-de-race x chef-de-race nicks can be identified by studying the pedigrees of superior racers over a suitable period of time. There are excellent books* ** which help us perform this task. When you are studying each pedigree note the chefs-de-race and their positions. See whether a number of superior racers have the same chefs-de-race. If they have, there could well be a nick between the chefs-de-race concerned.

INCORPORATING NICKS IN A BREEDING PROGRAM

Now let us learn how to incorporate nicks in breeding. Frequently less experienced breeders go astray here. Consider the Nasrullah x Princequillo nick. Can you breed any stallion with a cross of Nasrullah to a mare with a cross of Princequillo and expect superior progeny? Obviously not. The results are sure to be disastrous. We *cannot* ignore the normal rules of selection which we laid down earlier. We must include nicks within the rules.

Imagine a young stallion, a grandson of Nasrullah, who has made a bright start. We want to take advantage of the Nasrullah x Princequillo nick by breeding to him. How must we go about our task?

First we must study his performance in depth and determine the types of mares most compatible with him. Let us assume that he excelled with well-bred mares. Now we must look out for well-bred mares with a cross of Princequillo, as close-up in their pedigrees as possible. It would be ideal if they are granddaughters of Princequillo. Suppose we have been able to identify half-a-dozen such mares. We must then study their conformation and temperament and see if any of them is particularly suited to the stallion. Then undoubtedly that mare has an excellent chance of producing superior racers out of the stallion.

---

* *Winners of the world's major races from 1900* published by The Thoroughbred Press,, Sydney.

** *Pedigrees of Leading Winners 1960-1980,* compiled by Martin Pickering and Michael Ross, published by J.A. Allen and Co., London.

The significance of the above procedure is obvious. We have everything to gain but nothing to lose. We are breeding to a successful sire. The mare we have selected is compatible with him in several respects. *Therefore they have every chance of producing superior racers, even if the nick is not intense or there is no nick at all.* The nick will, hopefully, give their progeny an ''extra'' bit of talent. This crucial extra is the difference between a stakes-placed and a stakes winner, a stakes winner and a classic winner and a classic winner and a champion.

Hence a nick is not a substitute for the class and compatibility of the sire, and dam.

But a breeder who always breeds for nicks and tendencies toward nicks, in addition to class and compatibility, will definitely be more successful in the long run than one who does not bother about nicks.

We can go a step further. We can draw up a breeding program incorporating two or more nicks. We can breed for a sire x maternal grandsire and sire x chef-de-race nick, or a sire x maternal grandsire and chef-derace x chef-de-race nick.

ROLE OF NICKS IN STUD SUCCESS

We have just seen the phenomenal number of classic winners, champions and stakes winners produced by nicks between different progenitors. Readers would have surely noticed one more aspect: Many of the horses involved not only excelled on the course but also in stud. They were hugely successful stallions and broodmares. Did nicks play a role in their stud success? In other words do nicks help produce not only superior racers but also superior progenitors? An easy answer would be to say yes. After all look at Bold Bidder, Bold Lad, Mill Reef, Riverman, Secretariat and others. Let us also look at Thong the stakes-placed filly I referred to earlier.

Thong (B, 1964)	Nantallah	Nasrullah	Nearco / Mumtaz Begum
		Shimmer	Flares / Broad Ripple
	Rough Shod II	Gold Bridge	Swynford or Golden Boss / Flying Diadem
		Dalmary	Blandford / Simon's Shoes

She won 5 races and placed 2nd in the Alcibiades Stakes. She was a hugely successful broodmare getting:

Thatch (colt by Forli): 7 wins in England and Ireland, champion 2-yr-old in Ireland, champion miler in England, Sussex Stakes, St. James Palace Stakes. Sire of 16 stakes winners.

King Pellinore (colt by Round Table): 11 wins, as described.

Lisadell (filly by Forli): 2 wins from 4 starts in England and Ireland, Coronation Stakes, Athasi Stakes. (Dam of Yeats a stakes winner.)

Espadrille (filly by Damascus): 3 wins, Busanda Stakes.

Marinsky (colt by Northern Dancer): stakes-placed winner; 2nd St. James Palace Stakes, July Cup. Unfortunately died at 3.

Special (filly by Forli): unplaced in 1 start. Dam of Nureyev (colt by Northern Dancer): 2 wins from 3 starts in France and England, champion miler in France, Prix Thomas Bryon. (He finished 1st in the English 2000 Guineas, but was disqualified.) Note that Nureyev has the benefit of two sire x dam nicks. His grandam Thong was a part of the Nantallah x Rough Shod II nick, while his dam Special was a part of the Forli x Thong nick.

Thus we can easily identify hugely successful progenitors who were the products of different nicks. But it is also possible to identify a number of average and substandard progenitors who were a part of different nicks. So where does this leave us? We can try to answer the question in the following manner: We have to identify all the classic winners, champions and Group I winners who went to stud over a certain period of time. Then we must divide them into two groups: Those free from any nick and those with a nick or nicks. Then we must determine the number of successful stallions in each group and calculate each group's percentage of success. If the stallions with nicks were more successful, we can say everything else being equal a stallion with a nick has a greater chance of stud success. But I do not think any clear-cut result will emerge. This procedure can also be applied to broodmares.

CANCELLATIONS

We now come to a phenomenon that is equally important, if not more important, than a nick. What is it? It is the concept of a "negative" nick.

We know that nicks are a positive phenomena. Its negative equivalent obviously is:

The consistent ability of two bloodlines or crosses to produce inferior individuals.

You may smile but do not laugh. Which fool is going to adopt a breeding policy that consistently produces inferior horses? The question is easily answered. Just as nicks cannot be easily predicted, cancellations too cannot be easily predicted. The world's greatest breeders have produced quite a few substandard horses, for unless you fearlessly breed and race a number of horses, how will you know whether you are on the right track?

We understood that the word nick describes "total" and "intense" compatibility. The word "cancellation" or "nullification" describes total and intense *incompatibility*. The concept is not new. Just as breeders instinctively feel that a mare is intensely compatible with a particular stallion, they also feel that she is most incompatible with another stallion, and that the chances of the latter producing a superior or even average racer out of her are non-existent. Therefore we must be alert to pinpoint cancellations too.

The first type of cancellation is the sire x dam. We do come across this phenomenon. A number of broodmares produced superior racers out of different stallions, but all their visits to particular stallions resulted in very mediocre progeny. Remember the mares had visited the stallions in question not once but several times. An example will enlighten.

CLARINA

		Clarion	Djebel
			Columba
	Klairon		
		Kalmia	Kantar
			Sweet Lavender
Clarina			
(Ch, 1969)		Never Say Die	Nasrullah
			Singing Grass
	Athanasia		
		Hyrcania	Hyperion
			Kyloe

Clarina won 2 races in England.

Retired to stud she made a bright start, getting stakes winner Claddagh (colt, 1974, by Bold Lad). He won 3 races in England (2nd Brittania Stakes), 4 races in Germany and 1 race in Sweden — the Stockholm Cup

(Group 1). She then visited Roberto not once but 4 times with very disappointing results to say the least. 2 of the progeny, a filly and a colt, were unraced. Another filly won once at 2 in England while the 4th a gelding won once on the flat and once over jumps in England. *But do not think Clarina had forgotten the knack of producing a stakes winner.* After her futile visits to Roberto she visited Blushing Groom and promptly produced a classic winner' This was Rosananti who won the Italian 1000 Guineas. She was also 2nd in the Italian Oaks, Salisbury 1000 Guineas Trial Stakes and 3rd in the Irish Guinness Oaks. Clarina then had a colt by Tap on Wood who is in training.

Are we wrong in saying that there are certain elements in the pedigree, conformation, or temperament (in all probability in all three) of Clarina which cancel, nullify the corresponding elements in Roberto, thereby making her produce inferior progeny? Even if we agree to this concept in principle, of what practical use is it? It is unlikely that Clarina will again visit Roberto. The concept can be used practically as below.

Study all the mares who produced runners by Roberto and see whether he cancelled with any of them i.e. see whether any of them failed to produce a superior or average racer even after 3 or 4 visits. Let us assume that he cancelled with three mares. Now we must study these three mares in great detail and try to pinpoint the element or elements of cancellation. To do so we must see whether the mares have any element in common. In all probability they will. It could be a weakness in pedigree, a defect in conformation or even a flaw in temperament. If so, can we not emphatically assert that Roberto is unable to overcome this particular defect and in future it is inadvisable to send mares with that defect to him? Nobody can claim that a stallion, however superior he may be, can overcome all the defects and weaknesses in broodmares. We must endeavour to pinpoint the defects a stallion is unable to overcome at the earliest, and not breed mares with these defects to him. Therefore when you are studying the performances of stallions be alert for cancellations as well.

The sire x dam cancellation is not the only type of cancellation. We can also have sire x maternal grandsire and even sire x chef-de-race cancellations. These cancellations are particularly important in the case of specialist stallions. Think of a specialist stallion who gets stayers and extreme stayers out of staying mares only. Now think of a stallion who excelled in getting blazing fast sprinters, and who was also a maternal grandsire of sprinters. Do you think his daughters will be compatible with the stallion in question? Don't you think they are sure to cancel with him? This reasoning is also valid for sire x chef-de-race cancellations.

Timothy T. Capps* has given a specific example of a sire x maternal grandsire cancellation. Buckpasser is the sire in question. In the course of his stud career he served a number of Bold Ruler mares, but with very disappointing results. He got 37 foals from daughters of Bold Ruler but they included only 2 stakes winners and 3 stakes-placed. Clearly there was a cancellation, or at least a tendency towards a cancellation, between Buckpasser and Bold Ruler. Timothy T. Capps has also pinpointed the reasons for the cancellation. Conformation elements were involved. Buckpasser (who himself had conformation flaws) tended to get horses with knee and foreleg problems. Therefore most of his progeny found it difficult to stay fit, and they raced sparingly. Bold Ruler too passed on physical problems including arthritis (Buckpasser was also an arthritic) and therefore the progeny of Buckpasser out of Bold Ruler mares must have faced serious conformation problems.

In complete contrast Buckpasser really excelled with Northern Dancer mares. He got only 9 foals out of Northern Dancer mares but 5 were stakes winners and 2 were stakes-placed! Clearly he seemed to nick with Northern Dancer. But sadly breeders cannot take advantage of this nick today, as Buckpasser died in 1978. He had only 10 crops and a small 11th crop of 3 foals.

Chef-de-race x chef-de-race cancellations must be very rare, and I confess that I cannot pinpoint any straightaway. If a chef-de-race cancelled with too many chefs-de-race, he would not have become a chef-de-race in the first place! But still we cannot rule out the possibility.

The object of this exercise is to emphasize to less experienced breeders and owners, a fundamental truth known to senior breeders: The concepts of incompatibility and total incompatibility i.e. cancellations are as important as the concepts of compatibility and nicks. I am sure every breeder and owner believes in nicks. If the positive phenomenon exists then its negative equivalent must also exist. Therefore the concepts of incompatibility and cancellations are not a figment of somebody's imagination. *Your objective must be to breed towards nicks and away from cancellations.* Just as breeders rush to take advantage of nicks, breeders must be alert for cancellations and steer clear of them. Why carry out a particular mating when similar matings have failed badly? Therefore be alert for cancellations when you are studying the performances of sires, dams, maternal grandsires and chefs-de-race.

The moment you agree with the concepts of nicks and cancellations

---

* "Buckpasser",. *The Thoroughbred Record,* 18 July 1984.

a puzzling aspect of broodmare behaviour becomes clear. Why does a broodmare produce outstanding racers out of a particular stallion but very indifferent racers out of another equally illustrious stallion? It is because she has nicked with the former and cancelled with the latter. Consider the performance of Attache Case.

Attache Case (B, 1970)	Diplomat Way	Nashua	Nasrullah / Segula
		Jandy	Princequillo / Centenary
	Old Bess	Vincentive	Challenger II / Phenomenon
		Movie Lass	Kai-Finn / Dora W.

She won 5 races.

Retired to stud, she visited Explodent (sire of 14 stakes winners) 3 times and Nodouble (leading sire, sire of 39 stakes winners) once. The 4 progeny, all colts, were winners but were not stakes winners or stakesplaced. Clearly the Explodent x Attache Case matings were not very successful. We cannot immediately say there was a cancellation between them as all their 3 progeny were minor winners, but undoubtedly there seems to have been a tendency towards a cancellation. Then Attache Case visited Mr. Prospector. Readers will immediately see that this mating is on an entirely different footing as two nicks are brought into play:

The Mr. Prospector x Nasrullah and the Nasrullah x Princequillo, as Attache Case also has a cross of Princequillo.

Perhaps due to the benefit of these two nicks the offspring Widaad (a chestnut filly) won 2 races at 2 in England including the Queen Mary Stakes (Group II). She was also 3rd in the Flying Childers Stakes (Group II). Attache Case also had a colt by Baldski who is in training.

CONCLUSION

Even though we have studied about nicks and cancellations in some detail, we have not said the last word on the subject. You can write a book on nicks, nay you can write a book on one nick. We have only skimmed the surface. I am convinced that great breeders depended primarily on nicks for their success. All their breeding theories were based on nicks. I emphasized that it is very difficult to identify, pinpoint nicks in advance;

but they could do so. That was their greatness. An understanding of nicks and cancellations separates the ''men'' from the ''boys''. I wish to offer a spot of advice here: You too can base your breeding theories on nicks, *but make sure they are really and truly nicks.* If they are you will be hugely successful, otherwise the results will be disastrous.

EXERCISE

1) Identify at least three sire x dam nicks and cancellations. Also identify a sire x maternal grandsire and a sire x chef-de-race nick and cancellation. (The nicks and cancellations may be tendencies only.)

2) We discussed four types of nicks and cancellations. Are there other types? Can you think of a few?

3) We discussed a nick between two chefs-de-race. Can three (or more) chefs-de-race nick with each other?

4) I emphasized that greater the number of nicks functioning, greater the chances of success. But there could be a catch. Suppose we want to take advantage of the Nasrullah x Princequillo and Ribot x Hyperion nicks. We will naturally breed a number of horses with crosses of all the four chefs-de-race, which is not at all difficult to do. But can we be sure that the functioning of the Nasrullah x Princequillo nick will not interfere with the functioning of the Ribot x Hyperion?

CHAPTER 10

Inbreeding and Outcrossing

In our endeavour to breed superior horses we understood the importance of class and compatibility. Then we saw how "nicks" could help us. The next techniques we are going to learn are inbreeding and outcrossing.

INBREEDING

INTENSITY OF INBREEDING IN THE THOROUGHBRED TODAY

Dr. Nat M. Kieffer* has defined inbreeding as below:

Inbreeding in its broadest sense is the mating of relatives.

We will readily agree that all members of a breed are ultimately related, even though a large number will only be very distant relatives. Therefore our first task is to determine the intensity of inbreeding in the thoroughbred today. The thoroughbred is most ideal for inbreeding studies as we have his authentic ancestry for about 200 years. We only have to study a horse's pedigree to determine whether he is inbred, and the nature and intensity of the inbreeding. But before doing so let us go back to the very origin of the breed.

It is well known that all thoroughbreds have descended from only 3 stallions and about 50 mares. Therefore in the early days a tremendous amount of inbreeding must have taken place. Dr. Nat M. Kieffer explains:

Every horse has 2 parents, 4 grandparents, 8 great-grandparents and so on. This can be mathematically expressed as "2^n", where n = number of generations. For example to determine the number of ancestors in the 9th generation put n = 9 i.e. 2^9 = 512 ancestors. Since there are 9 generations to the century in the life of thoroughbreds, if we go back 20 generations we will go back to 1760 — the very origin of the breed. In the 20th generation a horse will have a staggering 2^{20} or 1,048,576 ancestors. Since that many horses were never present at any time, a tremendous amount of inbreeding obviously took place during the formative years.

---

* "Analysis of inbreeding trends in American-bred thoroughbreds from 1940-1971, *The Thoroughbred Record*, 22 October 1980.

275

Sir Rhys Llewellyn analyzed the pedigrees of the following horses and found:

Big Game was inbred to Old Bald Peg 3,67,162 times.

Sun Chariot was inbred to Byerly Turk 94,706 times and to Godolphin Arabian 2,33,579 times.

Hyperion was inbred to Darley Arabian 23,998 times.

But we need not go back 20 generations or even 10 generations to hit the first duplication of names. The past decades have seen a number of outstanding stallions, chefs-de-race like Hyperion, Nearco, Ribot etc who made an awesome impact on the breed. Breeders naturally flocked to them and to their sons, daughters, grandsons and granddaughters. Inevitably a certain amount of inbreeding to these stallions took place. The only alternative was to breed to mediocre stallions and mares. Therefore the first question we have to answer is: How far back must we go to hit the first inbreeding?

"Section A" of the *Thoroughbred Record Sire Book* (1983) lists 492 stallions These horses were all racing till recently — roughly between 1977 and 1982. They have just been retired to stud and their first foals are yet to race. If we assume that these horses represent a true cross-section of the American thoroughbred, then the intensity of inbreeding in them is the intensity of inbreeding in the American thoroughbred. (An overwhelming majority of the 492 horses in question are American.) I selected this source to study inbreeding trends, as the 5-generation pedigrees of a large number of horses are readily available. Most books and journals give only 4-generation pedigrees. Enlarging hundreds of 4-generation pedigrees into 5 generations is a time-consuming task, and I have not attempted it. I studied the 5-generation pedigrees of all the above horses and my findings are as below:

Among the 492 horses only 67 (about 14%) are 5-generation outbreds. All the others are inbred. Therefore we can immediately say: An overwhelming majority of American thoroughbreds are inbred within 5 generations. We need not go back further.

I then studied all the pedigrees up to 4 generations only and found that 341 horses (about 69%) were 4-generation outbreds. Combining this result with the earlier one we can say:

A majority of American thoroughbreds are 4-generation outbreds but inbred within 5 generations.

Therefore inbreeding in the American thoroughbred as a whole starts in the 5th generation. It may be the duplication of a name in the 5th generation or in the 4th and 5th generations — such a horse is a 4-generation outbred but is inbred within 5 generations i.e. a 5-generation inbred.

But can we assume a similar trend in European, Indian or Australian thoroughbreds? I personally feel we can. I then studied the 4-generation pedigrees of the "Major European Stakes Winners" of 1979, 1980 and 1981 from issues of *The Thoroughbred Record*. The findings are presented in Table 19.

TABLE 19

	1979	1980	1981
Number of stakes winners	178	169	183
Number of 4-generation outbreds	127	125	137
Percentage of 4-generation outbreds	71%	74%	75%

(Compare these percentages with the 69% 4-generation outbreds we got for American horses. These European horses include a few American-breds.)

	1979	1980	1981
Number of 4-generation inbreds	51 (178-127)	44 (169-125)	46 (183-137)
Percentage of 4-generation inbreds	29%	26%	25%
Among these 4-generation inbreds: Number of horses inbred within 3 generations or in the 3rd and 4th generations	14	15	14
Number of hor ses inbred in the 4th generation only	37 (51-14)	29 44-15)	32 46-14)
Percentage of horses inbred within 3 generations or in the 3rd and 4th generations.	8% ($\frac{14}{178}$ x 100)	9% ($\frac{15}{169}$ x 100)	8% ($\frac{14}{183}$ x 100)

In essence slightly less than 10% of the horses in question are "intensely" inbred i.e. inbred within 3 generations or in the 3rd and 4th generations. Assuming a similar trend in other parts of the world we can conclude:

A majority of present-day thoroughbreds (between 65% to 75% are 4-generation outbreds, but are inbred within 5 (or 6) generations. The 4-generation inbreds constitute about 25% to 35% of the breed. About 2/3rd of them are inbred only in the 4th generation and only the remaining 1/3rd are somewhat intensely inbred.

OBJECT OF INBREEDING

We now know the intensity of inbreeding in the breed today for good or for bad. Why must we breed horses with an even greater intensity of inbreeding? Why must we inbreed in the first place? What are the benefits of inbreeding? In the words of Sir Charles Leicester*:

The object of inbreeding is to increase the influence of the ancestor to whom we inbreed.

The ancestor was obviously an outstanding progenitor, a principal chef-de-race, who made a lasting impact on the breed. He gave his progeny all the qualities an outstanding racer requires. By inbreeding to him we hope our horse will inherit a "double dose" of the beneficial qualities he imparted. The horse will also get a double dose of all the bad qualities he transmitted, but that is unavoidable. However since the good qualities he transmitted greatly outnumbered the bad, we can boldly go ahead.

INBREEDING OR OUTCROSSING?

Before we proceed further we must understand that inbreeding or out-crossing *per se* is not going to help us breed classic winners or champions or even superior racers. Inbreeding cannot overcome all the weaknesses and defects of the sire and dam and enable them to get superior progeny. An intensely inbred horse is not going to become a classic winner or a stakes winner. Inbreeding (and outcrossing) is not a substitute for the class and compatibility of the sire and dam. All the principles we studied earlier are valid. Then what does inbreeding do? It may give the crucial "extra" bit of class to the individual. This extra may help a stakes winner develop into a classic winner and a classic winner into a champion.

While it is easy to identify scores of superior racers who were inbred, it is also possible to identify hundreds of utterly substandard horses who were similarly inbred. This is also true for outbreds. Therefore where does this leave us? Which technique is more successful? To give an accurate answer it is necessary to undertake the following research:

We must first identify all the superior racers of a particular genera-tion. Then we must study the pedigree of each horse of that generation and classify as 4-generation inbred or outbred. Then we must calculate the percentages of superior inbreds and outbreds and compare the figures.

---

* *Bloodstock Breeding,* by Sir Charles Leicester, revised by Howard Wright.

If we find that 8% of the inbreds were superior racers while only 3% of the outbreds were superior, we can boldly say inbreeding gives better results. But to come to such a conclusion we must analyze thousands of pedigrees and the result we get will be valid for that year only. To get a true result we must repeat the exercise for a number of years. However we cannot over-rule the possibility of inbreds coming out on top one year and the outbreds the next. The whole task is truly gigantic and I do not think anyone has undertaken it. I think we can safely say that both techniques are equally successful. But as we shall see, if we follow one technique through and through we will have a greater chance of success.

INBREEDING

Let us first study inbreeding in detail, and draw up different inbreeding programs. First and foremost I want readers to clearly understand the difference between incidental inbreeding and deliberate inbreeding. A mating is planned along usual lines. We are sure that a particular stallion and mare are compatible. When we draw up the pedigree of the offspring we find that he is inbred 4 x 5 i.e. in the 4th and 5th generations. This inbreeding is incidental. It is unplanned. The object of the mating is not to breed an individual who would be inbred 4 x 5 to a particular ancestor. The class and compatibility of the sire and dam decided the mating. For example the Epsom Derby winner Golden Fleece is inbred 4 x 4 to Nearco. Nobody is going to claim that the object of Exotic Treat's visit to Nijinsky was to produce an individual inbred 4 x 4 to Nearco. Exotic Treat visited Nijinsky because the breeder felt he was the most compatible and suitable stallion for her. The inbreeding to Nearco is purely incidental.

But now our object is different. We are going to inbreed deliberately. We are convinced that horses inbred to particular ancestors, chefs-de-race, will be superior. Therefore we will use only those stallions and mares who can give us the desired inbreeding. In other words matings are deliberately planned to get progeny who will be inbred as required.

Our first task is to fix the intensity of inbreeding. The inbreeding to the admired ancestor must be within 4 generations, as a majority of the breed is inbred in the 5th. Therefore if your horse is inbred in the 5th generation, he will not get any extra benefit. The benefit he gets will accrue to thousands of other thoroughbreds. Therefore the inbreeding should be in the 1st, 2nd, 3rd or 4th generations. But inbreeding in the 1st and 2nd generations is too incestuous and is repulsive to all of us. I do not think any breeder will even think of matings between full-brother and sister, parent and offspring or half-brother and sister. But technically there can be no objection. Such incestuous matings are common among wild horses, deer, rabbits etc. It has gone on for generations without apparently any ill effects. No doubt the substandard individuals have failed to survive, but a number of incestuously inbred animals lead perfectly normal lives. But such inbreeding is very rare among thoroughbreds.

Sir Charles Leicester gives the example of Coronation V who was the offspring of a half-brother and sister.

		Tourbillon	Ksar Durban
	Djebel		
		Loika	Gay Crusader Coeur a Coeur
Coronation V (B, 1946)		Tourbillon	Ksar Durban
	Esmeralda		
		Sanas	Asterus Deasy

In this case Tourbillon was obviously the admired ancestor and the mating was planned so that his influence would be maximum. This mating was successful as Coronation V was a brilliant (but nervous) filly who dead-heated for win in the French 1000 Guineas and who went on to win the Prix de l'Arc de Triomphe easily. Sadly she was barren in stud for 14 years, but this was due to a veterinary problem and not due to her inbreeding.

If you feel this inbreeding is too intense, you can decrease the intensity by breeding a grand-daughter of the admired ancestor to his son i.e. a 2 x 3 inbreeding, or to his grandson i.e. a 3 x 3 inbreeding. Similarly you can visualize a 4 x 4 inbreeding. Note that as you go back the influence of the admired ancestor on the offspring decreases. His influence on a horse inbred 5 x 5 to him will not be significant.

The methods we have just discussed are valid for inbreeding to any desired ancestor. We have got to suitably breed his sons, daughters, grandsons, granddaughters, great-grandsons and great-granddaughters among themselves to get the required intensity of inbreeding. This type of inbreeding is actually "linebreeding". We will discuss it further a little later.

Till now we restricted the inbreeding to only one admired ancestor. But having decided to inbreed, why not go all out and inbreed to as many admired ancestors as possible? A horse with such an intense inbreeding is the great Vaguely Noble.

		Hyperion	Gainsborough / Selene
	Aureole		
		Angelola	Donatello II / Feola
Vienna			
		Turkhan	**Bahram** / Theresina
	Turkish Blood		
		Risk	Manna / Baby Polly
Vaguely Noble (B, 1965)		Pharos	Phalaris / Scapa Flow
	Nearco		
		Nogara	Havresac II / Catnip
Noble Lassie			
		Big Game	**Bahram** / Myrobella
	Belle Sauvage		
		Tropical Sun	**Hyperion** / Brulette

He won 6 races including the Prix de l'Arc de Triomphe, Observer Gold Cup and the Prix de Chantilly. At 3 he was Horse of the Year in Europe and champion 3-yr-old in France.

Looking at his pedigree we find that he is inbred:

3 x 4 to Hyperion

4 x 4 to Bahram

4 x 5 to Phalaris

5 x 5 to Chaucer

5 x 5 to Spearmint

Let us analyze his pedigree.

His sire Vienna was a stakes winner and was 3rd in St. Paddy's St. Leger. But he was not a very successful sire. Vaguely Noble was by far his best get and none of his other progeny were anywhere near him.

Noble Lassie was a stakes winner of 2 races including the Lancashire Oaks. She had 9 progeny of whom 6 won, but none had the ability of Vaguely Noble. A full-sister Viva La Reine won in France at 3.

His tail female line — Noble Lassie — Belle Sauvage — Tropical Sun Brulette is definitely superior if not outstanding:

> Belle Sauvage : winner, dam of good winners
>
> Tropical Sun : states - placed, dam of good winners

Brulette   : winner of the Epsom Oaks,
dam of good winners

But it is his maternal grandsire component that is truly phenomenal. Nearco, Big Game and Hyperion do not require even the slightest introduction. They rank among the best maternal grandsires (and sires) of the 20th century. I do not know whether any other thoroughbred had these 3 horses as his maternal grandsires.

Summing up we have:

Sire   :   average
Maternal grandsires : outstanding
Tail female line   : superior to outstanding

This combination is sufficient to produce, and has produced, superior racers and champions. But in this case can we not boldly say that the intense inbreeding was also a factor in his success? For the horses involved Hyperion, Bahram and Phalaris were no ordinary individuals. It is unnecessary for me to describe their achievements. We can ignore the 5 x 5 inbreeding to Chaucer and Spearmint as its impact could not have been great. Therefore we can say that intense inbreeding proved very beneficial to Vaguely Noble and it helped him excel as a racer and in all probability as a sire and maternal grandsire too.

We are now in a position to lay down the rules, the guidelines, for inbreeding:

1) We must inbreed to as many admired ancestors as possible.

2) The admired ancestors must have been truly outstanding.

3) The inbreeding must be in the 3rd and 4th generations (unless you are prepared to inbreed incestuously), as inbreeding further back will not have a significant impact on the offspring.

It is possible to inbreed to most stallions and broodmares very advantageously. The difficulties arise, as we shall see, only when we want to inbreed continuously.

"ONE TIME" INBREEDING

Let us see how to inbreed to a particular stallion. The strategy I recommend is as follows: We will select a superior stallion, Front-line or Borderline classic, who has outstanding chefs-de-race in his 2nd and 3rd generations. We will inbreed to these chefs-de-race. Such stallions are most ideal for inbreeding. For notwithstanding Vaguely Noble, I am sure nobody would like to use average or inferior stallions just for the sake of inbreeding. The stallion selected must be capable of holding his own anywhere. Then we must study the stallion in detail and determine the types of mares most compatible with him. Among such mares we must select one or more mares who also have the required chefs-de-race in their 2nd and 3rd generations, so that the offspring will be inbred in the 3rd and 4th. *In essence we have made our inbreeding incidental.* We have selected a superior stallion. We are going to breed a compatible mare to him. Therefore we have every right to expect a superior offspring irrespective of the effect of the in-breeding. If the inbreeding is beneficial the offspring will be really top class; if it has no effect the offspring will still be above average and even if the inbreeding is detrimental (albeit slightly) the offspring will be marginally above average or at the worst average as all the other factors are in his favour. If you follow this policy you have everything to gain but nothing to lose.

But it may not always be possible to find compatible mares with the required pedigrees. Then if we are still keen on inbreeding we must use incompatible or even inferior mares; as only their pedigrees will give us the inbreeding required. There is no other alternative. In such matings we can only hope that the inbreeding will be potent enough to overcome all the deficiencies of the progenitors and enable them to produce superior offspring. This will not happen all the time and if the inbreeding has a negative effect the result will be a first class disaster. But if you practice such inbreeding continuously one outstanding racer may make the whole project worthwhile. I personally do not recommend such a program, but it is for the individual to decide.

Let us apply the above reasoning to a particular stallion. I have selected Ardent Knight.

	Nearco	Pharos / Nogara
Dante		
	Rosy Legend	Dark Legend / Rosy Cheeks
Ardent Knight (Br, 1953)		
	Hyperion	Gainsborough / Selene
Per Ardua		
	Ad Astra	Asterus / Pyramid

He started 6 times in England winning the Southampton Stakes at 2 and the Druids Stakes at 3. He also placed 2nd in the Rayners Stakes.

Imported into India and retired to stud, he was successful. His superior runners included Esquire (10 wins, Indian Turf Invitation Cup, South India 2000 Guineas and St. Leger, Bangalore Derby), **Prince Ardent, Noble Princess, Forest Hills, Our Little Prince, Yours Mine and Ours, Midnight Star, Amba** and **others.**

Studying his pedigree we find that we can inbreed very advantageously to Nearco and Hyperion. And happily for us there are hundreds of mares in the country with crosses of these 2 chefs-de-race. But it would be very difficult to study all of them in order to identify those most compatible. We need not do so if we fix the maternal grandsire first. We must identify the maternal grandsires most compatible with Ardent Knight. The maternal grandsire must also contribute to the inbreeding. Studying all the maternal grandsires we find that one successful maternal grandsire automatically selects himself — Star of Gwalior, a grandson of Hyperion and Nearco An offspring by Ardent Knight out of a compatible Star of Gwalior mare will have the required inbreeding and is sure to do well. In fact one horse bred along such lines was the classic winner Prince Ardent!

			Nearco	Pharos
				Nogara
		Dante		
			Rosy Legend	Dark Legend
				Rosy Cheeks
	Ardent Knight			
			Hyperion	Gainsborough
				Selene
		Per Ardua		
			Ad Astra	Asterus
				Pyramid
Prince Ardent (Ro, 1970)				
			Hyder Ali	**Hyperion**
				Eclair
		Star of Gwalior		
			Lady Emma	**Nearco**
				Divine Lady
	Mallika			
			Rajah II	Blandford
				Taj Mah
		Waikiki		
			City Fare	Cri de Guerre
				Skipper's Ship

Note the ideal 3 x 4 inbreeding to Nearco and Hyperion.

Prince Ardent, as we saw, won 7 races including the Bangalore Arc de Triomphe, South India 2000 Guineas, Madras Gold Vase (2000 m, 4-yr-olds, Madras) and Owners and Trainers Association Cup. He also placed 2nd in the South India Derby and Bangalore St. Leger.

Mallika won only 2 races. It is difficult to consider her Inherently superior or well-bred. We cannot assert that she was intensely compatible with Ardent Knight. But as she was a very successful producer, she had everything to gain and nothing to lose by visiting Ardent Knight. Her other superior racers were:

Al Mansour (colt, 1968, by Red Rufus): 8 wins, as described.

Regal Prince (colt, 1974, by Mr. Mauritius or High Commission): 8 wins, M.R.C. Hospital Cup, Ashoka Chakra Cup; 3rd Bangalore Derby.

I want to draw attention to the fact that Mallika produced a superior racer out of a stallion free from Nearco and Hyperion — Al Mansour by Red Rufus. This is what I mean by one time inbreeding. There is absolutely no need for you to produce only inbreds with your mare. You can inbreed and outcross. But if your mare is suitable for inbreeding, and compatible stallions are available, you must breed at least a couple of inbreds. As we saw, you have everything to gain but nothing to lose.

Till now we have restricted the inbreeding to outstanding stallions. But why not inbreed to outstanding *broodmares?* Most certainly we can and without doubt a number of superior horses were inbred to outstanding broodmares. I give below an example of a horse inbred to Lady Emma who, as explained, was very influential in India.

We saw that she had three sons and one grandson in stud. Therefore breeders could have easily worked out an inbreeding program involving these four stallions and their descendants. One individual who was inbred on such lines is the very successful Jaandaar. (Lord Jim is her grandson in stud.)

			Hyperion	Gainsborough
				Selene
		Hyder Ali		
			Eclair	Ethnarch
				Black Ray
	Star of Gwalior			
			Nearco	Pharos
				Nogara
		Lady Emma		
			Divine Lady	Papyrus
				Most Beautiful
Jaandaar				
(B, 1972)			Abernant	Owen Tudor
				Rustom Mahal
		Gul Mohar		
			Fatimite	Mahmoud
				Sister Anne
	Deep Mala			
			Chhote Khan	Flag of Truce
				Lady Emma
		Nanda Deep		
			Deepak Mahal	**Hyperion**
				Solerina

He is inbred 2 x 4 to Lady Emma and 3 x 4 x 5 to Hyperion.

Jaandaar, as described, was a genuine galloper who won 10 races including the R.W.I.T.C. Gold Cup, Sprinters' Cup (1200 m, 3-yr-olds and over, Pune) and Turf Club Cup (1400 m, 4-yr-olds and over, Pune). He won up to 1400 m. He was one of the best, if not the best sprinter of his generation.

His sire Star of Gwalior has been described. Deep Mala was retired to stud unraced, making it difficult to classify her. But her tail female line is really top class. Her dam Nanda Deep won 4 races including the Indian 1000 and 2000 Guineas and was the dam of 2 good winners from only 3 foals. Her grandam Deepak Mahal won 4 races in Ireland and 5 races in India and placed 2nd twice in the Eclipse Stakes of India. It is clear that the superior elements in his pedigree, plus the beneficial effect of inbreeding, enabled him to excel.

Retired to stud he made an excellent start getting:

Aztec (1979): 8 wins, champion, Stayers' Cup, C.N. Wadia Gold Cup.

Minicoy (1981): 5 wins, Golconda Oaks.

Lamarck: 3 wins, Maharaja of Morvi Cup; 2nd Indian 2000 Guineas.

Tanja: 5 wins, winner in class II.

(Unfortunately he died after only 4 crops. There is no doubt that he would have developed into a Front-line classic stallion.)

My third example is a daughter of a stallion we studied in detail — Everyday. Study his pedigree carefully. If you are going to inbreed to him, which chefs-de-race would you choose? You can inbreed to Alizier, Vatellor, Bull Lea, Tudor Minstrel, Vatout, Son-in-Law, Bull Dog or Hyperion. But "Arcturus"* was sure that inbreeding to Teleferique and Teddy would be very beneficial. But why Teleferique and Teddy? In his own words: ". . . Aurelie is by Teleferique and has enough lines of Teddy. Well. . . .!!"

I am sure readers have grasped the significance of Arcturus' suggestion. We saw that Aurelie's family has been consistently producing classic winners and superior racers. Therefore if mares from this very successful family visit Everyday, wouldn't they produce outstanding progeny? Arcturus' conviction that inbreeding to Teleferique and Teddy in the above manner would pay rich dividends was brilliantly proved by Classic Touch who won the 1983 South India St. Leger!

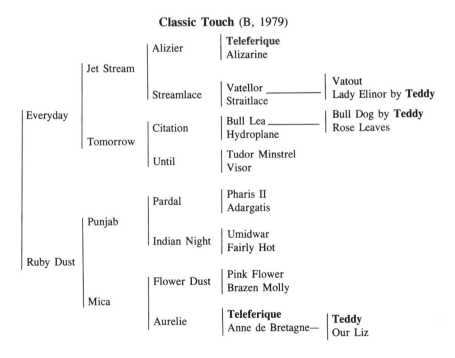

Classic Touch (B, 1979)

Everyday	Jet Stream	Alizier	Teleferique / Alizarine
		Streamlace	Vatellor ——— Vatout / Lady Elinor by **Teddy** / Straitlace
	Tomorrow	Citation	Bull Lea ——— Bull Dog by **Teddy** / Rose Leaves / Hydroplane
		Until	Tudor Minstrel / Visor
Ruby Dust	Punjab	Pardal	Pharis II / Adargatis
		Indian Night	Umidwar / Fairly Hot
	Mica	Flower Dust	Pink Flower / Brazen Molly
		Aurelie	**Teleferique** / Anne de Bretagne— **Teddy** / Our Liz

---

* *The Turfite,* December 16, 1979.

Study her pedigree carefully and note the inbreeding:

4 x 4 to Teleferique

5 x 6 x 6 to Teddy

Classic Touch has won 6 races in all including the Mysore Race Club Gold Trophy (2000 m, classes I and II, Mysore) and is in training. In fairness must say that the St. Leger field did not include any classic stayer the best horses in the country did not run as they were being specially prepared for the Invitation Cup. But the point is Classic Touch is a superior racer and she stays well.

Everyday has been described. Ruby Dust did not win but is Inherently superior due to her superior pedigree. Keeping this in mind readers will argue that the remote inbreeding had nothing to do with her success. They may well be right, *but it does not alter the logic of the mating.* Breeders with mares from the Aurelie family should seriously think of breeding them to Everyday. I, for one, am convinced that the resulting progeny will be outstanding. Classic Touch is only the beginning.

You can, of course, inbreed to the other chefs-de-race in Everyday's pedigree. This brings us to another dimension in inbreeding. You can inbreed to different combinations of chefs-de-race in the pedigree of a stallion. But do not forget the rules we have learned.

FORMULATING AN INBREEDING PROGRAM

It appears that it is very easy to prepare an inbreeding program. We have to only identify a handful of stallions and mares to get going. But on the contrary, practising inbreeding continuously is extremely difficult as we are going to see.

Suppose we wish to inbreed to Ribot, Donatello II and Bahram. Our first task is to identify stallions and mares who have these 3 outstanding progenitors within their 3 generations, so that the progeny will be inbred in the 4th. Here itself we are in difficulty. Studying all the stallions in the country I find that no stallion has the above 3 chefs-de-race in his pedigree! The first difficulty is now obvious. There may not be a sufficient number of successful stallions and mares with the required pedigrees for you to inbreed continuously.

But this difficulty can be overcome. Instead of selecting particular ancestors, we can inbreed to those influential ancestors who dominate the pedigrees of a large number of stallions and broodmares today. I quickly studied the pedigrees of a large number of stallions and broodmares in the country to identify the most influential ancestors. Clearly Nearco,

Hyperion, Fair Trial and Donatello II are most influential. Therefore we have to inbreed to the above chefs-de-race, whether we like it or not, as there is an insufficient number of stallions and mares with other chefs-de-race. We are cutting the suit according to the cloth. (But in Europe or North America you will have a greater choice.) Now we have to identify successful stallions and mares with the above chefs-de-race. The first stallion I have identified is Lord of Light.

		Hyperion	Gainsborough
			Selene
	Aureole		
		Angelola	Donatello II
			Feola
Lord of Light			
(Ch, 1973)		Court Martial	Fair Trial
			Instantaneous
	Night Court		
		Crepuscule	Mieuxce
			Red Sunset

Lord of Light met with a serious accident in his very first race and did not race again. He was imported into India and retired to stud. He has made a fine start getting 2 classic winners and several superior racers from only 3 crops:

Sunray (1978): 8 wins, Calcutta 2000 Guineas.

Raqsh-E-Rustum (1980): 5 wins, Hyderabad Colts Trial Stakes.

Pleasure and Leisure: 10 wins, R.C.T.C. Cup (1600 m, class II, Madras), winner in class I.

Young Diana: 9 wins, Esquire Cup (2000 m, classes I and II, Madras), Ootacamund Cup (1200 m, class II, Madras), winner in class I.

The Marvel: 11 wins, winner in class II.

Having selected the stallion, we must identify superior mares compatible with him and who have the pedigrees to give us the inbreeding required. Again we can simplify matters a great deal if we fix the maternal grandsires first. The maternal grandsires must be successful, must be compatible with the stallion and must contribute to the inbreeding. I have selected Jethro, Orbit and Satinello.

Jethro was only a fair sire. But his daughters are proving to be superior producers. He is already the maternal grandsire of **Punter's Delight** (7 wins, Calcutta 2000 Guineas, Bhutan Gold Cup, Grand Annual Handicap),

Tulipa (5 wins, Indian Oaks, Eve Champion Cup, Idar Gold Cup; 2nd Bangalore 1000 Guineas and Oaks, Nilgiris Derby) and several others.

Orbit, whom we studied earlier, is proving to be another successful maternal grandsire. He is already the maternal grandsire of **Charon** (4 wins, champion, Charminar Challenge Indian Turf Invitation Cup, Indian 2000 Guineas, R.R. Ruia Gold Cup) and others.

Satinello, a very successful sire, has also started well as a maternal grandsire.

Therefore we must select daughters of the above 3 stallions and breed them to Lord of Light. Do not forget that they must also be compatible with him. Happily this is not impossible as the above 3 horses had a large number of daughters who are active today. Among them several are sure to be compatible with Lord of Light. The pedigrees of the progeny will be as shown in the next pages.

LORD OF LIGHT X JETHRO MARE

Lord of Light	Aureole	**Hyperion**	Gainsborough / Selene
		Angelola	Donatello II / Feola
	Night Court	Court Martial	**Fair Trial** / Instantaneous
		Crepuscule	Mieuxce / Red Sunset
Daughter of Jethro	Jethro	Palestine	**Fair Trial** / Una
		Jet High	**Hyperion** / Jet Plane
	Various	Various	Various / Various
		Various	Various / Various

The offspring will be inbred:

3 x 4 to Hyperion

4 x 4 to Fair Trial

LORD OF LIGHT X ORBIT MARE

		Hyperion	Gainsborough / Selene
	Aureole		
		Angelola	Donatello II / Feola
Lord of Light			
		Court Martial	Fair Trial / Instantaneous
	Night Court		
		Crepuscule	Mieuxce / Red Sunset
		Crepello	**Donatello II** / **Crepuscule**
	Orbit		
		Urshalim	Nasrullah / Horama
Daughter of Orbit			
		Various	Various / Various
	Various		
		Various	Various / Various

The offspring will be inbred:

3 x 4 to Crepuscule

4 x 4 to Donatello II

LORD OF LIGHT X SATINELLO MARE

		Hyperion	Gainsborough / Selene
	Aureole		
		Angelola	**Donatello II** / Feola
Lord of Light			
		Court Martial	Fair Trial / Instantaneous
	Night Court		
		Crepuscule	Mieuxce / Red Sunset
		Crepello	**Donatello II** / **Crepuscule**
	Satinello		
		Saturnetta	**Hyperion** / Chanctonbury
Daughter of Satinello			
		Various	Various / Various
	Various		
		Various	Various / Various

The Offspring will be inbred:

3 x 4 to Hyperion

3 x 4 to Crepuscule

4 x 4 to Donatello II

Having bred the selected mares to Lord of Light once, or better still a number of times, we must breed them to other successful stallions with similar pedigrees in order to continue the inbreeding program. Such stallions are available and the name of Zelenko immediately came to my mind.

Zelenko (Br, 1974)	Welsch Pageant	Tudor Melody	Tudor Minstrel / Matelda
		Picture Light	Court Martial / Queen of Light
	Another Daughter	Crepello	Donatello II / Crepuscule
		Sybil's Niece	Admiral's Walk / Sybil's Sister

He won 2 races in England.

Retired to stud in India, he made a fine start getting in his first crop: **Maltese Prince** (6 wins, Calcutta and Nilgiris Derby, Mysore 2000 Guineas) and **Sugar Sweet** (5 wins, Armed Forces Handicap [1200 m, classes I and II Calcutta]). Readers can work out the intensity of inbreeding between him and the mares we have selected. It will naturally be different. But this is not the important factor. The question is: *Will the mares who are compatible with Lord of Light be compatible with Zelenko?* If they are well and good, but if they are not the inbreeding program collapses' For the only alternative is to breed to incompatible or substandard stallions just for the sake of producing inbred progeny. Needless to say, no breeder will be interested in doing so. It is this difficulty — the unavailability of compatible progenitors — that has frustrated, and continues to frustrate, many a well-intentioned inbreeding program. This is why breeders eagerly practise one-time inbreeding but are extremely reluctant to embark on elaborate inbreeding programs.

We have come to the end of the section on inbreeding. But no chapter on inbreeding is complete without a reference to Marcel Boussac — the breeder of Coronation V. A towering personality, a giant among giants, Marcel Boussac dominated racing and breeding in France for decades.

He became involved with thoroughbreds in 1912 and won his first French Derby with Ramus in 1922. 56 years later Acamas carried his colours — orange, grey cap — to victory in the same race. Altogether he won a staggering 124 Group I races in France and a further 18 in England. This figure does not include Akarad (Grand Prix de Saint Cloud; 2nd French Derby) and Akiyda (Prix de l'Arc de Triomphe; 2nd French Oaks) who ironically did not race in his colours. He won the French Derby an astonishing 12 times.

Marcel Boussac strongly believed in breeding and inbreeding to 3 chefs-de-race: Asterus, Pharis II and Tourbillon. Since his breeding program was so successful he could continue it for decades, using his own stallions and broodmares, without making any sacrifices whatsoever. We need not go deeper into Boussac breeding here, but readers would do well to study the pedigrees of his classic winners and champions.

OUTCROSSING

If in inbreeding our object was to increase the influence of a desired ancestor, in outcrossing it is to have the influence of as many desired ancestors as possible.

To put it crudely we want to "pack" the 5-generation pedigree of the horse with as many influential progenitors, chefs-de-race, as possible, since greater the number of influential progenitors greater the chances of the individual inheriting a lot of beneficial qualities from them. Further different progenitors may transmit different beneficial qualities. If a large number of them are present, the horse at least has a chance of inheriting all the different beneficial qualities. As I emphasized earlier every outbred is not going to be superior, but if we formulate a program for outcrossing scientifically and follow it continuously we have an excellent chance of success.

At the outset itself I emphasize that all the difficulties we faced in inbreeding will be present in outcrossing. We may not be able to find compatible stallions and mares with the required pedigrees. But undeniably outcrossing per se is far easier than inbreeding.

We can outcross with two distinct types of stallions. The first group consists of stallions with relatively obscure and unorthodox pedigrees, pedigrees with very few influential progenitors or chefs-de-race. Most of the names in their pedigrees are rarely found in the pedigrees of today. I near success on the course was a bit of a surprise. Even more surprising was the success of a few in stud. (I think we can safely say that a majority

of unorthodoxly bred horses fail as stallions, however outstanding their racing performances may have been.) Therefore we would like to patronize them in spite of their pedigrees.
Nijinsky [India] is one such stallion.

			Abjer	Asterus
				Zariba
		Nosca		
			Capella	Tourbillon
				Gracilite
	Zinosca			
			Mirza II	Blenheim
				Mumtmaz Mahal
		Zina		
			Drina	Chateau Bouscaut
				Dusky Maid
Nijinsky (India)				
(B, 1963)			Cockpit	Caerleon
				Merripit
		Asoka		
			Einga	Claro
				Loversland
	Natasha			
			Mas d' Antibes	Zionist
				Masse de Pommes
		Navvara		
			Crimson Rambler	Prestissimo
				Rosalia

He was a genuine galloper who won 8 races from 1000 m to 2800 m. His victories included the Indian Derby, St. Leger and R.R. Ruia Gold Cup. He was 3rd in the Invitation Cup.

When he was retired to stud breeders looked askance. His very unorthodox pedigree turned them away. Not surprisingly they were keen on the latest international bloodlines. But ultimately he had the last laugh.

It was his daughter the phenomenal Sweet Memories (1971) who first advertised his talent. She won 11 races including the Indian St. Leger, Bangalore Fillies Trial Stakes, Mysore 1000 Guineas and President of India Gold Cup. Her achievements are even more creditable as she had a bad setback in training. But she had the courage and tenacity to come back and win prestigious races. If she had raced normally she would have won several more classics.

Nijinsky then proceeded to get a number of superior racers like:

Muffin (1974): 7 wins, Indian Oaks.

Star Appeal: 5 wins; 2nd Calcutta 2000 Guineas; 3rd Calcutta Derby and Oaks.

Well Connected: 10 wins, Hyderabad Silver Vase (1200 m, class I, Bangalore) thrice, Ardent Knight Cup, R.W.I.T.C. Cup (1400 m, class I, Bangalore); 3rd Bangalore Arc de Triomphe.

There are only 4 chefs-de-race—Asterus, Tourbillon, Blenheim and Chateau Bouscaut in his 4-generation pedigree and all of them are in the 4th generation. This makes him an excellent outcross for most chefs-de-race and other influential progenitors. We can easily breed 5-generation outbreds from him. Naturally we will select those mares who are compatible with him and who have the desired ancestors. In fact inbreeding to him is next to impossible as there are very few mares in the country with the 4 chefs-de-race present in his pedigree.

Red Rufus, whom we studied in detail, is another excellent example. Note that he too has only 4 chefs-de-race in his 4-generation pedigree — Vatout, Teddy, Fairway and Blandford. Therefore he too is ideal for breeding 5-generation outbreds.

But it is not at all necessary to breed to only unorthodoxly bred stallions in order to produce 5-generation outbreds. We can use orthodoxly bred stallions as well. But there will be practical difficulties. Orthodoxly bred stallions will have a larger number of chefs-de-race and other influential progenitors in their pedigrees than unorthodoxly bred stallions. They may have anywhere from 8 to 12 chefs-de-race within their 4-generation pedigrees. Therefore to breed a 5-generation outbred, we must find a compatible mare who is free from the chefs-de-race in the pedigree of the stallion, and who, hopefully, has a significant number of other chefs-de-race. This is not impossible but is difficult. The only alternative then is to use incompatible or inferior mares just to breed 5-generation outbreds. But obviously no breeder will be anxious to do so. This is why a majority of thoroughbreds are inbred within 5 generations.

But instead of endeavouring to breed 5-generation outbreds, we can breed 4-generation outbreds. Now we are on very solid ground. We have before us the widest possible choice of stallions and mares. We can pick and choose. Our objective here is to include select chefs-de-race and other influential ancestors in the 4-generation pedigree of the offspring instead of any ancestor.

The procedure for doing so is simple. Select a number of successful stallions who have the desired chefs-de-race within their 3 generations. Select compatible mares who have other desired chefs-de-race within their 3 generations. Their progeny out of the above stallions will naturally be 4-generation outbreds with the desired ancestors. Here we are not bothered about the inbreeding further back which is inevitable and purely incidental. At this stage readers will immediately query: "But will such a horse have an 'extra' advantage over the others? Remember a majority of thoroughbreds are 4-generation outbreds with a number of chefs-de-race and other influential ancestors." Such horses will have an "extra" advantage as they have "selected" chefs-de-race and ancestors and not "any" chef-de-race or ancestor. I emphasized that in outcrossing our object is to pack the pedigree of the horse with as many chefs-de-race as possible. We can assume that all chefs-de-race are equally powerful and identical in behaviour and breed accordingly. Alternately we can breed for particular combinations of chefs-de-race, convinced that one "combination", one "set", is superior than the others. As readers will see, this aspect is of awesome importance. It will be dealt with in exhaustive detail in the next chapter.

In short: The object of outcrossing is to include as many selected chefs-de-race and other admired ancestors as possible within 5 or 4 generations of the individual, thereby giving him the chance to inherit a lot of beneficial qualities. But while we are doing so, we must not ignore the class and compatibility of the sire and dam.

THE "INTERNATIONAL" OUTCROSS

We now come to a subject that is truly fascinating. Its scope is immense and the possibilities are virtually limitless. The surface has been barely scratched. I look at the "International" outcross as below:

The thoroughbreds of different regions of the world differ in their inherent strengths and weaknesses. These differences are "subtle" and "invisible", but nevertheless exist. These differences are sharper in horses whose pedigrees have evolved exclusively in one particular region over an extended period of time. Imagine a sire line that has evolved exclusively in North America for over a 100 years. A descendant of that sire line today, will possess certain characteristics unique to that sire line, characteristics which are not found in other horses. Arguing on the above lines we can say: The thoroughbreds of region A possess a little more speed than the breed as a whole; the thoroughbreds of B are just a little more robust; the thoroughbreds of C are a little more precocious and so on. Therefore our endeavour must be to breed horses whose ancestors come from different regions of the world instead of a single region. For only then will the individual have a chance of inheriting beneficial qualities unique to different regions, qualities which he cannot otherwise inherit. This "inheritance" may hopefully give him an "extra" bit of talent. I readily concede that this idea seems far-fetched. A hundred years of evolution is too brief — far too brief — a period for the environment to interact with the breed. But still a number of outstanding horses were bred on the above lines. To understand the concept fully we would do well to study a few of them.

My first example is the great Nearco.

			Polymelus	Cyliene Maid Marian
		Phalaris	Bromus	Sanfoin Cheery
	Pharos		Chaucer	St. Simon Canterbury Pilgrim
		Scapa Flow	Anchora	Love Wisely Eryholme
Nearco (Br, 1935)			Rabelais	St. Simon Satrical
		Havresac II	Hors Concours	Ajax Simona
	Nogara		Spearmint	Carbine Maid of the Mint
		Catnip	Sibola	The Sailor Prince Saluda

Sir Charles Leicester has made a particular reference to his "cosmopolitan" pedigree. Analyzing the pedigree he found that his 30 nearest ancestors came from different regions of the world as below:

20 ancestors came from England

3 " " " Ireland

3 " " " France

2 " " " America

1 ancestor " " New Zealand

1 " " " Italy

Truly an International outcross! So the Italian bred Nearco had only one Italian ancestor. His breeder the legendary Federico Tesio was obviously far ahead of his times. It is unnecessary for me to describe his achievements on the track or in stud. It is also unnecessary and futile for us to try to determine the precise role played by each ancestor. The concept of the International outcross is definitely valid and it can be used with great success. (Readers would have noted that Nearco is inbred 4 x 4 to St. Simon. This inbreeding obviously does not alter the cosmopolitan, international nature of his pedigree.)

I am anxious to emphasize that conditions are now particularly favourable for breeding International outbreds. Transportation and communication between countries — continents — have become safe, easy and reliable. Horses bred in one country race in another and go to stud in a third. There are top class stud farms in every country and a breeder in one country can boldly send his mares to another. Just a couple of decades back breeders did not have all these advantages. Now everything is tailor-made, everything is in the hands of professionals. You only have to pick up the telephone! I am convinced that the International outcross will become the dominant philosophy of breeders. As its advantages are becoming very clear, its popularity is sure to increase by leaps and bounds.

Just as I was writing this chapter, the most prestigious race in the world was, to my intense delight, won by a true International outbred. I am naturally referring to Teenoso. Let us study his pedigree.

Teenoso (Dk B or Br, (1980)				
	Youth	Ack Ack	Battle Joined	Armageddon / Ethel Walker
			Fast Turn	Turn-to / Cherokee Rose
		Gazala II	Dark Star	Royal Gem II / Isolde
			Belle Angevine	L'Admiral / Bella II
	Furioso	Ballymoss	Mossborough	Nearco / All Moonshine
			Indian Call	Singapore / Flittemere
		Violetta III	Pinza	Chanteur II / Pasqua
			Urshalim	Nasrullah / Horama

It is unnecessary for me to analyze the bottom half of his pedigree. His maternal grandsires are well-known and his tail female line needs no introduction — it is one of the finest in the world. It is the top half of his pedigree — his direct male line — that is of very great interest. *This direct male line is exclusively American and had its origin there a hundred years ago.*

The line began when Eclipse, a son of Orlando (not to be confused with foundation stallion Eclipse who preceded him by about a hundred years), was imported into America from England in the 1850's. He had an outstanding great- grandson in Domino (1891). A fine racer, Domino had a stud career of only 2 seasons! But during that limited time he was able to get Cap and Bells II who became the first American-bred filly to win the Epsom Oaks. He also had an outstanding son in Commando (1898) who stood for only 4 seasons! Nevertheless he was able to get several superior racers including the phenomenal Colin. What Domino and Commando would have done had they had full stud careers can only be imagined.

A word about Colin (1905). He was unbeaten in 15 starts and his victories included the Belmont Stakes. His owner James R. Keene then sent him to England to race. There he showed that he had not lost his top class form, but unfortunately he broke down. Interestingly his owner kept him back in England as a stallion! Notice the foresight and wisdom of James R. Keene. He must have had several reasons for doing so but undoubtedly one of them was to breed International outbreds i.e. the progeny of an ''American'' stallion out of typical ''English'' mares. And since he raced Colin in England, he must have been anxious to compare the form of horses of both countries, and also see whether American horses could acclimatize themselves in England. For this he was prepared to use his best horse. But unfortunately English breeders did not fully understand American racing and breeding (remember this was during the early days of the 20th century) and Colin did not get much patronage. He returned to his native country but sadly did not get opportunities there too. But fortunately the line survived through Neddie. (There is another stirp of this line which we will study a little later.)

Neddie was not an outstanding galloper but managed to keep the line going through Good Goods — Alsab — Armageddon — Battle Joined — Ack Ack — Youth. Battle Joined (1959) was a stakes winner of 7 races (from only 10 starts) and a successful sire. Ack Ack (1966) was an outstanding galloper who won 19 races. At 5 he was Horse of the Year, champion handicap horse and champion sprinter. His victories included the Arlington Classic, Los Angeles Handicap, Hollywood Gold Cup and Santa Anita Handicap. Retired to stud he is already the sire of 26 stakes winners.

We now come to Teenoso's sire Youth. He scored 8 times from only 11 starts. His victories included the Prix du Jockey Club, Prix Lupin, Washington D.C. International and Canadian International Championship.

He was champion 3-yr-old in the Handicap Optional and champion grass horse in North America. His progeny have just started racing and 3 of them have won stakes.

Teenoso's dam Furioso won only once but was 2nd in the Epsom Oaks and 4th in the Irish Guinness Oaks and Sun Chariot Stakes. She was therefore among the best of her generation.

Youth has undoubtedly inherited certain special, unique characteristics from his direct male line ancestors. We can call them "American" characteristics. In my opinion the unison of these American characteristics with the typical "English" characteristics in Furioso helped Teenoso win the Derby. I am convinced that this is the major reason for his success. Teenoso is a perfect example of an International outbred. (Note that Slip Anchor is also an International outbred!) Incidentally Furioso is a successful producer. Her offspring by Habitat, Topsy, was a stakes winner of 5 races including the Sun Chariot Stakes, Fred Darling Stakes and Prix d'Astarte.

Readers may be interested in the actual breeding of Teenoso. Furioso after visiting Habitat and Grundy in England went to Kentucky where she visited Riva Ridge, Youth and The Minstrel. She then returned to England with Teenoso as a foal at foot, in foal to The Minstrel. Her journey was most successful and I am convinced that this will be the breeding schedule of most mares in future.

It is therefore possible to produce a large number of International outbreds by breeding European mares to Ack Ack and Youth and by breeding daughters of Ack Ack and Youth to European stallions. A few readers may be interested in working out the details.

The other branch of the Domino — Commando line descends to Double Jay. In order to get a clear picture I have given both the lines below:

Orlando	Orlando
Eclipse (U.S.A.)	Eclipse (U.S.A.)
Alarm	Alarm
Himyar	Himyar
Domino	Domino
Commando	Commando
Colin	Peter Pan
Neddie	Black Toney
Good Goods	Balladier
Alsab	Double Jay (1944)
Armageddon	
Battle Joined	
Ack Ack	
Youth (1973)	

		Black Toney	Peter Pan
			Belgravia
	Balladier		
		Blue Warbler	North Star III
			May Bird
Double Jay			
(Dk Br, 1944)		Whisk Broom II	Broomstick
			Audience
	Broomshot		
		Centre Shot	Sain
			Grand Shot

We can draw up another program for producing International outbreds based on the descendants of Double Jay. They too are sure to possess all the special characteristics of the Domino — Commando line.

Double Jay won 17 races from 6 furlongs to 1-3/16 miles. He was a successful sire but a phenomenal maternal grandsire. His daughters produced as many as 106 stakes winners. (He is the maternal grandsire I referred to earlier.) We can therefore use his daughters to produce International outbreds, by breeding them to compatible stallions with European elements in their pedigrees. But not many of his daughters will be active today. However we can go a step further. We can use his granddaughters as well. Specifically I have daughters of Bagdad in mind. Bagdad won 9 races including the Hollywood Derby and became the sire of 28 stakes winners. But what is important to us is that his daughters are showing a lot of promise as broodmares. Therefore breeders are sure to get excellent results if they breed them to superior and compatible European stallions. Such horses would be bred on the reverse pattern as Teenoso.

Incidentally Double Jay was not a sire of sires. Therefore very few of his direct male line descendants are stallions today. Breeding horses similar to Teenoso could be a bit difficult.

There is another outstanding stallion, with an American direct male line, whose sons and daughters are eminently suited for breeding International outbreds. The stallion I have in mind is In Reality. He is a descendant of the great Man o' War. The Fair Play — Man o' War line is an American branch of the Matchem sire line.

The line began when Australian (1858) a son of Triple Crown winner West Australian went to America in his early days. He was very successful getting among others 3 Belmont Stakes winners. One of them Spendthrift (1876) was the sire of Hastings (Belmont Stakes winner in 1885) who in turn got Fair Play (1905). Then the line developed as below:

West Australian
Australian
Spendthrift

Hastings
Fair Play
Man o' War
War Relic
Intent
Intentionally

In Reality (1964)

In Reality (B, 1964)	Intentionally	Intent	War Relic
			Liz F.
		My Recipe	Discovery
			Periette
	My Dear Girl	Rough'n Tumble	Free For All
			Roused
		Iltis	War Relic
			We Hail

In Reality won 14 races including the Florida Derby. He has proved to be a very successful sire with 44 stakes winners, and happily for us is emerging as a sire of sires. Several of his well performed sons have just entered stud. Readers can easily work out a program in which European mares visit In Reality and his sons and another program in which his daughters and granddaughters visit European stallions. (In Reality is inbred 3 x 3 to War Relic. This makes him all the more suitable for the International outcross as he will possess a greater number of elements unique to his sire line.)

I am anxious to make a special mention of one of his sons — Known Fact. A beautifully bred horse of great quality, he won 6 races including the English 2000 Guineas and William Hill Middle Park Stakes. He was Co-champion miler. Interestingly he has been retired to stud in Berkshire, England. This gives English breeders the opportunity to breed International outbreds without leaving the country! I have not looked at his mares but I presume that most of them are ''English'', thereby making most of his progeny International outbreds. As I write these lines his first foals would have just started hitting the ground. I look forward to their performances with immense interest. The success of Known Fact will be very sweet for those who believe in the International outcross and it will also be an additional seal of approval.

Another direct male line descendant of Man o' War is himself a prime example of the International outcross, and his services too can be most profitably utilized. I am referring to Olden Times, a grandson of War Relic.

Olden Times
(B, 1958)

Relic	War Relic	Man o' War	Friar's Carse
	Bridal Colors	Black Toney	**Valla**
Djenne	Djebel	Tourbillon	Loika
	Teza	Jock II	Torissima

He was a stakes winner of 17 races including the Metropolitan Handicap, San Juan Capistrano Handicap etc.

His stud career has been truly fascinating. Never a fashionable stallion, he finally got the recognition he deserved — at the age of 25! Recognition came because he is the first stallion in American Turf history to head the Maternal grandsire and Juvenile sire lists! In the words of Timothy T. Capps*: "It is a shame that Olden Times cannot talk, for his travels and the reasons behind them would make fascinating reading."

In spite of frequent changes in residence he has excelled, getting 50 stakes winners including 2 champions. He was second leading sire in 1977. He was leading sire in number of winners twice and in number of races won thrice.

His pedigree is of truly enormous interest and it makes him the most suitable stallion for the International outcross. As explained his direct male line is American. Notice that the bottom half of his pedigree is essentially French. In the words of Timothy T. Capps: "It contains some of the momentous names and concepts of the breeding dominion of Marcel Boussac." Therefore if we breed English mares to him or his sons, the progeny will have elements of American, French and English breeding — truly most appealing! And since his daughters are doing so well you can think of breeding them to English stallions.

I am sure the principles of the International outcross have become very clear. But I must add a note of caution. Since the expenses involved are far greater you must formulate your breeding program with extra care. The International outcross is not a panacea. The stallions and mares involved must be compatible. It would be better if you visit the stallion personally, and also see his progeny race, even though they may be thousands of miles away. (English and French breeders need not travel far; they only have to cross the Channel!) If you plan carefully I am sure you will be very successful.

---

* "A time to be recognized", *The Thoroughbred Record*, 19 January 1983.

EXERCISE

Readers must very carefully analyze the pedigrees of Genuine Risk, Pleasant Colony and Ma Biche. They are all International outbreds. Peter Willett* has described the first named as below: "A most complete and unusual outcross . . . for her sire Exclusive Native is a product of strains that have been developed in the United States for many generations whereas her dam Virtuous brings together some of the choicest strains developed in Europe during the twentieth century and represents in particular inbreeding to the 'flying filly' Mumtaz Mahal.''

LINEBREEDING

From the outcross and the International outcross we come back to inbreeding — to a special type of inbreeding called "linebreeding" which we referred to earlier. Dr. Nat M. Kieffer** has defined linebreeding as below:

"Linebreeding is a kind of inbreeding that is directed toward an outstanding ancestor, the purpose of which is to produce offspring that will be closely related to the admired ancestor but will themselves be only mildly inbred."

In inbreeding we decided to go all out and inbreed to as many outstanding ancestors as possible. In linebreeding we will inbreed to one desired ancestor only. There are enormous advantages in doing so. We saw that the non-availability of compatible stallions and mares with the required pedigrees greatly hampers inbreeding and frequently makes it impossible. This major difficulty does not arise in the case of linebreeding. For we are interested in only one influential ancestor like Nasrullah, Ribot, Princequillo or Northern Dancer. We are sure to find dozens of superior and compatible stallions and mares who have descended from the above horses.

Secondly if the linebreeding is not too incestuous the risk of bringing recessive defects and diseases to the surface is avoided. Remember both inbreeding and linebreeding increase the number of gene pairs fixed in double dose. The horse inherits not only the desirable qualities of the inbred ancestor, but also his undesirable qualities.

---

* "Rich dividends from an unusual outcross", *Horse and Hound,* January 23, 1981.
** "Linebreeding", *The Thoroughbred Record,* 15 April 1981.

Peter Willett* writes: "Estimates have been made that inbreeding at a level above 3% (roughly corresponding to the duplication of an ancestor in the 3rd generation) involves the risk of bringing recessive defects and diseases to the surface." Therefore the risks involved are very real. Peter Willett continues: "While the present average level of inbreeding in the thoroughbred is significantly below that danger point the reluctance of most breeders to exceed it understandable."

This automatically fixes the limits for linebreeding. You must restrict your linebreeding to the 3rd and 4th generations i.e. a 3 x 3 (a bit risky), 3 x 4 or 4 x 4 linebreeding.

Readers will recall that Prince Khartoum is a perfect example of a linebred horse. He is linebred 2 x 3 to Rockefella. There is no other inbreeding in his 5-generation pedigree.

```
                                                           Gainsborough
                                        Hyperion           Selene
                         Rockefella
                                                           Felstead
               Rock of                  Rockfel            Rockliffe
               Gibraltar
                                                           Monarch
                                        Premier Baiser     Passez Muscade
                         Toquade
                                                           Dark Legend
                                        Tonkette           Tonka
Prince Kartoum
(Ch, 1968)
                                                           Hyperion
                                        Rockefella         Rockfel
                         Elopement
                                                           Felicitation
                                        Daring Miss        Venturesome
               Pink Bamboo
                                                           Fair Trial
                                        Palestine          Una
                         Paeonia
                                                           Tehran
                                        Tenerezza          Masala
```

Let us take this opportunity to analyze his pedigree. Rock of Gibraltar has been described in detail. For quite some time he was the leading sire in the country. His maternal grandsires Elopement, Palestine and Tehran are definitely superior by Indian standards. His tail female line is as below:

---

* "Advantages of Line-Breeding", *Horse and Hound*, 20 April 1979.

PINK BAMBOO: ran only thrice at 2 in England. Dam of:

Prince Khartoum: as described.

Royal Highness: did not win in her short racing career.

PAEONIA: 1 win in England. Dam of:

Globe of Light: placed 3rd in the Prendergast Stakes.

Pink Bamboo: as above.

TENEREZZA: won Prix de la Lorie in France. Dam of:

Philodendron: 4 wins, Liverpool Summer Cup, Grand Stand Handicap; 2nd Hanging Stone Handicap.

Pachira: winner in France.

Twenty Francs: winner in North America.

Bunya-Bunya: did not win.

Sandbox: did not win.

Paeonia: as above.

This tail female line lacks quality. For real talent we have to go back to Tenerezza's grandam Mrs. Rustom. She won the Gimcrack Stakes and was 2nd in the Middle Park Stakes.

Therefore 2 of Prince Khartoum's 3 pedigree components are superior. This in itself is sufficient to produce a champion, but we would not be wrong in saying that the intense 2 x 3 linebreeding to Rockefella also helped. But readers will immediately query: ''Is Rockefella a stallion worthy enough to linebreed to? He is not even a chef-de-race.'' The question is a bit hypothetical. In this case it helped produce a champion. In another case it may not. The point is if you linebreed continuously using outstanding and compatible stallions and mares to whichever ancestor you like, you are sure to produce more than a few superior, if not outstanding, progeny.

There is yet another technique which we can use to breed superior horses. This technique consists of breeding horses whose pedigrees are ''identical'' to the pedigrees of classic winners and champions. (Here we are not referring to full-brothers and sisters. If you believe in the Derby Dictum, you will naturally breed a large number of full-brothers and sisters. Even if you do not believe in the Derby Dictum, you will be anxious to breed a full-brother or sister to a classic winner or champion.) One way of doing so is to breed the ''three-fourth'' brother (or sister) of an outstanding racer, in the hope that he too will excel. This term is reserved for horses out of the same dam but by sires who are father and son. It could also be used for horses out of the same sire but by dams who are mother and daughter. An excellent example of the former is King's Lake and Salmon Leap.

King's Lake (B, 1978)	Nijinsky	Northern Dancer	Nearctic Natalma
		Flaming Page	Bull Page Flaring Top
	Fish-Bar	Baldric	Round Table Two Cities
		Fisherman's Wharf	Alycidon Herringbone

King's Lake was a classic winner of 5 races in Ireland and England. His victories included the Airlie Coolmore Irish 2000 Guineas, Joe McGrath Memorial Stakes (Gr. I) and Sussex Stakes (Gr. I).

In 1980 Fish-Bar produced his three-fourth brother Salmon Leap.

Salmon Leap (Ch, 1980)	Northern Dancer	Nearctic	Nearco Lady Angela
		Natalma	Native Dancer Almahmoud
	Fish-Bar	Baldric	Round Table Two Cities
		Fisherman's Wharf	Alycidon Herringbone

Salmon Leap too has developed into a superior racer. His 2 victories include the H.M. Hartigan Tetrarch Stakes (Gr. III). In this case King's Lake's talent would not have been known at the time of Fish-Bar's visit to Northern Dancer. No doubt the breeder felt that Northern Dancer too was compatible with Fish-Bar, and that they were sure to produce a superior offspring, irrespective of the success or failure of the Nijinsky x Fish-Bar offspring. Incidentally Fish-Bar has proved to be a very successful producer getting superior racers out of Habitat and Sir Ivor also.

But undoubtedly the most outstanding and influential pair of three-fourth brothers of the 20th century are Nijinsky and The Minstrel.

		Nearctic	Nearco Lady Angela
	Northern Dancer		
		Natalma	Native Dancer Almahmoud
Nijinsky (B, 1967)			
		Bull Page	Bull Lea Our Page
	Flaming Page		
		Flaring Top	Menow Flaming Top

		Nearctic	Nearco Lady Angela
	Northern Dancer		
		Natalma	Native Dancer Almahmoud
The Minstrel (Ch, 1974)			
		Victoria Park	Chop Chop Victoriana
	Fleur		
		Flaming Page	Bull Page Flaring Top

It is unnecessary for me to describe their staggering achievements on the course or in stud. But in this case Nijinsky's success would have surely been the motivation for Fleur to visit Northern Dancer. (Interestingly Nijinsky and The Minstrel are vastly different in conformation and temperament.)

Some breeders like to breed full-sisters to the same stallion. This policy was very successful in the case of Request and Reward. Both the mares excelled with Prince Pradeep.

		Migoli	Bois Roussel Mah Iran
	Prince Pradeep (B, 1960)		
		Driving	Watling Street Snow Line
		Decorum	Orthodox Dignity
	Request (B, 1957) Reward (B, 1958)		
		Repay	Pay up Silver Loan

The former, as we saw, produced:

Reprint (1973): 6 wins, Indian 1000 Guineas and Oaks; 3rd Indian Derby.

Reflect (1974): 8 wins, Indian 1000 Guineas, Bangalore St. Leger,

Eclipse Stakes of India, Eve Champion Cup, C.N. Wadia Gold Cup; 3rd Indian Derby and Oaks.

The latter was responsible for:

Round-Up (1967): 6 wins, Grand Annual Handicap ; 2nd Indian Produce Stakes; 3rd Bangalore Derby.

Redouble (1969): 6 wins; 2nd Indian Oaks, Gen. Obaidullah Khan Gold Cup.

Round Off (1972): 4 wins, Bangalore St. Leger; 2nd Indian Derby.

Another variation is to breed half-sisters to the same stallion. Readers would have noted that this was successful in the case of Queen O'Scots and Mark Over.

My Opinion (Br, 1976)	Everyday	Jet Stream	Alizier Streamlace
		Tomorrow	Citation Until
	Queen O' Scots	Glasgow Paddock	Big Game Annetta
		Big Bess	Hindostan Empress Catherine
Royal Game (Dk B, 1978)	Everyday	Jet Stream	Alizier Streamlace
		Tomorrow	Citation Until
	Mark Over	The Wing	Major Portion Gondook
		Big Bess	Hindostan Empress Catherine

I have pointed out only a few variations. Readers can easily determine other methods of breeding "identically bred" horses. But I must add a note of caution. Full-brothers and sisters, half-brothers and sisters, fathers and sons and other close relatives can vary widely in class, aptitude, conformation, temperament and stud behaviour. It would be unwise to breed a horse just because his or her pedigree will resemble a stakes winner's. There must be a number of elements of compatibility between the sire and dam. If you are sure there are, you can boldly go ahead. The added advantage is that such horses are sure to sell for big prices.

CHAPTER 11

Dosage Analysis

THE CONCEPT OF A CHEF-DE-RACE

In the first part of the book we understood the significance of a pedigree and. learned how to analyze it in terms of its three components. But this is not the only method by which we can analyze a pedigree. Now we will learn how to analyze pedigrees by making use of a radically different concept — the concept of a "chef-de-race".

What is the meaning of this expression? Who is a chef-de-race? This expression (it is French) was first used by Lt. Col. J.J. Vuillier, a French Cavalry officer who did extensive research in thoroughbred pedigrees, in his book *Les Croisements Rationnels dans la Race Pure* published in the 1920s. The English translation of the expression would be: "heads of the thoroughbred" or "leaders of the thoroughbred".

Now who are the leaders of the thoroughbred? Look at pedigrees in any part of the world today. What do we find? The names of a handful of stallions keep appearing over and over again, lakhs of times. It is undoubtedly these stallions who have literally "shaped" and "moulded" the thoroughbred into what it is today. It is their blood that flows through the arteries and veins of the horses of today. Such outstanding progenitors, who were breed-shaping stallions in the truest sense of the term, are chefs-de-race.

Readers will have absolutely no difficulty in identifying a number of chefs-de-race. Nearco, Hyperion, Ribot, Bahram, Fairway, Court Martial, Princequillo, Djebel, Native Dancer, Teddy etc are all chefs-de-race. Turf historians have identified 147 stallions who deserve chef-de-race status.

I emphasize that we cannot give chef-de-race status to all successful stallions. A chef-de-race is on a higher plane. *He must have been a breed-shaping stallion in the truest sense of the term.*

Preparing the chef-de-race list is no easy task as it involves researching hundreds of stallions. A list prepared by one may not be agreeable to another. I have no hesitation in admitting that readers may not entirely agree with the list given.* One reader will ask: "Can Petition be given

---

* "Applications of Dosage", by Dr. Steven A. Roman, *The Thoroughbred Record*, 14 October 1981.

chef-de-race status? Was he really such an influential progenitor?'' Another may assert that Rockefella should have been included, while a third may be shocked at the non-inclusion of Migoli. In the words of Dr. Steven A. Roman**:

''The chef-de-race list, however, should be considered as dynamic and flexible, capable of refinement through modifications, additions or deletions.''

For example stallions like Nijinsky, Mill Reef, Habitat and Great Nephew are sure to have qualified for chef-de-race status.

Now we would all be very eager to take advantage of all the chefs-de-race. We would like our horse to inherit a lot of beneficial qualities from as many chefs-de-race as possible. How can we do so? We can plan the mating such that the individual has a large number of chefs-de-race within his 4-generation pedigree i.e. we are ''packing'' the pedigree with as many chefs-de-race as possible. Then the individual has an excellent chance of inheriting a lot of beneficial qualities from them, qualities which will enable him to excel on the course.

To check whether the above assumption is correct, let us analyze the pedigrees of a few outstanding gallopers and determine the number of chefs-de-race in them. It is unnecessary for me to give their race records.

(Here readers must note that we are ignoring the chefs-de-race in the 5th and subsequent generations as they could have played only a marginal role in shaping the individual. Readers must also understand that this concept is universal. The influence of the chefs-de-race is not restricted to one region; their influence is undoubtedly world-wide.)

** ''Applications of Dosage'', by Dr. Steven A. Roman, *The Thoroughbred Record,* 14 October 1981.

(Chefs-de-race are in **bold** letters.)

Sassafras
(B, 1967)

- Sheshoon
  - **Precipitation**
    - **Hurry On**
      - Marcovil
      - Tout Suite
    - Double Life
      - **Bachelor's Double**
      - Saint Joan
  - Noorani
    - **Nearco**
      - **Pharos**
      - Nogara
    - Empire Glory
      - Singapore
      - Skyglory
- Ruta
  - Ratification
    - **Court Martial**
      - **Fair Trial**
      - Instantaneous
    - Solesa
      - **Solario**
      - Mesa
  - Dame d'Atour
    - Cranach
      - Coronach
      - Reine Isaure
    - Barley Corn
      - **Hyperion**
      - Schiaparelli

Bustino
(B, 1971)

- Busted
  - **Crepello**
    - **Donatello II**
      - **Blenheim**
      - Delleana
    - Crepuscule
      - **Mieuxce**
      - Red Sunset
  - Sans Le Sou
    - Vimy
      - **Wild Risk**
      - Mimi
    - Martial Loan
      - **Court Martial**
      - Loan
- Ship Yard
  - Doutelle
    - **Prince Chevalier**
      - **Prince Rose**
      - Chevalerie
    - Above Board
      - Straight Deal
      - Feola
  - Paving Stone
    - **Fairway**
      - **Pharlaris**
      - Scapa Flow
    - Rosetta
      - Kantar
      - Rose Red

```
                                              │ Polynesian
                              Native Dancer   │ Geisha
                Raise a Native
                              │               │ Case Ace
                              Raise You        │ Lady Glory
  Majestic Prince
                              │               │ Nearco
                              Royal Charger   │ Sun Princess
                Gay Hostess
                              │               │ Alibhai
                              Your Hostess    │ Boudoir II
Coastal
(Ch, 1976)
                              │               │ Menow
                              Tom Fool         │ Gaga
                Buckpasser
                              │               │ War Admiral
                              Busanda          │ Businesslike
  Alluvial
                              │               │ Princequillo
                              Hill Prince     │ Hildene
                Bayou
                              │               │ Stimuls
                              Bourtai          │ Escutcheon
```

```
                                              │ Nearco
                              Nasrullah       │ Mumtaz Begum
                Never Bend
                              │               │ Djeddah
                              Lalun            │ Be Faithful
  Riverman
                              │               │ Princequillo
                              Prince John     │ Not Afraid
                River Lady
                              │               │ Roman
                              Nile Lily        │ Azalea
Policeman
(B, 1977)
                              │               │ Prince Bio
                              Sicambre        │ Sif
                Barbara
                              │               │ Fair Trial
                              Barbara          │ Mistress Ford
  Indianapolis
                              │               │ Prince Chevalier
                              Charlottesville │ Noorani
                Iberide
                              │               │ Mossoborough
                              Candytuft        │ Cretan Belle
```

Perrault
(Ch, 1977)

- Djakao
  - Tanerko
    - Tantieme
      - Deux Pour Cent
      - Terika
    - La Divine
      - Fair Copy
      - La Diva
  - Diagonale
    - **Ribot**
      - Tenerani
      - Romanella
    - Barley Corn
      - **Hyperion**
      - Schiaparelli
- Innocent Air
  - Court Martial
    - **Fair Trial**
      - **Fairway**
      - Lady Juror
    - Instantaneous
      - **Hurry On**
      - Picture
  - Aldousa
    - **Vatellor**
      - **Vatout**
      - Lady Elinor
    - Aurora
      - **Hyperion**
      - Rose Red

Providential
(B, 1977)

- Run the Gantlet
  - **Tom Rolfe**
    - **Ribot**
      - Tenerani
      - Romanella
    - Pocahontas
      - **Roman**
      - How
  - First Feather
    - First Landing
      - **Turn-To**
      - Hildene
    - Quill
      - **Princequillo**
      - Quick Touch
- Prudent Girl
  - Primera
    - **My Babu**
      - **Djebel**
      - Perfume II
    - Pirette
      - Deiri
      - Pimpette
  - Bride Elect
    - **Big Game**
      - **Bahram**
      - Myrobella
    - Netherton Maid
      - **Nearco**
      - Phase

The pedigrees of all these fine gallopers are bursting with chefs-de-race. Each of them was obviously influenced by the chefs-de-race in his pedigree, and it definitely appears that it was this influence that enabled him to excel. In other words it seems that the inherent strength of a pedigree is directly proportional to the number of chefs-de-race in it.

However this conclusion does not stand up to close scrutiny. For note that thousands of other thoroughbreds also have the above chefs-de-race within their 4-generation pedigrees. But they were not classic winners or champions. Far from it, most of them were content to race in the lowest classes! This is not really surprising as, by definition, it is the chefs-de-race who have literally "built" the breed. Therefore their names are sure to be found in an overwhelming majority of pedigrees — in the pedigrees of superior, average and substandard racers.

Therefore the presence of a large number of chefs-de-race in a pedigree is not a guarantee for success.

Turf historians have found that horses with few chefs-de-race have also excelled. Some of them are:

Czaravich (Ch, 1976)	Nijinsky	**Northern Dancer**	Nearctic	**Nearco** Lady Angela
			Natalma	**Native Dancer** Almahmoud
		Flaming Page	Bull Page	**Bull Lea** Our Page
			Flaring Top	Menow Flaming Top
	Black Satin	Linacre	Rockefella	**Hyperion** Rockfel
			True Picture	**Panorama** Verity
		Panaview	Panaslipper	Solar Slipper Panastrid
			April View	Atout Maitre Distant View

		Nasrullah	Nearco / Mumtaz Begum
	Fleet Nasrullah		
		Happy Go Fleet	Count Fleet / Draeh
Gummo			
		Determine	Alibhai / Koubis
	Alabama Gal		
		Trojan Lass	Priam II / Rompers
Flying Paster (B, 1976)			
		Hillsdale	Take Away / Johann
	Acroterion		
		Stage Fright	Native Dancer / Petrify
Procne			
		Tudor Minstrel	Owen Tudor / Sansonnet
	Philomela		
		Petrovna II	Blue Peter / Straight Sequence

		Grey Sovereign	Nasrullah / Kong
	Sovereign Path		
		Mountain Path	Bobsleigh / Path of Peace
Wolver Hollow			
		Caracalla	Tourbillon / Astronomie
	Cygnet		
		Mrs. Swan Song	Sir Walter Raleigh / Donati's Comet
Galaxy Libra (B, 1976)			
		Le Haar	Vieux Manoir / Mince Pie
	Exbury		
		Greensward	Mossborough / Stargrass
Garden of Eden			
		Zarathustra	Persian Gulf / Salvia
	Mesopotamia		
		Agar's Plough	Combat / Fair Fallow

Lyphard's Wish
(B, 1976)

- Lyphard
  - **Northern Dancer**
    - Nearctic
      - **Nearco**
      - Lady Angela
    - Natalma
      - **Native Dancer**
      - Alhahmoud
  - Goofed
    - **Court Martial**
      - **Fair Trial**
      - Instantaneous
    - Barra II
      - Formor
      - La Favorite
- Sally's Wish
  - Sensitivo
    - **Sideral**
      - Seductor
      - Starling II
    - Ternura
      - Embrujo
      - Bien Aimee
  - Garden Clubber
    - Intent
      - War Relic
      - Liz F
    - Locust Time
      - Spy Song
      - Snow Goose

Argument
(B, 1977)

- Kautokeino
  - Relko
    - Tanerko
      - **Tantieme**
      - La Divine
    - Relance III
      - Relic
      - Polaire II
  - Cranberry
    - **Aureolel**
      - **Hyperion**
      - Angelola
    - Big Berry
      - **Big Game**
      - Red Briar
- Arntellea
  - Tapioca
    - **Vandale**
      - Plassy
      - Vanille
    - Semoule D'Or
      - **Vatellor**
      - Semoule Fine
  - Neptune's Doll
    - Neptune II
      - Crafty Admiral
      - Timely Tune
    - Dzena
      - Tornado
      - Doria

Light Cavalry (B, 1977)			
Brigadier Gerard	Queen's Hussar	March Past	**Petition** / Marcelette
		Jojo	Vilmorin / Fairy Jane
	La Palva	**Prince Chevalier**	**Prince Rose** / Chevalerie
		Brazen Molly	Horus / Molly Adare
Glass Slipper	Relko	Tanerko	**Tantieme** / La Divine
		Relance II	Relic / Polaire II
	Crystal Palace	Solar Slipper	Windsor Slipper / Solar Flower
		Queen of Light	Borealis / Picture Play

Now I want readers to compare these pedigrees with the earlier ones. Can we not say that these are relatively unorthodox? They have very few chefs-de-race. Most of the other names in these pedigrees arc rarely found in the pedigrees of today. Therefore:

An orthodoxly-bred horse is one with a large number of chefs-de-race while an unorthodoxly-bred horse is one with a small number of chefs-de-race.

Till now we have ignored the position of a chef-de-race in a pedigree. Admittedly it is necessary to consider his position before we can determine the magnitude of his influence on the individual. A chef-de-race in the 5th or 6th generation, however outstanding, can only play a marginal role in shaping the individual. If a chef-de-race is to play a dominant role, he must be "close up" in the pedigree. But how close can he get? The sire and maternal grandsire positions are the closest that can be occupied' In other words an individual whose sire and maternal grandsire are chefs-de-race has the greatest chance of inheriting a lot of beneficial qualities from them and developing into a superior racer. Several outstanding racers had chefs-de-race as heir sires and maternal grandsires. A few of them are:

Citation (B, 1945)	Bull Lea	
	Hydroplane	Hyperion

Grey Dawn II (Gr, 1962)	Herbager	
	Polamia	Herbager

Hoist the flag (B, 1968)	Tom Rolfe	
	Wavy Navy	War Admiral

Mill Reef (B, 1968)	Never Bend	
	Milan Mill	Princequillo

Roberto (B, 1969)	Hail to Reason	
	Bramalea	Nashua

Secretariat (Ch, 1970)	Bold Ruler	
	Somethingroyal	Princequillo

Little Current (Ch, 1971)	Sea Bird	
	Luiana	My Babu

Foolish Pleasure (B, 1972)	What a Pleasure	
	Fool-Me-Not	Tom Fool

But again this is not a formula for success as readers will know scores of badly performed horses who also had chefs-de-race as their sires and maternal grandsires. The reasons for their failure are also known to us. Remember the maternal grandsires constitute only one of the three components of a broodmare. Even if the maternal grandsires (all chefs-de-race) are compatible with the sire (also a chef-de-race), *the mare need not be compatible with the sire. She need not even be Inherently-superior.*

We cannot claim that a sire — even if he is an outstanding chef-de-race — will be compatible with all mares. Therefore if the mare is incompatible, her chances of producing a superior offspring out of the sire are almost nonexistent. The fact that she is a daughter of a chef-de-race does not alter this conclusion. *Therefore the presence of a number of chefs-de-race, even if they are close up in the pedigree, is no guarantee for success. Then how can we take advantage of chefs-de-race? To do so we have to use the concept of "Dosage".*

THE CONCEPT OF DOSAGE

' The "Dosage System" was invented by Lt. Col. J.J. Vuillier. It was the logical extension of his work on chefs-de-race and this research was also published in his book. Col. Vuillier analyzed the 12-generation pedigrees of hundreds of superior horses and identified 16 horses (15 stallions and 1 mare) who deserved chef-de-race status. The names of these 16 horses — chefs-de-race — kept on occurring thousands of times. He then studied the distribution of these 16 chefs-de-race in the pedigrees and quantified his findings. He laid down a "Standard Dosage" for each chef-de-race i.e. the "quantity" of the chef-de-race necessary for an ideal thoroughbred. How can we express this quantity mathematically? It is simple.

For a chef-de-race in the 12th generation count	1 strain
For a chef-de-race in the 11th generation count	2 strains
For a chef-de-race in the 10th generation count	4 strains
For a chef-de-race in the 3rd generation count	512 strains
For a chef-de-race in the 2nd generation count	1024 strains
For a chef-de-race in the 1st generation count	2048 strains

(We are merely applying Galton's Law. We halve the strains for the next generation.)

Therefore calculating the dosage of a chef-de-race is very simple. Study the 12-generation pedigree of the horse and see in which generations he comes. Suppose he comes once in the 4th generation and once in the 5th. Then his dosage will be: 256 (for the 4th generation) + 128 (for the 5th generation) = 384. Likewise we can easily calculate the dosages of the other 15 chefs-de-race and compare with Vuillier's standard dosages. *The object is naturally to breed horses whose dosages are as close as possible to Vuillier's standard dosage.*

This can be easily done. First analyze the pedigree of the stallion and calculate the dosages of all the chefs-de-race. Suppose the stallion is free from 2 or 3 chefs-de-race say Touchstone and Hermit. Then the mare you select must have crosses of Touchstone and Hermit so that the offspring will have all the necessary chefs-de-race. Suppose the stallion's St. Simon dosage is higher than the standard. In such a case you will naturally breed a mare whose St. Simon's dosage is less than the standard so that the off-spring will have the required dosage. Therefore you must plan the matings such that the offspring's dosage is as close as possible to Vuillier's standard dosage.

But readers are sure to ask: "If my mare visits a particular stallion the offspring will, no doubt, have a dosage that is close to the standard. But unfortunately the stallion in question is *incompatible* with the mare. Will the mating be successful?" *It will not.* There is absolutely nothing to be gained by breeding incompatible or substandard stallions and brood-mares just to get progeny with standard dosages. The results are sure to be disastrous as several found to their chagrin.

Then how can we use the system? First identify a number of superior stallions who are also compatible with your mare. Now if you are unable to decide on one stallion you can use the system. Calculate the dosage of the offspring out of each -selected stallion and see which is closest to the standard. Then you can use that stallion.

The Vuillier Dosage System should not be used per se to finalize matings. It is an excellent aid, an instrument which gives additional support.

Before concluding this section I would like to emphasize: Very few horses would have had a dosage identical to the standard; but undoubtedly several were close. Secondly there were several outstanding horses whose dosages differed greatly from the standard: Gainsborough had over 100% excess Galopin, Nearco had a great excess of St. Simon and Tourbillon was free from Hampton.

Therefore we can say that several "mixtures" of chefs-de-race can produce outstanding horses. Vuillier's standard dosage is only one among the several.

In conclusion I must state that Vuillier's dosages cannot be used today. Remember he was analyzing pedigrees early in the 20th century. The chefs-de-race identified by him were naturally the outstanding stallions of the 19th century like Touchstone (1831), Hermit (1864), Bend Or (1877), St. Simon (1881) and Pocahontas (1837) the only mare in the list. We will not come across these names in the pedigrees of today. (This is one of the reasons why I have not given his standard dosages. However those who are interested can refer to *Bloodstock Breeding* by Sir Charles Leicester, revised by Howard Wright, where they are given.) It is therefore necessary to determine the standard dosages of 20th century chefs-de-race like Nearco, Hyperion, Ribot and others. But remember to do so it is necessary to analyze hundreds of pedigrees. I do not know whether anyone has done so, but if you want to breed according to this system you must undertake the task.

Dr. Franco Varola was the next person to take up the dosage thread. He made a crucial break-through by giving a qualitative aspect to the concept. He published his work in his book *Typology of the Racehorse*. Firstly he updated the chefs-de-race list by identifying 120 stallions of the 20th century who deserved chef-de-race status. Then Dr. Varola argued on the following lines: We saw that the mere presence of chefs-de-race in a pedigree, however close-up they may be, does not help. Could it be that one set, one combination, of chefs-de-race is inherently superior than another? It is very unlikely that each chef-de-race transmitted every beneficial quality. In all probability one chef-de-race would have transmitted one beneficial quality while another chef-de-race another. Therefore the task is to classify, categorize, chefs-de-race according to the qualities they transmitted to their progeny. Then if you breed a horse with chefs-de-race from each category, he has every chance of inheriting every type of beneficial quality.

This is precisely what Dr. Varola did. He divided all the chefs-de-race into five aptitudinal groups: Brilliant, Intermediate, Classic, Solid and Professional, depending on the degree of ''brilliance'' or ''stoutness'' the chef-de-race imparted to his progeny. What exactly do we mean by brilliance and stoutness? *We would not be wrong if we equated brilliance with speed and stoutness with stamina.* In other words brilliance is essentially manifested through speed and stoutness essentially through stamina.

We all know that several outstanding stallions, chefs-de-race, imparted brilliant speed to their progeny. Several of them may have stayed but undoubtedly their principal, dominant characteristic was speed. Such a chef-de-race is a Brilliant chef-de-race. Similarly we all know that several chefs-de-race at the other end of the spectrum imparted superior stamina and extreme stamina to their progeny. Such chefs-de-race would naturally come in the Professional category. Obviously all the other chefs-de-race belong to the three categories in between. An Intermediate chef-de-race is one who imparted slightly less brilliance than a Brilliant chef-de-race. Similarly a Solid chef-de-race is one who imparted slightly less stoutness than a Professional chef-de-race and a Classic chef-de-race is one who imparted an equal amount of brilliance and stoutness.

Readers must note that the chef-de-race's own aptitude on the course does not come into the picture. He may have been an outstanding miler but a sire of stayers and extreme stayers. Then he will naturally be classified as a Solid or Professional chef-de-race. Readers must also not be under the impression that a Brilliant chef-de-race is superior to an Intermediate chef-de-race and so on. All the chefs-de-race were breed-shaping stallions, otherwise they would not have got into the list.

The concept of dosage was further enlarged by Dr. Steven A. Roman. It is this extension that is of interest to us and we will study it in detail. Dr. Roman determined a method by which we can analyze a pedigree solely in terms of the chefs-de-race in it. In his words*: "Our approach which has appeared in detail as a series of articles in Leon Rasmussen's 'Bloodlines' column in the *Daily Racing Form* just prior to this year's Kentucky Derby, is a synthesis of Vuillier and Varola into a system of practical utility, amenable to statistical verification of its accuracy."

Let us analyze the pedigrees of two horses to understand this concept very clearly. To do so we have to use the Table given in Dr. Steven A. Roman's article**, which lists all the chefs-de-race in their aptitudinal groups. (I urge all readers to obtain the above article, study it very carefully, and keep it for future reference. Readers must also study Dr. Roman's subsequent article, "An analysis of dosage", which appeared in *The Thoroughbred Record*, 18 April 1984. This article has an updated list of chefs-de-race.)

---

* "Applications of Dosage", *The Thoroughbred Record*, 14 October 1981.
** "Applications of Dosage", *The Thoroughbred Record*, 14 October 1981.

Let us first analyze the pedigree of Riverman.

STEP 1

Write down the 4-generation pedigree of Riverman. This is done below:

```
                                                  Naerco         Pharos
                                                                 Nogara
                                  Nasrullah
                                                  Mumtaz Begum   Blenheim
                                                                 Mumtaz Mahal
                  Never Bend
                                                  Djeddah        Djebel
                                                                 Djezima
                                  Lalun
                                                  Be Faithful    Bimelech
                                                                 Bloodroot
Riverman
(B, 1969)
                                                  Princequillo   Prince Rose
                                                                 Cosquilla
                                  Prince John
                                                  Not Afraid     Count Fleet
                                                                 Banish Fear
                  River Lady
                                                  Roman          Sir Gallahad III
                                                                 Buckup
                                  Nile Lady
                                                  Azalea         Sun Teddy
                                                                 Coquelicot
```

STEP 2

Identify all the chefs-de-race in his 4-generation pedigree.

The chefs-de-race in his 4-generation pedigree are: Never Bend, Nasrullah, Prince John, Nearco, Princequillo, Roman, Pharos, Blenheim, Djebel, Prince Rose, Count Fleet and Sir Gallahad III.

STEP 3

Put the chefs-de-race into their respective aptitudinal groups. This is done below:

Chef-de-race	Generation	Aptitudinal group
Never Bend	1st	Brilliant and Intermediate
Nasrullah	2nd	Brilliant

Chef-de-race	Generation	Aptitudinal group
Prince John	2nd	Classic
Nearco	3rd	Brilliant and Classic
Princequillo	3rd	Intermediate and Solid
Roman	3rd	Brilliant and Intermediate
Pharos	4th	Intermediate
Blenheim	4th	Classic and Solid
Djebel	4th	Intermediate
Prince Rose	4th	Classic
Count Fleet	4th	Classic
Sir Gallahad III	4th	Classic

STEP 4

Construct the ''Dosage Profile'' (D.P).
This is done as below:

A chef-de-race in the 1st generation gets 16 points.
A chef-de-race in the 2nd generation gets 8 points.
A chef-de-race in the 3rd generation gets 4 points.
A chef-de-race in the 4th generation gets 2 points.
(We are merely following Galton's Law.)

Now we must gather together all the Brilliant chefs-de-race and allot points according to the generations in which they are present.

Never Bend comes in the 1st generation. He therefore gets 16 points. But as he is placed in the Brilliant and Intermediate categories, we will allot 8 points to the Brilliant category and 8 points to the Intermediate category as shown in the Tabular column below.

Nasrullah comes in the 2nd generation. He therefore gets 8 points. He is a Brilliant chef-de-race. Hence these 8 points are written below the 8 points contributed by Never Bend in the Brilliant column.

Nearco comes in the 3rd generation. He therefore gets 4 points. But as his influence has been divided between the Brilliant and Classic categories, we will give 2 points to each category.

Roman also comes in the 3rd generation. He therefore gets 4 points. Since he is placed in the Brilliant and Intermediate categories, we will allot 2 points to each category.

Now we can add up all the points in the Brilliant column: $8+8+2+2 = 20$. *What we have actually done is determine the magnitude of influence — of the Brilliant chefs-de-race.* Similarly we can determine the magnitudes of influence of the Intermediate, Classic, Solid and Professional chefs-de-race as shown in the Tabular column.

Brilliant		Intermediate		Classic		Solid		Professional
Never Bend	8	Never Bend	8	Nearco	2	Princequillo	2	Nil
Nasrullah	8	Roman	2	Prince John	8	Blenheim	1	
Nearco	2	Princequillo	2	Blenheim	1			
Roman	2	Pharos	2	Prince Rose	2			
		Djebel	2	Count Fleet	2			
				Sir Gallahad III	2			
	20		16		17		3	0

The row of 5 figures we have just obtained—20-16-17-3-0—is Riverman's "Dosage Profile". What does it mean? What does it signify? Our task now is to analyze and understand the Dosage Profile.

It is clear that his pedigree is dominated by Brilliant, Intermediate and Classic chefs-de-race. Since Brilliant and Intermediate chefs-de-race, by definition, impart a lot of speed, we can say that speed would have been Riverman's forte. But as Classic chefs-de-race are also well represented, we can assert that he would have carried his speed up to 2000 m. Notice that Solid chefs-de-race are poorly represented and that Professional chefs-de-race are absent. Therefore the chances of Riverman inheriting top class stamina or extreme stamina were definitely remote.

Now if we study his racing performance we will find that our deductions are substantially correct. At 2 he made a winning debut in the Prix Yacowlef (1000 m). At 3 he was champion miler in France with victories in the French 2000 Guineas (1600 m), Prix d'Ispahan (1850 m) and Prix Jean Prat (1800 m). I am anxious to add that he was also 2nd in the Champion Stakes (1-1/4 miles) and 3rd in the King George VI and Queen Elizabeth Stakes (1-1/2 miles). Undoubtedly he excelled up to 2000 m but did not seem to relish longer distances.

Therefore the Dosage Profile of a horse helps us determine his aptitude.

From the Dosage Profile we can calculate a quantity called the "Dosage Index". We simply add the points contributed by the Brilliant and Intermediate chefs-de-race to half the points contributed by the Classic chefs-de-race. Then we add the points contributed by the Solid and Professional chefs-de-race to half the points contributed by the Classic chefs-de-race. The significance of these two numbers is at once obvious. The first number is the total points that can be attributed to speed and the second number the total points that can be attributed to stamina. If we divide the first number by the second, we will get the ratio of speed to stamina. This is the Dosage Index (D.I.). Riverman's Dosage Index is:

$$20+16+17/2 \div 17/2+3+0$$
$$44.5 \div 11.5$$
$$= \underline{\underline{3.87}}$$

Readers would have grasped the significance of the Dosage Index. *Higher the Dosage Index greater the speed the individual will possess and lower the Dosage Index greater the stamina the individual will possess.* (There is one more quantity called the "Centre of Distribution" which can be calculated from the Dosage Profile. We will not go into it here, but readers who are interested can refer to Dr. Steven A. Roman's article.)

Let us determine the D.P and D.I. of Big Spruce. His pedigree is given in the next page and from it I have directly constructed the Dosage Profile.

Big Spruce (Dk B or Br, 1969)	Herbager	Vandale	Plassy — Bosworth / Pladda
			Vanille — La Farina / Vaya
		Flagette	Escamillo — Firdaussi / Estoril
			Fidgette — Firdaussi / Boxeuse
	Silver Sari	Prince John	Princequillo — Prince Rose / Cosquilla
			Not Afraid — Count Fleet / Banish Fear
		Golden Sari	Ambiorix — Tourbillon / Lavendula
			Banta — Some Chance / Bourtai

Brilliant	Intermediate		Classic		Solid		Professional	
Nil	Princequillo	2	Herbager	8	Herbager	8	Vandale	8
			Prince John	8	Princequillo	2	La Farina	2
			Prince Rose	2			Tourbillon	1
			Count Fleet	2				
			Tourbillon	1				
0	2		21		10		11	

His Dosage Profile is: 0 - 2 - 21 - 10 - 11.

His Dosage Index is:

$$0 + 2 + \frac{21}{2} \div \frac{21}{2} + 10 + 11$$

$$= 12.5 \div 31.5$$

$$= \underline{\underline{0.4}}$$

Readers would have immediately noticed that Big Spruce's D.P is diametrically opposite Riverman's. Whereas Riverman's pedigree is dominated by Brilliant, Intermediate and Classic chefs-de-race, Big Spruce's pedigree is dominated by Classic Solid and Professional chefs-de-race. And his D.I is as low as 0.4. It is clear that Big Spruce was bred to stay and genuine stamina rather than speed would have been his forte.

Studying his race record we find that our deduction is correct. He won 9 races including the San Luis Rey Stakes (1-1/2 miles, turf) and Gallant Fox Handicap (1-5/8 miles). He was also 2nd in the Washington D.C. International (1-1/2 miles, turf) and San Juan Capistrano Handicap (1-3/4 miles).

I deliberately selected two horses whose D.Ps and D.Is are relatively easy to interpret. Further they ran true to their D.Ps and D.Is. But I emphasize that this need not always be the case. We can easily name several superior stayers who possessed high D.Is and conversely several brilliant sprinter-milers who possessed low D.Is. But the D.I is undoubtedly an excellent aid, an additional technique that is available at our disposal.

I am anxious to stress that the Dosage Profile and Dosage Index cannot throw light on the class of the individual. This follows from the definition itself. We emphasized that a significant number of chefs-de-race are present in most pedigrees. Therefore every thoroughbred will have a Dosage Profile and Index. These two quantities only attempt to describe the aptitude of an individual in terms of the aptitudes of the chefs-de-race in his pedigree. To determine the class of the individual, we have to analyze his pedigree in terms of its three components as we did earlier.

EXERCISE

Readers must calculate the D.Ps and D.Is of a number of horses, interpret them and compare their findings with the race records of the horses.

Before we proceed further I would like to stress a fundamental aspect of this concept. We analyzed the pedigrees of Riverman and Big Spruce solely in terms of the chefs-de-race in them. We assumed that they alone shaped and moulded them. But not all the names in a pedigree are chefs-de-race. What about the non-chefs-de-race? Don't they play a role — however small it may be — in shaping the offspring? The non-chefs-de-race can be divided into two groups: The stallions who did not qualify for chef-de-race status and all the mares. The mares in a pedigree obviously play an equal role in influencing the offspring; yet we are completely ignoring them. To this extent our conclusions are incorrect. But, as explained, we cannot precisely determine the aptitudes of broodmares. Therefore are forced to ignore them.

But can we ignore the non-chef-de-race stallions? A non-chef-de-race stallion, by definition, does not play a dominant role, for if he did he would have qualified for chef-de-race status! Therefore we are not far wrong in ignoring them.

We now come to the crux of the subject. Dr. Roman has determined the Dosage Indices for selected performance categories in America. Let us go category by category. He found the average D.I of winners of sprint races to be as high as 5.61. This is not surprising as we emphasized that higher the D.I greater the potential for speed. The pedigrees of sprinters are obviously dominated by Brilliant and Intermediate chefs-de-race. Otherwise an individual would find it very difficult to develop into a sprinter. Not surprisingly the average D.I. of 2-yr-old winners is an almost identical 5.59. Remember that most of the races for 2-yr-olds are sprints and only "speedy" individuals can score. A stayer or extreme stayer will find it very difficult to defeat brilliant, precocious sprinters. *Therefore if you want to breed superior 2-yr-olds make sure that their pedigrees are dominated by Brilliant and Intermediate chefs-de-race.*

The picture for 3-yr-olds is different. They have to run over the range of distances with a strong emphasis on middle distances and routes. To excel in these races and in the classics, an individual must possess elements of stamina. A sprinter cannot obviously make an impact in these races.

This is reflected in the fact that the average D.I of winners of middle distance races falls to 4.1 and the D.I of winners of routes falls still further to 3.04.

Then Dr. Roman determined the average D.I. of classic winners* (between 1971-80) to be 2.43 and the average D.I of male champions, all ages,(between 1971-80) to be 2.65. These two figures are of enormous importance for they help us to answer a question breeders have been attempting to answer for years: *"Which blend of speed and stamina is the ideal blend of speed and stamina?"* An easy answer would be to say: ''Equal parts of speed and stamina constitute the ideal blend of speed and stamina. In other words a D.I of 1 represents the ideal blend of speed and stamina.''

Let us check whether this answer is correct. To do so we have to first identify horses who possessed an ideal blend of speed and stamina. Readers will agree, without the slightest hesitation, that classic winners, champions, Horses of the Year and leading earners i.e. the true ''elite'' of the breed possessed an ideal blend of speed and stamina. If we calculate their D.Is we will at once know the ratio of speed to stamina they possessed. Dr. Roman carried out this step and found that the above horses possessed average D.Is between 1.9 and 2.65. This finding is of awesome importance as it clearly establishes that *the ideal blend of speed and stamina is not one part of speed to one part of stamina but two to two and a half parts of speed to one part of stamina.* Therefore if you are interested in breeding outstanding racers, make sure that their D.Is are between 2 and 2.5.

In all honesty we must say that knowledgeable breeders were fully aware of the above finding. *That is why they repeatedly emphasized the importance of speed in a thoroughbred.* Readers will be interested in the views of Federico Tesio. Sen. Tesio analyzed the pedigrees of over 1000 winners of prestigious races going back 7 generations in all cases and 12 generations in some. He found that staying power in order to keep winning must occasionally be enlivened with the blood of top sprinters over 3/4 mile or 1 mile. He also found that if the first 62 ancestors of a racehorse, both stallions and mares, had staying power only, the horse rarely won a valuable race over any distance. He emphasized that a great horse, a superior horse, requires among his first 62 ancestors individuals who showed classic quality over 1, 1-1/4, 1-1/2 and 2 miles. Sen. Tesio continues**: ''Without a

---

* ''Winners of the Kentucky Derby and Belmont Stakes only.
** *Breeding the Racehorse,* by Federico Tesio, translated by Edward Spinola, J.A. Allen & Co.

representative of the 1 mile race in his pedigree it will be difficult to produce a horse of outstanding quality, because he will be incapable of those bursts of nervous energy which are synonymous with speed. *The principle to bear in mind is that speed over a long period of time means staying power, but staying power over a short period of time never means speed.''* (Italics mine.)

INCORPORATING THE CONCEPT OF DOSAGE IN A BREEDING PROGRAM

We have dwelt at length on the concept of dosage. Let us now learn how to incorporate it in a breeding program.

A number of chefs-de-race have been identified. The horse you plan to breed cannot obviously have all the chefs-de-race in his pedigree. Therefore even at the outset you must ask yourself: ''Must I treat all the chefs-de-race equally or must I give importance to a few chefs-de-race?'' The breeding programs of several eminent breeders hinged on ''key'' chefsde-race. Readers will recall that Marcel Boussac's breeding program rested on Asterus, Pharis II and Tourbillon. Therefore this is the first decision you must take.

You must then fix the D.I of the horse you plan to breed. If you want to breed a brilliant sprinter, you will naturally aim for a D.I above 5. If you are anxious to breed a classic contender you will try for a D.I between 2 and 2.5. How exactly will you go about this task? As we shall see there are several alternatives. But before we proceed further I am anxious to repeat: ''We are not claiming that a horse with a D.I less than 5 cannot develop into a superior sprinter. We are only saying that his chances of doing so are less than those with a D.I. above 5. This is obviously true for all other categories as well.''

The first technique is to breed horses with chefs-de-race from every aptitudinal group. This is the best and safest approach. Such a pedigree will be completely balanced and the horse has an excellent chance of inheriting every beneficial quality.

An alternative would be to avoid the Brilliant and Professional chefs-de-race and restrict the breeding to the Intermediate, Classic and Solid. Study carefully the chefs-de-race in these three categories. Can we not breed outstanding individuals with crosses of Prince John/Princequillo, Native Dancer, Buckpasser/Tom Fool, Big Game and Persian Gulf/Bahram Mahmoud, Blenheim and others? The D.P of such a horse would read: o-x-y-z-o. But a few readers will question: ''Such a horse will not have the benefit of qualities passed on by Brilliant and Professional chefs-de-race. Can he develop into a really top class galloper?'' My answer is positive. We need not worry too much. Intermediate and Solid chefs-de-race are present and the qualities they transmit are similar to those transmitted by the Brilliant and Professional. Even though we divided chefs-de-race into five distinct categories, a certain amount of ''overlapping'' obviously takes place, which is why several chefs-de-race have been placed in two categories. This overlapping, which is inevitable, takes place for almost all chefs-de-race (albeit to a small extent) and can compensate for the absence of chefs-de-race of one or two categories. Horses with this pattern of D.P include: Raise a Native (his pedigree is free from Professional chefs-de-race and Brilliant chefs-de-race contribute only 2 points) and Stage Door Johnny (free from the Professional and with only 1 point in the Brilliant column).

The next alternative is to ignore the Intermediate and Solid. The D.P of such a horse would be: x-o-y-o-z. Caro is the best example of this type of pedigree. He is free from Intermediate and Solid chefs-de-race.

You will have no difficulty in breeding horses without any one category of chefs-de-race.

An intriguing possibility is to breed horses with only the Brilliant and Professional or Intermediate and Solid. But I cannot recommend such a course of action. We cannot leave out three aptitudinal groups. There is no way in which the individual can inherit the beneficial qualities of those groups. The pedigrees of such horses would be severely unbalanced. Even though I stick to this view, a few horses have pedigrees dominated by the chefs-de-race of only two aptitudinal groups. Graustark, Halo and Naskra are examples.

Another variation is to omit the Solid and Professional categories. This seems to be the method of several breeders. A number of outstanding horses have been bred on this pattern: Sir Ivor, Exclusive Native, Nashua, Roberto, Riverman and Vaguely Noble.

Readers will readily understand that breeding with only Solid and Professional or even Classic, Solid and Professional chefs-de-race is not advisable. For such Horses, completely lacking in elements of speed, will find it very difficult to develop into superior racers. However I must add that a few horses with this type of pedigree have managed to excel.

Several breeders may be anxious to breed horses with pedigrees dominated by classic chefs-de-race. The D.Is of such horses will be near 1. But as we observed, such horses will not possess an ideal blend of speed and stamina. Nevertheless such horses have also done well.

We can also breed horses with only Brilliant and Intermediate chefs-de-race. What will be the D.I of such a horse?

LIMITATIONS OF THE CONCEPT

Earlier we made a distinction between orthodoxly and unorthodoxly-bred horses. Consider Known Fact. His dosage Profile is: 4-2-4-2-0. The very low points in all the columns show that his pedigree has very few chefs-de-race or that the chefs-de-race are in the later generations. Here the former is true. There are only 4 chefs-de-race in his pedigree: Tom Fool, Tudor Minstrel, Discovery and Bull Lea.

			Intent
		Intentionally	My Recipe
	In Reality		
		My Dear Girl	Rough'n Tumble
			Iltis
Known Fact			
(Dk B or Br, 1977)		Tim Tam	Tom Tool
			Two Lea
	Tamerett		
		Mixed Marriage	Tudor Minstrel
			Persian Maid

I consider such Dosage Profiles to be trivial Dosage Profiles. It is clear that chefs-de-race do not play a dominant role in such pedigrees. It is the non-chefs-de-race who play the dominant role, who shape and mould such individuals. Other horses with trivial D.Ps include:

In Reality	: 2 - 0 - 0 - 8 - 0
Ack Ack	: 9 - 6 - 7 - 2 - 2
Dust Commander	: 9 - 4 - 3 - 3 - 1

Therefore there have been quite a few outstanding horses with trivial Dosage Profiles. Instead of defining a trivial Dosage Profile, I will present a rough rule, a thumb-rule for identifying them.

A Dosage Profile without even one double digit column is a trivial Dosage Profile.

Therefore the four D.Ps given above are trivial D.Ps. Here we are not bothered about the number of chefs-de-race in a pedigree. Rather we are interested in the magnitude of their influence. A horse with only 2 chefs-de-race, but in the sire and maternal grandsire positions, will not have a trivial D.P. But a horse with a number of chefs-de-race in the 3rd and 4th generations may have a trivial D.P. A D.P without chefs-de-race in two, or even three, categories need not be trivial. Le Fabuleux's D.P at first glance certainly appears to be trivial: 0-0-6-0-24. But note that the Professional chefs-de-race are strongly represented and they have obviously influenced him.

Do not calculate the Dosage Index of a trivial Dosage Profile as we have done, as it is bound to be very misleading. Instead you must adopt the method formulated by the staff of *The Thoroughbred Record*. When they were calculating the D.Ps and D.ls of classic contenders, they found that several had very few chefs-de-race in their immediate generations i.e.. they had trivial Dosage Profiles. Therefore they classified every stallion appearing within the first four generations of the pedigree. In their own words: ''That step was to classify every stallion appearing in the first four generations according to our view of their primary aptitudinal traits.''

The logic behind this procedure is at once obvious. The non-chefs-de-race play the dominant role in horses with trivial D.Ps. Therefore we arc including them (together with the few chefs-de-race) in the D.P. From this ''modified'' D.P we can calculate the D.l — the ''modified'' D.l. The modified D.P and D.l are sure to give a clearer and more accurate picture of the individual. Remember you must attempt this modification only in the case of trivial D.Ps and not for regular D.Ps. If we recalculate the D.Ps and D.ls of horses like In Reality and Ack Ack by this method, an altogether different picture is bound to emerge.

But there is a more serious and fundamental limitation to the concept as used by us. This will become clear after the following discussion. Let us calculate the D.ls of two horses: Aced and Local Suitor.

		Ace of Aces	Vaguely Noble
Aced			Sofarsogood
(B, 1976)		December Delivery	Prince John
			Vailoa

		Blushing Groom	Red God
Local Suitor			Runaway Bride
(B, 1982)		Home Love	Vaguely Noble
			Homespun

Look at the pedigree of Aced. Vaguely Noble comes in the 2nd generation. Since he is a Professional chef-de-race, we will put 8 points in the Professional column. Now look at the pedigree of Local Suitor. Vaguely

Noble again comes in the 2nd generation contributing 8 points to the Professional column. But in the pedigree of Aced Vaguely Noble is the paternal grandsire — a sire — whereas in the pedigree of Local Suitor he is the maternal grandsire. I emphasized strongly that a horse's behavior as a maternal grandsire can be entirely different from his behavior as a sire. *Therefore a chef-de-race can be in one aptitudinal group as a sire and in another aptitudinal group as a maternal grandsire.*

This is true in the case of Vaguely Noble. Study closely his performance as a sire. What type of stallion is he? What qualities did he give his progeny? It is clear that he imparted qualities imparted by Professional chefs-de-race and has therefore been placed in that category. Now study his performance as a maternal grandsire very carefully. We emphasized that his daughters are proving to be extremely successful, having produced several classic winners. Therefore in which category would you put him as a maternal grandsire? Don't you think he belongs to the Classic category or even to the Brilliant and Classic categories? Therefore while calculating the D.P of Local Suitor, we have to put the 8 points contributed by Vaguely Noble in the Classic category and not in the Professional category. This will obviously change the D.P and D.1 of Local Suitor considerably, but don't you think this improved D.P and D.1 will give a clearer and more accurate picture of him?

Coming back to Aced, it is clear that Vaguely Noble plays the role of a sire — he is the sire of Aced's sire. Therefore his contribution of 8 points must be put in the Professional category. Similarly when we are (calculating the D.Ps and D.Is of Vaguely Noble's sons and daughters we must put his contribution of 16 points in the Professional category. But when n he appears as a maternal grandsire, we must put his contribution of 8 points in the Classic and not Professional category.

Therefore we must determine the behavior of every chef-de-race as a sire and as a maternal grandsire.

Undoubtedly several chefs-de-race would have shown the same aptitudes as sires and maternal grandsires. Naturally the contribution of such horses depends on the generation only. But I am convinced that a significant number of chefs-de-race exhibited different aptitudes. In which categories would you put Double Jay, My Babu and Big Game? Hence we have got to prepare one more table: *chefs-de-race — maternal grandsires.* Then we must recalculate the D.Ps and D.Is of all the horses using both the tables: chefs-de-race — sires and chefs-de-race — maternal grandsires (to be prepared). This improvement will naturally give us a clearer and more accurate picture of the individuals.

A very important fact reveals itself the moment we resolve the chefs-de-race into sires and maternal grandsires. Several stallions who are not present in the chefs-de-race — sires table come into the chefs-de-race — maternal grandsires table! In other words several horses were breed-shaping maternal grandsires, rather than breed-shaping sires! Similarly it may be necessary to drop a few chefs-de-race — sires from the chefs-de-race — maternal grandsires table i.e. such stallions were breed-shaping sires but were not breed-shaping maternal grandsires.

Let us determine the D.P of Super Concorde.

| **Super Concorde**
(Dk B or Br, 1975) | Bold Reasoning | Boldnesian
Reason to Earn |
| | Prime Abord | Primera
Homeward Bound |

His maternal grandsire Primera has not qualified as a chef-de-race — sire. Therefore when we draw up the D.P in the traditional way, Primera is not present. But we know that Primera was a very successful maternal grandsire, definitely a breed-shaping maternal grandsire. He therefore contributes 8 points. We cannot ignore his contribution. The next question is: "In which column must we put these 8 points?" Naturally we must determine his aptitude as a maternal grandsire and put the 8 points in that column.

Consider pedigrees in which Primera era the sire of the maternal grandsire, What will be his contribution to the D.P? It is zero as he is not a chef-de-race — sire. Primera makes a contribution only as a maternal grandsire. Similarly the contribution of a chef-de-race — sire who is not a chef-de-race — maternal grandsire, is zero when he appears in the maternal grandsire position.

Primera is not unique. There are several like him. These horses made an impact as maternal grandsires and not as sires. Hence it is necessary for us to study carefully the maternal grandsires of the 20th century, identify the breed-shaping maternal grandsires and put them into their respective aptitudinal groups.

It is not only chefs-de-race who exhibit this behaviour. We saw that even average and marginally above average stallions do so. Therefore even when you are using the method formulated by the staff of *The Thoroughbred Record*, you must classify the horses as sires and maternal grandsires. The dichotomy is an integral part of stallion behavior.

We have so far restricted ourselves to the 1st maternal grandsire only. But is there only one maternal grandsire in a 4-generation pedigree? Are all the other horses functioning as sires? No they are not. If we study a 4-generation pedigree very carefully we will find that there are 8 sires and 7 maternal grandsires!

Let us once again study the pedigree of Riverman. First we will take up his 2-generation pedigree.

Riverman	Never Bend	Nasrullah
		Lalun
	River Lady	Prince John
		Nile Lily

It is clear that Never Bend and Nasrullah function as sires while Prince John functions as a maternal grandsire. Therefore in a 2-generation pedigree there are 2 sires and 1 maternal grandsire.

Now let us look at his 3-generation pedigree:

Riverman	Never Bend	Nasrullah	Nearco
			Mumtaz Begum
		Lalun	Djeddah
			Be Faithful
	River Lady	Prince John	Princequillo
			Not Afraid
		Nile Lily	Roman
			Azalea

How many sires and maternal grandsires are there? Never Bend, Nasrullah and Nearco i.e. the direct male line stallions obviously function as sires. Prince John and Roman are maternal grandsires. But what about Djeddah and Princequillo? Note that the former functions as a maternal grandsire. He is the maternal grandsire of Never Bend, the sire of Riverman. But the latter functions as a sire. He is the sire of Riverman's maternal grandsire i.e. he is in the direct male line of the maternal grandsire. Therefore every 3-generation pedigree has 4 sires and 3 maternal grandsires.

We can similarly analyze his 4-generation pedigree.

```
                                              │ Nearco          │ Pharos
                                              │                 │ Nogara
                           │ Nasrullah
                           │                  │ Mumtaz Begum    │ Blenheim
                           │                  │                 │ Mumtaz Mahal
              │ Never Bend
              │            │                  │ Djeddah         │ Djebel
              │            │                  │                 │ Djezima
              │            │ Lalun
              │            │                  │ Be Faithful     │ Bimelech
**Riverman**  │            │                  │                 │ Bloodroot
(B, 1969)     │
              │                               │ Princequillo    │ Prince Rose
              │                               │                 │ Cosquilla
              │            │ Prince John
              │            │                  │ Not Afraid      │ Count Fleet
              │            │                  │                 │ Banish Fear
              │ River Lady
              │            │                  │ Roman           │ Sir Gallahad III
              │            │                  │                 │ Buckup
              │            │ Nile Lily
              │                               │ Azalea          │ Sun Teddy
              │                               │                 │ Coquelicot
```

Never Bend, Nasrullah, Nearco and Pharos function as sires. Princequillo and Prince Rose also function as sires. Note that Djebel and Sir
Gallahad III are also sires. They are the sires of Never Bend's and River
Lady's maternal grandsires. Prince John, Roman and Sun Teddy are maternal grandsires. We saw that Djeddah also acts as a maternal grandsire.
In the 4th generation Blenheim, Bimelech and Count Fleet also act as maternal grandsires. Therefore a 4-generation pedigree has 8 sires and 7 maternal
grandsires. In Riverman's pedigree the sires and maternal grandsires are:

Sires	**Maternal grandsires**
Never Bend	Prince John
Nasrullah	Djeddah
Nearco	Roman
Princequillo	Blenheim
Pharos	Bimelech
Djebel	Count Fleet
Prince Rose	Sun Teddy
Sir Gallahad III	
———	———
8	7

Now we must recalculate Riverman's D.P and D.I based on the Table given. There is no problem as far as the sires are concerned. All 8 have qualified for chef-de-race status and points will be allotted as usual. Among the 7 maternal grandsires 4 have qualified for chef-de-race — sire status, and it is clear that they will also qualify for chef-de-race — maternal grandsire status. But their aptitudes may be different. The remaining 3 maternal grandsires are not chef-de-race — sires, but we must check whether they qualify for chef-de-race — maternal grandsire status. Then we must determine their aptitudes. We can draw up the Dosage Profile of Riverman only after obtaining this information. I cannot do so now as I have not attempted to study the performances of the 7 maternal grandsires in detail. But I am sure readers have understood the principle. We must use the chef-de-race — sires and chef-de-race — maternal grandsires lists simultaneously. Therefore our task now is to prepare the chef-de-race — maternal grandsires list which can be used profitably by one and all.

Even though we have come to the end of this section, we have not said the last word on the subject. There is unlimited scope for research in this area. The sky is the limit. For example the methodology for giving chef-de-race status must be refined further. The non-inclusion of Nearctic in the chef-de-race — sires list is truly baffling. He was the sire of 49 stakes winners including 6 champions. He was also a sire of sires. A quick study will show that his influence has spread throughout the world. And I am very anxious to emphasize that his influence is not entirely through Northern Dancer (who has obviously qualified for chef-de-race — sire status). He is a chef-de-race — sire in his own right. He may have also qualified for chef-de-race — maternal grandsire status.

Even after this discussion there may be several who do not believe in the concept of dosage. They may even reject it outright. I was aghast to read that English breeders consider dosage to be "new-fangled nonsense"*. To them I say: "Be patient for just a little while. *There are a number of problems which cannot be solved until we apply the concept of dosage.* We will solve one such problem in the next part of the book. This will reveal the inherent merit of the system in no uncertain terms."

We now come to a small topic which we should have dealt with earlier. Nevertheless we would do well to take it up now. We discussed the qualifications necessary for broodmares and maternal grandsires to succeed. We found that those who satisfied particular criteria had greater chances of success. But we made no mention of stallions. Now let us deter-

---

* "Reading Habits of an English Racing Gentleman", by Tony Morris, *The Thoroughbred Record*, 12 September 1984.

mine the criteria stallions must satisfy in order to succeed in stud. In other words how must we select a stallion?

Readers will readily agree that a prospective stallion must possess:

1) A superior, if not outstanding, race record.
2) A superior, if not outstanding, pedigree.

Let us quickly discuss the former. There is nothing much for me to say. The horse must have excelled at 2, 3 and 4 years. Further it would be ideal if he scored over the range of distances. His form as a 2-yr-old is extremely important. He must have won or placed in prestigious races. He must have displayed precocious speed. If you look at the race records of all the successful stallions, you will find that an overwhelming majority of them excelled at 2. Then at 3 they carried their speed over a distance of ground. Without doubt they possessed an ideal blend of speed and stamina. Undeniably several late maturing stayers and extreme stayers also developed into successful stallions, but they were very small in number.

THE PEDIGREE REQUIREMENTS OF STALLIONS

The pedigree requirements of stallions are exacting and precise. An individual who is able to satisfy these requirements definitely has a greater chance of success. What are these requirements? Let us go component by component.

The sire of a prospective stallion must be a "sire of sires". Breeders know, and you too will be aware, that sons of a handful of stallions excelled, thereby making their sires "sires of sires". *The Thoroughbred Record Sire Book* (1982) lists 20 sires of sires (who were foaled after 1935). Horses like Nasrullah, Ribot, Native Dancer, Hail to Reason and Bold Ruler are naturally included. I urge all readers to obtain a copy of the above publication and study closely the 20 sires of sires. (A few outstanding maternal grandsires have also been included.)

But we cannot wait until a stallion has emerged as a sire of sires and then look among his sons for a prospective sire. We have to anticipate which sire is going to develop into a sire of sires. It is clear that only outstanding sires, world leading sires can develop into sires of sires. A stallion on the fringe of top class is not going to develop into a sire of sires. Stallions who have already emerged as sires of sires include Northern Dancer, Nijinky, Raise a Native, Lyphard, Mill Reef and In Reality.

The maternal grandsire of a prospective sire must be a maternal grandsire of sires. This phrase is not new to us. We have used it before. We saw that My Babu and Nashua are maternal grandsires of sires. Others include Double Jay (Nodouble, What Luck and An Eldorado and Prince John (Riverman, Big Spruce and Alleged).

It is necessary for me to say that only an outstanding maternal grandsire can become a maternal grandsire of sires. Readers can easily determine that The Axe is very close to qualifying.

We now come to a very important point. My Babu, Double Jay and others were not the only maternal grandsires of sires. Several sires of sires like Hyperion, Nearco, Nasrullah, Bold Ruler, Native Dancer and Princequillo were also maternal grandsires of sires. This behavior can be represented in steps as below:

TABLE 20

1) Successful sire

2) Qualify for chef-de-race-sire status

3) Qualify for sire of sires status
   (A sire who has got 3 successful sires is a
   sire of sires)

4) Successful maternal grandsire

5) Qualify for chef-de-race-maternal grandsire status

6) Qualify for maternal grandsire of sires status.

This Table calls for a detailed discussion. Let us commence at the very beginning. Several stallions qualify for chef-de-race-sire status. But they are not sires of sires, chefs-de-race-maternal grandsires or maternal grandsires of sires. Similarly several stallions qualify for chef-de-race maternal grandsire status. But they are not maternal grandsires of sires, chefs-de-race—sire or sires of sires.

Individuals who are still more talented qualify for chef-de-race sire and maternal grandsire status. But they are not sires of sires or maternal grandsires of sires.

Horses who are still more talented qualify for chef-de-race sire and maternal grandsire status and are sires of sires or maternal grandsires of sires.

Finally, right at the top, there are the handful of outstanding progenitors who passed all the six steps.

Therefore we must be careful. We must not jump to the conclusion that a chef-de-race — sire will automatically be a maternal grandsire of sires or that a successful maternal grandsire will be a sire of sires. Even among the finest progenitors, there are different degrees of talent. They specialize in particular roles. Only the finest among the finest excel in all roles

What are the qualifications of the 3rd component-the tail female lime? The tail female line of a prospective sire must be a "sire producing tail female line". Readers will know that a number of female families have been consistently producing superior sires. Therefore an individual from such a family has a greater chance of success. A few sire producing female families are those of Selene, Mumtaz Mahal, Marchetta, La Troienne, Simon's Shoes and Schiaparelli. Again it is clear that only an outstanding female family, which has produced a number of classic winners, champions, classic-placed and superior racers, can emerge as a sire producing family.

The concept of a sire producing tail female line was first enunciated by Bruce Lowe. In the latter part of the 19th century, he traced the tail female line of every mare to the first volume of the stud book. He found that every mare traced to one of the approximately fifty foundation mares in the first volume. Bruce Lowe then allotted a number to each of these families i.e. to the descendants of a foundation broodmare. He gave the number 1 to the female family that had produced the largest number of English Derby, St. Leger and Oaks winners. In other words all those winners traced back to that particular foundation broodmare in tail female line. Likewise he allotted numbers up to 43 in decreasing order of merit. Therefore higher the number lesser the number of superior racers produced by that family.

Bruce Lowe went further. He classified families 1 to 5 as "Running families", as they had produced the largest number of winners of the three classics mentioned above. He then specifically classified families 3, 8, 11, 12 and 14 as "Sire families" as horses from them, or inbred to them, excelled as sires. *Note that the Sire families (except family 3) are different from the Running families.* This clearly shows that the pedigree of the horse is a factor in stud success. If it were not, the Epsom Derby winner would become the leading stallion, the Epsom Derby 2nd the 2nd leading stallion and so on. But this is not the case as pedigree also comes into the picture. Bruce Lowe has emphasized the part played by the tail female line of the pedigree.

To sum up what we have learnt: A prospective stallion must possess a superior, preferably outstanding, race record and pedigree. (Do not forget his conformation and temperament.) Now go back to Miswaki (chapter 2). Clearly he satisfies the stringent conditions laid down. Therefore he is sure to be very successful. But we can boldly go a step further. Can we not assert that he will be among the top ten, if not the top six, stallions?

But readers will quickly point out that such stallions are very small in number, and at certain times there may not be a single individual who satisfies all the conditions' What must we do in such situations? My approach is as below:

First sacrifice one pedigree condition i.e. select outstanding racers whose pedigrees satisfy any two of the three conditions. My next preference is not for a classic winner or champion whose pedigree satisfies only one condition, but for a superior racer whose pedigree satisfies three and then two conditions. In all the above cases if a condition is not satisfied fully, it must be close to being satisfied. For example if the sire of the horse is not a sire of sires, he must be close to the status.

To summarize, our preferences would be as below:

1st preference
Outstanding gallopers with three superior pedigree components.

2nd preference
Outstanding gallopers with two superior pedigree components.

3rd preference
Superior racers with three superior pedigree components.

4th preference
Superior racers with two superior pedigree components.

Readers may be wondering whether dosage plays a role in the success of stallions. This question has been investigated in-depth by Dr. Roman who determined the D.Ps and D.Is of the sixty leading North American sires by Average Earnings Index. His findings are of enormous interest. The leading stallions possess every type of Dosage Profile. Note that several like In Reality, Ack Ack, Hawaii and Explodent have trivial D.Ps. Their Dosage Indices range from the very low to the very high. To summarize:

53 stallions have a D.1 Less than 4

18 stallions have a D.I between 3 and 3.99

9   "   "   "   "   "   2 " 2.99

14   "   "   "   "   "   1 " 1.99

12   "   "   "   "   "   0 " 0.99

In other words:

12 stallions have low D.Is i.e. Less than 1

23 stallions have medium D.Is i.e. between 1 and 3.

25 stallions have high D.Is i.e. 3 and above.

These findings are a bit surprising. One would have thought that stallions with D.Is between 2 and 2.5 i.e. the classic D.I would have an edge over the others. After all they possess an ideal blend of speed and stamina and can therefore pass on an ideal blend of speed and stamina. But the above figures show otherwise. It is clear that one particular D.I does not give an edge. This clearly shows that there are factors outside the scope of dosage which influence the success or failure of stallions. We already determined one such factor i.e. the sire producing tail female line. Superior stallions with low D.ls include the full-brothers Graustark and His Majesty, Grey Dawn II and Big Spruce. Vaguely Noble, Sir Ivor and Roberto possess medium D.ls. Mr. Prospector, What a Pleasure, Raja Baba and Nodouble possess high D.Is.

PREDICTING THE APTITUDE OF STALLIONS

It is possible to predict the aptitude of a stallion by studying together his race record and pedigree. Stallions who were themselves stayers and are bred to stay will, in all probability, get stayers. But it would be difficult for short distance horses with short distance pedigrees to sire superior stayers. It is unnecessary for me to state that there are several exceptions. Numerous stayers have failed to sire genuine stayers and several sprinter-milers have surprised us by getting superior stayers. Predicting the aptitude of stallions who did not run according to their pedigrees is obviously very difficult.

These predictions must be made by those breeding to, or buying the progeny of, first or second crop sires. They will become redundant when a sufficient number of the stallion's progeny have raced.

We have come to the end of the second part of the book, save for one topic. But that topic is the most important; it is the quintessence of breeding. *It is the procedure for choosing the most appropriate stallion for a broodmare.* Every breeder of thoroughbreds has got to use a procedure. A breeder who is able to formulate a superior procedure is sure to be more successful. Remember the best stallion in the country need not be the most compatible with your mare. I am sure readers can confidently formulate such a procedure, but for the sake of completion let us quickly formulate a simple procedure.

Firstly you must determine the precise behaviour of all the successful stallions in your region. This is a must. You cannot obviously identify a compatible stallion until you know the behaviour of all the stallions. The methods we used earlier can be profitably employed. Once you have done so you are ready to go forward.

Now we have to study the mare in detail. Instead of speaking vaguely about a hypothetical mare, I decided that we could undertake the following exercise: We saw that Om-Sakthi was a very successful producer (page 202). Let us identify the most compatible stallions for each of her daughters. She had five daughters—Santham, Pancharathnam, The Judgement, Perseverence and Weight in Gold. Let us first take up the last-named who was her best offspring.

		Red Rufus	Dark William
Weight in Gold			Red Belle
(Ch, 1978)		Om-Sakthi	Fighting Don
			Star of Vintage

As usual we must go component by component. We saw that she won 6 races including the South India St. Leger. She undoubtedly possessed an ideal blend of speed and stamina as she excelled over the entire range of distances.

We studied her sire Red Rufus in detail. Happily he is also emerging as a top class maternal grandsire. He is already the maternal grandsire of:

Almagest (Gombos x Red Surprise): 4 wins, Kunigal Stud Trophy, Sangam Cup; 2nd Charminar Challenge Indian Turf Invitation Cup; 3rd Indian Derby, Bangalore Arc de Triomphe and Colts Trial Stakes.

Wedding Gift (Sovereign Silver x Carte Blanche): 5 wins, Birthday Girl Cup, C.S. Loganathan Gold Cup; 2nd South India Derby and St. Leger. (In training.)

Viable Launch (Arrogant Lad x Bhairabi): 2 wins, Hyderabad Fillies Trial Stakes. (In training.)

His aptitude as a maternal grandsire is also clear. His daughters have the ability to get horses with an ideal blend of speed and stamina.

I unfortunately do not have much information about Fighting Don and Greek Star as maternal grandsires, but it is clear that (especially the latter) they had their share of success. Without doubt the maternal grandsire component is superior.

The tail female line is not outstanding, but Om-Sakthi by her efforts has raised its standard to the superior level.

OM-SAKTHI: as described.

STAR OF VINTAGE: ran only 3 times and retired to stud. Dam of:

Munthe: winner in England.

Trente Cing: winner in England.

Charente: 8 wins in the West Indies.

Star Fighter: winner in England.

Om-Sakthi: as described.

Bajagovindam: 17 wins, Tamil Nadu Commemoration Gold Cup (twice).

Minniehaha: 2 wins in India.

Vin Rogue: 3 wins in India.

LYONNAISE: 1 win in England. Dam of:

Blue Lion: 1-1/2 wins in England.

Petter Lion: placed.

Star of Vintage: as described.

Therefore all her 3 components are superior. Clearly Weight in Gold is an outstanding broodmare. Our objective naturally must be to breed classic winners and champions from her. She deserves the very best.

STEP 1

We will naturally select the leading stallions in the country for her. The name of Everyday was the first to come to my mind. He excelled with superior mares and in particular with superior racers. Further he did not miss getting stayers out of staying mares. An offspring of Weight in Gold by Everyday is sure to excel over the entire range of distances.

Malvado is another suitable stallion. We saw that he is a Border-line classic stallion. Since then he has gone from strength to strength and has qualified for Front-line classic status. His progeny too excel over the range of distances. In short outstanding stallions who consistently produce classic progeny are most compatible.

We can also select young or even first crop sires, provided they excelled over the range of distances and are extremely well-bred. I thought of Royal Tern and Everynsky. Therefore we must first make a list of about half-a-dozen (or even more) suitable stallions.

STEP 2

The next step is to determine whether any of the above stallions will nick with Weight in Gold. We cannot predict a sire x dam nick. At the time of writing, Red Rufus as a maternal grandsire does not seem to nick with any sire. There are no chefs-de-race in her 3-generation pedigree for us to take advantage of sire x chef-de-race or chef-de-race x chef-de-race nicks.

STEP 3

Now we must check the scope for inbreeding and outcrossing. As seen her pedigree does not have any outstanding progenitor to inbreed to. All her progeny are bound to be outbreds. The inbreeding if any will be purely incidental. However if certain stallions have chefs-de-race you particularly admire, you can consider them first.

STEP 4

Here we must determine the D.Ps and D.Is of the prospective foals by preparing their 4-generation pedigrees. See whether any D.I is near the classic D.I. If a stallion gives a classic D.I he must be considered first.

STEP 5

The final step is probably the most important. Do not forget conformation and temperament compatibility. It is absolutely necessary to inspect all the stallions to see whether they are compatible in these respects. It is also necessary to study the conformation and temperament of the progeny of all the stallions.

If we complete all these steps successfully, we will be able to identify stallions most compatible with Weight in Gold. She has the greatest chance of producing superior racers out of these stallions.

Now let us study her other daughters. Santham and Perseverence can be taken up together.

Santham (B, 1969)	Punjab	Pardal Indian Night
	Om-Sakthi	Fighting Don Star of Vintage

Perseverence (B, 1977)	Red Indian	Migoli Red Briar
	Om-Sakthi	Fighting Don Star of Vintage

They were not superior racers. Among them Perseverence was a stayer. Her victories included the Indian Republic Cup (2000 m, class IV, Madras). But we can claim that they are well-bred and hence Inherently superior. For their sires have started well as maternal grandsires. They are also developing into maternal grandsires of stayers. Punjab is already the maternal grandsire of:

> **Sun Lion** (Voluntary x Major Barbara): 15 wins, Calcutta Derby, Queen Elizabeth II Cup, Calcutta Gold Cup.
>
> **Classic Touch** (Everyday x Ruby Dust): as described.
>
> **Lorna Doone** (Lance Corporal x Margot Fontyn): 7 wins, M.R.C. Hospital Cup, Coonoor Cup.

Red Indian did not have many daughters in stud, but those who were active demonstrated the ability to get stayers.

Therefore it appears that Santham and Perseverence are predisposed to producing stayers. Should we try to breed classic stayers from them too? Or would such an effort be a gigantic waste of time and money? There is no doubt that Perseverence has the ability to get classic stayers. For her three-fourth sister Minniehaha was very successful.

		Migoli
	Red Indian	Red Briar
Minniehaha		
(B Rn, 1966)	Star of Vintage	Greek Star
		Lyonnaise

She was the dam of among others:

> **Half a Crown** (colt, 1971, by Scotch Crown): 15 wins, Bangalore Triple Crown, South India Derby and St. Leger, Deccan Derby; 2nd Indian Turf Invitation Cup. He won from 1000 m to 2800 m.
>
> **Anekta** (filly, 1972, by Orbit): 6 wins, South India Oaks.
>
> **Be My Guest** (filly, 1976, by Mr. Mauritius): 7 wins; 2nd Christmas Cup; 3rd Hyderabad Fillies Trial Stakes.

Scotch Crown would have been an ideal stallion for Perseverence as the offspring's pedigree would be ''identical'' to Half a Crown's. But he died long ago. Superior stallions who produced classic stayers out of staying mares and mares bred to stay are obviously most suitable for Perseverence. After identifying several such stallions, we have to complete all the other steps as we did earlier, to pinpoint the most compatible.

But what about Santham? The question we have to answer is: ''Is she predisposed to producing classic stayers?'' Honestly there is no easy answer. A few may answer in the affirmative while others may not. I would like to digress a bit here. We have all heard people say: "Always try to breed the classic horse." I honestly do not know who originally gave this advice, which is most presumptuous and foolish. If we all tried to breed classic horses out of every mare, we would very soon cease to be breeders. Allow me to say: "Always try to breed superior horses." Coming back to Santham it is clear that stallions who produced superior racers (sprinter-milers or stayers or both) out of well-bred mares are most suitable for her. (Her foal Clique by Rapparee was an average racer who won 5 races up to 1200 m.)

Pancharathnam and The Judgment are on an entirely different footing.

| **Pancharathnam** (Ch, 1974) | Rapparee | High Treason Libertine |
| | Om-Sakthi | Fighting Don Star of Vintage |

| **The Judgement** (B, 1975) | Voluntary | State Trumpeter Water Music |
| | Om-Sakthi | Fighting Don Star of Vintage |

Both were superior racers who excelled over 1200 m. The former won 10 of her races over this distance, while the latter 6.

However they are not well-bred mares. We studied Rapparee in detail. Even though it is too early to judge him as a maternal grandsire, the potents are not good. He has not made a bright start. Therefore to be on the safe side, we must not assume that he is a successful maternal grandsire.

This is also true for Voluntary. He is only an Average sire. Sun Lion was by far his best offspring and none of his other runners were anywhere near him. Readers will readily agree that the chances of Rapparee and Voluntary becoming maternal grandsires of stayers are almost non-existent.

It is clear that Pancharathnam and The Judgement are predisposed to producing sprinter-milers only, and stallions who get such horses are most suitable for them.

But there is an important point. We considered both these mares to be Inherently superior as they were superior racers. But they could not win in the highest class. They won only in class II. Therefore to be on the safe side we must assume that they were not superior racers. If we do so they are not Inherently superior, as then only one of their components (the tail female line) is superior. This automatically means only prepotent stallions can get superior racers out of them.

Frequently it is not possible to accurately judge whether a mare is Inherently superior or not. My advice in such cases is assume that the mare is not Inherently superior and plan accordingly. Therefore prepotent stallions who excel in getting sprinter-milers (or are versatile) are most ideal for Pancharathnam and The Judgement.

A few readers may argue that we can breed stayers out of these two mares also. They only have to visit stallions prepotent for stamina. My reply is: "Why go against the tide? Why swim against the current? Why try to breed stayers out of mares who are clearly predisposed to producing sprinter-milers? We must do so only when there are powerful extraneous factors at work. For example there could be a chef-de-race x chef-de-race nick, a sire x chef-de-race nick or perfect conformation compatibility between the stallion and mare. It is only in such cases can we ignore the normal rules of selection and go ahead. It is unnecessary for me to say that these factors must be very powerful. Otherwise the matings are bound to be disastrous.

Finally do not forget that mares will not always behave according to their pedigrees and aptitudes. You have every liberty to make changes even drastic changes — in the breeding program after seeing the first progeny of the mare race.

I thought it would be nice to end this part of the book with a quiz. The quiz concerns Satinello who is a very successful stallion in the country. I have given his produce record together with the pedigrees of his mares. You should determine his behaviour. What type of stallion is he? What is the quality of the mares he served? What type of marcs are most compatible with him? There is a spin-off for you. You can also determine the behaviour of Nijinsky [India].

QUIZ 3

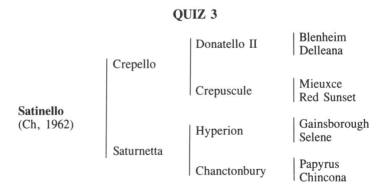

Satinello (Ch, 1962)	Crepello	Donatello II	Blenheim / Delleana
		Crepuscule	Mieuxce / Red Sunset
	Saturnetta	Hyperion	Gainsborough / Selene
		Chanctonbury	Papyrus / Chincona

He was bred in Ireland and exported to France. He won 6 races from 2 to 5 years including the Prix Ormonde, Prix Barcaldine, Prix Codoman,

Prix l'Express and Prix des Livres. He also placed on 15 occasions. He was imported into India and retired to stud in 1970. His produce record is as below:

TABLE 21

PROGENY OF SATINELLO WHO RAN

(First 8 crops only)

Dam	Offspring
1971	
Alkapuri	Our Emperor
Nanda Devi	Orange Lily
Rose Bud	Satin Rose
Sparkler	Prince Santio
Sparkling Rock	Moselle
1972	
Dinky	Sweet Angel
Donna Bella	Princess Yeti
Dusty	Red Cockade
Geisha Girl	Shogun
Our Grace	Bapu's Dauphin
Romantica	Recompense
1973	
Alkapuri	Red Satin
Mirabile Dictu	Recall
Port Gang	Reconcile
1974	
Dynamite	Diorella
Grecian Flower	Satin Flower
Mary Stuart	Grey Satin
Megh Jyoti	High Calibre
Portrait Attachment	Gioconda
Recovery	Crackerjack
Red Surprise	Satin Red
Shrimati	Psyche
Tudor Rose	Hampton Court
West Wave	Willow
1975	
Enthusiasm	Caradoc
Khublei	Khublei Khan
King's Pint	King's Satin
Ragamuffin	El Bravo
Red Surprise	Satinsky
Retained	Regency Satin
Serendipity	Shatrunja
Suparna	Crepella

TABLE 21 (cont.)

Dam	Offspring
1976	
Crystal Slipper	Crystal Star
Dear Heart	Miss Minstrel
Dilkhush	Anandini
Dusty	Roses For Me
Iona	Razzle Dazzle
Lorelei	Royal Brute
Never in Doubt	Hamiya
Petite Aureole	Impulse
Princess Saiqa	Sunlitta
Resourceful	Mahogany
Retained	Lone Star
Rolls Royce	Matinee Idol
Romantica	Satin Romance
Serendipity	Shankeshwar
1977	
Air Hostess	Marinsky
Dusty	Potential Champion
Hydrofoil	Zambo Anga
Iona	Natural Dancer
Joint Venture	Sweet Venture
Lady Madonna	Trinity College
Om Noori	Satin Splendour
Petite Aureole	Endurance
Pretendresse	Run Hard
Princess Saiqa	Pride of Kiliyanur
Recoup	Recoupere
Resourceful	Savoir Faire
Retained	Corniche
Rollicking Rachel	Kildare
Zifi	Zifinella
1977	
Air Hostess	Hawaiian Hostess
Dear Heart	Red Ranger
Goods and Chattels	Molly Brown
Hydrofoil	Satellite
Karthiayini	Thunder Wave
Majolica	Trevita
Only Girl	Only Satin
Petite Aureole	Satin Aurora
Radiance	Scintilla
Retained	Camargue
Shrimati	Jordache
Slip Rule	Golden Rule
Speedy Queen	That's the Spirit
Wavell's Lass	Satin Lass

(These 8 crops had 84 foals.)

Given below are the pedigrees of these mares together with the superior racers got by them. I have not described their average and substandard racers. Most of these mares have superior tail female lines.

1) ALKAPURI (B, 1956)

| Pippy | Watling Street |
| | Gainful |

| Superbe Rose | Tarquinius Superbus |
| | Rose Law |

ALKAPURI: 8 wins, Governor's Cup (1 mile 1-1/2 furlongs, Hyderabad); 2nd South India 1000 Guineas. Dam of:

Mighty Bear (by Pa Bear): 8 wins, Ramanatha Iyer Memorial Cup.

Red Satin (by Satinello): 13 wins, South India 2000 Guineas, Mysore Derby, Bangalore and Hyderabad Colts Trial Stakes. Sire.

2) NANDA DEVI (B, 1961)

| Golestan | Nasrullah |
| | Firanek |

| Evening Tide | Runway |
| | Crax |

NANDA DEVI: 6 wins, Radha Memorial Cup. Dam of:

Sun King (by Pindari): 9 wins, Daga Gold Cup, Sir Charles Forbes Cup, Chief of Kagal Gold Cup, Excelsior Stakes.

Orange Lily (by Satinello): 8 wins, C.D. Dady Gold Cup.

3) ROSE BUD (B, 1957)

| Kirkwick | His Highness |
| | Cherchez la Dame |

| Orchard Hill | Orestes |
| | Hampton Lucy |

ROSE BUD: 5 wins. Dam of:

Buttinsky (by Nijinsky [India]): 6 wins Tamil Nadu Commemoration Gold Cup, Governor's Cup; 2nd Stayers' Cup; 3rd South India St. Leger.

Rubaiyat (by Nijinsky [India]): 6 wins, Turf Club Cup, Governor's Cup.

4) SPARKLER (B, 1952)

Helios	Hyperion
	Foxy Gal
Golden Emblem	Hallmark
	Hasta

SPARKLER: 7 wins, August Cup, South India Turf Club Cup. Dam of:

Prince of Wales (by Star of Gwalior): good winner including Byculla Club Cup, Colts Handicap Stakes; 2nd Indian St. Leger.

5) SPARKLING ROCK (B, 1961)

Rock of Gibraltar	Rockefella
	Toquade
Sparkling	Hindostan
	Libation

SPARKLING ROCK: 4 wins, Surgeon General's Cup, Poona City Cup; placed Indian Oaks. Dam of:

Thunder Shower (by Pa Bear): 4 wins; 3rd Indian Oaks.

Sparkling Princess (by Prince Pradeep): 4 wins, Madras Race Club Cup (2000 m, class III, Mysore); 3rd Bangalore Oaks and Fillies Trial Stakes.

Tranquility (by Red Rufus): 13-1/2 wins, as described.

At My Best (by Red Rufus or Nijinsky [India]); 3 wins, Bahrain Trophy, April Handicap in only one season of racing.

6) DINKY (Dk B, 1957)

Moradabad	Blenheim
	Mirawala
Kalpna	Dennison
	Curfew III

DINKY: 9 wins; 3rd Dr. A. Karmally Memorial Cup, Nawabzada Rashiduzzafar Khan Gold Cup. Dam of:

Sheila's Gem (by Roccamare): 7 wins.

7) DONNA BELLA (Ch, 1958)

| Beldara | Djebel
Gandara |
| Belle Brandon | Havelock
Miss Otis |

DONNA BELLA: 7 wins, Guzdar Cup; 4th Indian 1000 Guineas and Oaks. She did not get a superior racer.

8) DUSTY (Ch, 1963)

| Sound Track | Whistler
Bridle Way |
| Blossom Gate | Big Game
Sea Fairy |

DUSTY: won Frickley Auction Stakes (Doncaster) and placed several times at 2 and 3 in England. Dam of:

Red Cockade (by Satinello): 9 wins (the first 7 in a row), Bangalore Colts Trial Stakes by a distance in record time, Nariman K. Irani Gold Cup; 2nd Bangalore Derby. He then had a setback in training and could not reproduce his form in the winter classics. In my opinion he is the best Indian-bred of all time. Sire.

Potential Champion (by Satinello): 5 wins, Indian 1000 Guineas and Oaks, F.D. Wadia Cup; 2nd Eclipse Stakes of India; 3rd Indian Turf Invitation Cup.

Gomos (by Gombos): 5 wins, Bangalore Arc de Triomphe, Rajajinagar Cup; 3rd Indian Turf Invitation Cup, Indian Derby.

9) GEISHA GIRL (B or Br, 1958)

| Cascadeur | Astrophel
Rose de Mai |
| Blue Pearl | Blue Lad
Vignette |

GEISHA GIRL: 2 wins. Dam of:

Shogun (by Satinello): 6 wins, The Republic Cup (1400 m, class II, Bangalore).

10) OUR GRACE (Ch, 1966)

Ouborough	Rockefella
	Intrigante II
Royal Grace	Kirkwick
	Grosvenor Belle

OUR GRACE: ran unplaced. She did not get a superior racer.

11) ROMANTICA (B, 1961)

Exaggerator	Hyperbole
	Benjamine
Maduri	Motky
	Whyna

ROMANTICA: 10 wins, C.D. Dady Cup, Sir Rahimtoola Chinoy Gold Cup; 4th Indian 1000 Guineas. Dam of:

Recompense (by Satinello): 4 wins, Rajyotsava Gold Cup; 2nd Bangalore Fillies Trial Stakes; 3rd Bangalore 1000 Guineas.

Sholay (by Red Rufus): 17 wins, as described.

Response (by Red Rufus): 5 wins, as described.

Malavika (by Malvado): 6 wins, as described.

12) MIRABILE DICTU (Ch, 1966)

Miralgo	Aureole
	Nella
Aspen Leaf	Hindostan
	Madam Jitters

MIRABILE DICTU: unraced. She did not get a superior racer.

13) PORT GANG (B, 1964)

Gang Bhup	Philderer
	Indefensible
Surya Mukhi	Sofferino
	Sunbeliever

PORT GANG: winner. Dam of:

Port Royal (by Orbit): 8 wins.

Honey Suckle (by Red Rufus): 6 wins, as described.

14) DYNAMITE (Ch, 1964)

Daneshill	Dante
	Life Hill
Surya Mukhi	Solferino
	Sunbeliever

DYNAMITE: 4 wins. She did not get a superior racer.

15) GRECIAN FLOWER (Dk B, 1967)

Flower Dust	Pink Flower
	Brazen Molly
Grecian Princess	Greek Star
	Peribanoo

GRECIAN FLOWER: 8 wins, Gen. Obaidullah Khan Gold Cup, Asaf Jah VII Memorial Cup. Dam of:

Well Connected (by Nijinsky [India]): 10 wins, as described.

Greek Tycoon (by Gombos or Malvado): 3 wins, R.W.I.T.C. Ltd. Gold Cup (1600 m, class II, Bombay); 2nd R.R. Ruia Cup (by a neck); 3rd Indian 2000 Guineas.

16) MARY STUART (B or Ro, 1969)

Scotch Crown	Jock II
	Sultan Mahal
Boudicca	Ardent Knight
	Regal Frolic

MARY STUART: unraced. Dam of:

Winfree (by Rapparee): 6 wins, as described.

Grey Satin (by Satinello): 4 wins; 2nd Indian Oaks; 3rd Indian 1000 Guineas.

17) MEGH JYOTI (B, 1969)

Asopo	Nimbus
	Assamenta
Realy	March Past
	Infiltration

MEGH JYOTI: unraced. Dam of:

Minsky (by Nijinsky [India]): 9 wins, Hill Sprinters Cup, Akkasaheb Maharaj Cup.

18) PORTRAIT ATTACHMENT (Gr, 1960)

Nearcolein	Nearco
	Grand Peace
Panoramic	Panorama
	Paloma

PORTRAIT ATTACHMENT: 2 wins in England. Dam of:

Benlitta (by Romiti): 6 wins, Hyderabad Fillies Trial Stakes, Govenor's Cup (1600 m, class I, Bombay).

19) RECOVERY (Gr, 1966)

Entanglement	King of the Tudors
	Filigrana
Eagle Don	Donore
	Gawthorpe

RECOVERY: 6 wins, South India Oaks. Dam of:

Crackerjack (by Satinello): 14 wins, Mount Everest Cup, Welcome Cup, Blue Ice Cup, Hyderabad Silver Vase.

20) RED SURPRISE (Ch, 1968)

Red Rufus	Dark William
	Red Belle
Some Surprise	Premi
	First Royalty

RED SURPRISE: 6 wins, Deccan Derby ; 2nd Indian 1000 Guineas. Dam of:

Satinsky (by Satinello): 9 wins, Farrokh K. Irani Gold Cup (1200 m, class I, Madras). (Track record holder over 1200 m in Madras.)

Almagest (by Gombos): 4 wins as described.

21) SHRIMATI (B, 1965)

| Daneshill | Dante |
| | Life Hill |

| Savitri | Decorum |
| | Solar Kiss |

SHRIMATI: ran only twice due to injury. Dam of:

Scrambler (by Nijinsky [India]): 4 wins, Ram Mahadevan Gold Cup: 2nd Bangalore Arc de Triomphe, South India 2000 Guineas.

22) TUDOR ROSE (B, 1967)

| Gul Mohar | Abernant |
| | Fatimite |

| Rang Mahal | Mackann |
| | Queen of Gwalior |

TUDOR ROSE: 2 wins. Dam of:

Miracle (by Nijinsky [India]): 8 wins, Daga Trophy (1200 m, class I, Bombay), Gool Poonawalla Memorial Gold Cup, Maharani Tripurasundarammani Avaru Gold Cup.

23) WEST WAVE (Br, 1954)

| Stalino | Stardust |
| | Inkling |

| West Light | Signal Light |
| | Westrol |

WEST WAVE: placed twice in England. 6 wins in India, Czecho-slovakia Cup. Dam of:

Enterprise (by Horatius): 12 wins, Farrokh K. Irani Gold Cup, Owners and Trainers Association Cup; 2nd Indian Gold Vase.

Flying Enterprise (by Horatius): 8 wins, Stewards Cup.

Rolls Royce (by Horatius): 7 wins.

24) ENTHUSIASM (B, 1964)

Khan Saeb	Atout Maitre
	Lady Emma
Enthusiasta	Erno
	Argyle Street

ENTHUSIASM: 5 wins, Meerut Cup. Dam of:

All That Jazz (by Nijinsky [India]): 7 wins, Ardent Knight Cup.

25) KHUBLEI (Br, 1967)

Ardent Knight	Dante
	Per Ardua
Equity	Petition
	Equiria

KHUBLEI: 7 wins, Beresford Cup, Bucephalus Cup. Dam of:

Khublei Khan (by Satinello): 13 wins, Coonoor Cup.

26) KING'S PINT (B, 1969)

Pinturischio	Pinza
	Natalina da Murano
Doreen's Choice	King's Bench
	Gavins Girl

KING'S PINT: unraced. She is yet to get a superior racer.

27) RAGAMUFFIN (B, 1966)

Lough Ine	Arctic Star
	Mindy
Princess of Gwalior	Hyder Ali
	Lady Emma

RAGAMUFFIN: ran unplaced. Dam of:

Muffin (by Nijinsky [India]): 7 wins, Indian Oaks, Sir Jamsetjee Jeejeebhoy (VI Bart) Gold Cup.

El Bravo (by Satinello): 7 wins, F.D. Wadia Gold Cup, Rajaram Chhatrapati Cup, Southern Command Cup; 2nd Indian Derby.

Bravissima (by Gombos): 2 wins, Thunder Storm Cup; 3rd Indian 1000 Guineas.

28) RETAINED (Dk B, 1971)

Star of Gwalior	Hyder Ali
	Lady Emma
Orcade Queen	Orcades
	Mumkin

RETAINED: unraced. Dam of:

Corniche (by Satinello): 4 wins, Mathradas Goculdas Cup, Chief Minister's Cup (1600 m, class II, Pune); 2nd Hyderabad Fillies Trial Stakes; 3rd Bangalore 1000 Guineas.

Camargue (by Satinello): 4 wins, Southern Command Cup, R.W.I.T.C. Ltd. Committee Gold Cup.

29) SERENDIPITY (Ch, 1970)

Young Lochinvar	Elopement
	No Angel
Minima	Macherio
	Mindy

SERENDIPITY: placed. Dam of:

Shatrunja (by Satinello): 9 wins, Mathradas Goculdas Trophy.

Shankeshwar (by Satinello): 5 wins.

30) SUPARNA (Ch, 1966)

Daneshill	Dante
	Life Hill
Winged Beauty	Chmo
	Jaishree

SUPARNA: unraced. Dam of:

Cremona (by Promontory): 10 wins, Southern Command Cup, Kailashpat Singhania Cup.

Supernal (by Never Never): 5 wins, Byculla Club Cup, Gen. Obaidullah Khan Gold Cup.

31) CRYSTAL SLIPPER (B, 1965)

Glasgow Paddock	Big Game
	Annetta
Celestial Slipper	Solar Slipper
	Divine Polly

CRYSTAL SLIPPER: 4 wins. She is yet to get a superior racer.

32) DEAR HEART (Gr, 1966)

Dear Gazelle	Petition
	Giselda
Locum	Constable
	Sea Chorus

DEAR HEART: 3 wins, Star of Italy Cup; 2nd Queen Elizabeth II Cup; 3rd Sassoon General Hospital's Centenary Gold Cup, Byculla Club Cup. Dam of:

Miss Minstrel (by Satinello): 10 wins, Golconda 1000 Guineas, Idar Gold Cup (1200 m, 4-yr-olds and over, Hyderabad), Allez France Cup; 2nd Nilgiris Fillies Trial Stakes.

Red Ranger (by Satinello): 6 wins, Highborn Handicap.

33) DILKHUSH (B, 1969)

Glasgow Paddock	Big Game
	Annetta
Prince Michiko	Chhote Khan
	Shenfield

DILKHUSH: 4 wins. She is yet to get a superior racer.

34) IONA (B, 1970)

Young Lochinvar	Elopement
	No Angel
Realy	March Past
	Infiltration

IONA: 6 wins, Mysore Race Club Cup. Dam of:

Master Key (by Gombos): 3 wins, Bangalore Arc de Triomphe, Chikkavaram Gold Cup; 2nd South India Oaks.

35) LORELEI (Dk B, 1970)

Cradle of the Deep	Doutelle
	Papoose
Topless	Gold Kale
	Sportsmen's Folly

LORELEI: 5 wins, Turf Club Cup; 3rd South India 1000 Guineas. Dam of:

Royal Brute (by Satinello): 7 wins, Thunder Storm Cup, K.M. Munshi Cup.

Proud Image (by Gombos): 8 wins, Bombay Cup, Welcome Cup.

36) NEVER IN DOUBT (Dk B or Br, 1958)

Empyrean	Hyperion
	Ad Astra
Manessa	Neapolitan
	Rhoda

NEVER IN DOUBT: 2 wins in Australia. Dam of:

Old Parr (by Asopo): 11 wins; 2nd Calcutta Derby.

Hamiya (by Satinello): 5 wins, winner in class II.

Negress (by Gombos): 2 wins; 2nd Indian Oaks; 3rd R.R. Ruia Gold Cup.

37) PETITE AUREOLE (Ch, 1969)

Aureole	Hyperion
	Angelola
Sweet Reason	Elopement
	Wyresdale

PETITE AUREOLE: unraced. Dam of:

Impulse (by Satinello): 7 wins, Ardent Knight Cup.

Endurance (by Satinello): 6 wins, C.N. Wadia Gold Cup, Christmas Gold Cup.

38) PRINCESS SAIQA (B, 1968)

Asopo	Nimbus Assamenta
Abeyance	Court Martial Bushire

PRINCESS SAIQA: 4 wins. Dam of:

Pride of Kiliyanur (by Satinello): 7 wins, winner in class II.

39) RESOURCEFUL (B or Br, 1968)

Hard Sauce	Ardan Saucy Bella
Railing	Nimbus Heala Ray

RESOURCEFUL: 3 wins in England, Duchess of York Handicap, Middle Distance Handicap; placed September Handicap, Primera Handicap. Dam of:

Mahogany (by Satinello): 7 wins, Homi Mody Trophy, Gen. Obaidullah Khan Trophy.

Savoir Faire (by Satinello): 7 wins, Rajaram Chhatrapati Cup, Glasgow Courser Cup.

Cartier (by Malvado): 3 wins, Indian 1000 Guineas, S.A. Poonawalla Cup.

Calibre (by Malvado): 2 wins, South India 2000 Guineas.

40) ROLLS ROYCE (Dk B or Br, 1965)

Horatius	Hyperion La Boulue
West Wave	Stalino West Light

ROLLS ROYCE: 7 wins. Dam of:

Marinee Idol (by Satinello): 7 wins.

Rollinsky (by Nijinsky [India]): 5 wins, Madras Race Club Cup.

41) AIR HOSTESS (Ch, 1970)

Denier	Dante
	Radiant Queen
Sky Flight	Exodus
	Sea Flight

AIR HOSTESS: 13 wins, South India 1000 Guineas, Oaks, Derby and St. Leger, Bangalore Oaks and Fillies Trial Stakes (dead-heat), Guindy Gold Cup. Dam of:

Hawaiian Hostess (by Satinello): 3 wins.

Air Ace (by Sovereign Silver): 4 wins K.M. Munshi Trophy.

42) HYDROFOIL (B, 1968)

Prince Pradeep	Migoli
	Driving
Helicraft	Golestan
	Hoverplane

HYDROFOIL: 6 wins, Calcutta Gold Cup, R.C.T.C. Gold Cup, Homi Mody Gold Cup; 2nd Calcutta Derby (by a short-head), Queen Elizabeth II Cup (twice), President of India Gold Cup. Dam of:

Zambo Anga (by Satinello): 6 wins, C.N. Wadia Gold Cup.

Satellite (by Satinello): 7 wins, winner in class I.

43) JOINT VENTURE (Dk B, 1970)

Cradle of the Deep	Doutelle
	Papoose
Rose Rock	Rock of Gibraltar
	Superbe Rose

JOINT VENTURE: 8 wins. Dam of:

Renowned (by Malvado): 5 wins, South India and Mysore Derby; 2nd Bangalore Arc de Triomphe.

44) LADY MADONNA (Ch, 1971)

| Never Never | Never Say Die |
| | Mixed Blessing |

| Donna Princess | Wilwyn |
| | Gaztelupe |

LADY MADONNA: 4 wins, Indian Oaks, Eve Champion Cup, C.N. Wadia Gold Cup, Homi Mody Cup; 2nd Indian St. Leger; 4th Indian Turf Invitation Cup. Dam of:

Trinity College (by Satinello): 7 wins, Idar Cup (2400 m, 4-yr-olds and over, Pune), Lady Tarquin Cup, Brindavan Cup.

45) OM NOORI (B, 1971)

| Crepollo | Donatella II |
| | Crepuscule |

| Krasny Bor | Parthia |
| | Karalyn |

OM NOORI: ran only once and retired to stud. She is yet to get a superior racer.

46) PRETENDRESSE (Ch, 1971)

| Pretendre | Doutelle |
| | Limicola |

| Suir Delight | Precipitant |
| | Persian Union |

PRETENDRESSE: placed 4th in the South Port Stakes, England. Dam of:

Mina de Ouro (by Gold Rod): 4 wins, Nawabzada Rashiduzzafar Khan Cup.

47) RECOUP (Br, 1969)

Forlorn River	Fighting Don
	Starflight
Righteous Girl	Right Boy
	Chamossura

RECOUP: 2 wins in England Rock Garden Stakes, Manton Stakes. 6 wins in India including the R.W.I.T.C. Gold Cup, Southern Command Cup, Rajpipla Gold Cup, P.D. Bolton Cup, Mathradas Goculdas Gold Cup. She is yet to get a superior racer.

48) ROLLICKING RACHEL (B or Br, 1971)

Crocket	King of the Tudors
	Chandelier
Arandena	Worden II
	Aranda

ROLLICKING RACHEL: 3 wins in England. Valentia-Handicap, Wicklow Handicap. She is yet to get a superior racer.

49) ZIFI (B, 1971)

Zinosca	Nosca
	Zina
First Lady	Hervine
	Desire

ZIFI: 3 wins, Calcutta 1000 Guineas; 2nd Bangalore Fillies Trial Stakes; 3rd Calcutta Oaks. Dam of:

Zifinella (by Satinello): 5 wins, P.D. Bolton Cup.

Vainqueur (by Gombos): 6 wins, Deccan Chronicle Gold Cup (1600 m, class II, Hyderabad), Red Surprise Cup.

50) GOODS AND CHATTELS (B, 1970)

Santa Claus	Chamossaire
	Aunt Clara
French Possession	French Beige
	Rose of Tudor

GOODS AND CHATTELS: unraced. Dam of:

Mahmoud (by Pieces of Eight): 10 wins, Allez France Cup.

51) KARTHIAYINI (B, 1968)

| Jethro | Palestine
Jet High |
| Miss Rebecca | Dumbarnie
Clara Rebecca |

KARTHIAYIN: placed. She is yet to get a superior racer.

52) MAJOLICA (Dk B, 1972)

| Punjab | Pardal
Indian Night |
| Majorca | Orcades
Farman |

MAJOLICA: 8 wins, South India and Bangalore 1000 Guineas, Bangalore Oaks, Tamil Nadu Commemoration Gold Cup (dead-heat with Jugnu). Dam of:

Attorney General (by Malvado): 7 wins, winner in class II.

53) ONLY GIRL (B, 1972)

| Sheshoon | Precipitation
Noorani |
| One Only | Sicambre
First One |

ONLY GIRL: did not win. Dam of:

Fair Helen (by Homeric): 2 wins, Queen Elizabeth Commemoration Cup (1600 m, 3-yr-olds, Madras). She was a filly well up to classic standard, but unfortunately had a setbck in training.

Solitaire (by Malvado): 11 wins, Golconda Derby, South India 2000 Guineas and St. leger, Guindy Grand Prix (1600 m, 3-yr-olds, Madras), Breeders' Cup; 3rd South India Derby (won by Renowned).

Nymph (by Sovereign Silver): 2 wins, Brindavan Cup (2000 m, classes II and III, Bangalore).

54) RADIANCE (B, 1972)

| Red Rufus | Dark William |
| | Red Belle |

| Sparkler | Helios |
| | Golden Emblem |

RADIANCE: ran unplaced. Dam of:

Sintilla (by Satinello): 3 wins, Gen. Obaidullah Khan Cup, Pune Fillies Gold Cup; 3rd Indian Oaks.

55) SLIP RULE (B, 1970)

| Privy Councillor | Counsel |
| | High Number |

| Identification | Ratification |
| | Dented Pride |

SLIP RULE: 4 wins in England, Lonsdale Stakes (Doncaster), Jack Jarvis Memorial Nursery (Ayr); 2nd Buggins Farm Nursery (Haydock Park). Dam of:

Highland Rule (by Highland melody): 12 wins, Indian 1000 Guineas, 2000 Guineas and Oaks, A.C.Ardeshir Gold Trophy (1600 m, 3-yr-olds and over, Bombay); 2nd Bangalore Fillies Trial Stakes.

56) SPEEDY QUEEN (B, 1970)

| Punjab | Pardal |
| | Indian Night |

| Lady Diana | Plumpton |
| | Passing Shower |

SPEEDY QUEEN: winner. Dam of:

That's the Spirit (by Satinello): 3 wins, Mother's Son Cup.

57) WAVELL'S LASS (Ch, 1970)

Young Lochinvar or Knight Valiant	Royal Charger
	Titanic
Affectionate	Infatuation
	Bienfaisant

WAVELL'S LASS: 5 wins. Dam of:

Satin lass (by Satinello): 7 wins, Winged Wonder Cup, C.S. Loganathan Memorial Cup.

Scaramouche (by malvado): 3 wins, Eve Champion Cup; 3rd Indian Derby; 4th Charminar Challenge Indian Turf Invitation Cup.

ANSWER

Satinello has been very successful. A Border-line classic sire, he has sired 33 superior racers including 4 classic winners. He got these 32 superior racers from only 75 runners — truly a magnificent performance. He was champion sire in 1980-'81, 2nd in '79-'80 and 3rd in '78-'79. He also topped other lists.

Percentage of classic winners and champions from runners $\dfrac{4}{75} \times 100 = 5.3\%$

Percentage of superior racers from runners $\dfrac{33}{75} \times 100 = 44\%$

His behaviour is Normal. He sired superior racers consistently. His colts and fillies were equally good.

We now come to his aptitude. It certainly appears that he is versatile. He has sired sprinter-milers, stayers and horses with an ideal blend of speed and stamina. But let us not jump to conclusions. Did Satinello really get genuine, high class stayers? A long and sometimes bitter debate went on in the country over this question. Readers will quickly reply in the affirmative, pointing out that Potential Champion, Red Satin, Red Cockade, El Bravo, Grey Satin, Trinity College, Endurance, Mahogany, Scintilla and Zambo Anga were stayers. But did they stay 2400 m or better still, 2800 m? To answer this question I studied their race records very carefully. I am convinced that they excelled up to 2000 m only. In other words, I feel they were horses with staying tendencies rather than true stayers. Only four of them excelled over 2400 m. They were: Potential Champion who won the Indian Oaks; Trinity College who won the Idar Cup (2400 m, 4-yr-olds and over, Pune); Endurance who won the C.N. Wadia Gold Cup

(2400 m, classes I and II, Bombay) and Mahogany who was an excellent 2nd to the Indian Derby winner Mohawk in the same race. Would these four horses have stayed 2800 m? There is no doubt that Trinity College would have. He was a good 3rd in the Northumberland Cup (3200 m, classes I and II, Pune) but carrying 47 kgs. Potential Champion did not even run in the Indian St. Leger. A word about her full-brother Red Cockade, whom I described as the best Indian-bred ever. While he stayed 2000 m, it is unlikely that he would have stayed longer distances. He was too brilliant. To make a long story short, Satinello could get only about half-a-dozen genuine stayers out of 32 superior racers. (He subsequently got Wild Obsession who won over 2400 m. He definitely has the ability to win over 2800 m.) Is such a sire a sire of stayers? Recall Rock of Gibraltar, Prince Pradeep, Everyday or Even Star of Gwalior. How did they perform? Therefore we are forced to conclude that Satinello is essentially a sire of horses who excel up to 2000 m only.

Let us now check the quality of his mares. Readers can judge them very easily. His mares are outstanding in every respect. They include the finest mares in the country. Count the number of got-abroad mares he served. Also count the number of classic winners, classic-placed and superior racers. It is unnecessary for me to say that most of these mares are also very well-bred. (Compare these mares with the mares served by the other stallions we studied.) You can easily see that about three-fourth of them are Inherently superior. Interestingly an overwhelming majority of Satinello's superior racers were out of these mares. In other words Satinello is not a prepotent stallion. He simply does not have the ability to get superior racers out of Inherently inferior mares. Literally less than a handful of his superior racers were out of Inherently inferior mares. This is our first finding.

His mares included a number of classic stayers, well-bred and got-abroad mares bred to stay. But we saw that he failed to get classic stayers from them i.e. he frequently missed getting classic stayers out of mares who clearly have the ability to get such horses. This debilitating weakness prevented him from developing into a really outstanding sire. He could not qualify for Front-line classic status even after 8 crops. In marked contrast Everyday qualified within 4 crops (3 crops if we include champion Every Time) and Malvado within 3 crops. Therefore Satinello is not a classic sire in the real sense of the term. He is only a sire of superior racers.

I would like to make a special mention of one of his offspring Fire Flash who was foaled later. His race record is given in page 18. His dam Fire Haven, who was undoubtedly the best of her generation, has also been described in page 18. Though Fire Haven had the ability to win from 1000 m to 2800 m, Fire Flash did not. Though he has the ability to win over 2000 m, he really excels up to 1600 m only. His best performance was in the Bangalore Colts Trial Stakes, where he was a game 2nd to Camino, who clipped 1/5th second off Red Cockade's course record. Camino was one among the handful of horses who could have gone close to Red Cockade. (Red Cockade had something in hand when he won his Colts Trial.) We are going to study Camino's sire in exhaustive detail in the next chaper. Coming back to Fire Haven, when she visited Malvado she got Vibrant who excelled over the entire range of distances. His victories included the Bangalore Triple Crown.

Let us now digress to other stallions, to Nijinsky [India] first. His pedigree, race record and stud performance have been given in page 293. But let us go deeper. Readers who studied Satinello's mares carefully would have found that his behaviour was diametrically opposite Satinello's. Clearly he is a prepotent sire. he consistently produced superior racers out of Inherently inferior mares as below:

Inherently inferior mare	Superior offspring
Enthusiasm	All That Jazz
Rose Bud	Buttinsky and Rubaiyat
Shrimati	Scrambler
Tudor Rose	Miracle

(Note that Satinello failed to get superior racers out of these mares.)

His other superior racers include Sweet Memories, Muffin, Star Appeal, Well Connected (who have been described in page 294), Sun Gold, Minsky, Rollinsky, Russian Wonder, Shaibya and Sweet Martini. Interestingly the dams of Star Appeal, Sun Gold, Russian Wonder and Sweet Martini are also Inherently inferior. But this is not all. A few of the horses out of these mares could also stay! They were Buttinsky and Rubaiyat, Scrambler (a fair 2nd in the Bangalore Arc de Triomphe) and Russian Wonder (a game 3rd in the Golconda Derby). Therefore Nijinsky is not only prepotent for class but also for stamina to a certain extent! Readers are sure to question at this stage: "If Nijinsky is so talented why didn't he develop into a Frontline classic sire?" The question can be easily answered. As explained, he just could not catch the attention of breeders. He just did not get Inherently superior mares. Though he did well with Inherently inferior mares, there is obviously a limit to which he can go. While stallions have the ability to get superior racers out of Inherently inferior mares, you cannot expect them to get classic winners and champions. To do so you need Inherently superior mares. Since Nijinsky was so successful with Inherently inferior mares, readers can well imagine what he would have done with the Inherently superior. But it was not to be. The outstanding mares, who visited Satinello did not visit him. Had they visited him he would have surely got more than half-a-dozen classic winners. Sweet Memories is the proof.

The behaviour of Satinello and Nijinsky helps us to grasp further the fundamental principle that we have been stressing all along. We must not focus our attention entirely on the produce record of a mare, ignoring her race record and pedigree. Imagine an Inherently inferior mare who got a superior racer out of Nijinsky. She now visits Satinello. Will the off-spring be superior? It is most unlikely, even though as per our definition he will be well-bred. Even outstanding mares cannot get superior racers out of every successful stallion. They must be compatible with the stallions concerned.

The outstanding mares who visited Satinello then visited Gombos and Malvado. Therefore a quick word about them is in order.

			Le Haar	Vieux Manoir
		Exbury		Mince Pie
			Greensward	Mossborough
Gombos				Stargrass
(B, 1969)			Hard Sauce	Ardan
		Gazpacho II		Saucy Bella
			Red Cloak	Big Game
				Manetta

A horse of quality, Gombos distinguished himself at the highest level. He won 4 races from 7f to 1-1/4 mi. He won his only start as a 2-yr-old and went on to win the Miss Harp Lager Stakes, Prix Matrico and Prix Orfeo. He also placed 3rd in the Prix Ganay (Gr. I) to Allez France and Tennyson and 2nd in the Brigadier Gerard Stakes (Gr. III) to Scottish Rifle. He also placed 4th in several other stakes. But his finest hour was in the Epsom Derby where he was a game 5th, only 5 lengths behind Roberto. Interestingly he beat Scottish Rifle and Steel Pulse, who were involved in the finish of the Irish Derby in which he did not run. He was then rated

130 by Timeform. He was also rated 60 1/2 kgs in the French Free Handicap behind only Allez France, Tennyson, Dahlia, Card King and Nonoalco. During the course of his career he defeated outstanding racers like Dahlia, Star Appeal. Steel Pulse, Scottish Rifle, Moulton and Minsky. He was imported into India and retired to stud in 1977.

Sadly for Indian breeding, his stud performance is nowhere near his race record. It is enough if I say that his behaviour is identical to Satinello's. He is not prepotent. He has sired stayers, but like Satinello frequently missed getting stayers out of staying mares. But tragically his percentage of success is much less than Satinello's. The net result is that after serving the finest mares in the country, he only has about a dozen superior racers to show for it. He is not even a Border-line classic stallion, unless you stretch a point and consider Almagest to be a classic winner. His best racers were Gomos and Master Key who have been described. (He has an outstanding youngster in Responsions [by Red Rufus' daughter Response] who is sure to develop into his best racer.) It is absolutely necessary for researchers in India to investigate why he was not successful. (You cannot fault the bottom-half of his pedigree. Could it be that Exbury was not a sire of sires? Did he have any acclimatization problem?)

MALVADO

			Pharos
		Nearco	Nogara
	Nearctic		
		Lady Angela	Hyperion
Malvado			Sister Sarah
(B, 1972)			Chop Chop
		Victoria Park	Victoriana
	Victory Chant		
		Orchestra	Menetrier
			Abondance

Another horse of great quality, Malvado won 6 races from 1700 m to 2400 m including the Prix Georges Baltazzi and Prix Maurice de Waldner. He also placed 2nd in the Prix de Guiche and Prix de la Coupe both Gr. III. He was weighted 61.5 kgs. in the French Free Handicap, only 5 kgs. below top-weighted Orange Bay. He was imported into India and retired to stud in 1978.

Happily for Indian breeding he is off and flying. We saw that he qualified for Front-line classic status within 3 crops. In addition to the classic winners described, he is also the sire of Prudential Champ who lifted the inaugural Splendour Deluxe Pune Derby (2000 m, 3-yr-olds, Pune), another "classic" which has just been introduced. There is nothing much to say about him except that he is a versatile stallion who invariably gets stayers out of staying mares and mares bred to stay. His percentage of success is obviously high. The question of his prepotence has not yet arisen, as most of his mares are superior if not outstanding.

It is time for us to come back to Satinello. To sum up his behaviour: He is not prepotent. Though he is versatile, he frequently fails to get stayers out of staying mares and mars bred to stay. But his percentage of success is high. Now which types of mares are most compatible with him?

Most surprisingly it is not easy to answer the question! Inferior mares are out as he is not prepotent. Outstanding mares are also out. Would you honestly breed mares of the calibre of Sparkling Rock, Grecian Flower, Red Surprise, Hydrofoil, Lady Madonna or Majolica to him? These mares are obviously predisposed to producing clasic winners and champions. Therefore you will naturally breed them to Front-line classic sires like Everyday or Malvado, not to Satinello. Therefore it seems that Inherently superior mares not predisposed to producing classic winners, champions or stayers are most suitable for him. This is the theoretically impeccable conclusion.

But it may not work out practically! Owners of Inherently superior mares will be anxious to breed them to Front-line classic stallions. Then they have a chance of getting classic winners, champions or superior racers. But if they breed their mares to Satinello they can get only superior racers. Therefore Satinello is unlikely to figure prominently in their breeding plans. market breeders too are sure to think on similar lines.

But I have no intention of denigrating Satinello. His percentage of success is his greatest asset. he too has qualified for Front-line classic status with Fire Flash, Wheels (a daughter of classic winner Rock Haven who has been described in page 19) and Goldie Brown. The last named, a full-sister to Red Cockade and Potential Champion, has won 5 races including the Nilgiris Fillies Trial Stakes, Guindy Grand Prix and Breeders' Cup (1400 m, 3-yr-olds, Madras). She also placed 2nd in the Nilgiris Derby and Bangalore Fillies Trial Stakes. (She is in training.)

PART III

CHAPTER 12

Miscellaneous

1

When I was young I committed the blunder of telling people that scientific methods and techniques could, and should, be applied to breeding and racing, only to be laughed at. Since then, needless to say, I have kept my mouth tightly shut. But I have had the quiet satisfaction of applying scientific methods to a variety of problems and situations in breeding and racing, with usually excellent results. I rest content by giving two examples, one below and another a little later.

This is about a trainer (now no more). He had a long innings and was successful. His horses won almost all the prestigious races in the country. He also had his share of success in the classics. Naturally he was accustomed to his share of winners every year, and his owners were very happy and content.

Then one year he had only half the number of winners he usually saddled. But his owners were not at all worried. Even the best trainers have lean seasons. You can't finish near the top every year. They were sure that they would quickly bounce back to the top.

Next year disaster! The trainer was struggling for a win — a single win! Now owners who had been patient started demanding results. Many of them removed their horses from him and others stopped buying young stock. Naturally the trainer was under intense pressure. His health suffered greatly. Tongues began to wag, filling the air with totally baseless rumors. Physically unwell and mentally upset the trainer migrated to another centre. But he never recovered from the setback.

Now what had actually happened? Did I — a mere stripling — know something that a veteran trainer and owners didn't! I remember the occasion well. It was a May afternoon in Madras, the temperature hovering around 105° F. Even the crows dared not stir. (Those who have experienced Madras summers will know that I am not exaggerating.) All the horses had naturally left for salubrious Ootacamund — the queen of the hill-stations. Examinations out of the way, I had nothing to do. Time was on my hands. Half-heartedly I took out a large sheet of paper and wrote the names of all the trainers. Underneath I wrote the names of the their youngsters with their pedigrees. When I came to this particular trainer I got a shock. For quite some time my temperature was more than the ambient. What had happened was this: half the youngsters had superior sires but disappointing dams; the other half had outstanding dams, but 1st or 2nd crop sires who were later disasters in stud. Therefore not even one youngster was average! A quick check showed that his 4-yr-olds were not well-bred either. Needless to say, the trainer was struggling for a win.

On top of this, this trainer had a penchant for buying horses with very obscure and unorthodox pedigrees. What exactly these horses are going to do, is impossible to predict. He was lucky a couple of times, but sadly all his misfortune came together.

There is a very important lesson tor us to learn here. Obviously you must not dabble with obscure and unorthodox pedigrees unless you really know what you are doing. More importantly, *if you are not familiar with pedigrees or are not sure with your pedigree analysis, you must buy horses whose sires have been consistently within the top twelve of the Sires lists and whose maternal grandsires have also been within the top twelve of the Maternal grandsires lists.* If you follow this rule you can't go far wrong. No doubt a particular sire and dam may be incompatible, but, in general, your horses are sure to be marginally above average or at least average. For you are very close to the source of superior racers. Remember, you must not touch a horse whose sire or maternal grandsire is not in the top twelve. I cannot think of a simpler rule to give to owners.

To use this rule easily, you must study the Sires and Maternal grandsires lists of the last ten years and prepare a consolidated list containing the leading sires, and another list containing the leading maternal grandsires. Keep these two lists in front of you when you are analyzing pedigrees. It will not take you more than a minute to check whether the sire and maternal grandsire are in the lists. You can go through the auction catalogue very quickly marking-off horses who satisfy the rule. Then inspect all the horses in question. If you are impressed with any individual you can buy him. This rule can also be used very profitably by those who give more importance to conformation and less to pedigree.

2

I have seen even veterans confuse the roles of an ''owner'' and ''breeder''. The two have very different objectives and are therefore very distinct personalities. The owner's task is to build up a strong racing stable, while the breeder's is to launch a powerful breeding program. These two operations are not the same and I straightaway say that the former is definitely easier. (In fact the dos of the former are the don'ts of the latter!)

As an owner you have the liberty of buying as many, or as few, horses as you like. You can, theoretically, buy any horse that comes for sale. You will obviously analyze their pedigrees with extreme care. You will study their conformation and straightaway reject Those with the slightest defect. What more, you will estimate the value of each horse and will be unwilling to pay more for him. Since the annual production of thoroughbreds runs in thousands, chances are you will find the horses you need even at your price.

You will naturally select an outstanding trainer and jockey for you, horses and plan their careers meticulously. They will get the best care and attention. They have everything going for them. If the results are not up to your expectations . . . well . . . you have only yourself to blame.

But breeding is an entirely different cup of tea. Let us start at the beginning. Every breeder has to go through three distinct stages before reaching the top. Let us study the first stage.

To start breeding there is no need to invest in land and buildings. There are scores of top class stud farms who accept boarders. There is no need for you to own a stallion. You can buy nominations to the stallions you like. (This is easier said than done. You cannot breed to a top class stallion unless you are a share-holder, as their nominations change hands at astronomical prices. And you cannot possibly be a member of every stallion syndicate. But as I explained, you can breed to young or slightly less fashionable stallions.)

Now you must buy broodmares. Here again things are not easy for the small breeder. You can't hope to buy stakes winners or superior racers, or even their near relations. You may not even be able to buy really well-bred mares. You may be forced to settle for marginally above average or even average mares. However you have managed to assemble a small broodmare band. These mares will visit the stallions you selected earlier.

Now recall all the uncertainties of breeding. This is the first obstacle you must cross. You must be able to overcome all the difficulties.

Let us assume you have done so. You have navigated the sea of uncertainty and have produced half-a-dozen superb yearlings. Now you have to market them successfully. This is easier said than done. It is unlikely that your yearlings will fetch fancy prices. You will be fortunate if they sell for fair prices. Do not forget the unpredictable swings of fashion. The market may be strong one year and weak the next. Your horses may not catch the attention of the leading buyers. You will be lucky if your whole operation breaks-even. This is the second stage, the second turning point. You must sell your horses and recover your costs fully.

Once you have crossed the second stage you are ready for the third: the stage where you sell your horses for a profit. This is the legitimate aspiration of every breeder — to sell horses for a handsome profit. But which breeders sell their horses for large profits? Those lucky enough to catch the swings of fashion are one group. But we must ignore them. Very successful breeders i.e breeders of classic winners and champions are sure to sell their horses for big prices. Their horses will be closely related to classic winners and champions. They will be in demand. In essence: If you want to make a profit in breeding you must have the ability to breed classic winners, champions and superior racers. Do you have this ability? You must answer the question from the heart of your hearts. If you have the ability you must become a breeder. But remember the profits will start coming in only after you have bred outstanding racers. Those outstanding racers may not have sold for big prices. When you study the lives of great breeders note how and when they crossed the different stages i.e. when did a particular breeder enter breeding? When did his operation break-even? When did he breed his first classic winner or champion? When did he make a profit? Such a study will give you an excellent idea of the time factor involved. You must be prepared to "stand" for that many years.

But what about those who have no hesitation in admitting their inability to breed classic winners or champions, but who really love breeding. Can't they become breeders? Most certainly they can — they can become owner-breeders.

If you become an owner-breeder you will be exactly midway between an owner and breeder. You will breed horses with the sole purpose of racing them yourself. Therefore straightaway your job is easier than that of a market-breeder. It is enough if you cross the first stage. You need not cross the third stage. You need not also cross the second stage. If you are affluent you may not be very unhappy if your operation does not break-even. The winners you have bred will be compensation enough.

An owner-breeder is not bothered about the swings of fashion, or even the strength of the market. Now we come to an important point. As an owner-breeder you are going to race your horses. Therefore—you must select progenitors you really admire. You must not be bothered by the by the news that these progenitors are not held in high esteem by others. You think they are talented, that they have the ability to produce great horses. Therefore you are patronizing them.

But even this is easier said than done. If you fail to cross the first stage you will surely lose money. But assume that you have crossed the first stage. You have horses ready to race. But at the auction sales you find that you are attracted towards several horses bred by market breeders. You really like these horses more than your own. Now what will you do? Buy the horses you like, as any other owner would do, and sell your horses for whatever prices they get even if it means incurring a loss? Or will you buy the horses you like and keep your own thereby doubling the strength of your racing stable? Will you be able to afford it? Alternately will you bite the bullet and keep your own horses, ignoring the rest? This is the dilemma faced by owner-breeders. They may not be happy with their stock. However several owner-breeders have solved this problem. They race their own horses and also buy a few horses every year.

In conclusion I would like to emphasize that an owner, owner-breeder and market-breeder are three distinct personalities. They have different duties, different responsibilities — different obstacles to cross. (A market-breeder can, of course, become an owner at any time by retaining one of his horses.) Consider all the facts once again and then decide who you want to be.

3

I have so far not made a mention of one type of horse — the "freak" horse. *The Concise Oxford Dictionary* describes a freak as: "an abnormally developed specimen". In our context it refers to horses with extremely unorthodox, abnormal conformation. Their pedigrees too may be very unusual and unorthodox. Such horses are the first to be rejected at the auction sales! By text-book rules such horses should be incapable of winning a race and without doubt an overwhelming majority of freaks are useless on the course. But a handful have broken the rules. They not only won, but developed into champions. They were obviously large-hearted, tenacious, determined, intelligent horses who scored in spite of their conformation and pedigree. Such horses are naturally very, very rare, may be one a decade.

The New Zealand wonder horse Phar Lap was a Freak. In the words of Tony Morris*: ". . . such a horse was Phar Lap, bred on no kind of principle at all, unless it was breed the worst to the worst. He looked first what might have been expected, a coarse ugly brute. But he proved himself the greatest racehorse of his era, and in Australasia his name is uttered with reverence to this day." He won 37 of his 51 races, giving an un-

---

* *Great Moments in Racing,* edited by Tony Morris.

forgettable performance in the Agua Caliente Handicap, Tanforan, Mexico. Eddie Arcaro, who rode a winner at Tanforan that day, insisted that Phar Lap was the greatest thoroughbred ever to race in America.

Mount Everest, winner of the first Invitation Cup, was also a bit of a freak He was a big, gangling top-heavy colt who gave a difficult ride. But he was talented enough to win 11 other races including the Indian St. Leger, South India 2000 Guineas and Kunigal Derby. He was also a very controversial 2nd in the Indian Derby to Rocklie, a story which must be told. In the Derby, both Mount Everest and Rocklie went locked past the post. Most unfortunately the photo-finish camera failed and the judge awarded the race to Rocklie. Needless to say, the supporters of Mount Everest were aghast. They were absolutely sure that their colt had won and several will swear to it even today. But this was not all.

The next day newspapers revealed that an entire family, which had apparently staked everything it had on Mount Everest, had committed suicide by drowning of Juhu beach. Racing is not all fun and games.

However Mount Everest got his revenge in the St. Leger where he beat Rocklie. She did not run in the Invitation Cup.

Mount Everest was not a successful sire though he was orthodoxly Bred. This is not really surprising as freak horses win entirely due to their own tenacity, will-power and sincerity of purpose. It would be too much to expect their descendants to take after them.

4

We are living in an era of change. Not a week passes without a dramatic break-through in one branch of science or another. Breeding and racing have not been immune to these developments. The last few years have seen the meteoric rise of "Sportsmedicine". Suddenly scientists of different disciplines began to vigorously research breeding, training and racing. Inevitably their findings are dramatic and often fly in the face of conventional wisdom.

Sportsmedicine* has been defined as: "The application of science to athletic excellence." It is a multi-disciplinary activity embracing genetics, nutrition, bio-medical engineering, physiology and every branch of veterinary science. Scientists seek to eliminate "guesswork" and put "rigor" into every aspect of breeding and training. The thoroughbred and other breeds have been made the subject of innumerable experiments, and

---

* "Perspectives and prospects", by Matthew Mackay-Smith, *Equus*, March 1983.

out of these have emerged the very exciting concepts of gait analysis, muscle fibre typing, interval training etc. Expressions like "aerobic glycolysis", "recovery slope" and "packed cell volume" may soon become a part of every horseman's vocabulary. The principal aims of sportsmedicine are as shown in the next page:

1) To evolve training programs that enable a horse to perform at his peak throughout his career.

2) To anticipate illnesses and injuries and prevent them.

3) To predict the performance of a young horse.

I hasten to add that sportsmedicine cannot give you a formula for quick success. Rather it is a supplement, an important addition, a vital adjunct. You have got to make use of its findings to further develop and refine your methods and techniques. You have got to try out its ideas in the field. You cannot run races in a laboratory.

A few may be of the opinion that conventional knowledge and methods are the safest and best. After all the horse himself has not changed. Why spend time and money experimenting with new ideas? I have no hesitation in replying that those who refuse to take cognizance of the latest developments in science are going to be hopelessly left behind. It would be foolish on your part to imagine that you are immune to these developments. This brings us to the point I was anxious to make. You must be constantly upgrading your knowledge, you must have a thirst for new ideas and innovations and be eager to implement them. Remember we are learning all the time. Coming back to sportsmedicine, readers can understand its status, promise and scope by reading the articles by Matthew Mackay-Smith, Bobbie Lieberman and Matthew Mackay-Smith in the March 1983 issue of *Equus*.

5
QUIZ 4

Readers know the performances of most of the leading stallions of the country. But now I want you to forget completely all that you have learnt about them. Instead I want you to focus your attention on the stallions themselves — something which we have not done till now. I have given in the following pages the pedigrees and race records of 20 stallions who dominated Indian breeding from the late sixties to the early eighties. (We have studied most of these stallions, but in order to avoid turning back frequently, I have once again given their pedigrees and race records.) Most of them were imported into the country specially for breeding. A few raced in England and India. The only exception was Prince Pradeep who was imported in-utero. (Indian stallions like Red Rufus and Nijinsky have not been included in the list.) After studying their pedigrees and race records carefully I want you to answer the following questions:

1) What type of racers were they? What was their aptitudes on the course? There is one very important quality which most of them lacked. What is it?

2) What do you think of their pedigrees? What are their dominant features?

TABLE 22 — LIST OF STALLIONS

1) ARDENT KNIGHT (Br, 1953)

Dante	Nearco	Pharos	Pharlaris / Scapa Flow
		Nogara	Havresac II / Catnip
	Rosy Legend	Dark Legend	Dark Ronald / Golden Legend
		Rosy Cheeks	St. Just / Purity
Per Ardua	Hyperion	Gainsborough	Bayardo / Rosedrop
		Selene	Chaucer / Serenissima
	Ad Astra	Asterus	Teddy / Astrella
		Pyramid	Papyrus / Trestle

2 wins in England. At 2 he won the Southampton Stakes (6f). At 3 he won the Druids Stakes (1-1/4 mi).

2) ASOPO (Dk Br, 1957)

Nimbus	Nearco	Pharos	Phalaris Scapa Flow
		Nogara	Havresac II Catnip
	Kong	Baytown	Achtoi Princess Herodias
		Clang	Hainault Vibration
Assamenta	Norseman	Umidwar	Blandford Uganda
		Tara	Teddy Jean Gow
	Assylia	Plassy	Bosworth Pladda
		Apulia	Apelle Verveille

1 win in Italy. At 2 he placed. At 3 he won the Italian 2000 Guineas (1 mi, Rome) and placed 2nd in the Italian Derby (1-1/2 ml, Rome) by a neck.

3) HIGH COMMISSION (B, 1960)

Tehran	Bois Roussel	Vatout	Prince Chimay / Vasthi
		Plucky Liege	Spearmint / Concertina
	Stafaralla	Solario	Gainsborough / Sun Worship
		Mirawala	Phalaris / Miranda
Queen of Arabia	Nimbus	Nearco	Pharos / Nogara
		Kong	Baytown / Clang
	Queen of Basrah	Fair Trial	Fairway / Lady Juror
		Queen of Baghdad	Bahram / Queen of Scots

5 wins in France. At 3 he won the PrixRadis Rose (1500 m) and Prix Sec Saw (1600 m). At 4 he won the Prix Tantieme (1600 m), Prix de Chemoitou (1500 m) and Prix de Lastours (1500 m).

4) KING OF PIPPINS (Ch, 1953)

Persian Gulf	Bahram	Blandford	Swynford / Blanche
		Friar's Daughter	Friar Marcus / Garron Lass
	Double Life	Bachelor's Guide	Tredennis / Lady Bawn
		Saint Joan	Willbrook / Flo Desmond
The Poult	Mr. Jinks	Tetratema	The Tetrarch / Scotch Gift
		False Piety	Lemberg / St. Begoe
	Golden Pheasant	Gold Bridge	Swynford or Golden Boss / Flying Diadem
		Bonnie Birdie	Buchan / Columba

1 win in England and 7 wins in India from 1200 m to 2000 m. At 3 he won the Hull Handicap Plate in England. In India he won the Czechoslovakia Cup, Berar Gold Cup and Republic Cup.

5) KING'S SON (Ch, 1958)

Supreme Court	Persian Gulf or Precipitation	Hurry On	Marcovil Tout Suite
		Double Life	Bachelor's Double Saint Joan
	Forecourt	Fair Trial	Fairway Lady Juror
		Overture	Dastur Overmantle
Pensacola	Marsyas II	Trimdon	Son-in-Law Trimestral
		Astronomie	Asterus Likka
	Bouillabaisse	Blenheim	Blandford Malva
		Becti	Salmon-Trout Mirawala

1 win in England and 5 wins in India. At 2 he won the Soltykoff Stakes (Newmarket) and placed 3rd in the New Ham Stakes (Goodwood). He was rated 8 st 9 Lbs in the Free Handicap and his June Timeform rating was 117. In India his victories included the Metropolitan (6f), Galstaun Cup (6f), Nepal Gold Cup (1-1/4 mi) and R.C.T.C. Gold Cup (1-1/2 mi).

6) LANDIGOU (Ch, 1964)

Mourne	Vieux Manoir	Brantome → Blandford / Vitamine
		Vieille Maison → Finglas / Vielle Canaille
	Ballynash	Nasrullah → Nearco / Mumtaz Begum
		Ballywellbroke → Ballyferis / The Beggar
Lady Djebel	Djebelilla	Djebel → Tourbillon / Loika
		Sevilla → Chateau Blouscaut / Biweh
	Fast Lady II	Fastnet → Pharos / Tatoule
		Charbonniere → Dampremy / Char Lady

2 wins in England. At 2 he placed. At 3 he won the Shipley Bridge Stakes (1ı1/2 mi) and placed 6th in the Epsom Derby, 6 lengths behind Royal Palace. At 4 he won the Mid-day Sun Handicap (2 ml) and placed 3rd in the Queen Alexandra Stakes (Ascot).

7) MIGHTY SPARROW (Gr, 1964)

Native Dancer	Polynesian	Unbreakable	Sickle Blue Glass
		Black Polly	Polymelian Black Queen
	Geisha	Discovery	Display Ariadne
		Miyako	John P. Grier La Chica
Kampala	Vieux Manoir	Brantome	Blandford Vitamine
		Vieille Maison	Finglas Vieille Canaille
	Sonibai	Solario	Gainsborough Sun Worship
		Udaipur	Blandford Uganda

He raced in France. He met with a mishap early in training and could not be trained seriously. He placed a few times at 2 and 3.

8) NEVER NEVER (Ch, 1961)

Never Say Die	Nasrullah	Nearco	Pharos / Nogara
		Mumtaz Begum	Blenheim / Mumtaz Mahal
	Singing Grass	War Admiral	Man o'War / Brushup
		Boreale	Vatout / Galady II
Mixed Blessing	Brumeux	Teddy	Ajax / Rondeau
		La Brume	Alcantara II / Aquarelle
	Pot-pourri	Rose Prince	Prince Palatine / Eglantine
		Sweet Lavender	Swynford / Marchetta

4 wins in England. At 2 he ran only once. At 3 he won the St. James Stakes (1-1/2 mi) and Manton Plate (1-1/4 mi). At 4 he won the Barnet Handicap Stakes (1 mi 5 f) and Wye Handicap Stakes (1-1/2 mi).

9) ORBIT (B, 1962)

Crepello	Donatello II	Blenheim	Blandford
			Malva
		Delleana	Clarissimus
			Duccia di Buoninsegna
	Crepuscule	Mieuxce	Massine
			L'Olivete
		Red Sunset	Solario
			Dulce II
Urshalim	Nasrullah	Nearco	Pharos
			Nogara
		Mumtaz Begum	Blenheim
			Mumtaz Mahal
	Horama	Panorama	Sir Cosmo
			Happy Climax
		Lady of Aran	Orpen
			Queen of the Nore

2 wins in England and 2 wins in India. At 2 he ran only twice. At 3 he won the St. Oswald Stakes (1 mi) and Blackhall Handicap (1-1/4 mi). In India he won the Cooch Behar Cup (2200 m) and Governor's Cup (2800 m).

10) PADDYKIN (B, 1964)

St. Paddy	Aureole	Hyperion	Gainsborough Selene
		Angelola	Donatello II Feola
	Edie Kelly	Bois Roussel	Vatout Plucky Liege
		Caerlissa	Caerleon Sister Sarah
Kilifi	Relic	War Relic	Man o'War Friar's Carse
		Bridal Colors	Black Toney Vaila
	Ethelreda	Prince Chevalier	Prince Rose Chevalerie
		Blue Gem	Blue Peter Sparkle

3 wins in England. At 2 he won the Somerville Tattersall Stakes (7f). At 3 he won the Abbot's Hill Handicap Stakes (1 mi, 110 yds) and Old Chester Stakes (1 mi, 2f, 10 yds).

11) PRINCE PRADEEP (B, 1960)

Migoli	Bois Roussel	Vatout	Prince Chimay Vasthi
		Plucky Liege	Spearmint Concertina
	Mah Iran	Bahram	Blandford Friar's Daughter
		Mah Mahal	Gainsborough Mumtaz Mahal
Driving	Watling Street	Fairway	Phalaris Scapa Flow
		Ranai	Rabelais Dark Sedge
	Snow Line	Ujiji	Umidwar Theresina
		Winter Sport	Hyperion Toboggan

He won the Indian Triple Crown and 6 other races.

12) PUNJAB (Dk B, 1963)

Pardal	Pharis II	Pharos	Phalaris
			Scapa Flow
		Carissima	Clarissimus
			Casquetts
	Adargatis	Asterus	Teddy
			Astrella
		Helene de Troie	Helicon
			Lady of Pedigree
Indian Night	Umidwar	Blandford	Swynford
			Blanche
		Uganda	Bridaine
			Hush
	Fairly Hot	Solario	Gainsborough
			Sun Worship
		Fair Cop	Fairway
			Popingaol

At 2 he ran only twice in England. At 3 he placed 2nd twice, his only starts.

13) RAPPAREE (Ch, 1964)

High Treason	Court Martial	Fair Trial	Fairway Lady Juror
		Instantaneous	Hurry On Picture
	Eastern Grandeur	Gold Bridge	Swynford or Golden Boss Flying Diadem
		China Maiden	Tai-Yang Bibi Sahiba
Libertine	Ballyogan	Fair Trial	Fairway Lady Juror
		Serial	Solario Booktalk
	Travelling Flash	Winalot	Son-in-Law Gallenza
		Drifting Flame	Hurry On Fire Mist

At 2 he won the Englefield Green Nursery Handicap Plate (5f) in England. At 3 he won the Forest Handicap Plate (6f) and Newchapel Club Handicap (5f). In India he won 6 races from 1200 m to 1600 m including the Southern Command Cup (1600 m) and Sir Charles Forbes Cup (1200 m).

14) RED INDIAN (Gr, 1953)

Migoli	Bois Roussel	Vatout	Prince Chimay
			Vasthi
		Plucky Liege	Spearmint
			Concertina
	Mah Iran	Bahram	Blandford
			Friar's Daughter
		Mah Mahal	Gainsborough
			Mumtaz Mahal
Red Briar	Owen Tudor	Hyperion	Gainsborough
			Selene
		Mary Tudor II	Pharos
			Anna Bolena
	Infra Red	Ethnarch	The Tetrarch
			Karenza
		Black Ray	Black Jester
			Lady Brilliant

He won 2 races in England, the Boscawen Stakes (6f) and Sandwich Stakes (6f). He won 7 races in India up to 1600 m including the P. Natesan Memorial Cup.

15) ROMNEY (B, 1962)

```
                                            |  Prince Rose
                          | Prince Bio      |  Biologie
         | Sicambre       |
         |                |  Sif            |  Rialto
         |                |                 |  Suavita
| Shantung
         |                |                 |  Gainsborough
         |                |  Hyperion       |  Selene
         | Barley Corn    |
         |                |  Schiaparelli   |  Schiavoni
         |                |                 |  Aileen

         |                |                 |  Phalaris
         |                |  Pharos         |  Scapa Flow
         | El Greco       |
         |                |  Gay Camp       |  Gay Crusader
         |                |                 |  Parasol
| Romanella
         |                |                 |  Tracery
         |                |  Papyrus        |  Miss Matty
         | Barbara Burrini|
                          |  Bucolic        |  Buchan
                                            |  Volcanic
```

He won 3 races at 3 in Italy, the Premio Casperia (1 mi, 110 yds), Premio Villa Torlonia (1 mi, 3f) and Premio Mandela (1-1/2 mi).

16) ROYAL GLEAM (Br, 1969)

```
                                         Nasrullah        Nearco
                                                          Mumtaz Begum
                        Grey Sovereign
                                         Kong             Baytown
                                                          Clang
       Sovereign Path
                                         Bobsleigh        Gainsborough
                                                          Toboggan
                        Mountain Path
                                         Path of Peace    Winalot
                                                          Grand Peace

                                         Hyperion         Gainsborough
                                                          Selene
                        Owen Tudor
                                         Mary Tudor II    Pharos
                                                          Anna Bolena
       Tudor Gleam
                                         Nearco           Pharos
                                                          Nogara
                        Riding Rays
                                         Infra Red        Ethnarch
                                                          Black Ray
```

He won 3 races at 3 in England, the Monkgate Maiden Stakes (1 mi), Tanshelf Handicap (10f) and Bloxwich Handicap (9f).

17) SATINELLO (Ch, 1962)

Crepello	Donatello II	Blenheim	Blandford / Malva
		Delleana	Clasissimus / Duccia di Buoninsegna
	Crepuscule	Mieuxce	Massine / L'Olivete
		Red Sunset	Solario / Dulce II
Saturnetta	Hyperion	Gainsborough	Bayardo / Rosedrop
		Selene	Chaucer / Serenissima
	Chanctonbury	Papyrus	Tracery / Miss Matty
		Chincona	Buchan / Chinchilla

He won 6 races at 2, 3, 4 and 5 in France, the Prix Ormonde, Prix Barcaldine, Prix Codoman, Prix l'Express and Prix des Livres.

18) SIMEAD (Ch, 1968)

Silver Shark	Buisson Ardent	Relic	War Relic / Bridal Colors
		Rose o'Lynn	Pherozshah / Rocklyn
	Palsaka	Palestine	Fair Trial / Una
		Masaka	Nearco / Majideh
Meadow Pipit	Worden II	Wild Risk	Rialto / Wild Violet
		Sans Tares	Sind / Tara
	Rising Wings	The Phoenix	Chateau Bouscaut / Fille de Poete
		Skylarking	Precipitation / Woodlark

3 wins in England. At 3 he won the Spiddal Handicap (12f) and Cabinteely Stakes (9f). At 4 he won the Spiddal Handicap (9f).

19) VALOROSO (B, 1962)

Vimy	Wild Risk	Rialto	Rabelais La Grelee
		Wild Violet	Blandford Wood Violet
	Mimi	Black Devil	Sir Gallahad III La Palina
		Mignon	Epinard Mammee
Bellaggio	Hyperion	Gainsborough	Bayardo Rosedrop
		Selene	Chaucer Serenissima
	Belleva	Stratford	Swynford Lesbia
		Passee	Tetratema Part Worn

3 wins in England. At 2 he won the September Stakes (7f), at 3 the Newbury Summer Cup (1-1/2 mi) and at 4 the Doncaster Spring Handicap (1 mi, 6f, 132 yds). At 6 and 7 he placed 2nd in the Queen Alexandra Stakes, Royal Ascot. He also won 3 races under N.H. rules.

20) YOUNG LOCHINVAR (Ch, 1959)

Elopement	Rockefella	Hyperion	Gainsborough / Selene
		Rockfel	Felstead / Rockliffe
	Daring Miss	Felicitation	Colorado / Felicita
		Venturesome	Solario / Orlass
No Angel	Nasrullah	Nearco	Pharos / Nogara
		Mumtaz Begum	Blenheim / Mumtaz Mahal
	Fair Angela	Fair Trial	Fairway / Lady Juror
		Pomme d'Amour	Apple Sammy / Angela

He won 4 races in England, the Upend Stakes (6f), Severals Stakes (1 mi), Old Newton Cup (1-1/2 mi) and Mentmore Stakes (1-1/2 mi). He had a Timeform rating of 121.

ANSWER

Let us first study their race records. At first glance it appears that most of them possessed an ideal blend of speed and stamina. But a closer examination shows otherwise. They were essentially stayers, horses who preferred long distances. Several did not win over short distances. When we were discussing stallions, we said that a prospective stallion must possess an ideal blend of speed and stamina. These stallions fail to satisfy this very important requirement.

But this is not all. Most of these stallions did not have brilliant speed, precocious speed, another very important quality prospective stallions should possess. Several of them could not win a race at 2. At 3 and 4 they needed a distance of ground to win. They just could not excel over distances less than 1600 m.

Now we come to their pedigrees. Again at first glance everything appears to be all right. Most of them are well-bred and several are very well-bred. They were all sons of classic winners, champions or Group I winners who were successful sires, even chef-de-race sires. Their maternal and paternal grandsires were equally illustrious. We have names like: Nearco, Bois Roussel, Native Dancer, Bahram, Vieux Manoir, Nasrullah, Hyperion, Aureole, Crepello, Pharis II, Sicambre, Court Martial, Wild Risk and others.

Their tail female lines are undoubtedly top class. Nobody dare fault the families of Horama, No Angel, Romanella, Black Ray, Per Ardua, Udaipur, Chincona, Popingaol or Marchetta. Their descendants are winning the most prestigious races today.

Therefore it seems that Indian breeders have done a fairly good job, especially if we keep in mind their limited resources. They have endavoured to import moderately performed but very well-bred horses.

However a closer look at the pedigrees reveals flaws — very serious flaws. Let us focus our attention on the key positions of sire and maternal grandsire. What do we find? Do we not find unprecedented concentrations of stamina? I give below the race records of a few sires and maternal grandsires:

Norseman: 2nd Prix de l'Arc de Triomphe; 3rd French St. Leger.

Tehran: English St. Leger; 2nd Epsom Derby, Ascot Gold Cup.

Owen Tudor: Epsom Derby, Ascot Gold Cup.

St. Paddy: Epsom Derby, English St. Leger.

Elopement: 2nd English St.Leger.

Never Say Die: Epsom Derby, English St. Leger.

Brumeux: Jockey Club Cup (3600 m), Prix Edgard de la Charme (2600 m).

Marsyas II: Prix du Cadran (French equivalent of the Ascot Gold Cup) 4 times.

(Old-timers in England will be delighted that the St. Leger and Ascot Gold Cup figure prominently in the plans of Indian breeders!)

But readers are sure to object to the above analysis on two grounds. They will say: "Though the above horses stayed well, they also possessed a lot of speed. And what is more important, they were versatile sires and maternal grandsires. Secondly you cannot analyze a pedigree by isolating one horse and determining his aptitude. You must determine the aptitude of a pedigree by analyzing all the horses in it together." Both the objections are upheld. Let us analyze the above pedigrees as a whole i.e. Let us determine their D.Ps and D.Is.

Instead of calculating the D.Ps and D.Is of all the 20 stallions, I selected 6 at random and my findings are as below:

TABLE 23

Stallion	Traditional D.P	Traditional D.I
Satinello	4 - 0 - 16 - 4 - 34	0.26
Prince Pradeep	7 - 0 - 9 - 12 - 4	0.56
Mighty Sparrow	0 - 16 - 26 - 4 - 4	1.38
Young Lochinvar	18 - 4 - 7 - 1 - 2	3.92
Never Never	10 - 2 - 25 - 9 - 2	1.04
High Commission	10 - 2 - 6 - 12 - 6	0.71

These D.Is at once confirm all our findings. The pedigrees of the stallions in question are indeed dominated by horses who imparted a lot of stamina to their progeny. This is true for all the other stallions as well, as readers can check for themselves. Royal Gleam is the only stallion with a relatively high D.I. I am not saying that the above pedigrees are lacking in elements of speed. Brilliant and Intermediate chefs-de-race are present, but their influence has been more or less neutralized by the Solid and Professional. Consider the pedigree of Rapparee. Court Martial, Fair Trial and Fairway are neutralized by Hurry On, Solario and Son-in-Law! We can now sum-up our findings:

1) The stallions in question were essentially stayers. They lacked brilliant, precocious speed.

2) Stamina, rather than speed, is the dominant characteristic of their pedigrees.

What type of progeny do you think these stallions would have sired? They obviously could not have sired really top class i.e. international class sprinters or even milers. But they could have very well sired really outstanding stayers or extreme stayers. Keeping all these facts in mind readers would have come to the conclusion that a majority of Indian thoroughbreds are genuine stayers, and that long distance races are the most popular in the country. Readers will be shocked to hear that less than 5% of a crop are stayers and that long distance races are the least popular! This conclusion is confirmed by the number of horses who ran in different long distance races as below:

The Indian St. Leger has never attracted more than 5 runners since 1974. The South India St. Leger has never attracted more than 6 runners since 1961. In '70 and '77 only 2 ran In 1959, '69, '78 and '79 only 3 ran! The South India Oaks has never attracted more than 5 runners since 1973, except in 1981 when 7 ran. The Calcutta Oaks could not attract more than 6 runners since 1974. (In 1980 8 ran.) The Calcutta St. Leger's story is similar. The Queen Elizabeth II Cup could not attract more than 8 runners since 1967. For the last ten years the Byculla Club Cup has been attracting between 3 to 5 runners.

Further do not think that all the horses who ran in the above and other long distance races were true stayers. They were not. In fact the effort enfeebled several of them to such an extent that they could not win again. Ironically long distance races offer the maximum prize money!

We must now summarize what we have learnt. We established that the leading stallions of the country were stayers and were bred to stay. Yet they could not get genuine international class stayers. Why? Federico Tesio has already answered the question. Recall his words: "Speed over a long period of time means staying power, but staying power over a short period of time never means speed." Since the Indian thoroughbred lacks speed, it is unable to excel over any distance. It is inferior to the thoroughbreds of other countries. Readers may want to know why breeders persistently imported such stallions. It is because they were all anxious to breed "classic horses" i.e. horses who can stay 2400 m, or better still, 2800 m. You can't breed classic horses by importing stallions who were sprinter-milers can you? But as we have seen, since breeders ignored speed in their enthusiasm for stamina, Indian horses can neither sprint nor stay at the international level. We now come to the crux of the issue: What type of stallions must Indian breeders import in order to breed international class horses? The avowed object of importing stallions (and mares) is obviously to breed horses of international standard. (To digress a bit. In the sixties the country faced a foreign exchange crisis and the import of stallions and broodmares was banned. However F.D. Wadia, a veteran breeder, appealed directly to prime minister Jawaharlal Nehru requesting him to lift the ban. The prime minister readily agreed and allowed the import of a small number of horses every year. Incidentally the prime minister was a total horseman, deeply interested in equestrian activity. When he was in Madras he took time from his busy schedule and inaugurated the new school of the Riding Club in a very colourful function.) I have answered this question in the very next section, but I am very anxious that readers determine the answer first.

6

QUIZ 5

After studying so much about Indian stallions, we now come to one stallion who is a contrast to the others in every respect. To say that he is phenomenally successful would be an understatement. Among all the imported stallions only he (and Everyday) can claim to have brought about a significant improvement, a visible improvement, in the Indian thoroughbred. There is no need for me to sing his praise; readers can judge for themselves. The stallion in question is Grey Gaston. (Readers in India will be very angry with me for bringing up the greatest stallion in the country at the very end of the book. They would have expected me to analyze his performance much earlier. My apology for not doing so, but I waited so long as I wanted to devote a section to him exclusively. Now we can take our time and study him in detail.

GREY GASTON (Gr, 1969)

Fortino II	Grey Sovereign	Nasrullah	Nearco / Mumtaz Begum
		Kong	Baytown / Clang
	Renavalo III	Relic	War Relic / Bridal Colors
		Navarra II	Orsenigo / Nervesa
Baroda Princess	Skymaster	Golden Cloud	Gold Bridge / Rainstorm
		Discipliner	Court Martial / Edvina
	Delicious Ashaa	My Babu	Djebel / Perfume II
		Oatflake	Coup de Lyon / Avena

At 2 he won the King's Gap Maiden Plate (7f) from a field of 42 and placed 4th in the Tankerville Nursery Handicap and Lavy Shine Stakes. At 3 he won the Teddington Handicap (10f) and placed 3rd in the Britannia Stakes (Royal Ascot) and Yellow Pages Summer Cup. He was imported into India and retired to stud in 1973. In 8 crops of about 50 runners he got:

Manitou (1974, by Dusty Marta by Martial): 12 wins, champion, Indian Turf Invitation Cup, Indian Derby, Bangalore Derby, R.W.I. T.C. Ltd. Invitational Cup, Bicentenary Cup (2000 m, 4-yr-olds and over, Madras).

Track Lightning (1977, by Traxana by Sound Track): 15 wins, champion, Indian Turf Invitation Cup, Indian and Bangalore Derby, President of India Gold Cup.

Revelation (1981, by Monica by Prince Pradeep): 4 wins, champion, Charminar Challenge Indian Turf Invitation Cup, McDowell Indian Derby, Indian Oaks.

Carnival (1977, by Yoko by State Trumpeter): 7 wins, champion, Sprinters' Cup, Mysore Derby.

Enterprising (1980, by Salvation by Salvo): 5 wins, Indian Derby; 2nd Charminar Challenge Indian Turf Invitation Cup.

Nelston (1979, by Nelciana by Nelcius): 5 wins, Indian and Deccan Derby; 3rd Charminar Challenge Indian Turf Invitation Cup.

Camino (1979, by Celandine by Roan Rocket): 13 wins, Indian 2000 Guineas, Bangalore Derby and Colts Trial Stakes, President of India Gold Cup.

Blue Ice (1978, by Amber Forest by Yellow God): 9 wins, South India 1000 Guineas, 2000 Guineas and Oaks, Bangalore Fillies Trial Stakes, Mysore 2000 Guineas.

C Minor (1977, by C Major by Sea Hawk II): 7 wins, Golconda St.Leger, Bangalore Oaks, South India 1000 Guineas.

Caminetto (1980, by Celandine by Roan Rocket): 6 wins, Bangalore 1000 Guineas, Derby and Fillies Trial Stakes.

Eminence (1981, by Tina's Way by Palestine): 4 wins, Indian 1000 Guineas; 2nd McDowell Indian Derby, Indian Oaks, Bangalore Derby.

Snow (1980, by Amber Forest by Yellow God): 5 wins, Indian 1000 Guineas; 2nd Indian Oaks, Bangalore Derby and Fillies Trial Stakes.

Amber Flash (1979, by Amber Forest by Yellow God): 3 wins, South India 2000 Guineas; 2nd Bangalore Arc de Triomphe.

Tick Tock (1979, by Clocked by Compensation): 6 wins, South India 1000 Guineas, Hyderabad Fillies Trial Stakes.

In addition to the above horses he has sired several classic-placed and superior racers like Track Flame, Rose of Shiraz, Grey Flash, Quintana, Don Corleone, Aureole Queen, Trocadero, Swiss Bank, Replican, La Lagune, Galileo and Silver Meteor. (His sudden death is an irreparable loss to Indian breeding.)

But readers may not be very impressed. They will point out that Rock of Gibraltar, Prince Pradeep and Everyday were equally successful. Then what is so special about Grey Gaston? Undoubtedly his best progeny were markedly superior than the best progeny of the above three and other stallions. This is confirmed by their record-breaking runs as below:

Horse	Centre	Distance	Mins.	Secs.
Manitou	Bombay	2400 m	2	31 4/5
Manitou	Madras	2000 m	2	5 1/5
Track Lightning	Madras	2400 m	2	30 2/5
Camino	Bangalore	1600 m	1	37 1/5

I also give below a Table showing the typical times taken by the progeny of Grey Gaston and by the progeny of the twenty stallions referred to earlier.

Distance	Time taken by the progeny of Grey Gaston	Time taken by the progeny of the twenty stallions
1600 m	1-38 1/2	1-40 1/2
2000 m	2 - 6	2 - 8 1/2
2400 m	2 - 32	2-34 1/2

Clearly Grey Gaston's progeny were visibly superior. They towered over their rivals and frequently left them standing. They won the most prestigious races in the country with plenty in hand. They excelled over the entire range of distances. Without doubt Grey Gaston fulfilled the purpose for which he was imported: *To improve the Indian thoroughbred to international standard.* He has succeeded to a certain extent while dozens failed. Several have asked me why Grey Gaston was phenomenally successful. Before I answer the question, I would like you to do so. Try to determine in what way he is different from the twenty stallions we discussed earlier. (I will give you a clue: Study his pedigree.) If you answer this question you will be able to answer the next easily: "Which type of stallions must be imported into the country? What qualities must they necessarily possess in order to be breed-shaping?" (I will give you another clue: These stallions must be capable of getting outstanding racers out of daughters of the twenty stallions discussed earlier.)

ANSWER

Several have tried to explain Grey Gaston's staggering success. Different ideas have been presented. It is necessary for us to study all of them before we can come to a conclusion.

"One expert felt that Grey Gaston had acclimatized himself well in his new home and was therefore successful."

There is a kernel of truth in this view. If a stallion is to succeed he must acclimatize himself well. While several do so very quickly, others do not. But would it not be far-fetched to attribute all his success to the fact that he settled down well? Surely he is not the only stallion who settled down well? Therefore we must look elsewhere for the answer.

"Another emphasized that Grey Gaston's progeny were reared on scientific lines."

Again, there is a grain of truth in this view. The importance of scientific management can hardly be stressed. Foals and yearlings must be looked-after well. Farm management must be of very high order. But again can scientific management by itself produce classic winners and champions? Obviously not. The horses must possess inherent talent. While scientific breeding and training will help this talent blossom, it is not a substitute for it.

A third quickly presented this view: "Grey Gaston had excellent mares; in fact most of them are got-abroad. Therefore it is not surprising that he did well."

This explanation seems to be the most plausible. We must research deeper. The fact is most of the dams of Grey Gaston's classic winners are got-abroad mares. But Grey Gaston is not the only stallion in the country who served got-abroad mares. Almost every stud farm in the country has got-abroad mares, and therefore most stallions serve them. We saw that Rapparee and Satinello served a lot of got-abroad mares. Then why weren't they as successful? I will go a step further. Readers can take my word that the got-abroad mares served by other stallions were superior to the got-abroad mares served by Grey Gaston! There is no doubt in my mind about it. Therefore Grey Gaston himself was the principal architect of his success. He is an enormously talented stallion. Make no mistake about it.

The above conclusion is confirmed by the fact that he could get classic winners out of Indian mares too. Revelation and Carnival are examples. Monica, the dam of Revelation, is absolutely top class. She won only 3 races but placed 2nd in the Indian 1000 Guineas. Her sire Prince Pradeep and maternal grandsires Rock of Gibraltar and Flower Dust were very successful. Her grandam Remembrance won the Indian Oaks. Her greatgrandam Nava Ratna won the Indian 1000 Guineas and Oaks. Therefore Revelation's success is not at all surprising.

But the same cannot be said of Yoko, Martini (dam of Swiss Bank) and May Day (dam of La Lagune). They cannot claim to be Inherently superior. Therefore Grey Gaston is prepotent as well. But as most of his mares are got-abroad there was no need for him to use his prepotence.

We now come to the answer. The answer is in his pedigree. Let us analyze it. At once it seems different, radically different, from the pedigrees we studied earlier. Let us first focus our attention on his sire and grandsires.

Fortino II was a stakes winner of 8 races in France including the Prix de l'Abbaye de Longchamp (5 furlongs, Group I, Longchamp). His maternal grandsire Skymaster won 7 races including the Middle Park Stakes, Windsor Castle Stakes and Stewards Cup. His paternal grandsire Grey Sovereign was another horse of great speed who won 8 races.

Now look at the other horses in his pedigree: Nasrullah/Nearco, Relic/War Relic, Golden Cloud/Gold Bridge, Court Martial and My

Babu/Djebel. What type of horses were they? Were they all St. Leger and Ascot Gold Cup winners? And more importantly what qualities did they impart to their pregeny? Did they impart a lot of stamina (like the horses in the pedigrees we studied earlier) thereby enabling them to develop into stayers and extreme stayers? On the contrary we find that almost all of them imparted brilliant, precocious speed! This, was their hallmark.

Therefore Grey Gaston's pedigree has unprecedented concentrations of brilliant, precocious speed in complete contrast to the pedigrees of all the other stallions which have unprecedented concentrations of stamina!

The above conclusion can be easily verified by calculating his D.P and D.I. But I must warn readers — you are going to get a shock. The chefs-de-race in his 4-generation pedigree are:

Chef-de-race	Aptitudinal Group
Grey Sovereign	Brilliant
Nasrullah	Brilliant
My Babu	Brilliant
Nearco	Brilliant and Classic
Court Martial	Brilliant
Djebel	Intermediate

Allotting points in the usual manner we find that his D.P. is:

$$19 - 2 - 1 - 0 - 0$$

Therefore his D.I. $= \dfrac{21.5}{0.5} = 43.0$

This figure is truly mind-boggling, unbelievable, unprecedented. But we can go further. Imagine for a moment that Nearco is a Brilliant chef-de-race and not Brilliant and Classic. Then what will Grey Gaston's D.P be? It will be:

$$20 - 2 - 0 - 0 - 0$$

Therefore his D.I $= \dfrac{22}{0} = \infty$ — Infinity!

After readers have recovered from the shock they are sure to ask: ''Can there be a horse with infinite D.I?'' Most certainly there can. A horse with only Brilliant and Intermediate chefs-de-race will have an infinite D.I, as any positive quantity divided by zero is infinity. (This is the answer to the question I asked earlier.)

Now we have to interpret infinite D.I or very high D.I. Clearly horses with very high D.Is lack stamina. In this way their pedigrees are unbalanced. But if this is true, how did Grey Gaston sire record-breaking stayers? "Surely", readers will say, "he must have sired a set of brilliant sprinters." This question is easily answered.

Look at his pedigree once again. Though the stallions in it were noted for imparting brilliant, precocious speed, their progeny could carry that speed up to 1600 m and sometimes over even longer distances. And do not forget, speed carried over a distance is stamina. For example Fortino II himself was the sire of horses like Caro (French 2000 Guineas, Prix Ganay; 3rd Prix du Jockey Club), Pidget (Irish 1000 Guineas and St. Leger), No Mercy (champion European sprinter), Fortissimo (winner between 1-1/2 and 2 miles), Fine Blade (Duke of Edinburgh Stakes, Waterford Stakes), Shamson (Premio Presidente della Republica) and Knockroe (Yorkshire Cup).

The second reason for his success in getting stayers lies in Indian mares. I have been stressing that Indian stallions possessed tremendous concentrations of stamina. Their daughters too are obviously similar. Therefore it would not be an exaggeration to say that the Indian thoroughbred is "overstout". Therefore if a stallion is to sire top class racers out of Indian mares, he must be able to neutralize the overstoutness first. Naturally only "overbrilliant" stallions like Grey Gaston will be able to do so. After neutralizing the overstoutness the stallions must still be able to impart some brilliance to the offspring. Then he will have an ideal blend of brilliance and stoutness ,and will be able to excel over the entire range of distances. This is precisely what Grey Gaston did.

I am most anxious to say that a "normal" stallion will not be able to overcome the overstoutness. All his brilliance will go in neutralizing the overstoutness, and he will not have any residual brilliance left to give the offspring. Therefore the offspring, completely lacking brilliance, can only be a mediocre performer.

We are now in a position to pinpoint horses who will make admirable stallions in the country. Recall the conditions we laid down earlier for stallion selection. Among the conditions I would like to stress one: The horse must have possessed brilliant speed as a 2-yr-old. He must have won over 1000 m or 1200 m and then raced in prestigious races for 2-yr-olds. At 3 he must have carried his speed up to 2000 m. His pedigree must naturally satisfy the conditions we laid down. In addition he must satisfy one more which is the most important: He must have a high D.I, the higher the better. His D.I must exceed 5, which can be taken as the cut-off point. There is no doubt in my mind that such stallions and only such stallions can be breed-shaping in the truest sense of the term. Only they can raise the Indian thoroughbred to international standard. Others cannot.

Sons of Raise a Native, Never Bend and Mill Reef, Noholme II and Nodouble, Intentionally and In Reality, T.V. Lark, Nashua, Habitat and grandsons of Nearctic and Bold Ruler are sure to excel in the country. The maternal grandsires too must be among the above horses i.e. the sire, maternal and paternal grandsires should be Brilliant or Intermediate chefs-de-race, or horses close to that status. Only then will the stallion be able to impart sufficient brilliance. Solid and Professional chefs-de-race should be conspicuous by their absence, or not contribute more than a handful of points.

Readers in India can easily check whether recently imported stallions satisfy the above conditions. Sad to say, most of them do not. It seems breeders are still importing St. Leger/Ascot Gold Cup horses. Therefore it is not surprising that they are unable to make a big impact. They are unable to sire superior racers of the calibre of Manitou or Revelation, let alone horses of international standard. But it is never too late to implement new ideas, new theories. If breeders scrupulously adhere to the above rules, every stud farm in the country can have a stallion like Grey Gaston!

A few may maintain that Indian breeders will find it very difficult to import horses who satisfy the above conditions due to their limited resources. I refuse to subscribe to this view. In fact it has been the other way round. Breeders have gone out of their way to import St. Leger/Ascot Gold Cup horses, labouring under the impression that only they can sire superior stock. If it is not possible to satisfy all the conditions, go close to satisfying as many conditions as possible. Remember that high D.I stallions with precocious speed must be imported until the overstoutness in the Indian thoroughbred is removed. The moment overstoutness is removed, breeders can start importing stallions with normal D.Is.

Readers may be surprised to hear that this problem is not unique to the Indian thoroughbred. The German thoroughbred too is overstout as breeders there neglected speed and gave undue importance to stamina. This point is stressed by David Conolly-Smith* who wrote: "German bloodstock has a crying need for sires who are able to impart precocity and speed to their stock. . . ."

Experienced readers may be wondering whether it is advisable to breed

* "Precocity and speed needed by the German Bloodstock Industry", *The European Racehorse*, December 1984.

horses with very high D.Is. After all, it is not difficult to breed horses with crosses of Bold Ruler, Nasrullah, Raise a Native, Royal Charger, Native Dancer, Never Bend, Northern Dancer and others. I cannot recommend such breeding. Overbrilliance like overstoutness is very harmful to the breed. We will study the havoc it is wreaking a little later. We must all endeavour to breed horses with an ideal blend of brilliance and stoutness. Any deviation is very injurious to the breed.

We have just solved an important problem by using the concept of dosage. Note that the problem cannot be solved without applying the concept. Mere study of the pedigrees of the imported stallions yields no information. As I said, there is apparently nothing wrong with them. They are all nicely bred. But the mist cleared the moment we applied the principle of dosage. We proved conclusively that the Indian thoroughbred is overstout. We then identified the type of stallions who could neutralize this overstoutness and get superior racers. But a few readers may still be unconvinced. I urge them to wait. The very next section will confirm all our findings.

You must therefore make use of dosage in all your work. Calculate the D.Is of different groups of progenitors and racers. Several intractable problems will be solved.

7

This is the story of Star Kingdom, the horse who revolutionized Australian breeding and who made a lasting impact world-wide. I have written it specially for the benefit of breeders in India and therefore implore them to pay the fullest attention. Star Kingdom gloriously vindicates all that we have learnt.

		Hyperion	Gainsborough
			Selene
	Stardust		
		Sister Stella	Friar Marcus
			Etolle
Star Kingdom (Ch, 1946)			
		Concerto	Orpheus
			Constellation
	Impromptu		
		Thoughtless	Papyrus
			Virgin's Folly

He was bred in England. He was purchased by Wilfred Harvey at the Tattersalls Doncaster Sale (1947) and sent to trainer Jack Waugh. An outstanding 2-yr-old, he started off with a bang by winning 3 races over 5 furlongs. He then had to face the great Abernant in the National Breeders'

Produce Stakes. Both the horses gave everything they had and went locked past the winning post. The jockey of Star Kingdom was sure he had won, but the judge gave the race to Abernant — there was no photo-finish in those days. Star Kingdom then won the Richmond Stakes (6f) and Gimcrack Stakes (6f). He was rated 131 lbs. in the Free Handicap, only 2 lbs. below leader Abernant.

As a 3-yr-old he started by winning the Greenham Stakes (7f). In the 2000 Guineas Abernant and he were strongly fancied, but both had no answer to Nimbus. Star Kingdom then won the Jersey Stakes (7f) and Hungerford Stakes and in-between was a poor 3rd to Abernant in the July Cup. At 4 he won the Coronation Stakes (6f), his only success. Clearly he was an outstanding 2-yr-old who trained-on to excel up to 7 furlongs at 3 and 4.

Stanley Wootten must enter the story at this stage. An experienced trainer based at Epsom, his knowledge of breeding was total. In the words of Timothy T. Capps*: "Stanley Wootten was convinced that he had found, in Star Kingdom, an ideal horse to sire fast-maturing stock and nick well with the stoutly oriented sire lines then dominant in Australia. Accordingly, he purchased the horse from Harvey in 1951 and took him down under. . . ." He was a staggering success. He was champion stallion 5 times, champion juvenile stallion 7 times and champion maternal grandsire 3 times. He got 61 stakes winners and 14 champions from only 374 named foals. His progeny pulverized the opposition. They included:

> **Skyline:** won A.J.C. Derby in record time of 2-28.8 for 1-1/2 miles. He was champion 3-yr-old.
>
> **Todman:** 10 wins from only 12 starts at 2, 3 and 5, co-champion 2-yr-old, A.J.C. December Stakes. He established a course record by covering 5f in 0-57.8.
>
> **Sky High II** (full-brother to Skyline): 29 wins from 5f to 12f, setting course records over 9f (1-49.1) and 10f (2-00.75).
>
> **Noholme II** (full-brother to Todman): 12 wins, Horse of the Year at 3, Champagne Stakes, December Juvenile Handicap, Epsom Handicap (he covered the mile in 1-34.9), Linlithgow Stakes.
>
> **Fine and Dandy:** champion 2-yr-old. At 4 he ran a mile in 1-34.4.

His superior racers included **Kingster** (champion 2-yr-old), **Star Over** (champion 2-yr-old), **Time and Tide** (leading sprinter-miler) and several others.

---

* "From start to finish he was a shining star from Down Under", *The Thoroughbred Record*, 23 March 1983.

We must now pause. Note the class and aptitude of the above horses. "Weren't they international-class racers who dazzled over the entire range of distances? Are you now willing to concede that even a 7 furlong horse can be a breed-shaping sire and get horses who excel over the entire range of distances? Will you deny that Stanley Wootten was dead on target when he felt that the Australian thoroughbred was stout and therefore required brilliant, precocious speed? Will you disagree with me if I say that the Indian thoroughbred today is exactly where the Australian thoroughbred was before the arrival of Star Kingdom? *Clearly stallions like Star Kingdom, and only stallions like Star Kingdom, can improve the Indian thoroughbred.* All that we emphasized in the earlier section is cent percent correct. If breeders adhere to the rules we laid down, I am sure we will get our Star Kingdom sooner, rather than later. I am convinced that every breeder in the country can breed horses of the above calibre.

Coming back to Star Kingdom, we find that his sons are continuing the good work. Todman was champion juvenile sire (twice) and champion maternal grandsire. Another son Biscay was champion juvenile sire and developed into a sire of sires. His grandsons too are equally talented. Bletchingly, by Biscay, was champion sire thrice. Zephyr Bay also by Biscay was champion juvenile sire in New Zealand and Luskin Star by Kaoru Star was leading first-crop sire in Australia. In fact in the 1985 Australian Premier Yearling Sale at Sydney, Star Kingdom was represented by 4 sons, 17 grandsons and 6 great-grandsons!

The influence of Star Kingdom is not restricted to Australia and New Zealand. Noholme II and Nodouble have been mentioned. The former, without being fashionable, managed to sire 51 stakes winners including 4 champions. The latter (his son) won 13 races (including the Arkansas Derby) and became champion handicap horse at 4 and 5. He is already the sire of 51 stakes winners and topped the North American Sires list in 1981. Another son of Noholme II, Shecky Greene was a champion sprinter who won 15 races. He is the sire of 25 stakes winners. This proves that Star Kingdom was truly breed-shaping.

The beneficial influence of Star Kingdom has not yet reached India. Breeders must therefore start making plans to import suitable progenitors. (Incidentally I cannot understand why breeders go only to England to import breeding stock. The time has come to visit U.S.A, Canada, France, Australia and New Zealand. They have much more to offer.) There is one more beneficial factor. Star Kingdom produced superior racers out of mares with Hyperion i.e. inbreeding to Hyperion seemed beneficial. If his descendants exhibit the same trait, they are sure to excel in the country.

It would be fitting if a descendant of Star Kingdom gives to Indian breeding what Star Kingdom gave Australian breeding.

8

In the earlier sections I was emphasizing that breeders are making every effort to upgrade the Indian thoroughbred to international standard. One of the reasons why they have not succeeded till now lies in the system of racing in the country. Most surprisingly this crucial factor does not seem to have caught the attention of breeders or owners. You will readily agree that the system of racing, the standard and quality of racing greatly influence the breed. You cannot separate racing from breeding. You cannot have top class breeding without top class racing. In the words of Joseph A. Estes*: "The conditions of racing will determine the shape of the breed."

Is the system of racing in India guaranteed to bring out the best in horses? Is it modern? Is it scientific? Sad to say, it is not. It is totally obsolete and hopelessly out of date. In fact it has done immense harm to the Indian thoroughbred. Readers will be astounded and aghast to know that it actually discourages horses from performing instead of giving encouragement. I doubt whether any other country in the world follows such a system.

Instead of dwelling on its deficiencies and drawbacks, let us concentrate on the alternative. (Incidentally you cannot blame the system per se. It was not designed for Indian thoroughbreds. It was meant to accommodate the large number of got-abroad horses who came into the country to race before independence.) The alternative is of course a true Pattern, race and Allowance race system, as in the principal racing countries. In fact there is a desperate need for such a system. Remember the country has emerged as a major thoroughbred producer by breeding over a thousand foals a year. Any delay in introducing the new system will be most detrimental. Merely giving Group race status to a few races will not do. The existing system must be scrapped altogether and replaced by a new system designed on scientific lines.

Firstly the race clubs must get together and constitute a "Pattern Race Committee" as in other countries. The Committee must study the systems of racing in different parts of the world and then evolve a system most suitable for the country. Introducing a new system is not going to be easy. It cannot be done by one race club. All the clubs must act in unison. But

---

* Quoted by John R. Gaines in *The Thoroughbred Record*, 28 December 1983.

with a little determination a new system can be introduced with great success.

There is no need for us to go into all the details here. They can be worked out by the experts. Here I would only like to say that there is a valuable spin-off. When the Pattern race system is introduced, each of the Pattern races can be sponsored. No doubt we are moving in this direction. Several races in the country have attracted sponsors. There is no doubt in my mind that the Pattern race system will double the number of owners (who are now totally frustrated and are therefore unwilling to invest in horses even though they love the sport) thereby doubling the demand for horses and treble the incomes of the race clubs and governments.

9

Major David Swannell is an unhappy man writes Peter Willett*. The reason for his unhappiness is the regression in the thoroughbred. The regression is obvious through the ''International Classifications'' formulated by Major Swannell himself. The horses of England, France and Ireland are classified every year according to age, and the 3-yr-olds and 4-yr-olds and over are further subdivided according to distance. In 1977, 148 horses were worthy of inclusion in the classifications, whereas in 1982 the number crashed to 57! While this concerns only England, France and Ireland, the situation in the U.S.A. is no better. They are in direct straits. In Italy the regression is almost complete. Australia, New Zealand and South America seem to be holding their own.

Let us try to determine the reasons for the regression. Do not try to minimize the gravity of the situation. The regression is eating into the vials of the industry. It bodes ill for all of us.

The regression is due to the entry of ''fashion'' into thoroughbred breeding. I am unable to say when exactly this happened, but since then it has been a rapid down-hill journey all the way. The pernicious influence of fashion is as below:

Certain sires and sire lines suddenly become fashionable. Every breeder rushes to take advantage of them, completely ignoring the fact that they may not be very compatible with his mares. Such progeny cannot hope to be superior, but this does not seem to worry breeders in the least, who then concentrate on ''marketing'' them. If a majority of horses are bred this way, a regression is inevitable.

---

* ''Innovator Swannell saddened by regression in the thoroughbred'', *Horse and Hound*, December 24, 1982.

Fashion has also condemned stayers and extreme stayers as freaks and their breeders as renegades. Till recently breeders took pride in, and made every effort, to breed horses who excelled over the entire range of distances. But no more. Stamina has become dirty. A horse with an ideal blend of speed and stamina is a liability and not an asset! Until a few years ago horses who ran in the Epsom Derby used to meet again in the St. Leger. But no more. In fact things have come to such a pass that a small but vociferous group want to tamper with the race, ostensibly to make it more competitive! Mercifully their "revolutionary" advice has been rejected, but when are we going to regain our balance? Overemphasis on speed and neglect of stamina is most detrimental to the breed. In fact the ill-effects are already visible. We will discuss this point, which is of awesome importance, in the very next section.

Overcommercialization has also contributed to the regression. We all know owners who really raced their horses, who tested their horses. But not any more. The fact that horses are prematurely rushed to stud is only half the story. Owners seem to be interested only in the horse's stud value throughout his racing career. His natural talent and aptitude are virtually ignored. Owners have also lost traditional values. Even the classics don't seem to interest them. Kentucky Derby winner Spend a Buck did not run in the Preakness!

The decline of the owner-breeder has greatly accelerated the regression. Few will deny that most owner-breeders were men and women of rare talent. Each of them methodically and painstakingly developed a very specialized and sophisticated breeding theory. They were willing to experiment fearlessly. This naturally resulted in a profusion of outstanding horses with different pedigrees, different aptitudes; horses who enriched the breed. Can anybody fail to recognize an "Aga" pedigree, a "Derby" pedigree or a "Boussac" pedigree? As owners they raced their horses sympathetically, but at the same time tested them fully.

But no more. The owner-breeders have been replaced by syndicates and corporations. There is absolutely nothing wrong in this, but the question is will they be able to innovate and experiment fearlessly? Remember they have to keep an eye on the bottom-line. Inevitably they play safe. They are very orthodox in all their actions.

At this stage the uninformed or the short-sighted may ask: "So what if there is a regression?" They do not realize that the regression is showing in the bottom-line the world over. The popularity of racing is decreasing steadily. Less fans means less income to the race clubs which in turn means less stake money to the owners. This forces owners to decrease their investment in horses, which means less money to the breeders. Therefore every segment of racing and breeding is under tremendous strain. Do not think you are immune from it.

It is not difficult to halt the regression. In fact it must be halted before it is too late. Firstly owners, especially owners of classic winners and champions, must race their horses fearlessly. They must race at 4. They must not rush their horses to stud after a single defeat, saying that something has gone wrong. Do not forget your duty towards racegoers who are very anxious to see their stars. Secondly we must respect all aptitudes. We must give an equal chance to all horses. Similarly we must give a fair chance to all stallions and mares. And last but not least, owners must strain to develop their own breeding theories. For this is the only way to enrich the breed. Would it not be disastrous if every breeder followed fashion and adopted more or less the same breeding program? No doubt there will still be classic winners and champions, but will it benefit the breed?

10

The Breeders' Cup Series is undoubtedly the most important innovation to have taken place in the thoroughbred world in the last decade. The Board of Directors, heartened by the spontaneous response, have framed an ambitious program. As I am writing these lines several important matters are being debated, sorted and settled. Further changes are inevitable. Still I would like to make a suggestion, which I feel is extremely important.

The Breeders' Cup Series scheduled for October 1984 features seven races up to 1-1/2 miles. The absence of a 1-3/4 mile or, better still, a 2 mile race is shocking. It is the same old story; give extreme stayers a bad name and hang them. It has apparently not occurred to anyone that a percentage of thoroughbreds foaled every year (however small it may be) will be extreme stayers due to their temperament, if for no other reason. Even if each and every breeder strives to breed sprinter-milers, a handful of horses will turn out to be stayers or extreme stayers. Therefore to do justice to them, it is necessary to organize long distance races. There are a handful of races for stayers and extreme stayers in Europe, but U.S.A is deficient in this respect. Further do not forget that a number of progenitors are predisposed to producing stayers or extreme stayers irrespective of their aptitudes and pedigrees. Therefore a 1-3/4 mile or 2 mile race in the Breeders' Cup Series would do justice to all thoroughbreds.

But there is an even more important reason why long and extreme distance races should be retained, nay encouraged. *Continuous emphasis on short and middle-distance races inevitably leads to skewed development of the breed.* This is not a glib statement. Sufficient evidence is available to show that the American thoroughbred has become dangerously overbrilliant. What exactly do I mean by this? Recall the D.Is calculated by Dr. Roman for select performance categories. Did you ponder over them for some time at least? What did you think? In particular what do you think about the D.Is of sprinters (5.61) and 2-yr-old stakes winners (5.59)? Aren't they on the high side? Let us discuss the behaviour of horses with such high D.Is.

Clearly brilliant, precocious speed will be the dominant characteristic of such a horse. He is sure to come to hand early and excel at 2 up to 7 furlongs. But what will happen at 3 and 4? Will he improve and mature? Will he train on well? Will he be able to carry his speed over longer distances? With such a high D.I it is most unlikely. Even at 3 and 4 he will be forced to compete up to 8 furlongs only.

But readers may not see anything wrong in this. If this individual is unable to carry his speed, others with lesser D.ls will be able to do so. Unfortunately most of the others too have high D.Is: Middle distance stakes winners — 4.16 and older horses — 4.41. The net result of these high D.Is is that most American horses seem to peak at 3 years and several at 2 years itself! They dazzle at 2 but are unable to train on at 3, much less at 4. In other words they "burn-out" even at 3. This is due to lack of stamina. *The lack of stamina not only prevents them from staying, but more seriously, prevents them from maturing into sound, robust horses at 3 and 4. What I am trying to say is that even sprinter-milers require an element of stamina.* But American sprinter-milers seem to have lost that element. This conclusion of mine is confirmed by two phenomena. (Here I would like to stress that the D.Is of classic winners (2.43) male champions [all ages] (2.65) and stayers (3.04) are perfect. It is the D.Is of the others that are on the high side.)

Firstly note that European bred horses are sweeping prestigious races for older horses in the U.S.A, over the entire range of distances. There is really no need for me to give examples. This clearly shows that American breds are unable to give their best at 4. They are frequently outclassed. However note that American breds are winning a high proportion of prestigious races for 2 and 3-yr-olds not only in the U.S.A but also in Europe!

Secondly there seems to be an alarming increase in setbacks and injuries. American horses are not what they were. They are less healthy, less robust. Can such a trend be allowed to continue? Is it not the duty of breeders to produce horses who are able to race soundly at 2, 3 and 4? I am convinced that this unhealthy trend is partly due to overbrilliance. Readers would have noted that the make-up of the American thoroughbred is diametrically opposite that of the Indian thoroughbred, which we found to be overstout. Both are harmful to the breed and remedial measures must be quickly taken. In the case of the Indian thoroughbred, we stressed the need to increase brilliance by increasing the D.I. Naturally the opposite must be done for the American thoroughbred. American breeders must decrease the overbrilliance by decreasing the D.I. I suggest an upper limit of 4. Breeders must see that the D.Is of the horses they breed does not exceed 4. This can be easily done as there are sufficient progenitors in the U.S.A.

Similarly we can say that a D.I of 2 is the safe lower limit. If the D.I is outside this range, the breed becomes overstout or overbrilliant, and all the adverse effects will automatically follow.

Quite a few readers may doubt the validity of the above arguments. They will say that there is absolutely nothing wrong with the American thoroughbred, and that the more brilliant it is the better. My reply is: "Is there no limit to brilliance? If you think there is no limit, you need not stop with a D.I of 5. You can go all the way to infinity (remember Grey Gaston) by breeding horses with only Brilliant and Intermediate chefs-de-race. Since such progenitors are available, you will have no difficulty in doing so." But is it really advisable to breed horses with all speed and no stamina? Theoretically one part of speed and one part of stamina is the ideal blend of speed and stamina, but we saw that this is not the case. Undoubtedly up to four parts of speed and one part of stamina is most beneficial.

But why did the American thoroughbred become overbrilliant? It is because race clubs, consciously or unconsciously, kept encouraging sprinter-milers by framing lucrative races for them and ignored stayers and extreme stayers. There is only one Grade I race over 1-3/4 miles (San Juan Capistrano) in the U.S.A, while there should be at least half-adozen. Therefore breeders naturally concentrated on producing brilliant horses and ignored stoutness altogether. (Recall the words of Joseph A. Estes.) To redress the balance prestigious races over 1-3/4 miles and 2 miles should be organized. Naturally one such race should be included in the Breeders' Cup Series. This will be incentive enough to breed genuine stayers and extreme stayers.

The avowed intention of the Breeders' Cup is to bring together the best horses in the world. Most North American breds are eligible. Most European breds are also eligible, thanks to the cross-registration agreement with the European Breeders' Fund. But what about the others? To make the Series truly international the Board of Directors can "invite" one horse each from Asia, Africa, South America and Australia/New

Zealand to take part in any one event. This will make the Breeders' Cup Series a true world championship.

I hasten to add that the above suggestions may be premature, as plans are yet to be finalized. I am, like innumerable others, really looking forward to October 1984.

11

The motion-picture industry which produced scores of brilliant actors, actresses, directors, musicians, singers and photographers could produce only one genius — Charlie Chaplin. The breeding industry too, which was responsible for dozens of outstanding breeders, owners, trainers and jockeys, could produce only one genius — Federico Tesio. I do not think anybody in the breeding or racing world is unaware of Senator Tesio's staggering achievements. A lot has been written about him. His champions have been studied in detail and his breeding theories analyzed threadbare. Here I am anxious to stress only one factor, which I consider to be the most significant — his versatility. *Federico Tesio was a versatile genius.* No other individual combined so many roles so successfully and, needless to say, it will be very difficult for others to even try.

Tesio was a total horseman. He was a breeder, owner and trainer. He won a staggering 73 classics (remember that there are only five classics in Italy) including an unprecedented 20 victories in the Italian Derby. Yet his stud farm in Dormello, on the banks of the lake Maggiore, did not average more than a dozen Foals a year! Tesio worked directly with his horses from dawn to dusk. He did not brook the interference of managers, assistant trainers or head lads. He himself gave all instructions to his jockeys. This enabled him to get an unparalleled insight into the character, behaviour and aptitude of horses. He understood horses like no one ever did, or is likely to do.

But Tesio's knowledge was not all practical. He was an outstanding theorist and Turf-historian too. I do not think any other individual has analyzed thoroughbred pedigrees to the extent he did. He analyzed 5-generation and frequently 7-generation pedigrees. His research took him to the very origin of the breed. He understood and applied principles which we are just mastering. A couple of examples will be of great interest.

Tesio was very alert for nicks. He identified several such as the Bend Or (sire) x Macaroni (maternal grandsire), Galopin (sire) x Hampton (maternal grandsire) and Isonomy (sire, chef-de-race) x Hermit (chef-de-race). He made use of the last nick. There was a mediocre stallion called Melanion by Hermit in Italy. Tesio went to England and purchased a grand-daughter of Isonomy, with the specific intention of breeding her to Melanion. Naturally he would have made sure that the mare was compatible with Melanion in several other respects too. He would have also determined that the beneficial effects of the nick would overcome the deficiencies of the progenitors, Melanion in particular. Needless to say, Tesio was correct. The offspring Guido Reni (1908) was his first Derby winner!

We need not go into all the theories formulated by Tesio here. But I am very anxious to give one of his observations to show how far ahead of his time he was: "A mixture of oil, salt and vinegar is pleasant in any salad. Coffee, salt and vinegar invariably form a repulsive mixture." Readers should strive to understand the above statement. What exactly did Tesio have in mind?

There is yet another dimension to his personality. He was a scientist and biologist in the truest sense. He was, in fact, attracted to thoroughbreds as he considered them most ideal to study heredity. He was not a mere breeder but a fearless experimenter. He possessed extraordinary powers of observation. He studied each horse as an individual. He studied the intelligence and instinct of horses. He also studied horses in their natural state.

Interestingly he was also an explorer. In his youth he travelled far and wide in search of adventure, but only where he could be with his beloved horses. He explored the interior of Patagonia on horseback. He was also an amateur steeplechase jockey and rode about 500 races in Europe.

Tesio did not straightaway start breeding classic winners and champions. He readily admitted that he made mistakes and was in fact forced to reject most of his original progenitors. It took him more than a decade to stabilize his operations. He then bred national champions and only then international champions like Nearco (1935). Clearly he did not take any short cuts. He started at the very beginning, studying each and every aspect (both theoretical and practical) until he was fully satisfied. Therefore he progressed steadily but surely, reaching a height no breeder has reached or is likely to reach. Further do not forget that Tesio did not spend large sums of money on stallions and mares. He sold most of his best horses. Most of his mares were cheaply purchased.

Tesio's horses confirm his genius. They were not just classic winners or even champions. They were superior sires, sires of sires. Their influence has spread to every corner of the world. It is not difficult to breed a superior racer or even a classic winner. Hundreds have done so. But can you breed champion sires and sires of sires who are capable of making a lasting impact on the breed?

Tesio was not superhuman. (As in most cases his genius was 99%

perspiration and 1% inspiration.) In fact a handful of his theories are incorrect. This brings us us to the point. If you are unwilling to innovate and experiment fearlessly, how will you progress? We too can try to reach Tesio's high standards. But we must take up one area at a time. It would be unwise and foolish on our part to study several areas simultaneously. Once you feel that you have mastered a particular area, you can take up another.

In conclusion I would like to quote the beautiful words of Edward Spinola*: "But in Italy and throughout the world the breed of the thoroughbred will carry the indelible mark of his influence, for the little foals who ran their first races in the green pastures of Dormello have already taken their place in the pedigrees of many a great race-horse of today and of tomorrow."

12

Whenever we talk of team-sports we instinctively think of cricket, football, hockey etc. We rarely think of racing even though it is no less a team-sport than the above-mentioned. How is racing a team-sport? Who are the players? A "racing team" is made up of thefollowing:

1) Owner (captain)
2) Trainer
3) Jockey
4) Turf historian
5) Veterinary doctor
6) Assistant trainer
7) Head man
8) Travelling Head man
9) Syce
10) Farrier
11) Work rider

Let us discuss the role of each player. The owner (or owners) who is naturally the captain of the team, has to play the biggest role and shoulder the greatest responsibility. (Note that there cannot be a team without an owner!) The owner's first responsibility is to ensure a supply of good horses to his team year after year. To do so he has got to be very knowledgeable. He has got to plan well, budget well. He must stabilize his operation at the required level. His objective must be to continue being an owner for

---

* *Breeding the Racehorse,* by Frederico Tesio, edited and translated by Edward Spinola.

as long as he desires. But frequently this is not the case. We find owners coming in with a bang but going out with a whimper.

The owner's next responsibility is to bring out the best in his horses. He must plan their careers meticulously and race them sympathetically, neither over-racing nor under-racing them. This is easier said than done, but several owners have mastered this difficult art.

We now come to an important point. An owner must cooperate well with other team members and bind his team into a single unit, working steadfastly towards a single goal. But frequently we find that owners and trainers are working at cross-purposes, with the result their horses do not even Will half the races they should. Such teams are going to break up sooner or later.

An ideal owner docs not put pressure on his team. Instead he should gently and unobtrusively pinpoint errors, rectify defects and eliminate short-comings.

An owner's responsibility increases dramatically when things are going badly and the fortunes of the team are at a low ebb. At such a critical juncture he must be a tower of strength. Did not scores of leaders hold and inspire their teams in the most desperate circumstances to unprecedented victories?

There is no need for me to stress the duties of trainers and jockeys; instead I will focus on the Turf historian.

Why is a Turf historian included in the team? What can he do that an owner or trainer cannot? His first job is to analyze pedigrees at the auction sales. As we have seen, this is a specialized task. Since a Turf historian follows the progress of scores of sires and maternal grandsires and hundreds of broodmares, he will be able to do a better job than most others. Further he would have mastered the principles of breeding and racing. Then a Turf historian can prepare a sophisticated buying program, tailor-made to the owner's requirements. The owner must be very clear on the type, types of horses he wants to buy. Is he interested in classic contenders or handicappers? Sprinters or stayers? A Turf historian can also minimize risks. He can help an owner ''play-safe'' or be ''adventurous''.

(Turf historians with their vast and in-depth knowledge of breeding can also make an immense contribution in stud farms. Every breeder must have a Turf historian by his side when he is finalizing his breeding program. His views on the class and compatibility of the progenitors will be invaluable. He can prepare a powerful breeding program for each of the mares. He can also help the breeder buy new stallions and mares.)

I am convinced that an owner, trainer or breeder however knowledgeable cannot replace a Turf historian, as they have their own day-to-day responsibilities. Remember that a Turf historian is working full-time. Undeniably he can give owners and breeders an edge over the others. The duties of a veterinary doctor are well known. Here I will emphasize only one aspect. The veterinary doctor must he a good judge of the conformation of yearlings. He must have a keen eye. He must know the weaknesses that can be accepted. (If you are looking for a horse with perfect conformation, you will never buy a horse.) In fact the owner, Turf historian, veterinary doctor and trainer form a team within a team, a sub-team at the time of the auction sales. They must know how much pedigree to give for conformation and vice-versa. They must also work out detailed procedure for studying and buying yearlings. Teams who have done this are sure to walk away with the choicest yearlings year after year.

The duties and responsibilities of the assistant trainer, travelling head man, syce, farrier and work rider are well known. They are the unsung heroes of racing. They, together with their trainer, constitute another sub-team. Your horse would not last a week without their support and your trainer will find it very difficult to win races if they were lacking in knowledge or application. A trainer who receives the fullest support from his team is sure to win anywhere from 5% to 25% more races. Conversely a trainer who receives inadequate support will win only half to three-fourths the races he ought to win. You would have noticed that top trainers throughout the world frequently acknowledge the role of their teams in their success.

One of the characteristics of team sports is that individual brilliance is not enough (unless you are a Frederico Tesio!). Co-ordination among the players is more important. How many times have we seen teams with brilliant players lose to less talented teams due to lack of co-operation.

Last but not least, do not forget the time factor in building up a team. Great teams do not spring overnight. They are assiduously built and nurtured by great individuals. My guess is it will take you five years to really start functioning as a team. For you will require that much time to really know your team members and for them to know you. You will require that much time to really get a grip on the sport. Then even before you realize it, you would have started functioning as a single Unit, as an organic whole. Now you are ready to reach great heights. Therefore as captain (and selector and coach) you must start building your team from today. Good Luck!